4 Week Lc

This book is due for return ~

Educational Research in Britain 3

Educational Research in Britain 3

edited by H. J. Butcher and H. B. Pont

UNIVERSITY OF LONDON PRESS LTD

SB 23697 £4.60. 1.74

ISBN 0 340 16792 0

University of London Press Ltd
St Paul's House, Warwick Lane, London EC4P 4AH

Printed and bound in Great Britain by
Hazell Watson and Viney Ltd, Aylesbury, Bucks

Contents

THE CONTRIBUTORS   vii

INTRODUCTION   ix

British research in education: some aspects of its development   1
WILLARD BREHAUT

Support for educational research and development   19
WILLIAM TAYLOR

The study of schools as organisations   32
E. HOYLE

Child rearing practices   57
JOHN NEWSON, ELIZABETH NEWSON
and PETER BARNES

Reading   71
ELIZABETH GOODACRE

Personality and academic attainment   89
N. J. ENTWISTLE

Convergent and divergent thinking   112
DESMOND L. NUTTALL

Science teaching   130
P. E. RICHMOND

The Humanities Curriculum Project   149
LAWRENCE STENHOUSE

Language, social class and the curriculum 168
DENIS LAWTON

Handicapped children 180
ELIZABETH M. ANDERSON and SIMON H. HASKELL

Maladjustment 214
J. P. RYAN

Learning processes in the mentally handicapped:
the work of the Hester Adrian Research Centre 236
PETER MITTLER

Educational and vocational guidance 261
K. M. MILLER, B. HOPSON and PATRICIA HOUGH

Further education 285
W. VAN DER EYKEN

Teacher education 301
DONALD LOMAX

The work of the Society for Research into
Higher Education 328
HARRIET GREENAWAY

BIBLIOGRAPHY 345

INDEX 410

The Contributors

H. J. Butcher
Professor of Educational Psychology, University of Sussex

H. B. Pont
Lecturer, Department of Psychology, University of Strathclyde

Elizabeth M. Anderson
Research Officer, Child Development Research Unit, Centre for Advanced
Studies and Research, University of London Institute of Education

Peter Barnes
Teaching Fellow, Department of Psychology, Nottingham University

Willard Brehaut
Professor, Department of History and Philosophy of Education, The Ontario
Institute for Studies in Education

N. J. Entwistle
Professor, Department of Educational Research, University of Lancaster

Elizabeth Goodacre
Reading Consultant

Harriet Greenaway
Assistant Academic Registrar, The Polytechnic of North London

Simon H. Haskell
Lecturer on the Education of Physically Handicapped Children, Department
of Child Development and Educational Psychology, University of London
Institute of Education

B. Hopson
Director, Vocational Guidance Research Unit, University of Leeds

Patricia Hough
Research Officer, Vocational Guidance Research Unit, University of Leeds

E. Hoyle
Professor, School of Education, University of Bristol

Denis Lawton
Reader in Curriculum Studies and Head of Department of Curriculum,
University of London Institute of Education

Donald Lomax
Lecturer in Educational Psychology, Department of Education, University of
Manchester

K. M. Miller
Director, Independent Assessment and Research Centre

Peter Mittler
Professor in the Education of the Mentally Handicapped; Director, Hestor
Adrian Research Centre for the Study of Learning Processes in the Mentally
Handicapped, University of Manchester

Elizabeth Newson
Senior Lecturer, Department of Psychology, University of Nottingham;
Joint Director, Child Development Research Unit

John Newson
Reader in Child Development, Department of Psychology, University of
Nottingham; Joint Director, Child Development Research Unit

Desmond L. Nuttall
Principal Research Officer, Examinations and Tests Research Unit, National
Foundation for Educational Research in England and Wales

P. E. Richmond
Senior Lecturer in Education, School of Education, University of
Southampton

J. P. Ryan
Lecturer on the Education of Maladjusted Children, Department of
Education, University of Manchester

Lawrence Stenhouse
Director, Centre for Applied Research in Education, University of East
Anglia

William Taylor
Director, University of London Institute of Education

W. van der Eyken
Senior Research Fellow, Further Education Group, Brunel University

Introduction

In the two earlier volumes of this series, our practice has been to present a collection of review articles without commentary and with only the minimum of introduction. This still seems to us the best policy. It is now exceedingly difficult for any single person to have more than a superficial acquaintance with many of the rapidly developing areas of educational research in this country—especially of educational research broadly defined. It would therefore appear almost an impertinence to comment upon many of the contributions and would convey the incorrect impression that we are expert throughout the whole field. Our editorial comments will therefore be brief and will aim not so much to introduce or summarise the contents as to clarify objectives in producing such a series, to comment upon general trends in educational research where these are visible, and to think aloud in print, as it were, about policy for future volumes.

Our main aim is to provide a continuing summary of educational research in this country from year to year somewhat similar to what is provided for general psychology by the (American) Annual Reviews of Psychology. We assume that summaries of this kind meet a recurring need and also that it is still practicable to cover a wide range of topics in a single volume. The Annual Reviews of Psychology, faced with a more severe task of compression, still follow this policy—though with evident difficulty. They have become inordinately bulky and the point seems near when they will inevitably suffer fission. But the case of educational research in Britain is less acute and it will probably be many decades yet before a selective review needs to be produced more often than about once a year. It may well be however that with the steady increase in the quality of such research, many of the more central topics will require to be reviewed annually, and the relatively peripheral perhaps only every three or four years. If any such developments occur within the present series, it will be desirable to form an Editorial Board and not to rely upon the unaided judgment of the present Editors.

Trend spotting and the extrapolation of supposed current trends is a notoriously risky business. This is no less true of educational research than of other phenomena, especially since the growth of research in this country has certainly not progressed at all smoothly, but rather in a series of discrete jumps. The reasons for its slow start and jerky progress are discussed in detail by Brehaut in the first chapter, and it will be sufficient here to mention two of the main jumps forward. Such turning points appear to have occurred around 1945 and around 1963. The first date saw the beginning of the National Foundation for Educational Research and the second the publication of the Robbins Report and (at about the same time) the foundation of the Social Science Research Council. If one supposes a reviewer in the year 2000 looking back and commenting on the third such leap forward, one must suspect that he will date it considerably later than 1973. At best the next few years seem likely to produce a steady consolidation rather than any major breakthrough.

What form is such consolidation likely to take? We have no crystal ball or Old Moore's almanac and the best we can do is try to discern among the bewildering mass of detail some emerging tendencies. One such appears to be the increased predominance of large-scale team projects and the concentration of resources into a few very large researches rather than their dissipation over a lot of small ones. In view of the quite impressive sums invested in educational research during the last few years by government departments and other official bodies this trend has been almost inevitable (one of the most extensive projects to emerge so far is described in the chapter by Stenhouse). This change in scale has been quite rapid. Only a few years ago, for instance, two of the major investigations into the effect of environmental factors on school attainment were those of Fraser and Wiseman, which were executed single-handed or with one or two assistants. Similar enquiries today would almost inevitably be conducted on a larger scale, with greater resources of money and labour and with more elaborate analyses by computer. Cottage industry is being succeeded by the production line. It hardly needs spelling out that this is by no means pure gain. In the past, educational researchers have been recruited from the ranks of serving teachers, and have learnt their skills by a kind of apprentice system, possibly working also for a higher degree while serving as a research assistant under an experienced investigator. The expansion of recent years has made this procedure out-dated, and unable to provide the numbers of research workers required, but systematic alternative means of recruitment and training appear to be lacking, with the result that a seller's market prevails. If educational research in Britain is to make steady progress and to consolidate the gains recently achieved, probably the greatest obstacle to overcome will be this lack of adequate provision for the training of research workers.

As regards the prevailing content of educational research during the next few years, one can only indicate a few areas that are at present attracting considerable attention and note signs of others that are likely to.

One trend during the last few years that can be heartily welcomed is the increasing amount of research resources devoted to studying the problems of handicapped children. This emphasis is reflected in the composition of our present collection of papers. In particular research into severe mental handicap, once an unduly neglected field, has been greatly encouraged by the setting up of the Hester Adrian Centre, whose work is described in the paper by Mittler. With the transfer of responsibility for such children from Health to Education during the last couple of years it is to be hoped that research into their needs and education will be further extended.

Another area of research that is new and promising is described in the paper by Hoyle. Until very recently organisation theory as applied to education was the esoteric specialism of a small band of enthusiasts. Today all that has changed and there is a widespread recognition that the study of formal and informal structures of organisation in education is not only interesting in theory but vital to effective improvement of practice. Decision-making processes are being extensively studied from the primary school to the organisation of post-graduate courses in Universities.

In the last ten years also the status and extent of research into tertiary education have been completely transformed. Before the last decade Universities were open to the accusation that they studied almost every topic under the sun with the one exception of their own processes. Since about 1965 however research into higher education (broadly interpreted) has been one of the most rapidly developing areas of educational research. A selection of such work is described in our last three chapters.

H. J. Butcher and H. B. Pont

Willard Brehaut

British research in education: some aspects of its development

A prefatory note on the definition of educational research

The problem of defining the term 'educational research' has been dealt with in the Introduction to volume 1 in this series. There the editors state that the term 'is interpreted . . . as empirical research, based on experiment, on social surveys and on the clinical study of individuals. We have not been able to include historical or philosophical studies or accounts of the organization and economics of education' (Butcher, 1968, p. 13). A similar definition is offered by Thouless (1969) in the preface to his *Map of Educational Research*. It is of importance to note, however, that in Britain, as elsewhere, the term has been taken to mean several different things. For example, Oliver (1946, p. 11) offers a very broad definition of research, stating that 'whenever a teacher recognizes a teaching problem and tries faithfully to solve it he is researching in education'. Rusk's earlier classification of types of research is also broad, embracing historical, philosophical, survey or administrative, and experimental research (1932, p. 36). More recent British contributors to the discussion of the nature of educational research have tended to be more restrictive. K. M. Evans, in her *Planning Small-Scale Research* (1968), stresses experimental and survey research, drawing attention in her preface to certain other types of educational research which she did not include—history of education, philosophy of education, and comparative education. One of the latest British guides to research methods, that of Nisbet and Entwistle (1970, p. 7), restricts its attention to 'areas which involve quantitative or scientific methods of investigation', noting that 'there are other important forms of research in education, such as historical or philosophical inquiry'. The authors then go on to include a chapter dealing with curriculum development, an area wherein the line between innovation and research becomes blurred. Two definitions of educational research are offered by Lovell and Lawson in

1

Understanding Research in Education (1970). These authors comment that 'it is virtually impossible to give a definition of the term ... which would command universal acceptance, as there are innumerable meanings that can be given to the word "education" ' (p. 21). Another British writer, E. G. Shacklock Evans (1963, p. 16), has defined research broadly as 'a critical or scientific investigation directed to the discovery of new facts, categories or hypotheses by means of the careful observation and control of its data'. Morris (1955, p. 78) considered educational research to be 'a broad term covering not only experiments designed to discover new facts or the relations between facts, but including also those scholarly activities, whether historical or philosophical, which while they may discover new facts or rediscover old ones, are often mainly concerned with the reinterpretation of facts already well-known'. Similarly, Peters and White (1969) in objecting to the assumption in much of the literature 'that educational research is a branch of psychology or social science' (p. 1), define research as 'systematic and sustained enquiry carried out by people well versed in some form of thinking in order to answer some specific type of question' (p. 2), thereby drawing a circle large enough to include the philosopher and others engaged in 'the more reflective side of scientific work'.

Despite the importance of keeping the definition of educational research as broad as many of the above researchers would desire, the following account refers, for the most part, to empirical research. By this restriction the writer acknowledges that only one part of the research development is being dealt with.

Introduction

When, in 1969, the author set sail across the Atlantic to undertake a year's sabbatical study of the development of educational research in Great Britain, he travelled under a great misapprehension: he believed that the British development in this field was sufficiently limited to enable him to examine it, identify its more important aspects, and prepare a report on his findings before his sabbatical year had expired. It soon became obvious, however, that this was a many-faceted assignment, each part of which warranted much careful study. As the reader will find, the present paper deals only with certain limited, but important, aspects of this development, namely the slow growth of British educational research and the possible reasons therefor.

Contributing to this misapprehension was the infrequency of references by North American researchers to the educational research conducted by British scholars—an infrequency emphasised by the very large numbers of references to American research—and the relatively late development of centres for the conduct of research in education in Britain, particularly in England. In addition, some British educators—obviously not Scots—advised the writer that he might well disregard any educational research conducted before the formation of the National Foundation for Educational Research in 1946. Others maintained that educational research really didn't make any progress in Britain until the 1960s when public funds for large-scale studies became available and the Schools Council, 'that indefatigable instigator of curricular research' (Dent, 1970), and the Social Science Research Council came into existence. Looking back, it would appear that the long American dominance of educational research had led at least some British scholars to the conclusion that the research contributions of other nations, including their own, were insignificant in comparison. Perhaps Hearnshaw's statement regarding the worship of American gods by British psychology in recent years could be applied to British educational research as well (1964, p. vii).

Certainly it is true that Britain lagged behind the United States and some other countries in the organisation of educational research. The British would be ready to admit that, in terms of research activity, the lion's share has been much less than that of the eagle. However, to disregard the educational research conducted in Britain before the organisation of the NFER, the National Foundation for Educational Research in England and Wales, is to do an injustice to the Scottish Council for Research in Education which was established in 1928 and conducted many important research studies several years before the NFER was established—studies which have received world-wide recognition. Indeed, as in other aspects of Britain's history, any generalisation about British educational research must be made with caution. It is possible to speak of 'British educational research' only if one keeps the Cheviot Hills prominently in mind.

Beginnings of educational research in Britain

Whether one accepts Knight's (1951, p. 85) choice of 1893, the year in which the British Child Study Association was established, as the date marking the beginning of educational research in Britain, or the choice of London inspector W. H. Winch, namely 1888, the year in which teachers participated on a large scale in one of Francis Galton's studies of mental fatigue (Rusk, 1932, p. 16), or selects some other date, it is evident that the beginnings of British research in education date back to the latter part of the 19th century. Several of the relatively early research studies, conducted before national research centres were established, continue to be regarded as classics, e.g., those of Cyril Burt. It is obviously in terms of such contributions by individuals rather than by government or other national organisations that Sukhia *et al.* (1963, p. 13) were able to point to Britain as one of the pioneers of educational research.

Certainly Britain has not lacked brilliant scholars who have conducted important research in education. When one thinks of the early period of this development, the names of Francis Galton, Michael Sadler, James Sully, W. H. Winch, and others come to mind. Although Galton is not remembered primarily as an educator, he is credited by Boring, the Harvard psychologist-historian, as the originator of mental tests and of the statistical methods for dealing with the measurement of individual differences. The other three, primarily educators, conducted important investigations in education. One of these, W. H. Winch, was one of the earliest advocates of educational research and, at considerable personal expense, undertook, in 1905, to go to the United States to study this new development and its organisation. Almost from the earliest period, too, one meets the name of Cyril Burt, first appointed as part-time school psychologist of the London County Council in 1913, and recognised as one of the leading educational researchers of the century. Indeed, judged by their influence on subsequent work, there were British pioneer researchers in education whose work compared favourably with the best to be found anywhere. In addition, Britain's relatively small size and, for a good part of the first half of this century, its comparative wealth should have helped it to contribute to the organisation and development of educational research.

From the earliest part of this century frequent attempts were made to promote the development of educational research in Britain. The formation, in 1901, of an Education Section in the British Association for the Advancement of Science was an indication of growing interest in the contribution of more scientific methods to the study of educational problems. In 1905, Inspector W. H. Winch, in seeking leave from the London County Council to study educational research in America, stressed the need for

'a group or groups of workers competent in the psychology, experimental or otherwise, of their day, and also with much knowledge of schools and school conditions, having, as it were, a foot in either camp. . . . Such workers are now in actual existence in America as professors of educational psychology or chiefs of departments of pedagogical research.' (London County Council Education Committee Minutes, 1905, vol. 3, p. 3346.)

A decade later, the Education Reform Council, founded in 1916 at a conference called by the Teachers' Guild, placed strong emphasis on the need for research in education and its organisation. The Council, which included such notable scholars as Michael Sadler, Percy Nunn and A. N. Whitehead, reported that 'England at present lags behind other great nations in respect of giving official support to individual research and in organising large-scale research in education. Valuable research has been carried out by individuals, but the benefit which should result is largely lost through lack of organisation and insufficient publication.' The Council also called for the establishment of 'a central institute for educational research, which should work in close connexion with the Board of Education and the teaching profession' as well as 'local research institutes' (*Times Educational Supplement*, 30 November 1916).

Several years were to pass before the objectives of the Education Reform Council would be attained, however, and, in the interim, other groups took up the cause. Chief among these groups was the British Psychological Society which set up its Education Section in 1919 and its Committee for Research in Education in 1921. These groups provided a means of communication among BPS members and did much to maintain public interest in educational research. The fact that teachers were permitted to join with such distinguished psychologists as Susan Isaacs, Percy Nunn, Cyril Burt and others in the discussions of educational research added to the strength of the organisation and its effectiveness in maintaining close liaison with the schools.

Another vigorous proponent, one of the early giants in British educational research, was Robert R. Rusk, a Scot. Rusk, who demonstrated British versatility in making important contributions to both psychological research and philosophy of education, made strong pleas for more experimental work in education. His respect for the scientific approach to enquiry in education is evident in his *Introduction to Experimental Education* (1912, p. 7): '(The new method) will deliver (the teacher) from the tyranny of tradition and the caprice of the faddist, and bring him under the servitude of his science . . .' Rusk's promptings and those of a few other dedicated persons eventually led to the setting up of the Scottish Council for Research in Education in 1928.

Perhaps the most widely quoted statement used to promote educational research in Britain, however, was made by Fred Clarke, of the University of London Institute of Education, in *The Study of Education in England* (1943, p. ii):

> 'If we conducted our medical and engineering services and our industrial production with the same slipshod carelessness, the same disregard for precision of thought and language, the same wild and reckless play of sentimentality or class prejudice or material interest masquerading as principle, with which we carry on our public discussions about education, most patients would die, most bridges would fall down, and most manufacturing concerns would go bankrupt.'

Clarke's stirring challenge did not go unheeded and his biographer, Mitchell (1967, p. 118), is able to report that Clarke was regarded as the prime mover in the activity which led to the establishment of the NFER.

The slow development of organised educational research

Despite the outstanding work of individual educational researchers and the clear statement by respected scholars of the need for educational research, England continued until after the Second World War without a national centre for such research. This long delay in the face of an obvious need suggests that there may have been truth in Santayana's general observation about English researchers of this period being 'learned men whose researches are a hobby and almost a secret' (1922, p. 52).

After 1928, when the Scottish Council for Research in Education was set up, Scottish researchers were able to provide the type of research miracle that is seldom encountered anywhere today—first-class research on a shoestring budget. (Obviously Warburton, [1962], an educational psychologist at Manchester University, did not have the Scots in mind when he stated that 'the lack of adequate research funds to finance the large-scale inquiries essential to explore problems in sufficient depth to yield authoritative findings means an endless repetition of poky little researches with the same title and different results' [p. 372]. Indeed, the highest tribute Warburton could pay the NFER in 1962 was that its publications had reached the same high standard of accuracy and careful planning as those of the SCRE.) Despite this Scottish achievement in the third decade of the century, England did not set up its national centre until the fifth decade. In 1932 England was chided for its tardiness by Rusk (1932, p. 80), then Director of the four-year-old Scottish Council for Research in Education, who quoted Winch's statement that:

> 'England permits but does not financially support research in education; and the upshot is that, with the possible exception of France, there is less provision for educational research than in any of the leading countries of the world.'

Dr Rusk's diagnosis and remedy were stated in few words (p. 79):

> 'Research cannot be relegated to the haphazard efforts of individual enthusiasts, nor can it be effectively undertaken by a committee each member of which is engaged in other more pressing duties. If it is to be profitably installed, the Research movement must have a local habitation and a name, and must also employ permanent officials. . . . This implies the establishment of a Bureau or Institute of Educational Research.'

Attempts to establish some kind of central educational research agency in England were made throughout the 1930s but these came to naught. One foreign observer, K. S. Cunningham (1934), of the Australian Council for Educational Research, commented that 'educational enquiry in England is not yet organised. . . . This situation is, however, not likely to last long, for there is an increasing interest in the question of educational research. . . . The antipathy which such new movements may have to overcome tends to delay even a sound development for an undue length of time, but it has at least this advantage, that when action is eventually taken it is likely to be well thought out and well organised' (pp. 84–5). But Cunningham's forecast was premature and England had to wait for another decade before its National Foundation was established.

Some reasons for the slow growth of research in education

Why did England and, to a much lesser extent, Scotland, show reluctance to conduct educational research? Why did Britain wait until the 1960s—a time when her finances were not in the strongest position—before pouring massive amounts of money into educational research? In view of the fact that Britain was one of the leading nations of the world during most of the early history of the educational research movement and could, therefore, have afforded the early development of a strong programme of educational research, it is of interest to look at some of the possible reasons for its relatively late development in this field.

1) NATIONAL CHARACTERISTICS

There appears to have been no single reason for the slow development of educational research in Britain. Rather, a number of obstacles to rapid development can be identified. One of these is especially difficult to deal with because it represents a cluster of national characteristics—and there are great dangers in attaching labels to any individual, let alone a people. Despite these dangers, it appears that the British reaction to educational research can be looked at with greater appreciation after noting, for example, the keen comment of Fred Clarke, one of the founding fathers of the NFER. who referred to his countrymen as 'an insular and unanalytic people'. (*Times Educational Supplement*, 18 January, 1947, p. 36.)

What have been some of these national characteristics? Several observers have credited the British with a deeply ingrained distrust of the faddist, more particularly a fear of the foreign faddist. Collingwood's reference (1939, p. 15) to the British public as 'always contemptuous of foreigners' also lends support. One British commentator, for example, writing a review in 1916 of two of John Dewey's books, warned his countrymen that:

> 'We cannot wholly exclude the influence of foreign ideas. . . . If we repulse a direct attack, the stream flows in on us by the backwater of our Dominions. Both in Canada and in Australia the influence of

men like Dewey is widely accepted, and contends on equal terms with "scholastic" traditions derived from the Mother Country. It would be a great mistake, however, to try to ignore the trend of educational thought in the New World . . . a student of education cannot ignore the movements of thought in Illinois or Missouri. . . .' (*Times Educational Supplement*, 4 January, 1916, p. 3.)

This same distrust of the expert was seen in the school classroom where the teacher was referred to as 'the only expert in education', an attitude which did little to promote research.

A related national characteristic which has often been cited in reference to the English is a lack of interest in efficiency, an objective often associated with the development of educational research. According to Peter Sandiford, writing in 1918, 'obvious efficiency is distrusted, even despised, by the average Englishman . . .' (p. 187). Although organisation and efficiency may not always be synonymous, Matthew Arnold's observation that 'disbelief in government makes us slow to organise government for any matter' receives support from the comments of those who were most directly concerned with the organisation of educational research in Britain. Indeed, the whole history of the English educational system shows that efficiency has not been an important objective. Unlike the United States' educational system which spawned large numbers of professional administrative personnel who came to be specially trained in the techniques of administration, Britain, and England in particular, long maintained respect for the amateur in the organisation and administration of education. This respectful attitude for the amateur tended to discourage the scientific study of education.

An important characteristic of the British is one that reveals itself both in the attitude towards the conduct of educational research and in reported educational research, namely the long-held view that Man is a poor subject for science. For example, one British writer, in offering an assessment of an early American book, Norbert Melville's *Standard Method of Testing Juvenile Mentality by the Binet-Simon Scale*, commented in 1917 that:

'the measurement of the mind is not a less arduous task than that of weighing the Universe, but American investigators, and some English, are approaching the task in the case of children with a sense of certitude. . . . But the proof of capacity is probably beyond the power of experimental psychology and beyond the measurements secured by a process of averaging. Genius is impossible to test or measure, and there may be a spark of genius hidden away in every personality.' (*Times Educational Supplement*, 6 September, 1917, p. 347.)

To this day, the research most often commended by British scholars is that wherein, as one reviewer has said of Burt's contributions, 'the problem of the individual is never lost in the statistics of the group'. It would appear that the same spirit which moved the Cambridge Senate in 1877 to reject Ward and Venn's proposed laboratory of psychophysics on the grounds that it would 'insult religion by putting the human soul in a pair of scales' is not yet dead in Britain.

Important as national characteristics may be, however, several other possible reasons for British reserve in regard to research must be noted.

2) LACK OF A UNIFIED SYSTEM OF EDUCATION

The lack of a unified system of education in England has undoubtedly affected the development of educational research in Britain as a whole. This lack of organisation was pointed to as early as 1916 by those wishing to promote educational research. Again, in 1937, Reeve (1938, p. 56), then President of the London Head Teachers' Association, stated in a Presidential address: 'We are hindered in our fundamental conception of our educational problems by the fact that we have not a national system of education.' Fifteen years later, R. A. Butler (1952, p. 43), looking back upon the success of his Education Act of 1944, still could not point to any unified national system of education:

'. . . this marriage of past and future meant that, while we had to be hopeful, forward-looking and constructive, we had at the same time to be exceptionally tolerant of administrative untidiness.'

Although this lack of a unified system has been referred to with approval by English and non-English alike, it seems evident that such a system of education would have created a demand for the methodical collection of educational data and for research into the educational problems that would be brought into sharper focus by surveys of this kind. Indeed, Pidgeon (1968) considers the publication, in 1959, of the

Crowther Report, with its emphasis on the many areas of education in which little is known, as a turning point in educational research in Britain. Similarly, Elvin (1965) points to the impetus given to research by the Robbins Committee which reported in 1963.

3) ANTI-GERMAN AND ANTI-AMERICAN SENTIMENT

Another obstacle in the path of the few persons attempting to promote the conduct of educational research in Britain during the early years of this century was one whose effects are very difficult to estimate—that of anti-German and anti-American sentiment.

During the period when many American students and scholars were studying at German universities and becoming acquainted with, among other things, German psychological thought, Britain was engaged in a variety of contests with Germany. These contests were economic, political, territorial and, eventually, military. While Americans were eager to partake of what the German universities were offering, at least up to the First World War, the British scholars and general public expressed anti-German feelings long before 1914. Not only were German ideas and ideals considered by many to be unsuitable for Britain but any studies which showed the characteristics of German scientific thought were looked upon with suspicion and disfavour. Thus, while American psychologists who had studied in German universities, especially under Wundt and his successors, were returning to their homeland to establish psychological laboratories and to provide a beginning for educational research, British scholars returning from Germany met with little encouragement and, from most quarters, vocal opposition. It would appear that Michael Sadler did not speak for many British people in stating in a speech in Frankfurt in 1912 that one of the lessons England could learn from Germany was the application of scientific method and of cooperative research to educational problems (Higginson, 1958, p. 122).

Similarly, though in much milder terms, up to the Second World War the British tended to demonstrate an anti-American attitude in commenting upon educational research, despite repeated exhortations that they might 'listen without danger to the counsels of the West'. Particularly in such areas as the methodology of educational research, it was necessary to turn to American sources, as Rusk points out in his *Research in Education* (1932), the first British guide to the subject. Among the nineteen bibliographical references listed by Rusk there is not a single British entry, a fact that gives added weight to his statement that, although his book was the first of its kind in Britain, 'in America its publication might be regarded as superfluous' (p. 5).

But the lack of sympathy for American research in education had been evident for many years. Even in 1918, when Britain and America were military allies, one British reviewer, in comparing books on educational measurement—one by Philip Hartog of London, the other by Walter Monroe, one of the best known American educational researchers, praised the British volume and damned the American for a strange reason. 'We fancy' said the reviewer, 'that if Mr Hartog could give a few months' careful investigation to Dr Monroe's statistical tables and to the tests invented by various American statisticians, he would discover fallacies and pseudo-scientific faults of detail. We, ourselves, shrink from the laborious work entailed. . . .' (*Times Educational Supplement*, 12 September, 1918, p. 383.)

Two so-called weaknesses of American educational research proved particularly annoying to British readers. One of these was the tendency to use jargon instead of the English language; the second, the tendency to overlook what was considered to have been important research by non-American, particularly British researchers. Examples of such criticisms as the following are numerous.

Writing in *The Forum of Education* in 1926, 'F.A.C.' (Professor Francis Cavenagh) paid high tribute to Everitt Dean Martin's book entitled *Psychology* with the barbed compliment that 'an American book written in English is as welcome as it is rare'. (1926, p. 237.)

Even the highly regarded *Encyclopedia of Educational Research*, 3rd edition, published by the Macmillan Company for the American Educational Research Association, brought forth a stinging attack:

'There is nothing like educational research for bringing out the arid jargon. When the research is American in origin the tendency seems often too great to be denied. So we are used to seeing the portentous phrases come in their floods across the Atlantic to join the surging mass we produce at home.' (*Times Educational Supplement*, 6 May, 1960, p. 890.)

Typical of the comments of British researchers who found few references to non-American sources in American research reports was Foulds' analysis (1954, p. 311) of Anastasi's *Psychological Testing*. Noting that Anastasi had discussed factor analysis without reference to Cyril Burt, Godfrey Thomson or Philip Vernon, Foulds expressed his feelings forcefully: 'If the Monroe Doctrine is to apply to Psychology, Professor Anastasi's book would lose nothing by being renamed *Psychological Testing in America*.' In a similar vein Alec Rodger's review (1946) of another American book, Arthur Traxler's *Techniques of Guidance*, makes no attempt to hide annoyance at the writer's neglect of British contributions to the field, noting that 'Mr Traxler has been generous enough to include the names of two British psychologists in his list of approximately 800 authors'. In recent years, however, the critical tone has become more moderate as British researchers looked to America for leadership, and, in some instances, for funds.

4) ATTITUDES OF ACADEMICS AND OTHERS

One of the chief obstacles to the development of educational research in Britain has been the attitude of the academic community, especially in England, towards the study of education and psychology. Although the first professors of education in both England and Scotland were appointed in the 1870s, graduate schools of education where educational research might be conducted were slow in emerging. The attitude labelled by Hearnshaw (1964) as 'the philosophical resistance to the human sciences', particularly in the English universities, had a marked effect on the development of not only educational studies but also of psychology and sociology. Even after Departments and Institutes of Education were established, the situation did not improve rapidly, for these 'tended to be small, inadequately staffed, badly housed and held in poor regard within the university and in the schools'. (Taylor, 1969, p. 219.)

Clarke had drawn attention to this academic attitude towards education in *The Study of Education in England* (1943, p. 32):

'One may still meet in England—as surely nowhere else—men looked upon as authorities in education to whom there is something irresistibly comic about the idea, as they put it, of "teaching teachers to teach".... Their opinion rests upon no investigation or test of any kind. It is simply the assertion of blind faith in tradition, a man teaches by the light of Nature *in the safe blinkers that a sure tradition provides*.'

The 'sure tradition' to which Clarke referred deserves mention here because of the role played by tradition in British education. Although its strength and its effect in delaying change are impossible to assess, perhaps there is some accuracy in the analysis offered in 1903 by Peter McArthur, a Canadian writer, in his strangely entitled book, *To be taken with salt: an essay on teaching one's grandmother to suck eggs*: 'The average Englishman has so deep a reverence for antiquity that he would rather be wrong than be recent.' (p. 157.)

5) SUSTAINED CRITICISM OF RESEARCH

Of all the obstacles to the expansion of educational research in Britain, the steady criticism of the educational research conducted at home and abroad must be ranked high. In itself the result of some of the circumstances and attitudes referred to above, this widespread criticism constituted an important negative guide to the conduct of research. Very few guides to the conduct of educational research have been produced in Britain: 'how not to' and, on numerous occasions, 'why not to', have received more attention than the 'how to' guides. Indeed, as soul-searching and critical analysis in educational research continue, the contributions made to this process by several British writers become of increasing importance. I do not refer here to the contributions of those opponents of educational research who have labelled educational researchers as 'cooperative laundrymen par excellence' (*Times Educational Supplement*, 27 June, 1969, p. 2117) nor to a Mr Seaman from Surrey who, in 1952, issued a call for 'a sabbatical year for all, away from the matter of educational theory and research.' (*Times Educational Supplement*, 23 May, 1952.) Nor do I refer to Sir Walter Moberly's exhortation: 'For God's sake, let's stop researching and begin to think.' However, these and other forceful statements, if sounded as a warning note at the appropriate time, might be beneficial to educational research in the long run.

Among the most constructive criticisms have been those voiced by researchers who have emphasised classroom-centred research, one of the most difficult and important kinds of educational research. The relatively few British scholars who have written guides to the conduct of educational research have stressed the need for this research to remain close to the reality of the teaching–learning situation. The first of these guides, Rusk's *Research in Education*, leaves no doubt about the importance of pupil-centred and classroom-centred research. One of the latest guides, *Educational Research Methods*, by J. D. Nisbet and N. J. Entwistle (1970), makes the point emphatically:

'It is important never to be so far from children that one forgets the setting of educational research. Some of the nonsense stemming from research studies which has often been written . . . could only be written by someone who has spent too long away from the classroom.' (p. 135.)

W. D. Wall (1968), former Director of the National Foundation for Educational Research, stressed this same point in equally strong terms:

'We must remember that it isn't enough to have a degree in a social science and a couple of bright ideas. . . . There is a kind of intuitive knowledge of schools, teachers, children and parents that can be acquired only by some years of real teaching experience.' (p. 8.)

Other British researchers through the years have held similar views. Among these should be noted Cyril Burt, James Maxwell, R. A. C. Oliver, Frank Warburton, Kathleen M. Evans, and several others, some of whom have been closely associated with the work of the Scottish Council for Research in Education or the National Foundation for Educational Research. In this regard a specific piece of advice offered by Evans (1968, p. 12) must have drawn ready support from teachers: '. . . schools do not exist to provide material for higher degree theses. Their only purpose is the education of children, and this must not be hindered without good cause.'

This steady criticism undoubtedly served to delay the development of educational research in Britain. Although Monroe *et al.* (1928) in a survey study entitled *Ten Years of Educational Research*, were able to report that the United States had passed through the pioneer period of educational research and had entered the period of 'quantity production', it is only within the last decade that 'quantity production' may be said to have been reached in Britain. The pioneers of British educational research were at work in the same period as the American pioneers but were slow in developing the numerous research bureaux and graduate chairs of educational research needed to provide for training programmes and career structures in this field. Wiseman (1962, p. 222), however, maintains that because 'few of us really believe in education as an academic subject, let alone education as a field for research, we have, in fact, got as much research as we deserve'. Support for Wiseman's statement can be found in widely different sources. One of these, an anonymous reviewer of Rusk's book, *Experimental Education*, writing in 1919, puts forth a not uncommon view of educational research:

> 'It will be possible to have more faith in the further results of experimental education if we find that they are largely in accord with the great educationists on some of the broad elementary problems.' (*Times Educational Supplement*, 6 February, 1919, p. 63.)

Ten years later Kandel (1930), a noted scholar of comparative education, was able to report that England 'has not yet developed a faith in education as a science'. Writing nearly a half-century after Rusk's volume was published, Elvin (1965, p. 56), Director of the University of London Institute of Education, provided support for a commonly held view in stating that 'the resistances of experience and common sense to the alleged "findings" of research are not always wrong'.

Added to the force of the criticism of educational research which has come from teachers, editorial writers and the researchers themselves has been the continuing campaign by certain philosophers to have researchers spend more time in analysing the concepts used in their enquiries before gathering heaps of data. Among the most effective critics in this category have been Peters (1969) and his associates at the University of London and Bantock (1961) at the University of Leicester. Unlike many earlier British philosophers, these scholars are keenly interested in the development of educational research and the role that philosophers can play in that development. Both Bantock and Peters have offered criticisms of research in education which are intended to reduce the number of what they judge to be conceptually inadequate research studies. Of special importance here are their favourable references to the writings of Peter Winch, D. W. Hamlyn and others whose analyses point to the possibility, indeed the necessity, of avoiding the empirical study of essentially conceptual questions. Seen in the context of such statements, Moberly's advice to give up research and begin thinking takes on new meaning.

A closely related criticism of educational research and one that may well be of crucial significance to education both in Britain and elsewhere was stated most emphatically by Wall (1968, p. 5): 'One of the most important problems we are going to face in the future is the attempt—unconscious in many cases, conscious in some—to capture research in favour of an ideology.' Maintaining that the researcher must remain politically and ideologically uncommitted, Wall states that the NFER's philosophy has always been 'a scrupulous political and ideological impartiality. The purging of bias is, we believe, the important discipline in applied social and educational research. . . . Facts are sacred . . . they may not be and should not be manipulated, suppressed or sought for with ideologies in mind. . . .' (*ibid.*) That such impartiality is possible, let alone desirable, is questioned by Hudson (1966, p. 29), who maintains that 'in practice, scientific research is frequently a muddled, piratical affair. . . . Research . . . engages the individual's personality; and in psychology there is a disconcerting tendency for the psychologists' personalities to reflect themselves in their theories, and even in their results. This being so, there seems every case for dropping the mask of objectivity in reporting psychological research. . . .' Taylor (1966), too, manifests that 'research that is undertaken with the exclusion of value as its central concern is often of little use either theoretically or practically—the value-free is often the valueless' (p. 195). Such differences of opinion regarding the nature of research might be considered to be, in Morris's words, 'really concealed arguments about the nature of man' (1955, p. 96).

As many social analysts have noted, British society has undergone great changes in recent years, changes which have met with strong and determined opposition. It was inevitable that education should be a central arena for debate and that research in education would be affected by this controversy, both in the selection of problems to be investigated and the methods of research to be used. These differences of opinion reflect strongly held convictions about the relationship of man and society and are of interest and importance to the international community of educational researchers as well as the social scientist and intellectual historian. Fortunately for educational researchers both in Britain and elsewhere, the British reluctance to plunge into educational research did not extend to the area of comment on research. British educators have continued to be among the most forceful critics of the conduct of research in education; indeed, in the long run, their contribution to the area of research methodology may prove to be as great as that of the classic studies completed by British researchers.

Summary

The foregoing commentary upon the development of educational research in Great Britain has been focussed primarily on one aspect of that development, namely, the recognised British lag in this area, particularly in the organisation of educational research in England. Of all the factors which appear to have contributed to this lag, the steady criticism of educational research by teachers, researchers, philosophers, journalists and the British public must be given a high place. In their reluctance to become actively committed to the educational research movement, British educators have performed a valuable service for educational research. Their lively analysis of the research undertaken through the years since the turn of the twentieth century remains not only as grist for the intellectual historian's mill but as a continuing guide to the conduct of research and its evaluation.

William Taylor

Support for educational research and development

The background

Willard Brehaut has shown that educational research in Britain has a longer and more complex history than some accounts allow. But large scale spending on research and development in education in this country is almost entirely a product of the past ten years. If the number of team projects before this was small, the work done was often influential on both policy and practice. Douglas's MRC-financed longitudinal study (1964, 1968), Glass's work on social factors influencing opportunity (1954), Pidgeon and Yates's analyses of secondary selection (1957), and a substantial number of studies about individual and group assessment and problems of backwardness and retardation, all preceded the era of big spending. Further back still, the studies of Susan Isaacs in child development, of Lindsey on educational opportunity, of Burt on the assessment of abilities, of Hartog and Rhodes on the marks of examiners, and the mental surveys of the Scottish Council for Research in Education, had all influenced the educational climate of the thirties and forties.

But the resources devoted to this kind of activity were small. The National Foundation for Educational Research had been set up in 1946 on the basis of a farthing per head of the school population, but by 1960 the Foundation had an income from all sources of only £34 000 and a staff of 39. (By 1970 the Foundation's income was £470 000 and it employed some 150 staff [NFER, 1970].) The level of educational research and activity in universities was in 1960—and still is—variable. The independent Foundations were making funds available in support of specific projects. The number of doctoral and masters' theses in education was growing, but had only reached a total of just over a hundred for the country as a whole by the end of the fifties.

In 1962 the then Ministry of Education decided to spend £20 000 to support educational research projects. No distinction was made between research or curriculum development. The money was available to support promising projects wherever they arose, and the Ministry interpreted its support role on the same lines as the independent Foundations. Once the decision had been taken that a proposal was worthwhile, the money was paid out and the researchers left free to get on with the work. The sums available for these general disbursements rapidly increased, and the studies they supported led to some important and by now well-known findings. Ministry money contributed to Basil Bernstein's work on socio-linguistics (see the chapter by Lawton); the preparation of a new British Intelligence Scale was begun; the National Foundation's streaming studies were initiated. The activity of the independent Foundations also began to be stepped up. The Nuffield Foundation in particular provided money for curriculum development projects which are now making a major impact upon the practice of the schools. The University Grants Committee made available additional sums of a few thousand pounds annually to stimulate educational research in a limited number of universities. The curriculum study group in the Ministry blossomed into the Schools Council, and the flow of money into curriculum development projects increased dramatically—at least in relation to what had been spent before. Some substantial grants began to be made—£75 000 for a research and development project in compensatory education; £175 000 for Lawrence Stenhouse's humanities project (described by Stenhouse in a later chapter); £89 000 for the evaluation of primary French.

While the bases of these developments in research and development work were being laid in the Ministry (later the Department) of Education, in the curriculum development group and in the independent Foundations, arguments were going on about the possibility of establishing an Educational Research Council which could support both research and the training of educational research workers. Many educationists wanted such a council to be a separate body, parallel to the research councils in other fields. Many social scientists argued for the inclusion of education within a Social Science Research Council. The question was remitted to the Heyworth Committee; the social scientists' views prevailed, and, once established, the Social Science Research Council set up an Educational Research Board under the initial chairmanship of Lord James, parallel to its other committees for sociology, economics, psychology and the rest of the social sciences.

By 1968, money in support of educational research was coming from five main sources. The Department of Education and Science was still backing a wide range of research activity, and beginning to co-operate with the Schools Council and the ssrc in jointly financed projects. The ssrc had begun to spend money on educational research, and had also established a system of postgraduate studentships. The Schools Council had either agreed to back, or had under consideration, development projects in most areas of the primary and secondary curriculum. The independent Foundations—Nuffield, Leverhulme, Gulbenkian and others—were paying for a variety of individual and team projects in universities. The University Grants Committee, through their quinquennial grants, were providing money which paid the salaries of university staff in education and the social sciences who spent part, and in a few cases, all, of their time on educational research (Taylor, 1973).

All this activity had developed on an *ad hoc* basis, reflecting a feeling that research in education must be a good thing, rather than any central plan or set of assumptions about benefits and pay-offs. In a matter of six years the resources devoted specifically to educational research and development had increased by at least a factor of ten. But the production of people competent to undertake the work, the means for the monitoring of projects and for the collation of research information, and procedures for the diffusion and dissemination of research findings, had all failed to keep pace. The consequences of this soon became plain. Too much research was a doubtful quality; too few researchers and potential researchers knew what was going on else-where and had contact with their fellow workers in the same fields; many decision-makers and administrators were becoming sceptical about the pay-offs for the sums being spent; too few teachers were in touch with research relevant to their tasks and too many were un-sympathetic to research activity; too little attention had been given to conceptualising the relationship between different kinds of research and between research and development. Attempts to distinguish between curiosity oriented, mission oriented and applied work, between funda-mental, action and policy oriented research, using terminology borrowed from the natural sciences, proved to be more useful in justifying the different foci of interest that the main funding agencies were beginning to develop than in clarifying the types of research and development work that most needed support.

The present position

The last four years have seen the beginnings of policies and practices designed to remedy these deficiencies. Information about on-going research and development work has become more readily available. Until recently there has been no up to date published record of current research. The National Foundation for Educational Research has issued a register that fills in the period from 1963 to 1969, and the Office of Scientific and Technical Information has taken over responsibility for providing an 'address book' in the shape of a new section in Volume III of *Scientific Research in British Universities, Colleges and Government Departments*. This helps the individual who wants to find out who is active in a particular field, but at present the entries make no distinction between personal interest research and large scale team projects. The annual reports of the main funding agencies and of the NFER are helpful, particularly that of the SSRC, which is a model of clarity and organisation. But even when all these are put together, the record is by no means complete. To make it so would cost a great deal of money. It is not certain that such money would be well spent, or that a national abstracting and dissemination service such as the American ERIC (Educational Resources Information Centre) would, at the moment anyway, be worth introducing. Except to those that think that the only problem about educational research and the dissemination of research information is that there isn't enough of it, the costs of classifying, coding, and, no doubt, computerising the results of all the present activity does not seem to have an over-riding priority over other demands. But we could do a lot more, short of establishing a United Kingdom ERIC, to make information about research more widely available, both to other researchers and to potential users. The Schools Council and the NFER have both shown that research reports can be published in a way that makes them accessible to teachers and to a wider public. Discussions are at present going on among the major funding agencies about the possibility of employing a common format in the lists of current and completed researches included in their annual reports. This could contribute much to the availability of information at very little additional cost.

Among more pressing problems is the need to improve the quality of research and the relationship between researchers and potential users. The quality of research depends upon the training of those doing the work, the facilities they have available and the supervision they receive (Härnqvist, 1973).

What kinds of training and experience does an educational researcher need? There can be no simple specification. Large projects often require staff from a variety of social science fields, with a knowledge of statistics and research methodology and some experience of teaching in schools. Such people are in short supply. Bright young social science graduates, even those who do want to work in educational research, tend to gravitate towards social science rather than education departments. The SSRC postgraduate award scheme, which reflects not only bids made by university departments but also subject preferences expressed by potential students, provided 65 studentships in education in 1972 (there were 25 in 1969), against 196 for management and 167 for sociology. The experienced teachers who make up the bulk of the research-trained higher degree graduates from university departments of education are often unwilling to take the risks involved in short term research appointments, especially when having held such posts confers no very clear career advantages. Outside the National Foundation and a few universities, there are not many full-time permanent posts available for educational research workers. Some will argue that this is a good thing; researchers need to be in touch with the schools; to professionalise research is to encourage the proliferation of esoteric projects and even more esoteric languages. Others claim that greater professionalisation is essential if good people are to be attracted to work in the field. In practice, the best research teams are often a mixture of young, methodologically sophisticated and tough minded social scientists, and more experienced, school oriented educationists.

Such teams only learn to work together if there is adequate supervision; the professors and senior academics who obtain the grants often have departments to run as well as several projects to supervise, and many would like to give more time to their research colleagues than often proves possible. In the past, funding agencies took little part in the initiation and supervision of projects. Their role was mainly responsive; the grant once agreed, they were happy to receive properly audited accounts and an annual report. This has changed. From the beginning the Schools Council has taken an active and direct interest in the progress of the work it supports, and has prior claim to the publication of reports and the distribution of resulting teaching materials. The Department of Education and Science, in accordance with its policy of concentrating resources on policy oriented work, initiated mainly by branches, has almost ceased to act in a responsive capacity, and is giving more attention to monitoring and evaluating the studies that it commissions. The SSRC has recently identified a number of areas in which it is particularly interested in responding to initiatives from researchers, and seems likely to place greater emphasis on reviewing the results of the work it supports.

All this involves risks. The line between monitoring and interference is narrow. If most of the available funds come to be disbursed by bodies that have explicit research policies, control over the direction of future work shifts from the field to the agency. The possibility of obtaining support for unconventional projects, particularly those involving fundamental research, may be reduced. Too enthusiastic and far reaching coordination and contact between the major research agencies might mean that to be turned down by one of them involves rejection by all. But if research and development are to influence policy and practice in education, these are risks that must be faced. An absence of intervention often implies a lack of interest; in the present state of the art, both researchers and funding agencies will probably benefit from a more sustained relationship than used to be the norm.

Such a relationship is particularly important when the funding agency has decision-making responsibilities to which the research may be relevant, like the DES, or, as in the case of the Schools Council, has the duty of making the results of development work widely known. Research is unlikely to influence policy unless channels exist along which the necessary kinds of information can flow. Many administrators have neither the time nor the inclination to study long reports or a wide range of journal literature; if there has been inadequate contact between the initiating and/or funding body and the researchers, those who do read this material are likely to be disappointed. If research, development, dissemination, implementation, administration and policy making are mutually to benefit one another, the links between them have to be thought out and organised with greater care than has been the case in the past.

The various forms of the 'research—development—dissemination—

innovation—institutionalisation' model, whatever their usefulness elsewhere, do not help much in this field. Few projects have results which
can be directly applied in the classroom or in the administration of the
educational system. Heads who thought that the NFER's large scale and
impressive research on streaming would tell them whether or not to
unscramble their streamed classes have been disappointed. Administrators and policy makers who looked to the literature on the effect of
class size on teaching outcomes to help in allocating educational
resources failed to find any conclusions that would in themselves
furnish a firm basis for decision. The main way in which research *does*
influence policy and decision-making is by working on the climate of
public and specialised opinion and contributing to the rationality of
choice. An accumulation of research findings, varying in scope but
tending in the same general direction, can clearly influence policy. The
studies of educational opportunity in the Central Advisory Council's
reports of the fifties and sixties, together with the results of university
and LEA based surveys, played a big part in the spread of support for
the reorganisation of secondary education along comprehensive lines.
A head who is considering unstreaming, or a chief education officer or
minister contemplating resources allocation, would find many helpful
indications in the literature. But whether it is 11+ selection, or streaming, or class size, however good the research it cannot in itself determine
which way a decision should go. Education, like politics, is about how
we should live, and neither political science nor educational research
can replace the complex processes of judgement that enter into political
and into educational decisions, although they may do a good deal to
make these judgements more rational.

At the moment, by far the largest proportion of the money spent
on supporting R. and D. work in education goes on curriculum
development projects. Many would argue that these proportions are
wrong. Worthwhile curriculum development work needs to rest on
sound learning theory, on a sophisticated knowledge of the social
relationships characteristic of classrooms and schools, on a proper understanding of the dynamics of child and adolescent behaviour. As things
are, the research base is inadequate to support the increasing bulk of
development projects that rest upon it. Many of those responsible for
the allocation of funds for research have sympathy for this view. But
they point out that the shortage is not so much of funds to support
basic work as of high quality proposals. The absence of explicit theo-

retical underpinning for a large number of on-going curriculum development projects is not due to any lack of interest or concern on the part of the development people; it is due to the failure of basic work in the psychology, sociology and philosophy of education to keep pace with the rate of educational expansion, both in terms of quantity and of quality.

It is almost impossible to calculate accurately how much we are spending today on educational research and development. A notion of the overall project expenditure can be obtained from the annual reports of the various funding agencies. But a lot of research is being undertaken or supervised by university-funded staff, and there is only minimal information available about the numbers involved and the proportion of their time that is devoted to this kind of activity. The 1971 enquiry into the use of academic staff time undertaken by the Vice-Chancellors' Committee showed that staff in education spent an average of eight and a half hours per week on 'personal research', and a further three hours supervising 'graduate research', a total of 21 per cent of their working week. Recent attempts to add up expenditure on education R. and D. have yielded a figure of about £3·5 million, some 0·16 per cent of total public expenditure on education (Taylor, 1973). This includes the substantial sums now being spent on applied curriculum development work; the proportion of educational resources being devoted to basic studies of the dynamics and correlates of children's learning is very much smaller.

In the United States, it has been estimated that financial resources available for educational research and development in a recent year amounted to nearly 200 million dollars. When this is compared with total U.S. expenditure on education, it yields a proportion on research and development of approximately 0·3 per cent, about twice what we spend in the United Kingdom. The Americans now regard this sum as inadequate. There have been Presidential initiatives for the establishment of a National Institute of Education, 'to conduct and support educational R. and D., disseminate its findings, train educational R. and D. personnel, and promote coordination of educational R. and D. within the Federal Government' (Levien, 1971). The Rand Corporation has produced a plan for the Institute which identifies four areas in which new work is needed, each broken down into a number of related 'programme elements'. The four areas comprise, first, three programme elements aimed at the solution of major educational problems—the improvement of the education of the disadvantaged, improvements in the quality of education, and improvements in effectiveness of resource use in education. The second area, aimed at advancing educational practice, is seen as including programme elements concerned with improving method and content, organisation and administration, measurement and evaluation, and the education of educational personnel. The third area, 'strengthening the foundations of education—selective research programmes building basic knowledge concerning education', includes five elements; increased knowledge of the individual as learner, increased knowledge of group processes as they affect learning, increased knowledge of societal influences on education, increased ability to use technology and media effectively in education, and increased effectiveness of analytical and research methodologies. Finally, the fourth area is entitled 'strengthening the research and development system—funding to facilitate formation of the complex network of individuals and institutions needed to link research, development and practice' and includes elements designed to develop the supply of competent R. and D. manpower, and of effective R. and D. institutions, to strengthen the linkage between R. and D. and practice, and to develop structures for information transfer (Levien, 1971). The agenda is ambitious, perhaps over-ambitious, but at least the effort is being made to think through and to categorise the problems to which researchers might address themselves. There is no parallel effort in this country at the present time.

Prospects and possibilities

The money available in support of educational R. and D. grew rapidly up until the end of the sixties, but there has been little subsequent increase. Given the current rates of cost inflation, the amount of work that this money can sustain is diminishing, and looks likely to diminish still further. University money to provide the 'research floor' for projects and programmes will also be harder to come by in the remainder of the 1972/77 quinquennium (Taylor, 1972a). If the balance of teacher education activity moves from the universities to the colleges, polytechnics and other maintained sector institutions, senates and finance committees may find it even more difficult to maintain education's share of the budget. Against this background any speculations concerning likely future developments are hazardous. The best that can be done is to identify a few of the tendencies that are already visible and which may become more important in the years ahead.

Crucial to the whole enterprise is the political climate with respect to educational R. and D. in the world of education and beyond. As has already been suggested, the decisions that led to the setting up of the SSRC and the Schools Council, to the growth in DES funding for research and to the activities in this field of the independent foundations, were based not upon any clearly worked out model of educational change, but on an essentially political conviction that knowledge was better than ignorance, and that research-based knowledge was often to be preferred to hunch, trial and error and speculation. As reports of teachers' conferences and studies such as those of Cane and Schroder (1970) indicate, there is by no means unanimous support within the profession for the activities of the research worker and the curriculum development specialist. There is clearly much to be done before there exists the kind of positive attitude towards educational R. and D. within the rank and file of teachers' organisations, in local education offices, in Parliament and among the public that alone can ensure a sympathetic reception for major new initiatives and the maintenance of a high level of project funding. Readable and relevant reports of high quality on important topics are an essential element in shaping such attitudes. Another is introducing students and teachers to the possibilities and limitations of research at an early stage in their careers, and ensuring that the content of their studies takes full account of the results of such research. A third is finding ways in which teachers and administrators can become more involved than at present in helping to determine research agendas, execute projects and evaluate outcomes. The favourable reception among press, politicians and public accorded to some recent research reports is encouraging, as is the likelihood of considerable enlargement in the range and scope of in-service work with teachers. But more than this is needed. If students and teachers are to feel themselves consulted and involved, then the research net has to be spread more widely. There need to be more small-scale projects (Chanan, 1972), more money available to back the activities of local groups based upon colleges and teachers' centres, and more secondments of a kind that enable teachers to obtain research training, undertake individual studies, and participate in team projects.

But there are also dangers in attempting to spread resources too thinly. Up to now it has been easier to secure funds for projects of limited duration than for longer term programmes or for longitudinal studies. There are relatively few research units that have any kind of assured future. Those that do exist have to rely upon a wide variety of resources for their funds. The Higher Education Research Unit at the London School of Economics, for example, has received grants from the Nuffield Foundation (to establish the unit, start new projects and cover running costs) from the SSRC, from DES, and OECD, the Ford Foundation, the Ministry of Overseas Development, and Department of Employment and Productivity, the National Board for Prices and Incomes, the National Economic Development Office, the London School of Economics, the Leverhulme Foundation and the Carnegie Commission on Higher Education (HERU, 1972).

The Educational Research Board of the SSRC indicated in 1972 that it would 'prefer to support *programmes* in priority areas, and to award *small* grants for other research topics, rather than to fund a large number of short-term medium-cost projects' (Tizard, 1972). But the SSRC contributes only a small proportion of the funds available for educational R. and D., and it remains to be seen how far policies of this kind will be adopted by other funding bodies.

What many people would like to see emerge in the seventies is a pattern of major research centres with a guarantee of support for up to ten or fifteen years, and some freedom to initiate new work without the necessity of securing separate project finance, plus a broader spread of low-cost small-scale studies in colleges of education, polytechnics and elsewhere, involving large numbers of practising teachers and administrators. If the weaknesses of financial uncertainty, rapid staff turnover and lack of professional credibility are to be overcome, explicit efforts will be necessary both to concentrate manpower and resources where the nature of the problems to be tackled requires such concentration, *and* to spread research activity over a large number of institutions and individuals.

All this may require greater coordination among the funding agencies than at present. Reference has already been made to the advantages of a plural structure, but it is arguable that the existing pattern is too loose and uncoordinated, lacking both the means to identify the areas in which research practitioners should be encouraged to interest themselves and to exert the kind of political pressure that would help to secure a better hearing for research needs and outcomes. The possibility of establishing a national coordinating body is still raised from time to time, but none of the bodies or significant individuals on the research scene seems keen at the moment to reactivate the issue of an Educational Research Council. Informal meetings of representatives of funding agencies are being held, not yet on a regular basis, and it is possible that these may lead to the emergence of some kind of coordinating machinery.

Whatever new structures and systems of funding may become established, they will be called upon to support a wider variety of research efforts than can be contained within the classifications referred to earlier in this chapter. In addition to programmes and projects dealing with basic educational processes, small-scale team and individual investigations, longitudinal studies of various kinds and curriculum development activities, there are likely to be more examples of what has come to be called 'action research' and of intervention programmes requiring systematic evaluation and appraisal. The recently completed educational priority areas programme is of this type, and there are a number of new innovatory programmes under consideration. All this reflects a growing sophistication concerning the relationship between research, innovation, development and institutionalisation that has already led to shifts in the attention that bodies like the Schools Council pay to different stages of the studies for which they are responsible.

Another emerging trend is the scale and importance of international cooperation in educational research and development. The only publication that provides details of how educational R. and D. is funded in this country is in fact produced by the Council of Europe, as part of its biennial survey of research in European countries (Council of Europe, 1971). The Council is also engaged in stimulating the exchange of research workers between countries and the creation of national dissemination centres for educational R. and D., and in organising symposia at which research workers in particular fields may exchange experience and ideas. The first European Colloquium for Directors of Educational Research Institutes was held in London at the end of 1971 under Council auspices, based upon a simulation within which participants took the role of the Director of the as yet non-existent European Foundation for the Promotion of Educational Research and Development (EFPERD) (Taylor, 1972b). The OECD, with its Centre for Educational Research and Innovation (CERI) is also active in the field of educational research policy (Eide, 1971) as is UNESCO. British membership of the European communities may well increase the importance of this kind of international collaboration.

In conclusion, it is clear that the problems of educational research in the seventies will not be simply financial. Here, just as in the United States and in several European countries, it is being realised that a rapid increase in expenditure on projects, without a parallel concern with training, supervision, wider institutional support and a more sophisticated conceptualisation of the knowledge system of which research forms part, is unlikely to have pay-offs for either knowledge or action. And without such pay-offs, the positive political climate within which further advances can be made is unlikely to exist.

E. Hoyle

The study of schools as organisations

There has long been an implicit recognition amongst educationists and laymen that schools can be regarded as entities having a distinctive organisational character. This organisational character is, of course, partly a function of school type—public, grammar, secondary modern, comprehensive—but there are variations among schools of the same type. In recent years, the attempt to understand schools as entities has been one of the growth points in educational studies. Schools have been variously conceptualised as *complex organisations*, *social systems*, or, occasionally, as *social institutions*. These terms are often used inter-changeably, but they can have different theoretical implications. *Complex* or *formal* organisations may serve to overemphasise the formal structure of the school as against the informal structure. *Social system* usefully connotes an interrelationship of parts, but may overemphasise the degree of integration, consensus, and goal-seeking activities to be found in schools. *Social institution* has been given a rather specialised meaning which emphasises the values of an organisation (e.g. Selznick, 1957), but more generally in the sociology of education the term is best reserved for an institutional pattern (e.g. comprehensive education, private education) than for a specific organisation. In spite of the differences in terms, the central concern of these studies is to understand the functioning of schools and particularly the interplay of their various dimensions: formal structure, administrative processes, informal rela-tionships, culture, goals, and so forth. There have been many theoretical and methodological approaches to the study of schools as organisations in recent years; there has also been a degree of optimism about a possible convergence which would provide a distinctive theoretical perspective and body of research to illustrate the functioning of schools and to resolve practical problems arising from their day-to-day operations. These expectations have been fulfilled to a lesser degree than was anticipated in the early 1960s. Some convergence has taken place, but there remain considerable differences in approach, and it may well be that a full understanding of schools will be best derived from different sorts of study.

The study of schools as organisations emerged in the United States during the late 1950s. It was during this period that organisational analysis was in the process of becoming one of the major substantive areas of sociological study. The development of the sociology of organisations need not be documented here (see Mouzelis, 1967 and Silberman, 1970), but very briefly it was characterised by an attempt to develop middle-range theories of the functioning of organisations which would allow comparison between different types (e.g. factories, prisons, hospitals, schools and colleges). Thus the perspective was distinctively sociological; schools were studied more because they were organisations than because they were schools. As Corwin (1967) put it: 'sociologists are beginning to appreciate the relevance of educational organisations for extending and testing theory'. This orientation has had significant implications for the study of schools. On the one hand the comparative perspective of sociology has helped to identify some of the salient aspects of school organisation. On the other, the approach from sociology has not always been sensitive to the unique characteristics of schools. A concurrent development in the United States occurred in the field of educational administration. During the 1950s there emerged a dissatisfaction with the theory and research which was underpinning the administration of schools. As a result, what has come to be called the 'new movement' developed. This movement was characterised by a more sophisticated theoretical and research approach to educational administration (Griffiths, 1964a, Halpin, 1967). Clearly the sociological approach to organisations was relevant to the new movement, but in fact the two traditions remained relatively distinct and the relationship between them remains problematical (Hoyle, 1969). In particular, the new movement owed more to the managerialist tradition than to the sociological approach which, in fact, partly arose from a rejection of the 'classical' and 'human relations' approaches to the study of industrial organisations. Although the new movement aimed to be interdisciplinary, the major figures in the field tended to be educational psychologists whose focus was leadership, morale and communication rather than formal structure, goals and culture, although certain contributors (e.g. Carlson, 1962 and Bidwell, 1965) did take a more distinctively sociological perspective. The influence of the American approach to educational administration on British thinking can be seen in Baron and Taylor (1969) and Hughes (1970).

In spite of the attention paid in the British literature of the 1960s to these American trends, the actual research carried out in this country has been largely indigenous. As we shall see, sociological studies of schools in Britain have tended to be concerned with the relationship between the differentiation of pupils, pupil subcultures, and the opportunity structure. In addition, there have been a number of studies of the implications for school organisation of new trends in education, e.g. comprehensivisation, de-streaming, and curriculum development, which have not drawn at all upon the social science approaches to organisation. Research into school administration has been carried out mainly by studies of the role of the headteacher. Thus in this country, a number of different approaches to the study of schools have emerged, and this is not surprising given the options which any student has before him when he considers potential theories and methodologies.

Problems in the organisational analysis of schools

Like all organisations, schools have many dimensions which are to some degree interrelated. The researcher cannot hope to study all these relationships and must therefore make certain choices. As a means of throwing light on the problems of organisational analysis, we can consider a series of hypothetical choices—dichotomised here for the sake of simplicity—with which the researcher is confronted. (See Davies, 1970 for a valuable alternative approach.)

THEORY VERIFICATION OR THEORY GENERATION?

The investigator must decide what stance he is to take with regard to theory. He can choose to undertake a piece of research aimed at verifying a theory or he can allow the theory to emerge from the data. In the former case he would select a particular organisation theory and derive from this a series of hypotheses to test in the school situation. In the latter case he would begin his investigation without having in mind any particular theory (although as a social scientist he would not, of course, be innocent of concepts which serve to organise data) but would allow the theory to emerge. The case for generating grounded theory has been made by Glaser and Strauss (1968) who write: 'We believe that the discovery of theory from data—which we call grounded theory— is the major task confronting sociology today, for as we shall try to show, such a theory fits empirical situations, and is understandable to sociologist and layman alike. Most important, it works—provides us with relevant predictions, explanations, interpretations, and applications.'

GENERAL THEORY OR SPECIFIC THEORY?

If the investigator is concerned with verification, he must decide through his choice of theory what level of abstraction is appropriate. A range of options is open to him, namely:

1 An abstract theory of the formal properties of organisations. The most common form is *general systems theory* which has been utilised in a number of organisation studies and has been held to be relevant to the study of schools (e.g. Griffiths, 1964b).

2 A general theory of social systems. For example, Parsons (1966) examines the relevance of his theory of social systems to the understanding of school administration.

3 A comparative typology of organisations through which schools are classified according to a particular organisational type, e.g. Etzioni's (1961) comparative typology based upon the dimensions of power and compliance classifies schools as having normative power and moral compliance.

4 A comparative typology of educational organisations whereby schools are categorised as particular types, e.g. Carlson's (1964) typology categorises schools according to the two dimensions of control by the school over the admission of clients and the control by the client over his participation and derives hypotheses relating to the functioning of the different types.

5 A theory based upon one or more of the central dimensions of schools, e.g. decision-making (Griffiths, 1959), leadership role (Gross and Herriott, 1965), autonomy (Katz, 1964), bureaucracy (Anderson, 1969).

6 A theory based upon a substantive problem of educational organisations, e.g. the conservation of values (Selznick, 1951).

These different levels of abstraction serve different functions in research. The more abstract the theory, the easier it is to compare the functioning of schools with the functioning of other types of organisation; the more specific the theory, the greater the possibility of understanding schools *as such.*

CASE STUDY OR COMPARATIVE STUDY?

The investigator must decide whether he is to study one organisation or several. Each approach has its advantages and its disadvantages. The considerable advantage of the case study is that it enables the investigator to become well acquainted with the day-to-day functioning of the school. He can gain the confidence of the participants, use a variety of data-collecting techniques, and, importantly, become familiar with the undertow which is an important determinant of organisational character. The disadvantage of the case study is that the investigator is not entitled to generalise from his findings. The advantage of a comparative study is that generalisation is theoretically possible, and the disadvantage that only limited aspects of the school can be studied and these largely by standardised modes of data collection. The choice between case study and comparative study will depend upon many factors: the purpose of the study, its theoretical perspective, and, often decisively, on the resources available to the researcher.

SYNCHRONIC OR DIACHRONIC STUDY?

A synchronic study provides a snapshot of the organisation(s) being studied at one point in time. This approach is appropriate if the main object of the investigation is to compare some formal aspect of the school, e.g. degree of bureaucratisation. A diachronic study is essential where the investigator is concerned with organisational processes, e.g. socialisation, differentiation. In order to study these processes in the school situation, it is clearly necessary to study a cohort of pupils as it passes through the year grades.

STRUCTURE OR BEHAVIOUR AS INDEPENDENT VARIABLE?

The choice between these alternatives will usually turn upon the theoretical perspective of the investigator. The sociological approach tends to take structural aspects as the independent variable and explains the behaviour within the organisation in terms of the patterning imposed by the structure. On the other hand sociologists of the interactionist school, and most social psychologists, would take as their independent variable the interactions of members of the organisation and seek to demonstrate how these modify the formal structure. This choice is avoided at the theoretical level in the model of Getzels and Guba (1957) and Getzels, Lipham and Campbell (1968), which sees organisational behaviour as the outcome of the interaction among three dimensions: the *nomothetic* (institution-role-expectations) and the *idiographic* (individual-personality-needs) mediated by an intervening dimension: group-climate-intention, but the integration of these three dimensions at the operational level is difficult to achieve.

RESEARCH PROBLEM DERIVED FROM THEORY OR PRACTICE?

All investigators are concerned with a 'problem'. This may be a theoretical problem, i.e. one generated by a gap in existing theory, or a substantive problem, i.e. a practical difficulty which a school needs to resolve. This has something in common with the difference between theory verification and theory generation, but differs in that grounded theory can be developed in the absence of a specific operational problem of the school. The difference between theory-problem and practice-problem raises the difficult question of which approach ultimately has the greatest implications for practice, but we are concerned here with the initial orientation of the research. The implications can perhaps be illustrated by reference to the distinction between 'sociology of education' and 'educational sociology' (Hansen, 1967). The sociologist of education is not directly concerned with the resolution of practical problems but trusts that the educationist will derive his own solutions from the research findings. The educational sociologist on the other hand is centrally concerned with a school problem and draws upon sociological theory and research as and when necessary for the solution of the problem (Jensen, 1965). There is little doubt that the majority of organisational studies in education have been approached from the perspective of sociology of education. This is also true of studies in educational administration since the 'new movement' was particularly concerned to avoid the 'cookery book' approach which was not underpinned by a social science theory. These studies have consequently not been particularly compelling to the practising educationist. On the other hand, there have been many studies of practical school problems which have not been as useful as they might have been through not drawing on social science theory. Research on ability grouping is a good example. The rather ambivalent findings of research in this area could well have been due to the fact that ability grouping has been considered in isolation from other aspects of the school social system. The significance of factors other than grouping has been demonstrated in the NFER study of streaming in the primary school (Barker Lunn, 1970). This study took dichotomised teacher attitudes as well as streaming as a variable. Although there was no difference in the attainments of children in streamed and unstreamed schools, there were differences in attitude. In streamed schools it was the streaming structure which appeared to be important; in unstreamed schools it was the teacher. This approach might be extended to take account of the relationship between streaming and other aspects of the school social system, e.g. leadership, climate.

ONE MEANS OF DATA COLLECTION OR MANY?

Organisational analysis can be carried out via the usual modes of data collection: questionnaires, attitude and opinion scales, structured and unstructured interviews, diaries, participant and non-participant observation, content analysis of documents, etc. The investigator must decide whether he is to rely largely on one technique or a limited number of techniques or whether he will use a variety of methods. His decision will to some degree depend upon whether he is undertaking a case study or a comparative study and upon what resources he has available. A combination of methods gives the investigator the opportunity to see the organisation in the round and to use one technique to check the validity of another. On the other hand, this does not yield an elegant research design. The use of a single means of data collection, especially if a questionnaire is used, makes comparative studies possible and is amenable to a more sophisticated statistical analysis, but, of course, it limits the investigator to a limited number of organisational dimensions. The problem has been interestingly discussed by Halpin (1967) whose own contribution to organisational studies in education has been largely through the construction of the Organizational Climate Description Questionnaire (OCDQ). This is a sixty four item questionnaire designed to determine teachers' perceptions of the administrative climate of their schools. By means of factor analysis, Halpin identified eight dimensions of administrative relationships and, from the school profiles of these dimensions, six organisational climates. This measure has been widely used in several countries with some success. But Halpin is sensitive to the shortcomings of a single instrument and notes that it needs to be supplemented by studies within the schools themselves to establish whether the OCDQ climates were corroborated by studies carried out on the ground. As he notes: 'In a genuine sense we did not discover these Organisational Climates; we *invented* them.'

DETACHED RESEARCH OR ACTION RESEARCH?

The choice to be made by the investigator is whether he simply wishes to add to the understanding of the functioning of schools and leave the practical implications to practising educationists, or whether he wishes both to understand and to participate in change on the basis of his findings. It is likely that if the research problem has been theoretically derived, the stance of the investigator will be detached. If the problem has been derived from practice, the investigator may remain detached, but may also become actively involved in the problem-solving activity. Many sociologists and social psychologists perform consultancy roles as well as researcher roles, mainly in industrial organisations. At the present time there has been relatively little involvement of social scientists in the planned organisational change of schools (Hoyle, 1970). Where the investigator does become actively involved in the organisation through action research, his entire research strategy will be different from the approach of the detached researcher. In particular he will be required to relinquish traditional modes of verification in order to manipulate the situation which he is studying and in which he himself is involved. The reader is referred to Chin (1960) for a brief summary of the differences between the various types of detached and applied research. (Related points are discussed in the chapters by Richmond and by Stenhouse.)

ARE MEASURES OF OUTPUT TO BE USED OR NOT?

The input-output model has an immediate appeal to investigators who are particularly concerned with organisational effectiveness. The paradigmatic research design in these circumstances would be to seek to predict variations in output between various categories of input on the basis of the internal characteristics of organisations. But there are some obvious difficulties—theoretical and methodological—inherent in input-output studies, e.g.

1 The identification of school goals or objectives.
2 The conceptualisation of output. In the school situation pupil achievement is an obvious 'output'. But what about absenteeism, teacher turnover, or—the object of an interesting British study by Power *et al.* (1967)—delinquency rates?
3 The operationalisation of output. The cognitive outcomes of schooling are *relatively* easy to assess, but the social, moral, emc onal and aesthetic development of children is much more problematic. Organisational studies of schools have not so far been ntegrated with the movement towards the articulation and evaluation of curriculum objectives.
4 The identification of organisational patterns sufficiently different to account for variations in output. One recent review of American research (Robbins and Miller, 1969) estimated that: 'organisational arrangements of individual schools account for less than three per cent of the variance' (i.e. of pupil attainment). This review was admittedly of research which had taken school structure as the independent variable, and it could well be that other dimensions have more impact. Nevertheless, it is probably true to say that schools tend on the whole not to be very different in the internal arrangements and a low variance is to be expected in a random sample. A more appropriate method might be to study the outputs of schools which were very different in structure and process.

Students of schools as organisations have in the past been inhibited from studying outputs because of the lack of appropriate statistical models, but in recent years various models (e.g. stochastic, two stage input-output, path analysis) have been employed in assessing the effects of higher education and in some cases of schools (see Feldman, 1971 for a review of these techniques).

IS THE STUDY TO BE INTROSPECTIVE OR ARE ENVIRONMENTAL FACTORS TO BE INCLUDED?

A school is not a closed system. Its internal activities are affected by contextual factors. The investigator must decide whether he is to consider only the internal aspects of the school, or whether he is to take account of the influence of external factors (see Eggleston, 1967 for a review of these influences). If he decides to take account of external factors, the investigator is faced with the problem of limitation, for the school environment has its social, cultural, political, administrative, and economic components which range in extent from the immediately local to the national.

The above ten examples of the choices facing the analyst of educational organisations are by no means exhaustive. It is true that there will be a tendency for some of the solutions to these problems to be interdependent, but they nevertheless serve to illustrate perhaps why studies of schools as organisations do vary considerably in their theoretical and methodological perspectives. Each of the studies reviewed in the next section can be classified according to the particular solution adopted, but this is left to the reader rather than spelt out explicitly.

Organisational studies of British schools

Although there was considerable discussion of the potentialities of organisational analysis in education during the 1960s (e.g. Hoyle, 1965), very few empirical studies have been carried out in this country. There are a number of possible ways of grouping these studies for purposes of discussion, but perhaps the most profitable distinction is between case studies and comparative studies.

CASE STUDIES

It is probably true to say that the best organisational studies of British schools so far have been case studies of single schools. Hargreaves (1967) and Lacey (1970) have both reported studies arising out of a research project initiated by the Department of Sociology at Manchester University. The orientation of the project was the analysis of social relationships amongst small groups within a school. Thus the study began with a closer affinity to small group sociology than to organisational sociology with its emphasis on structure. Hargreaves functioned as an observer-participant over a period of one year in a secondary modern school in a northern city. The central concern of his study was the pattern of pupil relationships and their cultural norms, especially amongst the fourth year boys. He outlines his research orientation as follows:

'The study is thus socio-psychological and micro-sociological in orientation. Many limitations restrict the scope of the study. Differences in individual psychology, such as personality, have been excluded, and many sociological variables receive scant attention. The study does not intend to test specific hypotheses derived from current theories. Rather, the research is exploratory in nature and focuses broadly on the structure of informal groups of pupils and the influence of such groups on the educative process.'

He uses a variety of methods of data collection: observation, questionnaires with various types of item, e.g. sentence completion, orientation tests, sociometric tests, and analysis of school records, e.g. registers, house points, school fund contributions. The data on pupil subcultures revealed that these were to some degree generated by one aspect of the formal structure of the school—namely streaming. Hargreaves was able to demonstrate that in the fourth year the pupils in the A and B streams shared a distinctive 'academic' subculture whilst those in the C and D streams shared a 'delinquescent' subculture. He was also able to show that these subcultures had emerged over time, especially in the third and fourth years. Thus, apart from giving a valuable descriptive account of pupil subcultures, Hargreaves has made an important contribution to organisational studies by demonstrating a process of differentiation deriving from the interaction between a component of the formal structure—streaming, and a component of the informal structure—pupil interactions and friendship patterns.

As Lacey's investigation formed part of the same project as that of Hargreaves they not unnaturally have certain features in common: participant observation, the use of a variety of data gathering techniques, and a primary orientation towards studying relationships amongst pupils. Lacey begins with a detailed account of the historical development of the school and the current provision of secondary education in the city in which the grammar school which he studied was situated. This puts the study in a macrosociological context and establishes links between the internal operations of the school and the opportunity structure of Great Britain. The middle section of the study is concerned with the issue which was central to Hargreaves' work, i.e. the relationship between ability grouping and pupil subcultures. Lacey establishes a process model with two components: *differentiation*, i.e. 'the separation and ranking of students according to a multiple set of criteria which makes up the normative, academically orientated value system of the grammar school', and *polarisation* which 'takes place within the student body, partly as a result of differentiation, but influenced by external factors and with an autonomy of its own'. He tests some of the assumptions of this model, using sociometric techniques and various indicators of pupil subculture, at three levels: in the school as a whole, in a cohort study of one express stream, and through a number of individual case studies. Lacey is able to demonstrate that the intake of the grammar school becomes differentiated by streams in the first year, when classes are unstreamed, and further differentiated during the second year, when streaming occurs. The pupil culture is polarised into a pro-school subculture strong in the higher streams and an anti-school subculture which is strong in the lower streams. The final section of Lacey's work is concerned with the relationship between parents, teachers and pupils and is illustrated by means of case study material. As with Hargreaves' study, Lacey's work has considerable implications for the link between 'labelling', opportunity, achievement, and social stratification.

Julienne Ford (1969) carried out a case study of a comprehensive school, also drawing comparative material from a secondary modern school and a grammar school situated in the same area of London as the research school. In some ways the study resembles the work of Hargreaves and Lacey both in its methodology and in its substantive concerns—especially the relationship between friendship patterns, peer values, and streaming. But there are at least two important differences. Firstly, there are differences in the role which theory plays in the researches. Ford's study is basically concerned with verification, not of an organisation theory as such, but of the implicit theories of proponents of the comprehensive school. Her starting point is a set of seven propositions culled from the writings of these protagonists. Two of these propositions are used to generate five hypotheses:

1 Comprehensive schools will produce a greater development of talent than tripartite schools.
2 Comprehensive schools will provide greater equality of opportunity for those with equal talent.
3 The occupational horizons of children in comprehensive schools will be widened relative to those of children in tripartite schools.
4 Comprehensive school children will show less tendency to mix

only with children of their own social type than will tripartite school children.

5 Comprehensive school children will tend to have views of the class system as a flexible hierarchy, while tripartite school children will tend to see this as a rigid dichotomy.

Data were gathered to test these hypotheses by a variety of techniques: questionnaire sociometric testing, analysis of school records, and so on. The second difference between the studies is that whereas those of Hargreaves and Lacey begin with microsociological problems and allow the macrosociological implications of their findings to emerge, Ford begins with macrosociological issues such as occupational choice, class consciousness, and ideology, and uses a single school as a test situation—a point which has evoked criticism from sociologists and also from supporters of the comprehensive idea. In fact, Ford's study is a study of an institution—comprehensive education—through a single example rather than an organisational study as such. But there is no doubt that it has made an important contribution to organisational analysis of educational organisations in Britain.

Ford does not find support for any of the hypotheses which she tests. In other words, the hopes of the protagonists of comprehensive education are not being fulfilled in this one example. It emerges from the study that again the major barrier is the process of differentiation and the 'labelling' which is its consequence. In her final chapter, Ford discusses the fundamental problem of whether schools should differentiate and, if so, how this can be done in a manner which avoids the depressant effects on children who are labelled as low achievers. She offers her own solution, which is to have 'schools' for children up to the age of fourteen in which there would be no differentiation within the formal structure and from which children would then pass to 'colleges' offering differentiated courses.

King's (1969) case study of a grammar school was primarily concerned with the relationship between school values and pupil involvement. His three basic propositions were that education is a process of cultural transmission, that degrees of continuity exist between the culture of pupils' families and the culture transmitted by the schools, and that pupils are differentially involved in schools as social systems. From these propositions are derived a number of hypotheses which are tested by a variety of methods of data collection including interviews with pupils, questionnaires completed by staff, pupils and parents, analysis of documents including school records, and participant observation—King was a teacher in the school during the period of the investigation. For the most part the basic model is substantiated. The value system of the school was distinctively middle class. Children from middle class homes tended to hold the school-approved middle class values. But the holding of these values was associated with involvement in school only at a low level of significance. He sums up this finding as follows:

'For pupils with low stream status the degree of involvement was related to the acceptance or rejection of the school's values, but it was not so for those with higher stream status. In general, school involvement does not appear to be an important mechanism for value transmission.'

A research of rather a different kind is Wakeford's (1969) study of a boarding school. In one sense this is an institutional study of the public school, drawing upon documentary evidence from a variety of sources: prospectuses, lists of school rules, apologias, personal communications and interviews. But central to the study is the analysis of the single school. The main form of data collection was through observer participation—Wakeford taught in the school and had also been a pupil there—an approach which he justifies in some detail in a methodological appendix. The analysis is structured around a number of key concepts: relative deprivation, social control, adaptation. These, of course, are general sociological concepts and not specific to a middle-range theory of organisations. No distinctive theoretical perspective is adopted nor are any hypotheses tested. Wakeford's approach is to draw upon a wide range of sociological theory to give meaning to his material. For example, the section on adaptation is structured around Merton's well-known paradigm. But the main conceptual links are made with work on other forms of relatively closed organisations: prisons, military units and hospitals. The methodological orientation of Wakeford makes it difficult to summarise his main findings, since the objective of the investigation was to convey the feel of the life of such a school rather than to provide verified objective data. It is a difficult task to provide a descriptive account of the life of an organisation in all its manifestations and at the same time to make this sociologically meaningful in the sense that it articulates to familiar sociological concepts and theories. Wakeford chooses to use prior theoretical formulations to order his data in a sociologically meaningful way. The other possible approach, and the one of which Erving Goffman is the best exponent, derives new concepts from the observation of behaviour, to generate categories which cast new light on the familiar or which draw attention to the unfamiliar.

The above review of the best-known case-studies of British schools indicates that although these studies have made a substantial contribution to the understanding of educational organisations, they have not done so through testing established middle-range theories of organisation. With some exceptions (e.g. a study by Turner, 1969, which applies a paradigm by Blau, 1964, for relating the macrostructure and the substructures of an organisation to a secondary modern school), British studies have been less concerned with the formal properties of schools than with seeking to understand the significance of school as an agency of cultural transmission for different categories of pupil. They have been more concerned with the pupil's world than with the staff world—the studies tell us very little about teachers in any direct sense—and it is probably the case that extant theories of organisation are more applicable to the study of the élite of an organisation than its lower participants. This must be counted as a major shortcoming of current organisation theory.

COMPARATIVE STUDIES

Although there are very few comparative organisational studies of British schools at the present time, there are a number of comparative surveys of various dimensions of different types of school. The essential difference between a comparative organisational study and a comparative survey is that a survey is not concerned with the patterns of interaction which constitute a social system. It is concerned with comparing dimensions which are taken out of their organisational context rather than with comparing schools as entities. Surveys are valuable for many purposes, but they are not strictly organisational studies. One example is Kalton's (1966) study of sixty six public schools conducted by means of questionnaire. Data were collected on pupils (e.g. intelligence, social class, exam results), masters (e.g. age, degree class), school structures (e.g. staffing, sixth form size) and school finances. The study is subtitled 'A factual survey', and this is what it is in that it was not the

purpose of the research to try to determine the organisational characters
of the various schools, but to compare their dimensions. Interestingly,
Kalton's book has a foreword by Royston Lambert which puts the
study in a sociological context and in so doing offers a very neat account
of the nature of organisational analysis:

> 'Any information collected by postal questionnaires from one
> source in a complex institution such as a school will have inevitable
> limitations. It can tell us much of value but not all that we need to
> know about a community or a system of communities. Some
> essential features of a school cannot be reduced to facts by this
> method: the wider social system or macrocosm which the school
> serves, the aims and values which inform it, the ethos and attitudes
> which permeate it, the organisation and dynamics by which it works
> towards its ends, the culture and underlife which it generates in the
> process, the effects and modes of adaptation which it induces. To
> examine these and other aspects of the community of the school
> more diverse methods are obviously needed.'

Lambert has himself undertaken a comparative organisational analysis
of public schools. Although the final report has not yet been published
the project has so far yielded two publications: an account of pupils'
perceptions of their schools as revealed in written work (Lambert,
1968) and a manual on how to conduct a comparative analysis (Lambert et al., 1970).

A comparative study of direct grant schools was carried out on
behalf of the Donnison Commission and constitutes Appendix 6 of
Part 2 of the Report (HMSO 1970). This provided valuable background
data for the Commission but it did not provide an analysis of the
organisational character of different types of Direct Grant School
generated by the combination of different elements: degree of selectivity, religious affiliation, proportion of fee payers, etc. The Commission
was aware of the potential value of such profiles but was disinclined to
mount the necessary research which would have delayed the publication of its report.

Another large comparative study which has recently been undertaken and which will soon be published is the Sixth Form Study carried
out on behalf of the Schools Council by the Department of Education,
Manchester University, under the direction of Professor R. A. C. Oliver.
Part of the study was considered by the Donnison Commission and has

been separately published (Christie and Griffin, 1970). This showed that in a sample of highly selective schools when O-level achievements are used as a predictor of A-level achievements, there is a relative decline at A-level—although overall achievement remains high. As this is a survey rather than an organisational analysis it cannot yield the reasons for this. It might be hypothesised, however, that it could be another example of the effects of labelling whereby A-level achievements of intelligent pupils are depressed because they have not been labelled as potential Oxbridge entrants. Christie and Griffin (1971) point out that the answers could only be determined through a study of social and educational processes within the schools.

There have so far been reports of the first two stages of the Comprehensive Education Project which is being carried out by the NFER. The first report (Monks 1968) contains a survey of several of the dimensions of a comprehensive school, e.g. structure, staffing, pupil ability. The second stage has been reported in Monks (1971) and covers a sample of 59 out of the 222 schools identified as meeting the definition of 'comprehensive' in the initial survey. The report contains data on administration, attainments, friendship choices, curriculum and pupil welfare, extra-curricular activities and school-community contacts. The approach is descriptive, static, and considers one dimension at a time. The difference between a survey and an organisational analysis can be seen by comparing the chapter on administration—which includes material of pupil-teacher ratios, the distribution of responsibility allowances, and the amount of time which the head spends with visitors—with studies of school administration as a social process. One can also compare the chapter on friendship choices—which reports such data as the tendency for pupils to choose their friends from the same ability, social, behavioural and ethnic groups—with the work of Lacey and Hargreaves which considers the relationship between friendship choice, pupil subculture and streaming as a social process and examines its implications. The third stage of the project involves a study of twelve schools to determine the degree to which they are fulfilling their objectives. This stage will involve a comparative organisational study of the schools using measures developed by Banks and Finlayson.

The first major organisational study carried out on a comparative basis has been completed by King on a grant from the Schools Council. The conceptual basis of the research is given in King (1968) and a synopsis of the main findings in King (1970). The basic research problem is expressed thus: 'How does the organisation of the school affect the pupils' involvement in the school?' The basic methodological problem is expressed as follows by King: 'The intention of the research . . . is to advance the study of schools as organisations, by attempting to evolve objective criteria of observation, simple taxonomies and actual measurements of certain organisational dimensions, all of which may enable reasonably valid and reliable comparisons to be made between schools, and also account for some of the unique features of individual schools.' The basic research design involved a measure of the organisation of the school as it affects the pupils, the measurement of pupil involvement, and the relationship between organisation and involvement. The study of organisation was carried out in seventy-two secondary schools by means of questionnaire, interviews, documentary analysis and direct observation. Structural variables were characterised as being either *instrumental* or *expressive*, as being either *ritualised* or *bureaucratised*, as being age-, ability-, or sex-differentiating, and by reference to their subsystems, e.g. games, pastoral care. The results of this part of the investigation showed that the organisation of the school was most clearly related to the ability, social background and sex of pupils, its age range and its ideology; size was relatively unimportant. The study of pupil involvement was based upon 7 500 pupils drawn from a subsample of thirty schools who completed a mixed item questionnaire related to incidence in joining clubs, self-estimates of educational life, involvement, etc. The results showed that the degree of involvement varied by age, sex, ability and social class. The third element in the investigation which brought together the organisational measures and the involvement measures showed that the following organisational variables are significantly related to degrees and types of pupil involvement: the sex composition of the school, the social composition of the school, streaming, provision of out-of-school activities. This research is still very much in the British tradition, which was exemplified in the case studies, of focusing on the pupil dimension of the school, although in this case it is related to certain aspects of school organisation. As King himself notes, he has omitted from the investigation the role of teachers as agents of social control and of cultural transmission, and one might also add that the significance of the administrative process has been omitted. But this only serves to highlight the problem of attempting comparative organisational studies which will simultaneously handle all the major dimensions of the school. (The report of King's research is currently with the Schools Council from whom a synopsis can be obtained.)

There have so far been few comparative studies of the administrative dimension of schools. The issue of school administration is being largely dealt with in this country through studies of the role of the head-teacher which are currently being carried out at the Universities of Bradford (see Cohen, 1970), Bristol and Leicester. Compared with the voluminous American research, there has been little in this country so far on such issues as decision-making, communication, patterns of authority, administrative climate, etc. One of the most suggestive pieces of research in this area was carried out under the direction of R. W. Revans (1965). The basic concern of the research project was to evolve a method of measuring pupils' involvement in their school work through an analysis of films of their activities during lessons in ten schools where the teachers concerned had agreed the lesson content. Significant variations in pupil involvement emerged and Revans went on to investigate the possibility that this was a function of the administrative dimension of the school. He investigated the attitudes of children towards teachers and the attitudes of teachers towards the authority structure of the school in twenty seven schools. He summarised the findings as follows:

'. . . where teachers feel either that they have a hand in the internal running of the school, or that its outside directors are aware of their internal problems, they tend to be both liked by their pupils and seen as effective teachers. If the teachers see their superiors as remote or dictatorial, they, in their turn, are seen by their pupils as un-friendly and ineffective.'

A forthcoming study by Rose, Director of Research for the Central Lancashire Family and Community Project, and his colleagues will make a very valuable contribution to literature on school organisation, especially its administrative aspect. The research project was primarily concerned with the functioning of the school social workers who formed part of the project, but it became clear that the 'preventative' work of the project could only be fully understood if the functioning of schools was also taken into account. Information on the schools was collected by means of interviews and observation by the project workers who were in close contact with them. Aspects covered in the report include staff ideology in relation to social work based upon a typology of teachers, the categorisation of the formal and informal aspects of the school organisation, the influence of the head, the power situation in the schools, and the flow of information. This is a case where a concern with the school as an organisation arose out of a specific problem.

Potentialities and problems

The preceding review indicates that in this country the study of schools as organisations has only recently begun. The purpose of this final section is threefold: to indicate possible areas for future research, to refer to relevant American work from which ideas may be derived, and to raise certain methodological issues. These aspects cannot be dealt with exhaustively and therefore three topics have been selected for discussion which give the opportunity for bringing them out.

COUNSELLING

One of the most important recent developments in the social science of education has been the growing interest in the problem of 'labelling'. The ascription of status—especially academic status—to pupils has been shown to involve a self-fulfilling prophecy at three levels: at the institutional level of allocation to different types of school, at the organisational level, and at the classroom level (e.g. Rosenthal and Jacobson, 1968). This research has contributed to a movement towards mixed ability grouping at the primary and early secondary levels. But where pupils are not 'grouped by destination', as where a system of streaming operates, there arises the need for a more individualised form of guidance and counselling. This movement is only just beginning in this country, and although there are some useful studies (e.g. Moore, 1970), there is a need for further studies which will examine the relationship between guidance procedures and other elements of the school social system and particularly study the latent functions of guidance.

A number of American studies provide valuable insights in this area, and two in particular can be mentioned. Burton Clark (1960) carried out an organisational study of a Californian junior college established to provide mainly technical courses for terminal students and some academic courses for transfer students aspiring to enter a four year university course. But as an 'open door' policy allowed any student to enter the junior college and choose his own courses, the majority of students entered academic courses. The college had to reorganise its internal structure in order to provide more of these courses, but it also developed what Clark called 'cooling out' procedures whereby non-academic students were persuaded to revert to technical courses. A variety of devices were used, but importantly the counsellor, armed with his files and records, became the 'agent of consolation' in encouraging the less able student to drop out from academic courses on the basis of his scholastic record. Cicourel and Kitsuse (1963) studied counselling procedures in a large American high school. Using open-ended interview procedures with pupils, parents and counsellors, they demonstrated the ways in which the activities of counsellors affected the aspirations of students and parents, identified academic and other problems, and channelled students towards different courses. Their results suggested that the counselling system had become a bureaucratised form of talent hunt whereby students were differentiated on the basis of their school records, biographical and clinical data. But the bureaucratic procedures were not followed uniformly by the counsellors. They were modified on the basis of their perceptions of students as likely college material and the cases handled differently. It is clear from these two studies that that differentiation by counselling raises new problems of labelling and British investigators might begin studies of the organisation of comprehensive schools taking as the central problem of the social system the extent to which counselling replaces streaming as the basis of ascription.

Having cited these two American studies in relation to a substantive area of research, the opportunity can be taken to draw attention to the methodological contributions which they have made. Two aspects of Clark's study are of interest. Firstly, the study centres around an organisational problem which emerged during the course of the investigation. In other words, the theory emerged from the data. Secondly, the study is notable for its use of documentary material as an important source of data. The study by Cicourel and Kitsuse has considerable methodological interest in that it was one of the first studies to take a sociological perspective which has since become much more common. They note that most sociologists take the statistics collected by an organisation as 'given' and, whilst acknowledging their questionable basis proceed to correlate these statistics with such variables as sex, class, race, etc. They reject this approach and outline their own as follows:

'In formulating our research, therefore, we proposed to address specifically the problem of investigating the processes by which persons come to be defined, classified, and recorded in the categories of the agency's statistics. If the rates of college-going students, underachievers, "academic problems", etc. are to be viewed sociologically as characteristics of the high school as a complex organisation, then the explanation for such rates must be sought in the patterned activities of that organisation and not in the behaviour of the students *per se*. The theoretical significance of student *behaviour* for variations in rates is dependent upon how the personnel of the high school interpret, type, and process the behaviour.'

This orientation owes much to the work of Alfred Schutz and of Harold Garfinkel who emphasise the central importance of the perspectives of the actors whose actions produce the organisation which is under study and how organisations define persons as instances of given categories.

AUTHORITY

It has already been pointed out that there have so far been few studies of patterns of authority in British schools, and yet as these patterns are themselves undergoing change there would appear to be a need for research in this area. There are perhaps two major forces which are bringing about changes in authority patterns in British schools. Firstly, there is a change in the social climate which is leading to a demand by teachers for more participation in the running of schools. Secondly, changes in the curriculum and forms of organising for instruction (e.g. flexible grouping, team teaching, interdisciplinary enquiry) are bringing teachers into greater integration with each other at the level of their day to day work which *prima facie* might seem to be congruent with *collegial authority* whereby professional equals govern their work situation.

Research on administration has tended to conceptualise the question of authority in terms of leadership and administrative climate whereas sociologists have tended to rely upon the Weberian concept of bureaucracy. Most of the work which has operationalised bureaucracy has been carried out in North America. The standard procedure is to develop a scale of bureaucracy whereby teachers report their *perceptions* of their schools as being more or less bureaucratic. Summed scores give school profiles and it is then possible to compare schools or to correlate school scores with other variables, e.g. social class of intake, proportion of women employed, school size (Anderson, 1969), teachers' sense of power (Moeller and Charters, 1966), etc. There are, however, a number of difficulties arising from the use of the concept of bureaucracy. Firstly, it is not a unitary concept. Punch (1969) factor analysed teachers' responses to an adaptation of Hall's scale of bureaucracy and two distinctive factors emerged, a bureaucratic factor and a professional factor. Secondly, there is no single model of authority which applies to the school. Katz (1964) has suggested that the school is characterised less by authority than by autonomy, and Bidwell (1965) has suggested that the school is characterised by a mixture of authority and autonomy. This is true of the British school at the present time. The teacher has a relatively high degree of autonomy in the classroom, but relatively little involvement in decision-making on matters of school policy. The greater integration of teachers in their daily work is likely to lead to a decline in their autonomy. On the other hand, they are likely to gain a greater voice in the determination of school policy if integration is accompanied by collegiality. The paradox is that a loss in autonomy could actually increase the teacher's professionality. On the other hand, for some teachers this loss in autonomy might not be compensated for and a loss in satisfaction might result. In a highly perceptive article Lortie (1964) has pointed out that future research in team teaching should aim to assess the competing trends towards greater collegiality and towards a new form of bureaucracy.

SCHOOL COMMUNITY RELATIONSHIPS

A number of sociologists have argued that the central problem of organisation is that of boundary maintenance and that this, therefore, ought to be the central focus of research. The British school, as compared with its North American counterpart, has been relatively insulated from the local community and hence the problem of boundary maintenance has not been particularly acute. But at the present time there is a growing pressure to strengthen the links between school and community, particularly through the involvement of the parents in the life of the school but also through the involvement of teachers with the families of their pupils. There are obvious substantive problems here which suggest the need for research. There is little doubt that the effectiveness of the school would be improved through greater co-operation with parents, and research indicates that teachers see parental support as improving their effectiveness and satisfactions. On the other hand, there are indications that in certain circumstances teachers would see parental involvement as a threat and that a sizeable proportion of teachers do not see an involvement with the community as part of their role. Thus a boundary maintenance problem is likely to be generated by these trends. Again one can look to American experience and research in this area. The most sophisticated theoretical approach to the problem is that of Litwak and Meyer (1965, 1967) who conceptualise the problem in terms of the incompatibilities between social units of different kinds: a formal organisation (school) and a primary group (family). They develop their ideas at a theoretical level in terms of patterns of linkage which arose out of their participation in the Great Cities Project in Detroit where a variety of school-community links were established.

Apart from the work of the Central Lancashire Family and Community Project which has already been cited, the substantive problem of school community linkage is being handled in this country through the EPA Project directed by A. H. Halsey and especially through the Liverpool scheme of Eric Midwinter. The report of this project has not yet been completed and one must await its publication to see to what extent there is data which touches on this problem of the school boundary. The EPA project is a piece of action research and it may be, as Young (1965) has suggested, that school community relationships particularly lend themselves to this approach. But it is important in such a scheme to attempt to evaluate its impact upon the internal organisation of the school.

Conclusion

It has been the purpose of this chapter to review British research on schools as organisations. It has been shown that there are many possible approaches—both theoretical and methodological—to such studies, but that the best British studies so far published have tended to be case studies of single schools and have concentrated on pupil subculture and differentiation. A number of comparative studies have been carried out and are yet to be published, but comparative studies involve the solution of difficult problems of design. There has been little work so far in this country on the administrative dimensions of the school, perhaps partly due to the problems of access in this sensitive area but perhaps also due in part to the feeling that existing theories of organisation and administration are not particularly relevant in this context. It might well be the case that future studies will take as their starting point substantive problems rather than theoretical problems, and three possible areas have been cited—counselling, authority in a system of integrated teaching, and school-community relationships. In either case, there would appear to be scope for, and a need for, further organisational studies of British schools.

John Newson, Elizabeth Newson and Peter Barnes

Child rearing practices

One of the strongest threads running through much educational research is the general agreement on the important role played by the home in affecting progress and adjustment at school. This is hardly surprising when one considers that virtually all of a child's formative years until the age of five are spent under the supervision of home and family, and that this influence is maintained once he is at school. What *is* surprising is that we know comparatively little about the ways in which the child's upbringing influences his educational performance—attractive theories and hypotheses abound, but hard evidence is remarkably thin on the ground. As Klein (1965) commented at the beginning of her book on child rearing practices, 'there is a dearth of English studies on what parents think and do'. American research is more abundant, but it is necessarily excluded from consideration here by the terms of reference of this volume. Its direct application to the English situation has also been questioned (Klein, 1965).

It is our belief that, to understand fully what is happening in a child rearing situation, that situation must be seen in its widest context—to to look at supposed influential factors in detail will often lead to over-simplifications and misunderstandings if context is ignored. The frequency of smacking may be used as an indication of the nature of maternal discipline, but this will mean little unless information is also available on those situations in which the child is smacked, whether he is smacked in anger or in a cold dispassionate way some time after the event, and whether or not the smack is accompanied by a verbal explanation of why the punishment is necessary. The differences between breast fed and bottle fed babies may be the result, not of the particular technique used, but of factors which influence the mother to choose one method as opposed to the other (Bernal and Richards, 1970). The nature of the information on child rearing gleaned from a question-

57

naire, interview, or period of observation depends entirely on the questions asked (and the way in which they are asked), or the coding system used by the observer, and these in turn reflect the preconceptions and theoretical orientation of the researcher. The data can only be as good as the questions asked.

However, Swift (1965, 1968) has pointed out that, even amongst those who recognise the importance of taking context and the environment into account there are wide differences in understanding of the perspective involved; hence the basic failure of communication between the psychologist, whose interest is primarily in the individual, and the sociologist, whose concern is for the social process of which the individual is a part. In this confusion it is perhaps inevitable that contradictions will be commonplace. If we accept that in much of child rearing practice it is the parental *values* rather than specific techniques which are important, we also have to enquire after the source of the values. Because this source, however vaguely we may be able to define it, is certainly a part of the environment in its broadest sense, the distinctions made below between aspects of the child-rearing situation are merely an administrative convenience. The overlap between the subsections is unavoidable, and will, we hope, serve as a reminder to the reader of the way in which this interrelatedness operates in reality.

Language and communication

The importance of language in education is self-evident. It is the instrument with which thinking is conducted, so that impoverished linguistic ability is associated with limited cognitive power. Abstract thought and the ability to reason, upon which so much of academic education is based, are almost wholly determined by the possession of and the ability to use language. It seems reasonable to suppose that the seeds of such an ability are sown in the nature of the interaction between mother and child in the early years of life when language is first being acquired by the child, and in the value that the mother herself places upon the use of language in her dealings with the child.

Studies have shown that children reared in institutions where interaction with adults is low score lower on tests of linguistic development and verbal intelligence than do children in normal family situations (Pringle, 1965; Tizard and Joseph, 1970). Similar trends have been found in studies of twins for whom, it is argued, the need to communicate verbally is diminished, and the opportunities to develop a 'restricted code' form of speech (see below) are greater.

In the longitudinal study of children growing up in Nottingham (Newson and Newson, 1968) information has yet to be gathered on the intellectual and educational progress of the sample. However, sufficient information has been amassed on four year old children to illustrate the variety of ways in which language plays a part in child rearing, and to speculate on the likely educational consequences. These speculations are given strength by the similarity between the social class differences in language usage, and class differences in educational performance shown in other studies (Douglas, 1964; Wiseman, 1964). These differences will become clearer in the subsequent sections on Play, and Supervision and control, but some indication will be given here of the sort of differences encountered.

Middle class mothers tend to interact more with their children than do working class mothers, and this interaction tends to be of a more verbally articulate nature. For 48 per cent of middle class four year olds, telling stories and singing songs formed a regular part of the bedtime pattern, but this was so for only 24 per cent of the working class. At meal times, although middle class parents are more likely to be particular about manners, they place fewer restrictions on 'talking at table' than do the working class, who, in other respects, are more lax. Middle class mothers are also more likely to apologise to the child if they have broken one of the child's toys by accident, whereas the working class mother lays more stress upon restitution. The apology is an attempt to make explicit the principle of reciprocity—that the mother is prepared to treat the child in the same way that she expects to be treated by him—and to provide the child with a model of correct behaviour; it involves much greater effort on the mother's part than mere restitution, but it forces the child to consider her actions, and, maybe, in some way to recognise the use and power of words.

Certainly the most ambitious and comprehensive study of the interrelationship between language, education, and child rearing has been made by Bernstein and his colleagues at the Sociological Research Unit, in the Institute of Education, London University. Useful summaries of the development of this work have been given by Lawton (1968) and Ravenette (1970). (See also Lawton's chapter in the present book.)

The basic premise of Bernstein's approach (1965) is the distinction between the 'restricted' and the 'elaborated' speech codes. The former is a typical style of communication in all social groups which are characterised by a sense of common identity, purpose, and aspiration. This unity of outlook implies that a lot of meaning can be communicated by a little effort, perhaps only a gesture or an inflexion of the voice; language and syntax need only be simple. The 'elaborated' code, by contrast, is characteristic of situations in which this unity cannot be taken for granted, and where greater reliance has to be placed on the more elaborate use of language to communicate meaning, intention, and feeling. The difference between the codes can be shown in characteristic grammatical and syntactical features.

Bernstein has further argued that the nature of working class life is such that there will be a tendency for a 'restricted' code to be the dominant form, whereas the middle class style of life requires the children to become adept at using both forms so that they learn to switch from one to the other as the situation demands. Access to an 'elaborated' code brings with it certain educational advantages in terms of higher performance on verbal intelligence tests, the ability to use language in a way acceptable to the school, and an easier acceptance of modern educational theory and practice which is geared to the child capable of manipulating words and concepts. The codes are imparted to the child by the form and nature of the mother's interaction with him, which, in turn, is determined by the nature of the social relationship which they share.

Robinson and Rackstraw (1967) have illustrated this difference by contrasting the ways that mothers of five year old children said they would answer their children's questions (the assumption is made that this is how they *would* act in such a situation). The middle class mothers, it was concluded, were more likely to answer the question, to give more information, and to give more accurate information, than the working class. They were also more likely to use compound arguments and analogies, and to give a greater variety of causal and purposive answers. If mother–child interaction *does* differ in this way between the classes, this provides further evidence of differences in verbal and cognitive experiences which might be expected to affect the child's own cognitive development.

Bernstein and Henderson (1969), in an ingenious experiment, have continued this line of enquiry. A sample of mothers was asked to imagine that parents could not speak, and then to assess the extent to which this would add to the difficulty of dealing with certain specified situations that might arise with young children, such as showing them what is right and wrong, and teaching them everyday tasks such as using a knife and fork. Whereas all the mothers thought that being dumb would make it more difficult to deal with aspects of social control (referred to generally as the 'person' area) than with the transmission of skills (the 'skill' area), middle class mothers placed much *greater* emphasis on dealing with things in the 'person' area than working class mothers, and much *less* emphasis on the difficulty of transmitting skills. Bernstein and Henderson argue that the root of this difference is to be found, not in terms of the relevance of these two areas for the social classes, but rather in the nature of the social relationship when skills and personal relationships are transmitted. In the working class the receiver of knowledge is relatively passive, and the mother plays a didactic role, whereas in the middle class knowledge is transmitted through a social relationship in which the child learns at his own pace and on his own terms in an environment which is carefully supervised and controlled by adults to suit his needs. It is suggested that, as a consequence, the working class child learns skills in terms only of an understanding of the operations they entail, whilst the middle class child learns both the operations and the principles on which they are based.

After his early theoretical writings, Bernstein is now beginning to present some empirical findings. Inevitably these will lead to adaptations of the theory and will stimulate further research. The importance of this area of investigation to our understanding of the complex relationship between patterns of child rearing and intellectual and educational progress cannot be overestimated.

Supervision and control

One of the aspects of child rearing in which modes of communication are important, and almost certainly significant in terms of development, is the control that the mother exercises over her child. All parents attempt, by some means, to exercise some control over their children in an endeavour to guide them in the direction which they believe to be right. It is in the form and extent of this control, and the way in which it is achieved, that differences may occur. Once again, however, we are dogged by the fact that 'there is little systematic evidence on normal English practice' (Klein, 1965).

Judged by their writings, those who were in a position to advise on child rearing practices during the last century and the earlier part of the present one, e.g. Sir Truby King, Mabel Liddiard, J. B. Watson, advocated a strictly authoritarian approach (Newson, E., 1967). Thompson (1969) has queried whether this advice was necessarily taken. On the evidence of people's recollections of their childhood or parenthood during the period 1900–1918, he suggests that relationships were more relaxed than is generally imagined. It would be of interest to see whether this was still the case in the 1920s and 30s when advice was more widely available and would have reached a wider audience. It is certainly clear that nowadays parents are, in general, warmly disposed towards their children, and, from an early age, recognise and respect that the child has rights of his own. Over half the mothers of the four year old children in the Newson's sample were prepared to accept the child's excuse that he 'couldn't come because he was busy' to the extent of allowing him extra time to carry on with what he was doing. For the past twenty years or so these predominantly middle class values have been the accepted basis for ordinary primary school practice. It may be that the apparent hostility towards authoritarian control and attempts to overthrow traditional disciplinary procedures in some of our schools and colleges stems from this democratic attitude; in terms of the structure of the traditional school, children no longer know their place.

Nevertheless all parents agree, operationally, that children need to be controlled, even though some object to words like 'control' which recognise this fact. Some writers have suggested that there are class differences in the extent to which parents are permissive or restrictive (see Bronfenbrenner, 1958 for a review of the American literature on this question), but this seems to be making the wrong distinction. Evidence suggests that all parents are both permissive *and* restrictive, but about different things, and it is here that class divisions become apparent. Middle class parents may exercise strict control over the company the child keeps, his choice of recreation, and his application to school work. Working class parents, by contrast, may show little concern for such things, and instead be restrictive over sex play, access to sexual knowledge, and the asking of questions generally which might seem to pose a challenge to parental authority. Arising out of our current work with mothers of seven and eleven year olds we would argue that this includes challenges to their knowledge; the working class mother is more inclined than the middle class to attempt to 'pass it off' if the child asks a question to which she doesn't know the answer.

A further important difference which has been observed is the medium through which control is exercised. The middle class mother typically uses verbal methods to regulate her child's behaviour. She is prepared to embark upon seemingly endless explanations as to why a certain action is desirable or undesirable with the aim of providing her child with a set of rules with which, in time to come, he can assess his own behaviour and thus exercise his own control over himself. She may not always have time for these long drawn out procedures, and, in the heat of the moment and in the face of an irrational child (or, more disconcertingly, a child whose rationality runs counter to her own), she may have to resort to an appeal to her status as mother to insist that something be done. But her aim remains as a long-term one, and her technique one of consistent verbal pressure, despite the absence of short-term results. This approach is not reserved only for situations where the child's behaviour needs to be constrained; attempts to promote positive behaviour are also sought through verbal analysis and persuasion. Feelings and emotions are considered, and hypothetical situations may be suggested, forcing the child to think in abstract and general terms rather than concrete and specific ones. An indication of the extent to which this principle is followed to its natural conclusion can be seen in the greater preparedness of the middle class mothers in the Nottingham sample to admit that they are in the wrong, thus acknowledging the power of verbal argument. The child is rewarded for the skilful use of such verbal counter-argument, and comes to recognise its power. The fact that these techniques are also the ones on which the pursuit of knowledge on all levels is based, assures for him a position of advantage.

For the working class child, on the other hand, much of this is lacking. His mother's main emphasis tends to be more on the short-term effect of ensuring compliance with her immediate wishes rather than on the long-term inculcation of rules and standards, and although she may expect him to generalise these for himself, she does much less to assist him by spelling out general rules of conduct and by making them verbally explicit. Although the working class mother is concerned with the future in the sense that she hopes for her child's long-term reconciliation to and acceptance of her authority, internalisation of rules and identification with the rule-making person are not expected. As a consequence his powers of verbal reasoning are not so often called upon, and his understanding of the value of argument as a means of achieving his ends is limited. The study by Bernstein and Henderson (1969) has already been cited in support of the class differences in the extent to which parents conceive of the value of language in various aspects of child rearing.

One could add here that the encouragement toward explicit rational argument is also a preparation for adult middle class life, where the power to be a persuasive verbal advocate becomes an indispensable property for anyone occupying an administrative or organisational role.

Data from the Nottingham survey of seven year olds, currently being analysed (Newson and Newson, in preparation), throw light upon the contrasting amounts of supervision to which children of this age are subjected. Working class mothers are more likely to describe their children as 'outdoor' in their habits, and once out of doors they are more likely to be beyond the reach of adult control and surveillance. In other respects too the middle class children are more closely chaperoned, either by the physical presence of an adult (collecting them from school, or supervising their play in the house or its immediate vicinity), or by the imposition of rules about where and how far they may go alone. On this same measure a far greater difference was found between boys and girls, the latter being more limited in their actions. The long term effects of this cannot be stated with any certainty, but in this situation girls, and particularly middle class girls, come under consistently greater pressure towards conformity with adult standards and values. The common finding that girls of this age are superior to boys in their language development may also be related to this more frequent contact with an adult language model.

Play

Reference has been made already to the ways in which the pre-school child's experiences may stand him in good or poor stead when he begins school. Play is at the root of much modern infant education method, and also, of course, occupies most of the waking hours of the young child. These two facts have recently been grasped by the toy manufacturing industry in this country, and many toys currently on sale now bear the prefix 'educational' or 'child guidance', the implication being that they will give some kind of intellectual advantage which will carry over into school performance. Although toys may vary in their suitability for eliciting language or presenting the child with a problem to be solved, much of the value of the toy rests with the way the child plays with it, the way the parents introduce it into the child's play, and the concept of the purpose of play that the parents hold and manage to convey to the child. Similarly, parents' reaction to, and participation in, their children's play which need not necessarily involve toys can be seen to have results which also have fairly obvious educational implications. Once again, however, interpretation must be cautious since research is, in the main, only suggestive.

The Nottingham research at the four year old level provides information on play from various angles, but in each case one is struck by contrasting class attitudes and actions. Although the majority of parents see play as having some value in a broadly educational sense, there are differences in the ways in which they encourage and capitalise upon it. This is illustrated by the fact that fewer restrictions are placed upon children's noisy or messy play by the professional and managerial class as opposed to the rest. This difference may be attributable in part to the economic and material circumstances of this group—the ability to provide play space, and to employ someone to clean up the mess—but it probably also reflects the recognition among the parents in Social Classes I and II that such play has an educational and intellectual value that might not be immediately apparent. These mothers are able to justify the inconvenience in a way that the working class mother, with a more limited understanding of education, finds difficult.

Parental reaction to a further aspect of the child's play, his fantasy world, also gives an indication of the influence that the adult may have. The Nottingham data show that, after allowance has been made for family size, there is a significant increase in the number of fantasies (imaginary playmates and the like) communicated by children from Classes I and II to their mothers, and a significant decrease in Class V as compared with the remainder. Although the interpretation of this is not straightforward, there is some evidence that the middle class mother welcomes this sort of play, seeing in it an opportunity to encourage the child's imagination and creativity, whereas the lower working class mother discourages it, perhaps seeing in it an indication of oddity, or even mental disturbance, in her child. For the child, however, fantasy play is an important social exercise which enables him to take on the role of the other, and thus to understand himself better, in a way akin to adult sociodrama. Such dramatic play forms an integral part of infant and junior school education, so that, once again, the middle class child finds an environment in which he quickly feels at ease, whereas the working class child has to learn how to use the *medium* through which he is expected to express himself.

Further evidence on differing attitudes towards play has been provided by Bernstein and Young (1967). When they asked a group of mothers about their concept of play and the use of toys they found that the middle class had a more distinct concept of toys as a way for children 'to find out about things'. Working class mothers, by contrast, indicated that 'to keep the children amused by themselves' ranked as high in their estimation as 'to find out about things'. There was also a relationship between acceptance of this latter attitude and both the nature of verbal communication between mother and child, and the child's measured intelligence. Bernstein (1967) has also reported that middle class mothers, when buying a toy as a present, seem more aware of the need to choose one suited to the child's age, sex, and mental development.

Encouragement to do well at school

So far the emphasis has been placed on the ways in which certain styles of child rearing may affect the child's intellectual development and his preparedness for the school system. Once the child is at school the influence of the home does not disappear, but may be manifest in significant new ways. Perhaps the first way this is seen is in the choice of school made by the parents. This choice is far wider than that between private and LEA school, for it is often within the parents' power to exercise a choice in deciding which LEA school their child attends. A primary concern for some people when buying a new house is the quality of the schools which serve the area, a fact of which estate agents are well aware. For those already settled in an area the opportunity exists to request the transfer of their child to a school serving another locality. But although these opportunities exist for all, they are likely to be employed only by those with a concern for education, sufficient money to live where they choose, and an understanding of the alternatives open to them and the means by which they can be obtained; such people come, almost exclusively, from the middle class.

Once the child is attending school the start he has been given at home is enhanced by parental interest in his progress. The middle class parent is more ready to confer with his child's teachers (and is usually much more socially at ease in doing so). By knowing the right words to use he will make his educational expectations and aspirations known to the teacher and be quick to react if his child is obviously lagging behind. If the child is not meeting these parental expectations the teacher will, if only in self defence, communicate educational aims back to the parents, and will suggest ways in which they can help the child effectively at home. The working class parent may be just as concerned for the educational well-being of his child, but is less able to do anything effective about it; he finds talking to the teacher a strain, and is happy to place his trust in the teacher as a highly trained member of a well-esteemed profession, even though he may be unclear as to what the school is trying to achieve. It is arguable that without this pressure the school is not motivated to obtain the best from its pupils.

The Plowden Report (1967) was particularly concerned about home/school relations and suggested ways by which they might be improved. One of these, reported by Young and McGeeney (1968), was an attempt to encourage greater involvement by parents in their children's schooling and in their general educational activities at home. The results in terms of test scores suggested that, in this one school, greater parental involvement and closer home/school contact could produce beneficial effects for some children. But Bernstein and Davies (1969) have argued that attempts to generate interest among parents may prove to be more difficult than is envisaged in Plowden, since the social principles which are responsible for shaping parental attitudes run very deep; the interest produced by cooperation experiments may only be transient. They also point out that technical and curricular innovations in primary education (Cuisenaire and Dienes systems, i.t.a., binary operations, etc.) make it more difficult for parents to feel that they can plan an active role in their children's education; the inability of parents to understand these methods (and, one might add, the inability or perhaps unwillingness, of teachers to explain them coherently) places a further barrier against participation which affects the working class in particular.

It is likely that parents who are most adept in their dealings with the education system will also provide their children with an atmosphere most conducive to educational progress. Frazer (1959) found that the best environment in terms of achievement at school and motivation in the child to do well was a lenient, 'democratic' one, characterised by friendliness and spontaneity. Kent and Davis (1957) found that the most effective home in terms of the children's scores on intelligence tests was one where the parents were ambitious for the child, setting high standards from an early age. They rewarded the child infrequently and without generosity, and approval and affection were conditional upon achievement. Although apparently contradictory, these two descriptions taken together represent two facets of the typical middle class family. Jackson and Marsden (1962) found that grammar school children from working class homes had parents who were ambitious for them and drove them on; the fathers tended to belong to the sunken middle class, or to be foremen with little chance of being promoted to the ranks of management proper. Swift's (1964) study of 11+ success can be interpreted in a similar way; in a sample of forty-five middle class families ten were found to have fathers who were pessimistic about their job and their likelihood of advancement, and in each of the ten cases the child was successful in the selection examination. All pessimistic fathers had successful children. Swift suggests that, as well as the advantages normally attributable to the middle class home, the father's frustrated ambition and his belief in the importance of education (usually seen in terms of exam qualifications) led to considerable pressure being put on the child to do well at school. He is made aware of the importance of education in later life, the implication being that it will enable him to do better than his father.

The parental pressure may take the form of help with school work, making sure that the child completes work expected of him, and providing additional help at important times, such as 11+ examinations. Later in the child's school career it involves encouragement to stay at school, to obtain qualifications, and to find a suitable career. All of this implies a knowledge of the hurdles that the child is likely to face, making sure that he is prepared for them, and instilling in him the belief that the end is worth achieving. The former point is, once again, more likely to be within the province of the middle class family, subscribing to what Jackson (1968) has so aptly described as the 'ethic of postponed pleasure'. Middle class children, in keeping with their families, are future-oriented, a fact reflected in the apparently trivial finding that they are expected, on principle, to set aside a proportion of their pocket money as savings, even when they receive, on average, less of it each week than their working class counterparts (Newson and Newson, 1970).

Conclusions, and a look towards the future

When compared with other reviews in this volume, our report on research into child rearing and its educational significance may appear somewhat thin. The reason is, quite simply, that comparatively little research has been done in this area. This may be because of the commitment that longitudinal research demands, or it may be that the subject matter falls between the three stools of psychology, sociology, and education, and that the contrasting approaches are difficult to resolve.

In our view, however, more research needs to be done; child rearing practices change with time and location. The evidence from our own study refers only to Nottingham in the 1960s—other communities should be studied, and at regular intervals, to discover something about the reason for these differences and changes. We need to know in greater detail something of the nature of parent-child interaction and its effects on development; the work of the Unit for Research on the Medical Applications of Psychology, in Cambridge, is making headway here, but little has been published to date. Douglas et al (1968) have devised and validated a useful instrument for obtaining some measure of the amount of time which young children spend with different persons in varying patterns of interaction. Mothers have been shown to be accurate in their ability to recall, in detail, the events of the preceding 24 hours and a technique has been worked out for coding this information. The method has been used in a study of houseproud housewives (Cooper and McNeil, 1968). It is of interest to note that, by comparison with the U.S.A. (Lytton, 1971), only a few British researchers (e.g. Robertson, 1965) have employed direct observation as a method of obtaining information on the nature of mother-child interaction. The argument that the presence of an observer distorts the situation to such an extent that the interaction seen is atypical, is a strong one, particularly where the nature of the interaction is emotional as opposed to cognitive. Direct observation may well have an important part to play in uncovering the nature of communication as mother tries to teach child, but accurate accounts of situations which involve, for example, conflict, are best obtained at second hand. Although the report may be less detailed it does refer to a real event; the observer's account, by contrast, is of an interaction distorted by the very fact of his observing.

Most of our information on child rearing comes from the mother; the father's role has tended to remain in the background. At a time when fathers are participating more in the domestic side of family life and are taking a greater interest in their children this is an omission that should be rectified.

From a more immediately educational point of view, it would be of interest to investigate ways in which parents can be helped to help their children at home, bearing in mind Bernstein and Davies' stricture on treating this merely as a problem of attitude change.

In conclusion we would reaffirm our belief that it is the *values* behind child rearing techniques that are important, rather than the techniques themselves, and that those values need to be seen in the context of the whole situation in which the family lives. Until this is recognised results will continue to appear contradictory, and progress to be slow.

In one sense, to look for connections between child-rearing values and practices in the home on the one hand, and educational achievement at school on the other, is to look for something which is almost too obvious to require scientific validation. In our society the educational system as a whole clearly serves the function of maintaining social differences rather than eliminating them. In the final analysis, to become educated through this system means in part to become rationally articulate, and in part to become adept in the technique of articulate rationalisation. Having this unique blend of skills comes very close to the heart of what most ordinary people mean by saying that a person is educated; and to be educated in this sense is basically to be middle class. Thus the educational system is still widely—and probably correctly—regarded by the majority of parents as a series of hurdles to be surmounted by those children who have middle class expectations, either as a continuing way of life or as an aspiration to be strived for.

Elizabeth Goodacre

Reading

Jessie Reid reviewed the research in this field in the first volume of *Educational Research in Britain* (Butcher, 1968). This meant that she covered the research which appeared during the period 1960–67 approximately. As she explained in the introduction to her paper, her account could not be an exhaustive survey of all the research into reading being carried out and so she decided to concentrate on outlining some of the main areas in which important work had been done, relating the results to one another in as meaningful a way as possible. From the studies available she selected the following areas of research: general surveys; the Initial Teaching Alphabet; other studies of early learning; linguistics and reading; specific dyslexia; deprivation and reading.

Surveying the field of reading research approximately four years after her summary provides one with a certain degree of perspective, and the writer thought it might prove useful to examine reading research within these areas again, but trying to see whether and to what extent certain trends observed earlier had developed or whether changes of emphasis had occurred.

For instance, although no major general survey results were published during the period 1967–71, a series of surveys at local level added not only to our knowledge about standards in particular parts of the country, but also to the accumulating information about the size of the 'hard-core' of backward readers and the identifiable characteristics of specific dyslexia. Although little experimental work was being carried out in relation to the Initial Teaching Alphabet, inquiries into the use and effect of this medium led to further exploration of the factor of teacher effectiveness, and the study of the control of the teacher variable in reading research. Also, the work on i.t.a. concentrated attention on the function of signalling devices in clarifying the beginning stages of reading and on the importance of young children understanding the language concepts involved in learning to read. This meant not only attention being paid to children's comprehension of the technical terms used in teaching reading but also greater awareness of the way in which teachers can facilitate or hinder this understanding.

The work in the linguistics area seemed to be developing two distinct strands, which in time will probably be found to have more in common than is at present anticipated. One was the relationship between reading materials and children's language development and speech patterns, which led to a more critical look at existing reading schemes and materials. The second aspect seemed to be concerned with interpreting and assimilating work developed in the United States and New Zealand, which is based on the idea of reading being a 'psycholinguistic guessing game' in which children's oral reading errors or 'miscues' can be interpreted by the child's teacher as evidence of the strategies being used by the pupil to accomplish this learning task. Emphasis is placed upon the type rather than the number of mistakes or 'miscues' and researchers are gradually trying to collect sufficient evidence to determine whether stages in acquiring the skill can be identified by the types of mistakes made, or whether 'miscues' occur mainly as a result of the type of reading materials or approach adopted by the teacher in the classroom.

Both in the area of specific dyslexia and that of deprivation and reading, a great deal of the work being carried out seemed to be concerned with accurate identification of these children. Community surveys provided evidence of the way in which the number of children identified could differ in certain characteristics according to the type and number of tests used, as well as providing information about the distribution of such characteristics among 'normal' child populations of particular ages. Again attention was focused on the need for teachers, at all levels of the primary school, to have knowledge not only of the stages in children's physical and psychological growth but also of the various stages in the acquisition of this complex, abstract skill, so that they could more effectively identify and match a child's developing skills with the appropriate level of reading materials and approach. Inevitably this led to reappraisals of the adequacy of teachers' professional preparation, and consideration of the nature and function of in-service education.

Underlying most of the work in these areas was the realisation of the crude nature of the majority of measures of reading achievement available to researcher and teacher alike, and the need for improved diagnostic instruments. Running as a continuous thread through so much of the research of the last four years is concern for sharper, more accurate measuring instruments, particularly as researchers come to grips with their subject matter. This interest in improving their measuring tools, in clarifying terms such as 'reading readiness' and 'dyslexia', and realising the need to separate and control the teacher variable in research designs, reflects a more rigorous and one hopes 'scientific' approach by researchers to the study of teaching reading.

However, during the period there seemed few signs of the study of reading being accorded a higher level of academic status. The comparatively low status of reading research both in universities and colleges of education was reflected in the limitation of resources devoted to it. Often work appeared superficial and even lacking in scientific rigour, because insufficient resources were available to develop reliable, accurate assessment and measuring devices; to continue studies sufficiently long enough to provide longitudinal evidence; to evaluate, abstract and disseminate the information from valid studies while also incorporating ideas and work from related fields of study. If improvements in these three areas could be accomplished, reading research would appear more cumulative and would demonstrate that a concerted attack was being made on problems, both researchable and of educational importance.

Surveys

During the period, the National Foundation for Educational Research undertook a national survey of the reading attainment of eleven and fifteen year olds, which included the study of the influence of bilingualism in Wales on the teaching of reading. An adult literacy survey was also instigated by the Rank organisation during the period. The findings of these general surveys are of special interest, following the discussion which greeted the last DES survey findings *Progress in Reading 1948–1966* (1966). The general conclusion seemed to be that the reported improvement in reading standards was probably little more than a recovery from the set-back of the war, and that teachers had little about which to be complacent. Some of the heat engendered by this controversy may have resulted from the participants' personal experience of reading standards within their own local areas. Certainly, local surveys (Hammond, 1967; ILEA, 1969; Bookbinder, 1970; Devon LEA 1970; Rutter *et al.*, 1970; Clark, 1970) suggest that reading standards differ considerably throughout the country, and that the large urban areas in particular are faced with reading problems.

For instance, in some of these areas the problem is undoubtedly complicated by the proportion of immigrants. The proportion of the total school population who are immigrants (DES definition of an immigrant is a child born outside England and Wales, or one born in those countries to parents who have not lived there for ten years) is not large, but the distribution of immigrants is very uneven. Thus teachers, particularly in London and the industrial areas of the Midlands, find they have a large number of immigrant children with a variety of languages and customs in their classes, and it is often necessary to teach these children English as a second language before tackling the problem of teaching them to read in it. The London Literacy Survey (ILEA, 1969) found that the overall reading standards of the immigrants were markedly lower than those of non-immigrants both in regard to average scores and the proportion of good and poor readers; e.g. there were twice as many poor readers (reading age two years less than chronological age) in the immigrant group—one in four being poor readers.

During the period there was increasing interest in the content of teachers' professional courses, particularly from those teachers in their first appointments (Goodacre, 1969a). Not only was there dissatisfaction expressed with the preparation for the teaching of reading, but it was also noticeable that in several of these surveys of teachers' opinions, there were references to teachers asking for more courses on the teaching of immigrants.

Teachers have generally been advised to concentrate on the language development of immigrants and 'disadvantaged' pupils, but several studies are beginning to indicate that it might be equally important to encourage the use in classrooms of constructional materials which will develop the manipulative ability and the spacing and sequential skills of these children; e.g. understanding of the terms beginning and end, sequential order, scanning from left to right, etc. (Mundy, 1970; McFie and Thompson, 1970).

In the United States, Goodman (1970) has strongly criticised the view that differences in language imply deficiency, and contends that there is a deep language structure unaffected by dialect differences. (See the chapter by Lawton in the present book.) Uhl and Nurss (1970) have suggested that socio-economic factors and their effects may be more important than sex and race differences, and that phonological, morphological, syntactical and lexical differences assume most importance when the child is mastering the decoding stage of learning to read, particularly at the word by word matching stage; i.e. when coordinating the spoken and written word. Dialect may assume importance therefore in regard to beginning reading materials. A reading series such as *Nippers* (Berg, 1969) represents an attempt to make reading materials more realistic in content but does not present a solution of the dialect problem, as the 'working-class' language used in the books seems to have been tidied up; i.e. it does not accurately represent the speech patterns of such children and their families.

A recent survey (Goodacre, 1971) found that the majority of local education authorities preferred to leave the assessment of pupils' reading standards to the heads of individual schools, although there was some evidence that an increasing number of LEAs were becoming aware of the advantages involved in regularly carrying out reading attainment surveys; i.e. finding children 'at risk' early in their schooling when they benefit from short term remedial provision rather than having to be given long term treatment, including help for emotional difficulties; obtaining objective data on which to base decisions regarding the most effective use of scarce remedial resources; providing the opportunity to make a field evaluation of new or unfamiliar reading attainment tests. Also it was found in this survey that the heads of individual schools tend to assess their pupils either subjectively on the basis of their observation of a child's behaviour, usually in relation to their progress in a published reading scheme, or by using a reading attainment test, more often than not one of word recognition, emphasising a child's ability to pronounce a word without help from contextual or language clues. Such tests use criteria of reading progress often at variance with the professed reading aims of the school, especially at the infant level.

During the period there were several new reading tests published. (GAP, 1967; Young, 1969; Carver, 1970), and the NFER produced *Reading Test BD*, a timed sentence completion test of forty four items, still being standardised. Of the former tests, the Carver and the GAP seem to be useful measures, providing, respectively, a diagnostic test of word recognition, and comprehension using the 'cloze' procedure.

O'Kelly (1960) suggested the use of the English Picture Vocabulary Test as a means of screening late readers who might need special educational provision in their Junior years. She argued that because a child's comprehension vocabulary is critical to success in learning to read, an objective test of 'listening vocabulary' might be useful for assessing readiness for reading instruction. The Schools Council Research Project in Compensatory Education re-examined the concept of reading readiness, and in the publication *Reading Readiness* (Chazan, 1970) outlined the main forms of measuring readiness and concluded that a scale which measured early communication skills might be more useful to the infant teacher than a specific reading readiness test. Fisher and Williams (1969) experimented with the 'tell-a-story' technique pioneered by de Hirsch and her associates as a means of identifying young children likely to experience reading difficulties. Although in practice this method was found to have a major drawback in the time that must be spent transcribing the story from tape recordings in order to obtain the essential qualitative/quantitative scoring, the technique could be successfully used with individual children, even if not applicable as a 'screening' device at the infant school level. As part of the Compensatory Education Project, Sims and Williams (1969) studied the development of phonic skills in young children, using a sample of ninety six infants selected on the basis of their reading ages on the Southgate W.R. Test. They developed two parallel test forms containing the same seventy six phonic elements, each element being embedded in a nonsense 'word', and the child's phonic skill was assessed by asking him to recognise the nonsense word containing it. Highly significant differences were reported between reading age levels and the ability to recognise phonic elements in the nonsense words. This test has now been published (Williams *et al.*, 1971). The idea behind this type of test needs to be carefully assessed, and further experimental work is necessary to justify the claim that inability to identify specific phonic elements in nonsense words (where there are no linguistic or contextual clues to aid the reader as to pronunciation of the nonsense word) does in fact act as an impeding factor to the extent envisaged by the test designers. Also, further evidence is needed regarding the effectiveness of the test as a diagnostic instrument. Merritt (1968) has reported experiments with word tests using different types of word deletions, which may prove a useful technique for measuring the development of the intermediate reading skills.

Specific dyslexia

Local or community surveys conducted by a multi-disciplinary team, possessing a wide and varied experience of children with reading difficulties, can produce a considerable amount of information about normal and retarded readers which may be useful for examining the relevancy and validity of hypotheses suggested from experience with individual or atypical groups of children. Lovell and Gorton (1968) studied two groups of readers (9–10 years) of normal intelligence to discover whether normal and poor readers could be identified by their scores on visual-spatial and neuropsychological tests. While no single factor was isolated by the tests of auditory-visual integration and motor performance, the evidence suggested that neurological impairment and reading disability were linked even when the subjects studied were not from a clinical population. The aim of a survey of primary school children on the Isle of Wight (Rutter *et al.*, 1970) was to find out the incidence of a number of handicaps, intellectual, behavioural and physical. Using a sample of 2 300 children (9–12 years) the researchers found that approximately four per cent who were normal neurologically were severely retarded in reading; i.e. reading age more than two years behind chronological age. There were more boys than girls in this group, and there was evidence of delay in speech development and persistent speech problems, as well as a certain amount of emotional maladjustment. The latter appeared to be related to the children's learning difficulties rather than a precipitating factor in relation to their reading disability. (See also the account of this research in the chapter by Anderson and Haskell.) In the Scottish county of Dunbartonshire, Clark (1970) set out to discover the incidence figures for *continued* reading difficulty in children of average intelligence. She believed this information would indicate the size of the provision required and also provide evidence of the pattern of disabilities, thus throwing some light on the type of provision needed. Clark was also interested in exploring ways of identifying such children sufficiently early to prevent, if possible, the development of severe reading disability. She screened 1 544 children (7–9 years) and after two years of schooling found that 15 per cent were non-readers (Reading Quotient of 85 or less). This group was tested again a year later, and 69 pupils were found to be still retarded; i.e. 6 per cent of the boys and 3 per cent of the girls of the original sample. At nine years, only 9 children (15 boys and 4 girls) were severely and specifically retarded readers, representing 1·3 per cent of the original sample. She suggested that *severe* reading difficulty was not a problem of the magnitude envisaged by some authorities, but this was not to deny the importance of the fact that a number of children of average intelligence experienced prolonged reading difficulties. She found that absences from school, over-large classes, lack of parental help, frequent changes of school, emotional problems, relatively low intelligence (not amounting to mental subnormality), the presence of speech defects and poor auditory discrimination and poor visuo-motor coordination, were all important factors in relation to the acquisition of the skill.

Both the Dunbartonshire and Isle of Wight surveys noted the diversity of disabilities shown by the severely retarded group of children. It was noted that there was no underlying pattern of disabilities common to this group which could have provided a basis for one single remedial method for all the children so handicapped. However, work at the Word Blind Centre in London, before it closed in 1970, was beginning to indicate that it might be helpful to recognise different types of specific reading backwardness, i.e. 'visual' or 'auditory' clusters of disabilities. Another line or development is the consideration of causal factors in conjunction with environmental conditions, including differences in reading approach and method. For instance, when the approach to reading is more phonically based, children with poor auditory discrimination are likely to be vulnerable, while the more the approach emphasises the memorising of whole words, the more vulnerable are children with poor visual discrimination. In this connexion American tests such as the *Frostig Visual Perception Test* and the *Illinois Test of Psycholinguistic Abilities* provide battery type tests of these two areas relevant to the development of the reading skill. Mittler and Ward (1970) reported work on the use of the latter test with British four year olds, and Ward (1970) has examined the factor structure of the Frostig test. Farnworth (1971) has experimented with the Frostig test as a means of assessing children's reading readiness in terms of perceptual maturity. (See also the chapter by Mittler in the present book which describes research involving use of the ITPA.)

Gradually, it is being accepted that *some* children of normal intelligence (but a very small proportion of the total school population) experience severe reading disabilities, which appear to be constitutional in origin. It is not at all clear yet to what extent environmental factors, such as poor teaching or parental pressure, aggravate perceptual dysfunctions or interact with developmental delays in the maturational process. Reid (1968) examined the controversies centred on the understanding and use of the classification 'dyslexia', and a study of recent papers in the *British Journal of Educational Psychology* Symposium on Reading Disability (Miles, 1971; Ingram, 1971; Clark, 1971 and Naidoo, 1971) show that some agreement is being reached as to the incidence of severe reading disability and the absence of a single causal factor. Valuable work is being done in regard to the exploration of particular characteristics associated with retardation and disability. For instance, the Isle of Wight survey reported no significant difference regarding *handedness* between poor readers and the normal controls, and Shearer (1968), who compared consistency of hand preference, performance in right or left discrimination, and finger localisation for two groups of normal and backward readers (7-10 years) also found no significance differences in relation to these factors. In general, the retarded group performed less adequately, but there was sufficient overlap in the two groups to raise many questions about the importance of such characteristics as means of identifying the potential poor reader. It is of considerable interest then that Clark (1970) in her Dunbartonshire survey found that the number and type of tests of handedness used affected the incidence of crossed laterality reported. 'The more tests of eyedness or handedness, the smaller proportion who would appear to be consistent.' Left-handedness, left-eyedness, mixed dominance or crossed laterality, are not in themselves predictors of reading failure.

The realisation that some children have particular reading difficulties for some time, and a few have a number of severe difficulties over a lengthy period draws attention to the importance of providing different forms of remedial assistance and ensuring that teachers be made aware of the possibility of having to deal with a child with reading difficulty, whatever age of child they may teach. An incidental finding of the Isle of Wight survey was that the children in classes taught by teachers who had attended an in-service course of only three days' duration, made two months more gain in reading age than was anticipated (Rigley, 1968). Ways of improving children's reading ability which could be suggested to LEAs concerned with reading standards are the establishing of remedial reading centres, the greater use of peripatetic teachers, and the organisation of reading advisory services. However, there is little information available about the comparative effectiveness of these or other solutions (Rigley, 1968; Goodacre, 1971).

Cashdan and Pumfrey (1969) examined the effectiveness of weekly and semi-weekly treatment at the end of two terms and twenty-two months respectively, but found no significant differences between these groups or the untreated group. These findings are similar to those in the classic experiment carried out earlier by Collins (1961), but Cashdan and Pumfrey have questioned the 'natural' improvement of the control groups which seems to occur in such experiments. It is possible that the 'untreated' control groups do, in fact, receive help in the form of advice given to their teachers by remedial agencies and relief of pressure when some of their classmates, often those making considerable demands upon the class teacher, are taken out of the class and receive special attention. In more recent work Cashdan (1971) has drawn attention to the importance of the variable of group size. This factor assumed importance when groups were bigger than six.

The design of research into the effectiveness of remedial provision has improved during the last decade as researchers have become more aware of the different variables involved, but more information is still needed on the characteristics of children selected for remedial help, and the criteria for allocation to different sized groups. Sampson (1969) has provided more up to date information about the Remedial Education Service, including details of the incentives found to be useful in this work by remedial teachers. The most often mentioned category was related to the retarded readers' experience of success, and Lawrence (1971) suggested on the basis of his own somewhat limited experiments that in most cases of reading retardation it would be possible to increase the general level of pupils' motivation by planning a personal counselling programme, aimed at improving the 'poor' reader's self-image. Wooster (1970), using a Repertory Grid test has looked at the question of when children become aware of themselves as readers, and how failure in this task affects their self-concepts and their ability to accept responsibility for their level of reading attainment.

The survey by the Reading School of Education on LEA 'Provision for Reading' (Goodacre, 1971) provided some information about present practice in regard to remedial provision. Half the LEAs taking part in the survey thought of remedial provision solely in terms of the provision made by individual schools, although some LEAs evidenced considerable concern over their backward readers and were tackling the problem through a variety of different approaches, which included advice on reading materials (difficulty and interest level), forms of assessment and diagnosis, and remedial tecsniques; sustained in-service education programmes; special allowances for the reading material needs of backward readers; setting up of centres for the treatment of such children and the provision of facilities of use to remedial teachers working in schools. The School Psychological Service generally assisted backward readers, but in practice, because of heavy case loads, understaffing of the Service and the referral of 'difficult' children for emotional rather than attainment problems, the assistance of the Service was often limited to advice to the remedial teachers. These teachers were usually not specifically trained for the task, and where LEAs required special qualifications, these were usually in the field of slow-learning children, so there was no assurance that such teachers were familiar with recent developments in reading research and remedial techniques. Also, a common practice was to use part time teachers who might have only returned to the profession recently, or probationers beginning their teaching career, to teach groups of backward readers in schools.

i.t.a. and the beginning stages of learning to read

Downing and Latham (1969) reported the progress after five years of children from the first i.t.a. experiments. The i.t.a. children were superior in reading comprehension (NFER Sentence Reading) and on the NFER English Progress Test, which included sub-tests of capital letters, story comprehension, past and present tenses, spelling, sentence completion and abbreviation. Downing (1969a), in a re-analysis of the i.t.a. studies, looked at the proportion of failure occurring in the i.t.a. and t.o. groups, and found that all the tests except speed of reading showed that 'i.t.a. generally reduced the incidence of poor reading and poor spelling both before and after transition to t.o.' Downing suggested that this information might be of particular interest to teachers of classes containing slower learners, and cited the evidence from a survey he had carried out of the opinions of teachers in ESN schools using i.t.a. (Downing 1968) which suggested that i.t.a. helped slow learners by reducing the confusion resulting from dealing with the irregularities of t.o. Downing developed this idea of the importance of eliminating 'cognitive confusion' at this early stage of children's learning in several papers (Downing, 1969b, 1970a, 1970b). He continued the work initiated by Reid (1966) into children's understanding of the purpose of written language features and the development of their comprehension of the technical and abstract terms used in the teaching of reading. He used the following procedures to stimulate 13 five year olds to respond to concepts involved in reading and writing; an open-ended interview; an interview using concrete stimuli such as colour photos, books and model toy buses; the first two techniques and a yes/no game using tape recorded auditory stimuli involving non-human noises, phonemes, and words. He found considerable confusion amongst the children as to the use of categories such as 'word' and 'sound'. He suggested that children needed help with understanding the purpose and nature of written language, and concluded that an important function of i.t.a. was the way in which it facilitated children's understanding of the part played by linguistic structure in the reading process.

Downing has also been concerned about the transition stage from i.t.a. to t.o. Although according to their teachers the i.t.a. children showed no outward signs of having difficulty with the transfer, there was evidence from the objective reading tests that a setback occurred in the learning curve at that stage. Downing has shown interest in experimenting with the i.t.a. symbols and the English spelling system, with the idea of changing the forms in the light of children's difficulties. He is now carrying out work in Canada to determine which aspects of i.t.a. cause difficulties and therefore could lead to improvements in the i.t.a. symbols if this should be acceptable (Downing, 1971).

In 1969 the Schools Council's independent evaluation of i.t.a. was published. The report (Warburton and Southgate, 1969) included an evaluation by Professor Warburton of all the research evidence available at the time, including a detailed appraisal of the methodology used in the experiments. Southgate collected and evaluated the views of a sample of i.t.a. users and those closely connected with its use. The report also included suggestions for future research projects on i.t.a. and drew attention to the urgent need for the construction of suitable tests of reading for primary school age children. The verbal evidence collected by Southgate supported the view that children using i.t.a. learned to read earlier, more easily and at a quicker speed, and were better in writing and spelling than the children using t.o. However, some doubt must be cast on the validity of these subjective impressions, in the light of the fact that so many of these people were unaware of the set-back experienced by the i.t.a. children after transition which showed up clearly on the objective reading test results. Warburton was extremely critical of the design and the statistical methods used in most of the i.t.a. experiments. He considered the two British experiments the most satisfactory. Of course, it must be acknowledged that the second experiment benefited from the mistakes of the first. Somewhat surprisingly, following his critical examination of the research evidence, Warburton concluded that i.t.a. was a superior medium to t.o. in teaching young children to read.

Thackray (1971) made a comparison between the reading readiness and early progress of children learning with i.t.a. and children using t.o. He reported that the i.t.a. children were ready to read earlier but experienced a setback during the transfer stage. An interesting experiment by Milne and Fyfe (1969) involving i.t.a., examined the possibility of controlling and assessing the teacher variable. No approach to reading (children were taught by i.t.a., t.o. and Stott's Programmed Reading Kit) showed a significant superiority on any one of the tests or measures used at the end of the third year of schooling, although some schools were found to be significantly superior. Jones (1968) compared the results of the second i.t.a. experiement with his own Colour Story Reading experiment results and concluded that the latter produced superior results in both reading and spelling, for high, average and low achievers. However, Downing (1971) believes these conclusions to be invalid, the samples in the two experiments not being comparable.

Southgate (1971) has tried to place the work on the effect of changes in the medium (e.g. colour codes, i.t.a., signalling systems, etc.) in some perspective. Comparing colour codes with i.t.a., she summarised the results obtained in experimental work and analysed the main differences between these techniques, emphasising the way in which each medium sought to provide the child with a uniform method of decoding new words. These new media share a common attribute; they are based on the belief that the irregularities of t.o. increase children's difficulties at the beginning stage. The codes devised abolish or diminish the inconsistencies of t.o. at the initial stages, but involve areas of varying difficulty; i.e. supply of reading materials; size and nature of the basic learning 'load'; transfer stage; teacher's flexibility of approach; similarity between school and home regarding written language form. She clarifies the situation at present facing teachers by noting not only the advantages of particular new mediums, but also the features which could be considered as drawbacks. As she states 'Whether to use a new medium in preference to t.o. and, if so, which one to select, is a personal choice to be made by the staff of a school. They cannot make it until they have listed their own criteria of assessments based on their own priorities regarding children's acquisition of the skills of reading and writing, against the framework of their total beliefs, aims and plans regarding the whole sphere of primary education.'

Linguistics and reading

In the research on the effect of changes in the medium, it has been difficult to know exactly what occurs in the control groups. Some of the criticisms of the British i.t.a. experiments carried the implication that this research was dealing with the comparison of a structured with a comparatively non-structured or 'laissez-faire' approach to the teaching of reading (Haas, 1969). For instance, the writer's 1968 (Goodacre, 1969a) Survey of the teaching of reading in the infant school produced evidence that 'normal' practice in England probably placed less emphasis upon a systematic and structured approach than for instance in Scottish schools (e.g. comparison of differences in practice, Goodacre and Clark, 1971). The writer inquired into the use of published reading schemes and found that the group of English teachers placed great emphasis upon the reading scheme as a means of assessing their pupils' progress and few of the teachers adopted a diagnostic approach to 'hearing' their children read aloud, i.e. they seldom recorded pupils' difficulties or types of reading errors. Downing also noted this ritualistic aspect of teaching children to read in English classrooms, and as a result of his experimental work on the relationship of children's language concepts to their progress at the early stages, stressed the need for making reading more relevant to children's cognitive development, and less a ritual performed to gain adult approval (1970b). Also, the writer found in her survey that four out of five English teachers preferred 'incidental' phonics, i.e. telling children their 'sounds' or drawing attention to phoneme/grapheme correspondences when pupils encountered words they could not recognise by sight, rather than systematically following a planned phonic programme. The most popular published reading schemes were predominantly of the controlled vocabulary type, so it could be concluded that during the sixties 'normal' practice in English schools tended to be towards a comparatively non-structured approach.

Certain recent work deriving from linguistics has, however, had some influence upon the quality of teachers 'hearing' of children, and the writer's personal impression is that teachers are adopting a more diagnostic approach to teaching reading, although this is still primarily through the medium of informal methods—listening more actively to children's reading aloud and their errors—rather than through the use of diagnostic reading tests. Mention must be made at this stage of Clay's work which, although not carried out in Britain, is likely to be influential (e.g. Lavender, 1970; Goodacre, 1970a). A report appeared in 1969 of Clay's study of the learning strategies adopted when learning to read by New Zealand five year olds in their first year at school (Clay, 1969). She found that the children progressed from page matching to line matching, to locating words in relation to the spaces between words, thus coordinating spoken and written words. This expressionless, word by word, stage of reading aloud appeared to be an important stage in children's acquisition of the reading skill, and an absence of 'fluency' (a characteristic emphasised by many teachers as a criterion of progress, Goodacre, 1970b) did not necessarily imply a lack of understanding of what was being read. Discussing her analysis of the mistakes pupils made when reading aloud, and their self-correction behaviours, Clay concluded that the very complexity of reading material which provided rich cue scources for the child who could discover the regularities of the code involved in reading, might present confusion to the child of limited language skill. She suggested that information processing would be given the greatest scope if the method of teaching reading allowed the child's spontaneous speech as an aid to making a 'good' guess or word match, stressed flexible and varied word-solving techniques, and encouraged pupils to work at their errors or 'poor' guesses.

Mackay and Thompson (1968) in their book explaining the research behind the *Breakthrough to Literacy* reading materials, were very critical of the usual type of published reading schemes being used in schools, where the language is artificial, and the use of a controlled vocabulary makes for reading materials which seldom match the language of children or their wide interests. Peters (1970) studied the historical development of published reading schemes since the beginning of the century, and concluded that there was evidence to suggest that the impact of linguistics on reading would help to resolve the traditional conflict between look-and-say and phonic teaching methods,

> 'by clarifying and spelling out the various supportive and corroborative cues in reading. . . . It is this complexity of cues that will most successfully provide an integrated attack on reading. It makes heavy demands on a writer; for the material must be progressively phonic yet fulfil all readability criteria (and be within the child's idiom and interests so that at every word and within every word there are, as the child reads, *expectations easily and inevitably fulfilled*). These expectations derive from linguistic constraints acquired, at least in favoured children, long before coming to school . . .' (the writer's italics).

Peters suggested several aims which publishers of schemes might consider, including the use of words which made syntactic and semantic as well as phonic demands simultaneously on the young reader, so giving him the opportunity to use multiple clues, correcting himself when what he read failed to sound 'like language' (i.e. that children's errors are corrected and can be explained in the light of 'cognitive dissonance', Clay, 1969). Peters outlined the advantages of the early stages of schemes approximating very closely to young children's language (sentence length, sentence structure, word difficulty, word frequency, word depth), in other words, to what are generally accepted as readability criteria (Bormuth, 1966).

Several studies examined popular reading schemes from the point of view of language constraints. For instance, Garside (1968) studied two popular reading schemes in relation to sentence length and vocabulary, and compared them to the language of a group of normal and a group of ESN children in an interview and a play situation respectively. Latham (1971) examined six popular reading schemes and developed techniques for analysing schemes in regard to general teaching approach, increase of difficulty, content and general attractiveness. This analysis included a measure of vocabulary difficulty based on children's spoken language, as well as consideration of the introduction and progression of phonic work in the schemes studied. Latham was particularly concerned about the interchangeability of books within different reading schemes. Reid (1970) looked at the structure of four schemes, including the Downing i.t.a. Readers, using as the starting point for her study an earlier classic study by Strickland (1962) of the relationship between speech structures of children and their reading textbooks. The entire paper merits close reading. She suggested further experimental work into the effects of different language structures in published reading schemes, including the exploration of the use of compound structures, and the reading difficulty for children of deleting 'movable' elements in the sentence structure particularly for children coming from different types of home background. The construction of different types of trial materials was suggested, so that the elements within the sentence could be systematically manipulated in known directions and amount, and the resulting types of errors made by children studied. She suggested that the aim of reading materials should be to use children's linguistic resources in their strengths and their limitations, first matching and utilising these factors, and then 'carefully extended in ways which not only follow the chronology of acquisition but are of maximum usefulness in all aspects of communicative behaviour'. Reid's paper provides a number of insights into the way in which popular reading schemes can use linguistic structures which are unfamiliar and awkward for children because of the author's determination to repeat words often and in different contexts as a means of developing children's powers of word recognition. Birnie (1967, 1968 and 1970) examined popular readers from the point of view of the consistency of sound/symbol relationships encountered by children when the readers were written in i.t.a. or t.o.

Peters raised the question of the relevancy of illustrations in reading schemes in her paper on trends in schemes, and Keir (1970) reported a study into the use of word illustrations as phonic clues, which outlined some of the problems arising from the use of pictures with young children. The young reader may not be familiar with the conventions of illustrators, and may be misled by the use of shading or incomplete drawings, quite apart from identifying illustrated words by inappropriate or incorrect terms, e.g. *lamp post* (*l*) being used in reading apparatus but the child calling it a *streetlight* (*st*), an example from the writer's experience.

Conclusion

Reviewing the research which has been produced during the last four year period, it is possible to discern certain important trends. Some of these developments have not been as fully exploited as they might have been, because to a large extent the scope of reading research in this country is determined by the efforts of individual researchers convinced of the importance of their work, who must however cut their cloth according to the means available to them. As there is no central institution with responsibility for coordinating and guiding research and abstracting and disseminating the results, it can be difficult to discover the extent and scope of work being carried out in this country. It can be done but it is a time consuming operation. This communication difficulty acts as a limiting factor, affecting possibly both the quantity and the quality of reading research being done. Several national bodies have taken an interest in reading and relating areas of study, but unfortunately not on a sustained basis (e.g. NFER, National Children's Bureau, DES, Schools Council).

For instance, the attention of the Schools Council now seems to be directed away from the initial stages of learning to read, to the problem of how proficiency in the use of the reading skill can be developed and maintained. Interest is centred on how children can use the skill for their own interests and purposes (e.g. NATE study of children as readers; Sheffield Institute of Education investigation into children's reading habits, etc.). In this connection, work by Abernethy *et al.*, 1967; Alderson, 1968; and Wragg, 1968, is relevant, as well as Professor Merritt's consideration of the development of the intermediate reading skills (Merritt, 1970). Undoubtedly, the latter stages of the development of the reading skill merit further study, but it would be a great pity if the continued study of promising aspects of an area of research were always left to the enthusiasm and enterprise of individual researchers. It is as if the initial surveying and opening up of a mining area were carried out by large mineral firms with all their technological resources and then the actual mining was left to individual prospectors with their wash pans, picks and shovels, to get the most out of any rich deposit! This is a legitimate method, but a slow one for producing sufficient raw material for the consumer—in this case, the teacher in the classroom concerned about how to facilitate children's learning of this far from easy skill.

N. J. Entwistle

Personality and academic attainment

One of the recurrent themes to be found in educational research involves the attempt to unravel the complex determinants of academic
attainment. Early work concentrated on intelligence as the explanatory
variable and this is still the single most effective predictor of school
achievement. Subsequently a wide variety of research reports has drawn
attention to the importance of social factors and early experiences of
the child in the home. Environment affects both the development of
intelligence and the level of achievement. Almost unnoticed in the
research literature is a series of papers which describes the relationship
between personality and academic attainment. The results have been
far from clear-cut and consequently have attracted little publicity. But
any attempt to understand the complete causal chain associated with
school attainment must include the effect of personality on the child's
work in the school.

Personality has been defined by Allport (1963) as 'the dynamic
organization within the individual of those psychophysical systems that
determine his characteristic behaviour and thought' (p. 28). If this
definition is accepted, it appears inevitable that personality will be an
important determinant of classroom behaviour and ultimate scholastic
success. The measurement of personality is, however, far from simple
and the initial lack of success in isolating personality correlates of
school attainment can to a large extent be attributed to this difficulty.
The advent of pencil and paper group tests which have been carefully
developed and validated has stimulated renewed interest in this research
area. As a result there is now a sufficiently large literature for certain
trends to emerge. Most of the British studies have used the personality
inventories developed by either Eysenck or Cattell. This review thus
concentrates on these factorial approaches to the measurement of
personality.

Measurement and personality

Eysenck and Cattell have used different methods of identifying the factors which can be used to describe human personality. The resulting structures appear dissimilar at first sight. Papers by Burt (1965) and Adcock (1965) and a recent book (Eysenck and Eysenck, 1969a) have compared and contrasted the two approaches. Basically Eysenck had strong theoretical grounds for hypothesising two important, yet distinct, dimensions underlying human behaviour. Factor analysis designed to produce unrelated factors allowed Eysenck to choose items for his inventory which measured the traits of extraversion and neuroticism (emotional instability). Among children at least, the correlation between these two dimensions is generally found to be significantly negative and not zero as postulated. However these scales are still being developed and new versions are expected shortly.

An understanding of the terms extraversion and neuroticism, as used by Eysenck, demands a study of the items included in the various inventories (Maudsley or Eysenck in both junior and adult versions). Neuroticism is characterised by unnecessary worrying, by feelings of restlessness, by moodiness and by general nervousness. The stable person shows behaviour which is generally controlled; he tends to be reliable, even-tempered and calm. The typical extravert is 'sociable, likes parties, has many friends, needs to have people to talk to, and does not like studying by himself. He craves excitement, takes chances, often sticks his neck out, acts on the spur of the moment, and is generally an impulsive individual. . . . The typical introvert, on the other hand, is a quiet retiring sort of person, introspective, fond of books rather than people; he is reserved and distant except with intimate friends. He tends to plan ahead, "looks before he leaps", and distrusts the impulse of the moment' (Eysenck, 1965, pp. 59–60). Scores on these two dimensions are expected to be normally distributed with the majority of people being neither extraverted nor introverted, neurotic nor stable. For certain analyses, however, it is useful to identify individuals with above or below average scores on each trait and to describe four personality 'types'—stable extraverts, stable introverts, unstable extraverts and unstable introverts.

Cattell (1965) prefers to use an alternative method of factor analysis which produces inter-related factors. Out of a vast range of items he has isolated up to seventeen primary source traits which are given the alphabetic notation shown in table I. Because the factors are inter-related

TABLE I

*Cattell's Primary Source Traits and Second-order Factors**
(from Warburton, 1968a)

Anxiety	C−	instability v stability (low ego strength)
	L+	suspiciousness v broadmindedness (paranoid tendency)
	O+	insecurity v self-confidence (guilt proneness)
	Q_3−	undependability v self-discipline (low self-sentiment)
	Q_4+	tenseness v calmness (id pressure)
Extraversion	A+	friendliness v aloofness (cyclothymia v schizothymia)
	E+	dominance v submissiveness
	F+	surgency v desurgency
	H+	unreservedness v shyness (low reactivity to threat)
	Q_2−	group dependence v self-reliance
Tendermindedness	I+	sensitivity v insensitivity
	N−	tendermindedness v toughmindedness
Liberalism	Q_1+	radicalism v conservatism
	M+	unconventionality v conventionality
Moral attitudes	G+	moral attitudes v expediency (super-ego strength)

* Note the signs indicate the direction of scoring. Thus C− shows that low scores are an indication of instability, L+ that high scores indicate suspiciousness, and so on.

it is possible to simplfy Cattell's structure by repeated factor analyses which extract higher order factors. Warburton (1968a) provided a lucid summary of the pattern of higher-order factors. The five second-order factors are reduced by successive analyses down to two fourth-order factors, as shown below.

second-order	third-order	fourth-order
stability conservatism]	adaptation]	integration
extraversion toughmindedness]	thrust]	
conscientiousness or morality]	morality	morality

It is interesting to note that the two most important second-order factors are extraversion and stability, which are similar to Eysenck's major dimensions. Another two factors carry labels identical to what Eysenck sees as social attitudes (Eysenck, 1951). Eysenck has also moved away from the simple two-factor structure both by adding a psychoticism dimension (Eysenck and Eysenck, 1969b) and by subdividing extraversion into sociability and impulsivity (Eysenck and Eysenck, 1963). There is thus a considerable amount of overlap in the two descriptions of personality. In terms of the actual inventories the Cattell questionnaires (CPQ, HSPQ and 16PF for children, high-school pupils and adults) have the disadvantage of being lengthy and yet having short, rather unreliable, sub-scales. They also have American phraseology in places. Nevertheless the possibility of being able to investigate up to sixteen dimensions, rather than two, has an obvious appeal.

Investigations into the relationship between personality and academic attainment have used both types of inventory. Taken overall the findings appear somewhat contradictory, but a pattern emerges if the studies are examined separately at each of the main educational stages. As it is impossible to present detailed reviews of all the articles written about this topic, findings derived from large representative samples are used to illustrate the various approaches and to provide a relatively firm basis for systematising results from smaller studies.

RESEARCH AT SCHOOL LEVEL USING EYSENCK INVENTORIES

Two large-scale investigations of the relationships between personality and attainment have been reported among schoolchildren. Eysenck and Cookson (1969) were able to analyse the test scores of some 4 000 pupils in their final primary year from schools throughout Staffordshire. Entwistle and Cunningham (1968) used data from an almost complete age-group of 3 000 thirteen year olds in Aberdeen secondary schools. Even with two such large samples there is still no close agreement between the results. An examination of the differences does however draw attention to some of the complexities involved in this research area.

In the introduction to their article Eysenck and Cookson provide an excellent review of the literature, including studies using both types of inventory. They conclude, from examination of studies by Jones (1960), Morrison et al. (1965), Ridding (1967), Rushton (1966) and Savage (1966), that the extravert tends to be better at schoolwork in late primary and early secondary school. Similarly the work of Butcher *et al.* (1963), Callard and Goodfellow (1962), Hallworth (1961) and Lunzer (1960) is used to hypothesise a link between neuroticism and poor performance at this age level.

In their own study Eysenck and Cookson used the Junior Eysenck Personality Inventory (JEPI) and various standardised intellectual tests. Correlational analysis, analysis of variance and zonal analysis were used to investigate the relationship between personality and intellectual abilities. Results from boys and girls were presented separately. All the cognitive measures were found to correlate positively with extraversion for both boys and girls, the value lying between ·23 and ·19. With neuroticism the correlations were negative and rather lower (−·11). From these analyses it appeared that, taken as a group, stable extraverts are likely to be the more successful pupils in primary schools. However the zonal analysis which compared the mean scores of contrasting personality types, showed a less simple picture. Sex differences were found in this analysis with emotionally unstable extraverted girls being fairly successful, while boys of the same personality type achieved only low scores on both verbal reasoning and attainment tests.

It is interesting to note that for both boys and girls the least success-ful group at this age combined middling scores on neuroticism with low scores on extraversion. Elsewhere it has been suggested, by extrapola-tion from the results of experiments with mice and rats, that there should be an inverted-U curvilinear relationship between neuroticism (seen as an indicator of high 'drive') and performance in tasks of inter-mediate difficulty (Lynn and Gordon, 1961). In other words the group with middling scores on neuroticism would be expected to have the highest, not the lowest, level of performance. There is no suggestion of such a relationship in the results reported by Eysenck and Cookson, but Brown (1970) has found a curvilinear relationship of the postulated shape in a study of programmed learning in mathematics. Banks (1964), using secondary modern pupils again with a mathematical criterion, and Lynn and Gordon (1961) with students, have also reported similar results, but Entwistle and Cunningham (1968) demonstrated linearity of regression among their findings.

This last study is also the second of the large scale studies mentioned earlier. The authors made use of data obtained as part of a follow-up study concerned with the transition from primary to secondary school (Nisbet and Entwistle, 1969). The JEPI was given at age thirteen to pupils in all types of secondary school and teachers' rank-orders, scaled against a verbal reasoning test, were used as the criterion. The correlation between neuroticism and attainment was —·14 for boys and —·19 for girls. The correlations between extraversion and attainment were less than ·10, but there was a sex difference in the direction of the relationship. Extraverted girls but introverted boys tended to be more successful. This puzzling reversal was examined through zonal analyses which confirmed the superiority of stable introverts among boys and stable extraverts among girls. A recent re-analysis of these data by Wood (1971) using a multivariate analysis of variance technique, confirmed this sex interaction effect, but only for the original choice of partition defining high, middle and low scores on extraversion and neuroticism. Wood draws attention to the effect of using different cut off points. As Eysenck and Cookson chose their partitions to equalise the size of groups, while Entwistle and Cunningham chose theirs to bring out the effects occurring at low extraversion scores, some of the differences in the findings between these studies may be explained in this way.

The main difference between the studies lies in the lower correlation between extraversion and attainment in Aberdeen. Eysenck and Cookson attribute this effect to the age difference in the samples and point out that there is a tendency for introversion to be associated with academic success among older children and students. Ongoing research by Duckworth and Entwistle (1972) is probing this age effect further with samples of second year and fifth year pupils from grammar schools. In both groups there is a negative correlation between extraversion and examination performance, but the value is much higher among fifth formers (—·24) than among the second year (—·12). The correlations with neuroticism are uniformly low, but the direction of relationship moved from —·04 in the second year to ·05 in the fifth form. John (1973) reports similar correlations between the EPI and 'O' level grades. Extraversion correlated —·21 and neuroticism ·08 with the attainment measure. This pattern of result fits rather closely with some of the findings in investigations using the Cattell inventories.

RESEARCH AT SCHOOL LEVEL USING CATTELL INVENTORIES

One of the most important of these studies in Britain is that reported by Rushton (1966; 1968). He gave Cattell's Children's Personality

Questionnaire (CPQ) to 459 junior school boys and girls of above average intelligence. Attainment was measured by standardised tests in arithmetic and English. Significant correlations were found between C+ (stability) and both intellectual tests and between Q_4- (calmness) and English. Phlegmatic (D—) and self-disciplined (Q_3+) children tended to do well. There were also several positive correlations between the extraversion sub-scales and attainment. Perhaps the most important aspect of this study is that Rushton was able to retest 327 of his sample in the fifth form. Whereas at age eleven stable extraversion appeared to be related to high achievement, by age sixteen it was the anxious introverts who had the higher scores. At the trait level, however, the correlations were not consistent for all the examinations taken at 'O' level. The possibility of variations in the relationship between personality and attainment, subject by subject, will be taken up later.

Ballham (1965) also used a sample of grammar school pupils who had taken GCE 'O' level examinations. There was a clear tendency for introverts to obtain higher marks in all subjects. Cattell's primary traits of A— (aloofness), E— (submissiveness) and F— (desurgency) were associated with success. The results from the traits underlying neuroticism are of particular interest. While one dimension (Q_4+, tenseness) correlated positively with academic attainment, another (Q_3+, dependability) showed negative correlations. Furthermore the effects of the remaining neurotic traits appeared to vary from subject to subject. This shows how an examination of primary traits may help to explain non-significant relationships at the second-order level.

Ridding (1967) used a stratified sample of 600 pupils in their second year of secondary modern schooling. Children with intelligence quotients between 92 and 108 were chosen for an investigation into the relationships between personality and under- or over-achievement. Differences of eight points or more between attainment scores and verbal reasoning scores were used to define groups of over-achievers and under-achievers. Traits of E+ (dominance), F+ (surgency) and G+ (conscientiousness) were found to be associated with over-achievement. In terms of the second-order factors this suggests a positive correlation between extraversion and attainment, with intelligence held constant.

Two of the American studies are worth introducing at this point. Cattell, Sealey and Sweney (1966) have maintained that up to twenty five per cent of the variance in school attainment may be attributable to the effects of personality. This suggestion is, however, speculative as it is based on correlations corrected for the effects of unreliability in the measures. Even after these corrections, the value of correlations between the primary traits and attainment remained below ·3. Nevertheless some agreement is to be found between this study and that reported by Cattell and Butcher (1968). The primary traits of conscientiousness (G+), submissiveness (E—), friendliness (A+) and dependability (Q_3) are related to achievement in both samples. Cattell and Butcher report a regression equation, which, by including the dimension of intelligence (B), leads to a multiple correlation of ·7 with academic success. The constants in the equation indicate the weightings given to each trait.

$$Achievement = + \cdot 15A + \cdot 50B + \cdot 10C - \cdot 10D - \cdot 15E + \cdot 10F$$
$$+ \cdot 25G + \cdot 10H - \cdot 10I + \cdot 15J - \cdot 10O$$
$$+ \cdot 20Q_2 + \cdot 20Q_3 - \cdot 10Q_4$$

It is too soon, however, to put much trust in such a prediction equation. The variations in relationship between samples will lead to considerable fluctuations in the weightings. In fact, individual studies taken separately do not provide a coherent picture in terms of the primary source traits. The unreliability of the sub-scales, together with the small scale of many of the studies, makes this confusion inevitable. Fortunately a lucid summary of research using the Cattell tests is already in existence (Warburton, 1968b) and has been particularly valuable in preparing this chapter.

Warburton, who was closely associated with the work of Cattell for many years, chose twenty nine of the most satisfactory studies to demonstrate the existence of a pattern of relationships in terms of the second-order factors. Table 2 presents a condensation of Warburton's summaries, based on the twenty five studies which used Cattell inventories. The articles from which these results were derived are shown among the references, marked with asterisks.

Warburton drew attention to the same age trend noted by Eysenck. Stable extraversion is related to success in the primary school, changing over to introversion and possibly to emotional instability by age eighteen. From the pattern shown in table 2 it appears that the changeover both from stability to neuroticism and from extraversion to introversion in fact occurs late in the secondary school. The abrupt reversal of relationships after age fourteen, particularly that between intro-

TABLE 2

*Summary of results from studies using Cattell's inventories:
direction of correlation coefficients with scholastic attainment
(adapted from Warburton, 1968, Table 3)*

second-order factor	primary-source trait	age group							
		under 12		12–14		15–17		over 17	
		+	−	+	−	+	−	+	−
anxiety/ neuroticism	instability (C−)	0	3	0	1	3	0	3	2
	tenseness (Q₄+)	0	1	0	1	1	0	5	1
	insecurity (O+)	0	0	0	2	1	0	1	1
	bad-temperedness (D+)	0	1	0	2	2	0	0	0
	unreliability (Q₃−)	0	1	0	5	0	2	0	2
	suspiciousness (L+)	0	0	0	0	0	0	2	2
	total	0	6	0	11	7	2	11	8
introversion (1)	aloofness (A−)	0	0	0	6	3	0	0	1
	surgency (F−)	0	3	0	0	8	0	3	1
	shyness (H−)	0	2	0	2	3	0	1	0
	total	0	5	0	8	14	0	4	2
introversion (2)	submissiveness (E−)	0	1	7	0	4	0	1	2
	independence (Q₂+)	1	0	3	0	3	0	1	0
	total	1	1	10	0	7	0	2	2
tendermindedness	tendermindedness (I+)	0	0	1	0	2	0	3	0
	unaffectedness (N−)	0	0	0	0	0	0	1	0
	total	0	0	1	0	2	0	4	0
radicalism	bohemianism (M+)	0	0	0	0	0	0	4	0
	radicalism (Q₁+)	0	0	0	0	0	0	1	0
	total	0	0	0	0	0	0	5	0
morality	conscientiousness (G+)	2	0	6	0	4	1	2	3

version and attainment, is quite remarkable. All thirteen relationships obtained with younger children are negative, with extraverts being more successful; out of eighteen with older pupils and students only two are in this direction. Perhaps the change over from junior to senior versions of the inventories affects the results, but it is difficult to explain such a clear-cut change in the direction of the relationship in this way, but its coincidence with the school leaving age is more likely to be an indication as to its cause. Between fifteen and eighteen the majority of young people move into employment and out of the reach of educational research workers. The remaining captives are highly selected on both intelligence and social class. It may be that the different relationships between personality and attainment are a characteristic of this restricted population found in sixth forms and in colleges and universities.

RESEARCH AT COLLEGE AND UNIVERSITY LEVEL

Warburton's summary provides convincing evidence of the superiority of the introvert in higher education, but there are conflicting findings in terms of neuroticism. Pioneering research by Furneaux (1962) drew attention to the differing failure rates among students of the four personality types. Using a sample of ninety one male engineering students and the Maudsley Personality Inventory, he was able to show that stable extraverts had by far the highest failure rate in a first year examination (sixty one per cent). For neurotic extraverts the percentage was thirty six and for the stable and neurotic introverts the figures were twenty six per cent and twenty one per cent respectively. Also at London University, Kelvin, Lucas and Ojha (1965) found that students obtaining poor degrees had higher mean extraversion scores than those who obtained good degrees, although they commented that a nomal degree of extraversion appeared to be quite compatible with academic success. Savage (1962) in Australia and Lavin (1967), who reviewed the American literature, also found that introversion was positively related to academic performance at college or university level. To this extent Furneaux's findings have been confirmed by more widely based studies.

The precise relationship of stability–instability to good performance is much less clear. Furneaux suggested the importance of instability; Kelvin and his co-workers, however, showed that the first class honours graduates and those students who failed, both showed high neuroticism scores on the whole. But other studies by Savage (1962) and by Lynn and Gordon (1961) have found a different relationship in which students who had high or low instability scores did worse than those who had moderate scores. The American literature also produces contradictory evidence, in spite of the use of large samples in some studies. Lavin (1967) concludes that, on balance, the stable student is likely to be the more successful. Warburton and Eysenck both reached the opposite conclusion in Britain, but results from recent studies have been more equivocal. Kline and Gale (1971) administered the EPI to 455 students over a five year period. Only for one year group was there a significant relationship between either neuroticism or introversion and marks in a first year psychology examination. The remaining correlations were not only insignificant, but also in the opposite direction. Wankowski (1968) has suggested that it is stable introverts who do best at university. Smithers and Batcock (1970) find similar results for social scientists in a technological university, but not for health scientists. This last study points to the likelihood of variations in relationships among students taking different academic disciplines.

Entwistle and Wilson (1970) and Warburton *et al.* (1963) used samples of graduates training to be teachers. Entwistle and Wilson indicated a tendency for stable introverts in their sample to have obtained the best degrees, while Warburton, using the 16 PF scale, obtained significant correlations between the second-order stability factor and the examination results in educational theory. Traits of stability (C+), conscientiousness (G+) and unconventionality (M+) showed significant relationships with the attainment measure. The last trait mentioned above is part of the second-order factor of tender-mindedness and Warburton suggested elsewhere (1968b) that success in theory of education examinations might, in part, demand the adoption by the students of their tutors' attitudes towards education. Again the realisation that examinations in certain disciplines will assess more than cognitive skills and that examinations reflect the objectives of the course, helps to explain the different relationships being found in contrasting academic disciplines.

A recent study by Wilson (1971) at Aberdeen used a sample of 624 undergraduates who had taken the EPI, divided into groups by faculty (arts/science) and by sex. Analyses were also carried out separately for students who had failed and for those who had a high level of performance in first year examinations. The results emphasise again the importance of not assuming wide generality in the relationship between personality and academic performance. Extraversion was significantly related to failure for all students in the arts faculty. Stability was also linked with failure, but only for arts women. Merit performance was predicted by neuroticism and introversion, but only in isolated sub-groups. Neuroticism was related to high performance among male arts students, while introversion went with success for male scientists. Insignificant results emerged from analyses of the other sub-groups.

Not only are different relationships to be expected in contrasting subject areas, but it seems logical to anticipate similar variations between universities and colleges of either education or technology. Staveley (1967) obtained a sample of 351 students from three technical colleges. These students were taking a first-year part-time course in mechanical engineering, craft practice and general engineering. In two colleges introverts tended to be more successful in one or more of the examinations and in one of these colleges anxious introverts were best of all, but in the third college there was no significant relationship at all. As the relationships observed varied between first and second years, between different types of examinations and between different colleges, no general conclusions may be reached from this study. Cowell and Entwistle (1971) also failed to obtain significant relationships in a technical college among students taking ONC courses. On the other hand Venables (1967) did find a tendency for introverts to do rather better in academic work during the first year. In subsequent years anxious students, except those in the mechanical trades, reached higher levels of performance. There thus appears to be no clear-cut pattern of relationships emerging from research in technical colleges.

A confused picture is also found in research on students at colleges of education. Halliwell (1963) included students taking both a two year course and a three year course. In the former stability was related to success, while the reverse was found in the three year course. To complicate the situation even further Cortis (1966) obtained positive correlations for extraversion (A+) and stability (L—) with academic performance. Again tenderminded (I+) and unconventional (M+, Q+) students tended to do well.

Clearly it is important to have results from comparable studies in different types of institution. One small scale investigation of this type has recently been reported by Entwistle and Entwistle (1970). Using the EPI and first-year marks, correlations of —·25 (extraversion) and —·11 (neuroticism) were found for university students. Comparable coefficients for a college of education sample were —·11 (extraversion) and —·02 (neuroticism). This last study was in fact designed as a pilot for a large-scale follow-up study of students from all three sectors of higher education, which is still in progress. Preliminary analyses have been carried out on just over half the full sample (Entwistle, Percy and Nisbet, 1971); these were based on 898 students from three universities, 562 students from four colleges of education and 190 students from five polytechnics (actual and designated). All the students were taking degree level, teachers' certificate or HND courses and academic performance had been assessed after one year. Students were given, among other tests, the EPI, the Eysenck scales of radicalism and tendermindedness and the study of values. One interesting set of results showed that the profiles of mean scores on these tests varied considerably between students taking different disciplines. Comparing linguists with pure scientists distinct differences were found on nine out of the thirteen dimensions included in the analysis. Pure scientists tended to be stable introverts and to have conservative attitudes combined with high theoretical and economic values. Linguists were more neurotic and radical with high aesthetic values. It was also found that successful students tended to have more extreme scores on these dimensions than those who did badly in the examinations. While there were definite arts/science differences, there were also variations within faculties. For example neurotic introverts apparently make good engineers, as Furneaux found, but stable introverts do better in the pure sciences. Neurotic introverts are also good at languages, but stable introverts make better historians. Among social science students the correlations between both personality dimensions and attainment were near zero, which fits in with the findings of Kline and Gale.

Taken overall the greatest consistency in results occurs with the extraversion trait. On the whole introverts do tend to be more successful. Correlations ranged from —·26 to —·03 in different subject area groups at university, from —·21 to —·07 in comparable groups at colleges of education and from —·10 to —·08 at polytechnics. The neuroticism trait was much less consistent, equivalent ranges being —·24 to ·28, —·27 to —·07 and —·42 to —·05. Neuroticism is only positively correlated with academic performance in certain sub-groups of the student population, at least on the evidence of this particular study.

There thus appears to be some doubt about the generality of the earlier suggestion that unstable students tend to be successful. The findings are conflicting and, while the possibility of subject-area differences may help to resolve some of the confusion, there are likely to be alternative explanations for this situation. For example, Eysenck (1972) suggests that there have been fundamental weaknesses in previous discussions of this problem. It has usually been assumed that a high score on 'neuroticism' predisposes a student to act in one particular way for any given situation. The research problem has thus been seen as identifying the type of academic behaviour which unstable students most frequently display. This approach probably represents a misleading oversimplification; it ignores the important distinction between trait and state anxiety, and also the effect of existing habits.

> 'To say that a person is high on anxiety . . . means that his anxiety is easily aroused, and that he admits to many neurotic symptoms; nevertheless he is not always in a state of high anxiety. Thus a very intelligent, well prepared person who scores high on N may nevertheless enter the examination room quite calm and self-possessed because under the circumstances this situation does not provide the necessary stimuli for the arousal of his anxiety.' (p. 42)

Eysenck indicates that measurements of the 'state' anxiety aroused by particular situations may be necessary before the conflicting findings on the neuroticism dimension can be resolved. It also may be necessary to know in some detail how a student's previous habits interact with drive stimuli—such as an imminent examination—before accurate prediction of performance can become possible. Thus to reduce anxiety

> '(One) . . . student may go out on a drinking spree, . . . get home late and be in no fit state in the morning to cope successfully with his examination. Another student, perhaps more introverted, may reduce the strength of his (anxiety) by going over his notes again and again; this might prove beneficial and improve his chances of passing the examination.' (Eysenck, 1972, p. 43)

Eysenck suggests that the inclusion of measures designed to assess relevant habit systems might allow more accurate prediction of academic behaviour. Under this heading might be included variables such as academic motivation, study methods, attitudes to studying, and the dimension recently described by Hudson (1968) as 'syllabus bound/ syllabus free'. A number of studies have already shown that these dimensions are related to both personality and academic performance. Eysenck (1972) suggests that 'theoretically at least, introverted habit systems would seem likely to predispose students to engage in good study habits, so that high anxiety drive in introverts would lead to even more strenuous study' (p. 44). It is not known at present whether good study habits combined with introversion and neuroticism are particularly likely to lead to academic success, but empirical results do indicate that good study habits, as defined in two separate inventories, are related to stable introversion (Entwistle *et al.*, 1971; Cowell and Entwistle, 1971). Also academic motivation is linked to stability, that is to *low* drive (Entwistle *et al.*, 1971) and the syllabus bound dimension to introversion (John, 1973).

The link between stability (*low* drive) and either motivation or study methods is not ruled out in Eysenck's elaboration of the elementory theory of drive and performance. However it is possible to put forward alternative formulations of the effect of neuroticism on academic study. It may be precisely the combination of high motivation with emotional stability which summarises the characteristics of the student with 'high drive'—at least in the everyday use of this term. Descriptions of stability imply low reactivity to stimuli. Perhaps in this particular context we need to extend the neuroticism dimension further to include strong reaction in a non-neurotic direction. Then drive might be linked with high reactivity in either direction and both extremes might lead to success for differing groups of students. This would represent a parallel to the distinction met elsewhere in the literature between 'achievement motivation' and 'fear of failure' (Birney, Burdick and Teevan, 1969). The Eysenckian formulation, which modifies the direction of anxiety (drive) according to previous habits, may well coincide with the concepts of 'facilitating' and 'debilitating' anxiety as described by Alpert and Haber (1960). It certainly appears that the use of elaborate theoretical models may lead to more sophisticated investigations into the relationship between personality and attainment; there is also room for improvement in the research designs used in such studies.

Problems and growth-points

There is a variety of factors which may explain the contradictions between findings which abound in the literature reviewed in this chapter. Before attempting a final summary of the outcomes of this research, various aspects of research design which may have affected results, will be briefly discussed.

METHODS OF ANALYSIS

The commonest forms of analysis applied to data on personality and attainment have been correlation techniques and zonal analysis. Both approaches lead to difficulties. The major problem involved in zonal analysis is the definition of the various personality 'types'. Many studies have created four types simply by dichotomising the scores on each dimension at the median value. To equalise the size of groups it is better to plot the two dimensional scatter diagram of extraversion against neuroticism (Wood, 1971). But both these methods are specific to a particular sample and prevent direct comparisons being made between studies. Agreement to define personality types in terms of the norms presented in the test-manuals for each age level or sub group of the adult population would be a useful move, at least where the norms have been derived from samples of adequate size. As much of the research is done on rather small groups, it might be necessary to make the extreme groups fairly close to the overall mean. Personality types might then be created by taking scores of $\pm 0.5\ \sigma$ either side of the means reported in the manuals or, where necessary, dichotomising at this mean value. Studies having larger samples might be able to report additional analyses of more extreme groups (perhaps $\pm 0.75\ \sigma$). Nevertheless the advantage of comparability produced by a standard way of creating 'types' is off-set by the artificiality and rigidity of using arbitrary cut-off points which do not reflect, even in an intuitive way, variations in relationships existing in the data. Clearly other approaches and other methods of analysis should also be attempted.

Most of the research reported in this chapter has involved the use of various correlational techniques. While these methods of analysis have distinct advantages in terms of ease of communication, they do have definite weaknesses. It is possible to dismiss a non-linear relationship in reporting an insignificant product-moment coefficient and also to ignore the possibility of important interactions between variables. Correlations average out the relationships over the whole sample, ignoring possible differences between sub groups. It is certainly useful to apply correlational techniques to sub groups, where these are known in advance. But in view of possibilities such as the one discussed in the previous section, that anxiety may affect the performance of different students in opposite directions, alternative methods of analysis might be more appropriate. Whereas correlational techniques compare similarities between *tests* over the whole sample, the methods of cluster analysis and classification procedures compare similarities between *people* over the complete battery of tests. They provide indications of groups of people who have the same patterns of scores. It would thus be possible, in principle, to identify two separate groups of students both with high neuroticism scores, one showing high and the other low attainment scores. Recent developments in computers have made cluster analysis a more attractive possibility and some promising analyses of data have already been reported (Entwistle and Brennan, 1971). One classification procedure in particular (automatic interaction detection) allows sub groups to be produced on the basis of the various interactions existing in the data, rather than being created by arbitrary or subjective decisions. This method of analysis seeks to maximise the prediction of a criterion variable by forming sub groups in terms of a small number of 'explanatory' variables. It thus appears to be a potentially fruitful approach to the problem of isolating interactions between personality and other variables in relation to academic performance. Early results from an analysis of data from university students (Brennan and Entwistle, 1974) has thrown up the possibility that introversion is related more closely to attainment in a sub group of science students with moderate A-level results who see themselves as being 'hardworking', than in other sub groups.

MEASUREMENT OF ATTAINMENT

The results reported in earlier sections were all based on scores from either Eysenck or Cattell personality inventories, but academic attainment was measured in a variety of ways. Some of the differences in findings may be attributable to these variations.

In some studies attainment is measured by objective tests of English and mathematics; in others verbal reasoning tests are used. A few studies have reported analyses based on performance in programmed learning tasks, in which the time allowed for these tasks may be an important consideration in itself (Seddon, 1972). External or internal examination marks are found frequently in the literature. While all these measures may well show fairly high intercorrelations, they still represent differing definitions of attainment. 'Academic attainment' surely implies that pupils or students have been assessed in terms of their performance on the courses they have actually taken in school or college. Thus tests of verbal reasoning, though correlated with academic attainment, are not measures of success in school. Similarly objective tests of English and mathematics provide only two components of school attainment. Even in primary schools many other mental skills are important—for example, there is an increasing emphasis on individual expression in music, art and language. It seems improbable that a single set of personality correlates will adequately describe success in such different forms of intellectual activity.

There is some evidence that different personality characteristics are linked to success with contrasting definitions of attainment (W. Rudd, 1970; Bennett, 1971). Bennett, in a piece of ongoing research is using two contrasting measures of attainment in primary, middle and secondary schools. Early results from the primary stage are based on a conventional measure of school attainment (teachers' rank-orders scaled on a verbal reasoning test) and on impression marking of imaginative stories. As anticipated rather different relationships between personality and attainment are emerging from the two types of measure. Bennett has confirmed the superiority of stable extraverts in conventional attainment at this age level, but a sex difference was found when results from the imaginative stories were analysed. High scores were given to boys who were stable extraverts, but to girls who were unstable extraverts.

Similar differences might also be expected in secondary schools. Again standardised tests, used on their own, do not correspond at all closely to the teacher's view of school attainment. With a larger number of subjects included in the curriculum perhaps the only valid measure of overall achievement will be a sum or an average of marks taken from the whole range of subjects. These marks will generally have to be scaled against a standardised test of scholastic aptitude to allow comparisons between classes and between schools. The assumption here is that the consensus of opinion among teachers provides the best indication of the rank-order of achievement within a class, while an objective test is a more accurate way of deciding the standard of that class compared with others. During the later stages of secondary school sums (or averages) of grades at O- or A-level make satisfactory measures of academic success without any scaling procedure.

It is thus possible to devise appropriate ways of assessing overall performance in secondary schools, but the pattern of results found with students suggests the need to examine separately the relationship between personality and each individual school subject. Some of the investigations described in an earlier section included such analyses. Ballham (1965) reported that the effect of Cattell's anxiety traits in relation to GCE 'O' level marks differed according to the type of academic subject taken. In this sample more anxious pupils tended to do well in science and in practical subjects. It was also found that sensitive (I+) pupils were particularly successful in arts subjects. Rushton (1968) found that the more serious-minded (E—) pupils obtained high 'O' level marks in an English Language examination. These pupils also tended to be conscientious (G+). Successful mathematicians were more introverted (A—) and frivolous (G—).

The recent research of Duckworth and Entwistle (1972) obtained measures of attainment in eight separate subjects for second and fifth year pupils. No systematic variation in the relationships between personality and achievement in different subjects was found with the second year pupils, but among the fifth formers introversion and stability were associated with success in science O-level examinations. The relationship between introversion and performance in arts subjects was less close and there was a tendency for unstable pupils to be more successful in these subjects.

Finally in higher education the growing tendency to include both course work and examination marks in the overall assessment of students suggests a further division in the definition of attainment. Differences in the correlates of success from discipline to discipline have already been demonstrated. There is a distinct possibility that course work and examination may favour different personality types. Again research on this possibility is already being undertaken (E. Rudd, 1970).

INTERVENING VARIABLES

Repeatedly throughout the review of the literature the possible effect of intervening variables has been implicit in research reports. An intervening variable is one which affects the size or the direction of the relationship between the two main dimensions under consideration. It is already clear that sex and age have been acting in this way. Further analysis of the data obtained from the follow-up of Aberdeen secondary pupils by Entwistle and Welsh (1969) suggested that there might also be different relationships among bright children compared with those found for pupils of below average ability. Dividing their sample into top and bottom thirds in terms of ability level, they found that introversion was linked to high achievement for bright boys, whereas extraversion was the more favourable trait in the low ability group. The results for girls were similar, but less marked.

Some support for this finding can be obtained by comparing studies on secondary modern children with those on grammar school pupils. In a number of studies extraversion has been found to be related to achievement in non-selective schools (Fraser, 1967; Ridding, 1967). Introversion is generally related to success in grammar schools (Ballham, 1965; Rushton, 1968; Duckworth and Entwistle, 1972). While part of this difference in relationship may well be attributed to the age effect, there is a particularly interesting comparison which can be made between the results obtained by Fraser and by Duckworth. Both investigators used the JEPI with children aged 12–13 years and obtained separate correlations with attainment in English and mathematics. Fraser's secondary-modern sample showed a correlation of 0·16 between extraversion and English and of 0·28 with arithmetic. Duckworth's grammar-school sample produced comparable values of −0·12 and −0·05. It does seem probable, although the evidence is still tenuous, that introversion is related to success for the brightest children in secondary school even as early as the second year. Among the low ability group extraversion is still associated with high achievement at age 14 (Entwistle and Welsh, 1969).

There are other intervening variables which may affect the relationships between personality and attainment. A number of studies have observed differing relationships among urban children and rural children (Cattell and Butcher, 1968; Entwistle 1967), but these may be a reflection of differences in classroom organisation, in average class size or in methods of teaching. The range of approaches in primary schools, between formal and informal methods, suggests that different personality types would be successful in contrasting educational climates. These possibilities are being investigated at present (Sharples, 1971; Bennett, 1971; Eysenck, 1972).

Finally, it seems probable that there will be an interaction between the teacher's personality and the performance of children of differing personality types. There are formidable obstacles to research of this kind, but it may be crucial to overcome them. It is probably only in this way that the observed relationships between personality and attainment can be fully explained.

Conclusion

The last few sections have outlined a personal view of problems and growth-points in research into personality and attainment. Recent work at Lancaster has figured rather prominently in this subjective perspective, as the author is less familiar with ongoing research elsewhere. There are almost certainly important developments which have been undervalued or ignored altogether. Similarly the map drawn in describing the literature may represent the operation of selective perception. Nevertheless two major conclusions may be drawn with some confidence. First, it is dangerous to assume wide generality in statements about the relationships between personality and academic attainment. Age, ability, sex, geographical area, classroom organisation, class size, teaching methods and teacher personality may all affect these relationships to some extent. Nevertheless the second conclusion does indicate the existence of some overall pattern in this confused research area.

There is now considerable agreement as to the existence of an age effect. Many apparent contradictions in the literature are resolved by the recognition that stable extraverts tend to be successful in primary schools, while introverts, and possibly even neurotic introverts, predominate among outstanding students. Figure I represents an intuitive graph, based partly on research evidence, which indicates how the pattern of observed relationships may change with the age and ability level of the pupils forming the sample. Extraversion and stability remain advantageous longer for children of below-average ability. Introversion is related to success among bright children soon after entering secondary school. It may be possible to simplify even further the relationships shown in Figure I. If the correlation were to be plotted against *mental age* rather than chronological age, a single line could adequately describe each of the relationships. If a bright child of age 10 can be assumed to be equivalent intellectually to a child of low ability aged 16 or more, the four discrete lines would merge into two. However, such neatness is unlikely to coincide with reality in this particular research area.

Finally it may be salutary to look for practical, rather than theoretical, importance in the research findings. It still requires considerable faith and imagination to see where these results may lead. The lack of generality in relationships and the probable link between teaching methods and personality correlates of success, both reinforce the grow-

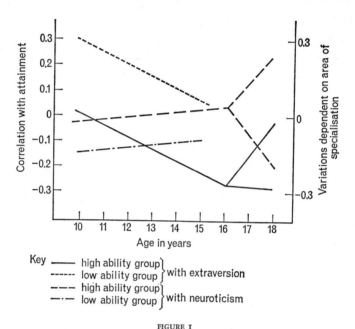

FIGURE I

Indication of variations in correlations between personality and conventional measures of academic attainment with age and ability.

ing realisation of the importance of variety in the presentation of material to be learned. Even at the same intellectual level no one teaching method or way of organising learning experiences will be ideal for all pupils or for all students. Ultimately it may be possible to allow the 'consumers' to choose the method of instruction, at least in the later stages of education. Formal, systematic presentation may still be preferred by some; unstructured freedom may suit others. An understanding of personality differences may help us to anticipate such preferences. Research into the relationships between personality and academic attainment, with an emphasis on changes with age, may provide guidance as to the appropriate provision of alternative methods of presentation at different educational stages.

Desmond L. Nuttall

Convergent and divergent thinking

While the analysis of thinking processes has a long tradition in British philosophy, stemming from the work of Hobbes in the seventeenth century (see Shouksmith, 1970), it is only relatively recently that processes other than logical reasoning have had any experimental or psychometric investigation. Despite isolated attempts to test imaginative thinking (e.g. Hargreaves, 1927), it was not until the early 1960s that the 'creativity' testing movement established a major foothold. The work of Torrance (1962) and Getzels and Jackson (1962) were mainly responsible for stimulating work in this country, and they themselves owe a major debt to Guilford's formulation of his Structure-of-Intellect model (Guilford, 1956, 1967).

In his now famous presidential address to the American Psychological Association, Guilford (1950) criticised existing tests of ability as being too limited in their scope and suggested that, in the study of creativity, tests to measure the fluency, flexibility and originality of thinking would be required. He and his colleagues proceeded to develop tests of these abilities and in later formulations of his model, they were classified in the Operations category of Divergent-Production. In general, each test presents a problem situation in which there are many, if not an infinity of, appropriate responses, requiring the individual to 'diverge' in his thinking. Divergent-Production thus stands in stark contrast to the remainder of the five Operations categories (Cognition, Memory, Convergent-Production and Evaluation) where there is usually a unique correct answer to the test problem to be chosen from among five alternatives. In tests in the category of Convergent-Production, the candidate has to produce the answer in his own words rather than to choose an answer as in a multiple-choice item, but the term 'convergent thinking' is most commonly used now to cover all those situations where the problem has a unique correct solution, whether the candidate has to generate his own response or merely to select it.

In the following review, convergent thinking is used in this broad sense. The review concentrates on five major areas: whether divergent thinking can be considered a unitary trait, the relationship of divergent and convergent thinking abilities, the validity of divergent thinking tests, the influence of environmental and educational conditions on performance in divergent thinking tests, and factors affecting the reliability of such tests. A number of studies, of course, produce evidence relating to several of these issues.

Is divergent thinking a unitary trait?

The majority of divergent thinking tests give rise to more than one score. Almost invariably, one score is simply the total number of responses produced, disallowing any responses that clearly do not meet the requirements of the problem (the fluency score); another very common score is for originality, which, in an attempt to avoid subjective judgement, is usually based on the statistical infrequency of the responses. A flexibility score is sometimes used: it consists of the number of different categories of response that a candidate uses and often gives rise to problems in defining the categories.

Nuttall (1971) found very high correlations between fluency, flexibility and originality scores within any one test, the median intercorrelation for four tests being 0·74. Ward (1967) and Fee (1968) in their re-analyses of the data of Wallach and Kogan (1965) found that uniqueness (originality) scores loaded on the same factor as fluency scores, although Ward's analysis also gave rise to a factor, accounting for only 6 per cent of the variance, on which fluency scores loaded but uniqueness scores did not. The factor analysis of Child and Smithers (1971) revealed that fluency and originality scores from the same tests always loaded on the same factor and the same is true, with minor exceptions, in the factor analysis of Richards and Bolton (1971) who also used flexibility scores with two of their tests. In both cases, the flexibility score loaded with the fluency score.

The method used to score divergent thinking tests thus seems to be largely irrelevant and Dacey, Madaus and Allen (1969) concluded from their own results that 'the task-specific measures are highly related, almost to the point of being redundant' (p. 263). No British study has produced results that in any way support the idea of separate factors of fluency, flexibility and originality that cut across tests, although this is implied by Guilford's model.

Although the correlations within a test may be high, the same is not necessarily true of correlations between tests. Many researchers write of divergent thinking as though it were a single dimension and have tended to add scores from different divergent thinking tests to produce a single score, even though the correlations among the tests have sometimes been quite low. For example, Getzels and Jackson (1962) formed a composite score from scores on five divergent thinking tests, all predominantly verbal in nature, and contrasted this score with IQ even though the correlations among the divergent thinking tests were of the same order as those between the divergent thinking tests and IQ. Hudson (1966), too, formed a composite score from scores from the Uses of Objects Test and the Meaning of Words Test even though these tests had a correlation of 0·30, little higher than their correlations with convergent thinking measures.

The most important single piece of evidence in favour of a single factor of divergent thinking stems from the work of Wallach and Kogan (1965). Their composite score based on fluency and uniqueness scores from each of five tests had internal consistencies of up to 0·93, but all their tests, administered individually under game-like conditions, required verbal responses even though some of the stimulus material was visual. Fee's re-analysis (1968) did suggest some slight differentiation between 'verbal' and 'visual' divergent thinking, but Ward's (1967) did not.

When tests sampling a wider range of content are used, there is a growing body of evidence to suggest that divergent thinking is far from being a unitary dimension. Lovell and Shields (1967), working with a group of 50 eight to ten year olds all with IQs greater than 140 on the WISC verbal scale, found that their divergent thinking tests (those used by Getzels and Jackson) defined a reasonable factor but that many of the tests showed substantial loadings on other factors identifiable as academic attainment factors. They concluded: '... while the remaining dimensions [factors] suggest that divergent thinking cannot be accounted for by one dimension; rather the able pupil is "creative" in different degrees according to the task that is set him' (p. 207). Child and Smithers (1971) found that the Circles Test loaded on a different factor from the Uses and Consequences tests, although there was a correlation of 0·30 between the two factors, and earlier Child (1968) found that his divergent thinking tests spread themselves across a number of different factors. Richards and Bolton (1971) found that their various divergent thinking tests all loaded on the same factor, but the loadings from the Circles, Consequences and Make-Up Problems tests were all low and there was another factor on which the Circles and Consequences tests had high loadings and the other divergent thinking tests low loadings. Nuttall (1971) found very low correlations between the Squares Test (an alternative form of the Circles Test), the Uses Test, the TH Test (five letter words beginning with TH) and a Number Routes Test (ways of reaching 12 starting with 6, e.g. $6+3+3=12$, $6+17-11=12$). The median correlation among a sample of secondary school fourth-formers broadly representative of the whole ability range was only 0·14 and among a sample of fifth-formers, 0·10.

Divergent thinking therefore appears to be far from a unitary trait and is better considered as a number of distinct abilities. These abilities seem to depend largely upon the stimulus material; that is, there is evidence for a verbal divergent thinking factor, a diagrammatic factor, a numerical factor and so on. Much more research is needed to demonstrate this conclusively and there is an added complication in that low correlations between divergent thinking tests may in large part be due to their unreliability (see below). There has been considerable looseness in applying the title 'divergent thinking' to open-ended tests and a clearer picture may emerge when divergent thinking tests are classified more carefully. Butcher (1968) has suggested that the possible number of responses to such tests may be an important consideration: many tests such as the Uses Test and the Circles Test have a seemingly infinite number of possible responses, whereas the Meaning of Words Test and the TH Test have a strictly limited number of possible responses and would also seem to be highly dependent upon the candidate's breadth of vocabulary. The mode of response is also likely to be important, as are the conditions of testing.

The relationship between divergent and convergent thinking abilities

Getzels and Jackson (1962) claimed to have differentiated between intelligence and 'creativity'. Reviewing their work, Burt (1962) suggested that they had adopted an oversimplified view of both concepts and Marsh's re-analysis (1964) of their data provided no evidence for separate dimensions of 'creativity' and intelligence. Both Burt (1962) and Vernon (1964) suggested that divergent thinking is better seen as a facet of general ability and, indeed, divergent thinking tests have been included as an integral part of early versions of the new British Intelligence Scale (Warburton, 1970).

The view is borne out by the results of Hasan and Butcher (1966). Using Getzels and Jackson's divergent thinking tests among others, they found positive and significant correlations between the Verbal Reasoning Quotient (VRQ) and all the divergent thinking tests, these correlations being higher than those among the divergent thinking tests. The correlation between VRQ and the Fables test was no less than 0·726, in contrast to a value of 0·131 in Getzels and Jackson's study. The mean VRQ of the 175 Scottish schoolchildren (aged twelve) in Hasan and Butcher's study was 102, while in Getzels and Jackson's sample of over 500 adolescents the mean IQ was 132; the standard deviations of the quotients in the two samples were comparable, so that restriction of range cannot explain the differing results.

Guilford's Structure-of-Intellect model and the results of his factor analytic studies suggest that the relationships between divergent and convergent thinking abilities are negligible. Guilford tends to employ samples which are highly homogeneous in ability and factor analytic techniques which maximise the chances of obtaining uncorrelated factors. Vernon (1969a) has argued that the British favour the hierarchical model of abilities, which implies substantial correlations between abilities, largely because their samples tend to be more heterogeneous in ability and because they prefer the group factor analysis technique. This latter point is demonstrated in a study by Sultan (1962) who used a wide variety of Guilford's Divergent-Production tests together with a number of conventional convergent thinking tests with a sample of 170 thirteen to fourteen year old grammar school pupils. Using Varimax rotation on his Principal Components, he found evidence for distinct Ideational Fluency and Originality factors (as postulated by Guilford, 1959), but no evidence for any of Guilford's three Flexibility factors, the marker tests for these factors tending to load with the convergent thinking tests. A group factor analysis of the same data led to the usual British hierarchical model of abilities with no evidence for any separate divergent thinking factors.

Hudson (1966), working with samples of very clever schoolboys all destined for university, found very little relationship between divergent thinking and intelligence, as measured by the AH 5 test. Cameron (1968), using the same tests with a similar group of pupils in Scotland, also found negligible relationships, the median correlation between the two divergent and two convergent thinking measures being 0·08. With university students, Christie (1970) obtained a correlation of exactly zero between the Miller Analogies tests and a composite divergent thinking score based on the Circles, Problems and Impossibilities tests, and Child and Smithers (1971) found a median correlation of 0·075 between six measures of divergent thinking and the two parts of the AH 5 test.

In samples more representative of the whole ability range, Vernon (1967) and Nuttall (1971) also found a distinct separation between divergent and convergent thinking measures. Haddon and Lytton (1968), however, found a correlation of 0.48 between VRQ and a composite divergent thinking test score among a sample of children aged eleven to twelve representative of the whole ability range. On retesting most of the same children with the same divergent thinking tests some four years later, Haddon and Lytton (1971) found a correlation between VRQ at age eleven and divergent thinking at age fifteen of 0·615. In contrast, Lytton and Cotton (1969) found a correlation of only 0·17 between VRQ and the divergent thinking tests used by Haddon and Lytton among a sample of fourteen year olds whose mean VRQ at 112 was some 10 points greater than the mean VRQ of the children in Haddon and Lytton's study.

While there is a tendency for correlations between divergent and convergent thinking measures to be higher among samples representative of the whole ability range than they are among highly selected groups, as would be expected on the grounds of restriction of range, the general picture is far from clearcut. An alternative explanation stems from the threshold hypothesis, which postulates that a minimum level of general ability is required for a high level of performance on divergent thinking tests, but that above that level there is little relationship between general ability and divergent thinking ability. This hypothesis is sufficient to explain the conflicting results of Getzels and Jackson (1962) and Hasan and Butcher (1966).

Haddon and Lytton (1968) also tested the threshold hypothesis. They found that the correlation between VRQ and divergent thinking was 0·076 among the group with VRQs of 115 or higher, 0·164 among the group with VRQs of 100 or higher (which included the first group) and 0·512 in the group with VRQs below 100, thus lending support to the hypothesis. The evidence of Nuttall (1971) also supports the hypothesis: among 100 fourth-year children attending grammar schools the median correlation between four divergent thinking test scores and two scores from a general ability test was 0·01, while among 524 fourth-year children attending secondary modern schools the median correlation was 0·16.

Barker Lunn (1970) isolated a group of pupils scoring in the top five per cent on her tests of divergent thinking (based on those of Torrance and scored for fluency in ideas, flexibility in ideas and associations and statistical originality of response) and found that approximately two-thirds of these pupils were above average in ability (as measured by both verbal reasoning and English attainment tests) and that one-third were of average ability. A number of American studies (e.g. Yamamoto, 1965) also tend to support the threshold hypothesis, but there is one exception in the results of Lytton and Cotton (1969): while the correlation between VRQ and divergent thinking was lower (0·037) in the group with VRQs of 116 or more than it was in the group with VRQs of 101 or more ($r = 0·141$; the second group included all members of the first), the correlation in the group with VRQs below 101 was unexpectedly even lower and slightly negative ($r = -0·058$).

In summary, it appears that divergent thinking abilities can fairly readily be distinguished from convergent thinking abilities among high ability individuals, but that among individuals of lesser ability, the distinction is far less marked. As was the case when examining relationships among tests of divergent thinking, there is always the danger that the correlations between convergent and divergent thinking tests are considerably attenuated because of the unreliability of the latter tests.

The validity of divergent thinking tests

Ten years ago, divergent thinking tests were usually described as tests of 'creativity'. For every ten studies using such tests and accepting the validity of this title, only one attempted an empirical validation of the tests against criteria of creativity and few of these met with any great success. For this reason, the title 'divergent thinking' has come to be increasingly preferred, but whatever title is used, few researchers would dispute Cronbach's statement that 'most of the tests have been announced to the world prior to any solid validity studies' (Cronbach, 1970, p. 395).

Two British studies have attempted to validate divergent thinking tests against teachers' ratings of the creativeness of their pupils. Lovell and Shields (1967) found that the teachers' ratings loaded on a factor orthogonal to that on which the divergent thinking tests loaded, but Haddon and Lytton (1971) met with slightly greater success. They obtained a significant correlation of 0·286 between the divergent thinking test composite scores and ratings of the pupils' creativeness by teachers of English, but found no relationships between either the test scores or the rating and a pupil's Interest Blank 'Things Done on Your Own' devised by Torrance (1962) as a possible criterion measure of creativity. In studies of this type, the criterion measures may legitimately be criticised as being of dubious validity and Shapiro (1968) presents a stimulating discussion of the criterion problem in creativity research. Ratings by teachers are particularly prone to 'halo' effect, and Lovell and Shields (1967) found a much higher relationship between ratings of originality and tests of logical thinking than between the ratings and divergent thinking tests, which suggests the presence of 'halo' in the ratings.

Convincing validation of the tests as measures of creativity thus appears to be lacking, but interesting relationships between the tests and other variables have been found. Hudson (1966, 1968) has based most of his work on a comparison of divergers and convergers. A diverger is not necessarily someone who scores highly on a divergent thinking test; divergence is a matter of bias: a diverger is someone whose standing relative to his peers is much higher on the dimension of divergent thinking than on the dimension of convergent thinking, while the reverse bias defines a converger. 'All-rounders', a group to which Hudson pays scant attention, demonstrate no bias, scoring equally well (or equally badly) on both types of test.

Hudson (1966) showed that male divergers were much more likely to specialise in arts subjects than in science subjects in the sixth form, and male convergers in science subjects rather than in arts subjects. There were exceptions (for example, more convergers than divergers specialised in classics, and there was an even split in biology) and, among girls, Hudson (1968) found that the association between specialisation and convergence/divergence was far less clear-cut: 'as with boys, divergent girls tend to avoid science subjects, but convergent girls are equally likely to go into arts or physical sciences' (p. 23). Haddon and Lytton (1971) also found a considerable difference between the sexes in this respect. Pont's review (1970) shows, however, that the majority of studies attempting to replicate Hudson's work have met with a fair degree of success (e.g. Child, 1968 and Mackay and Cameron, 1968). Christie's study (1970) is a recent exception; he found no association between cognitive bias and faculty (arts, social science, medicine, technology and science) among third-year university students, the testing having been done some years earlier while the students were in the grammar school sixth form.

Child and Smithers (1971) used a slightly different approach. Instead of classifying their sample of first year undergraduates studying science, social science and languages as convergers or divergers on the basis of test scores, they asked the undergraduates to complete the convergent/divergent self-rating questionnaire devised by Joyce and Hudson (1968). This questionnaire consists of twenty items (e.g. 'I seem to do rather well on intelligence tests'; 'I dislike the idea that science will one day explain every aspect of human experience') to which the respondent has to agree or disagree. The pattern of responses purports to provide an estimate of the individual's degree of convergence or divergence. Subsequent work (Child and Smithers, 1973) has shown that an individual's degree of convergence or divergence as assessed by the questionnaire is only marginally related to his degree of convergence or divergence as assessed by the use of convergent and divergent thinking tests. They found, in fact, that the results of the questionnaire were much more closely related to arts or science bias. The validity of the questionnaire as a measure of convergence or divergence is thus extremely suspect. The results obtained by Child and Smithers (1971) using this questionnaire are therefore not discussed further here.

Another of their findings was that science bias was associated with a high level of performance in the verbal divergent thinking tests. This illustrates the falsity of the conclusion that many have drawn on the basis of Hudson's results, namely that arts specialists (being divergers) score more highly on divergent thinking tests than science specialists.

Further evidence on the falsity of this conclusion comes from two studies. Haddon and Lytton (1971) found no significant differences between a group of arts specialists and a group of science specialists (as far as these were discernible at the age of fifteen) on their battery of divergent thinking tests and Mills (1970) found no significant differences on either the Uses of Objects Test or the Meaning of Words Test between five groups of ten upper sixth form boys classified by their intended university specialisation (physics/engineering, natural sciences, medicine, languages/law and English/history). The group with the highest mean score on both tests was composed of natural scientists. On the other hand, one study among undergraduates at the University of Keele (Hartley and Beasley, 1969) showed a tendency for arts specialists to do better than science specialists on the same two tests that were used by Mills, but no significant differences in test scores were found between a group of less extreme science specialists who were also taking at least one social science option and a group of arts specialists likewise taking a social science option.

These studies suggest that the *level* of divergent thinking test scores is not very different for arts and science groups. Since the association of the *bias* score between divergent and convergent thinking and arts/ science choice is fairly well established, it may simply be differences in *level* of convergent thinking scores that are giving rise to this relationship. Child (1969) showed that science and technology students obtained significantly higher IQ scores than social scientists and Child and Smithers (1971) found that science and language students scored significantly more highly than social scientists on both parts of the AH 5 test. While the differences were not significant, language students tended to score more highly than scientists on the verbal and numerical section, while the opposite occurred on the diagrammatic section. Mills (1970), using the AH 6 test (AG version) with sixth formers, found no differences between the five specialist groups on total score but did find significant differences between the groups on the verbal and the numerical sections, but not on the diagrammatic section.

Hudson (1968) has also looked at this problem. With a sample of 139 fifteen year old boys from three schools, he found a much sharper discrimination between arts and physical science specialists on convergent thinking alone than on divergent thinking alone; using both measures to provide a bias score, the discrimination was sharper still. It thus seems reasonable to conclude that divergent thinking tests are not just 'passengers' in this matter of arts/science differences, but that bias within the domain of convergent thinking abilities may be just as fruitful an area of study.

The divergent thinking tests used to establish cognitive bias have been almost exclusively verbal in nature. If there are indeed independent

dimensions of divergent thinking, it follows that an individual classified as a diverger with tests of verbal divergent thinking (and, of
course, a suitable convergent thinking test) may well be classified
differently with tests of, say, mathematical divergent thinking. The
present writer feels, however, that it is more profitable to enquire
further into differences between arts and science specialists, rather than
simply to pursue differences between convergers and divergers, however so classified. In this respect, it seems a pity that Hudson (1968) oscil-
lates between comparisons of divergers and convergers and comparisons of arts and science specialists, apparently equating convergers with
science specialists and divergers with arts specialists.

The relationship of academic attainment and divergent thinking
has often been investigated since Getzels and Jackson (1962) concluded
that divergent thinking was a more important determinant of attainment than IQ, among adolescents of high ability. McNemar (1964) has
neatly demonstrated that exactly the opposite conclusion may equally
validly be drawn from their results, and Hasan and Butcher's study
(1966) failed to replicate Getzels and Jackson's results. Hasan and
Butcher found very high correlations between divergent thinking
and attainment in English and arithmetic (0·76 and 0·62 respectively)
but the correlations between VRQ and attainment were even higher.

Richards and Bolton (1971) also investigated, indirectly, the relationship between divergent thinking and mathematical attainment. On
their first factor, identified as general ability, the attainment tests and
verbal reasoning tests had high loadings and the divergent thinking
tests low loadings. On their second factor, the majority of the divergent
thinking tests had high loadings and about half the mathematical
attainment scores had low loadings, the other half having negligible
ones. They therefore concluded 'that the most important determinant
of the performance in mathematics is general ability and that divergent
thinking plays only a minor role' (p. 34).

Nuttall (1971) correlated performance on divergent thinking tests
with performance in a wide range of CSE and GCE 'O' level examinations. Unlike the attainment tests used in other studies which tend to be
in multiple-choice or short-answer format, these examinations usually
require longer answers and the aims of the examinations in art and
English language, as set out in the syllabuses of a number of boards,
place some emphasis on the assessment of creative ability. Two of the
divergent thinking tests (the Squares Test and the Uses Test) showed

no significant relationships with attainment, but the TH Test and the Number Routes Test showed positive and significant correlations with about half the examinations studied. However, on the application of multiple regression techniques, it was found that the variance in attainment attributable to divergent thinking was negligible once the variance attributable to convergent thinking had been accounted for. Cronbach (1968) makes a strong case for the use of multiple regression techniques in this field, since it enables the burden of proof to be placed on the newer psychological variable of divergent thinking.

Freeman, M'Comisky and Buttle (1969) investigated the relationship of the A–C (Performance) Test to academic performance among architecture and economics students. They found that the ten best architecture students, as assessed by examination results, had achieved significantly better total accuracy scores on the divergent thinking section of the A-C test than the ten poorest architecture students. The test, described in some detail in Freeman, Butcher and Christie (1971), involves the classification of sixteen blocks varying in size, shape and colour into two groups of eight in each of four different ways, and then into four groups of four in three different ways, the principles of classification being left up to the candidate in the 'divergent' section. The facts that the test is scored for accuracy and that the number of classifications requested is limited suggest that this test is not, perhaps, a typical divergent thinking test, but this is not to deny its potential value. No significant difference in total accuracy scores ('divergent' thinking) appeared between the ten best and ten poorest economics students.

The studies reviewed above treat divergent thinking in the main as a cognitive variable. Just as many writers (e.g. Cattell and Butcher, 1968) consider that, above a certain minimum level of general ability, affective factors are of greater importance than cognitive abilities in the study of creative ability, so a number of writers feel that divergent thinking may better be considered as an affective dimension or, at the least, as bridging the artificial gap between cognitive and non-cognitive dimensions. For example, McHenry and Shouksmith (1970) obtained highly significant correlations between both the Uses and the Meaning of Words tests and a test of suggestibility, a factor which is hypothesised to be of importance in the study of creativity. They also found non-significant but positive correlations between the two divergent thinking tests and a test of visual imagination.

Shouksmith (1970) tested 98 first year university students with a battery of measures including divergent and convergent tests and new tests of cognitive style and problem-solving style. Among men, he found that high performance on divergent thinking tests was associated with inconsistency, as assessed by responses to a number of insoluble problems, but the same relationship did not obtain among women. Among both men and women, Shouksmith identified a dimension of 'divergent flexibility of style' which was not associated with performance in divergent thinking tests but which he hypothesised to be of importance in creativity.

There thus seem to be good grounds for extending the investigation of the validity of divergent thinking tests further into the realms of cognitive style and personality. Meanwhile, in the realm of cognitive abilities, it seems that we know much more about what divergent thinking tests are *not* measuring than about what they are measuring. This again may be a criticism of existing tests of divergent thinking more than it is a criticism of the concept of divergent thinking itself.

The influence of environmental and educational conditions

Critics of progressive education have suggested that progressive methods lead to lower attainment in the basic skills than do more traditional methods. Research (e.g. Barker Lunn, 1970) has shown that this is not necessarily so, but researchers have striven to find tests that might reveal a clear superiority of progressive methods and divergent thinking tests have been an obvious choice.

Haddon and Lytton (1968) tested 211 children, aged eleven to twelve, half coming from 'formal' and half from 'informal' primary schools who were matched for mean VRQ and socio-economic background. As hypothesised, the pupils from the 'informal' schools showed significantly higher performance on the verbal and non-verbal tests of divergent thinking than their peers from 'formal' schools. They also found that the correlation between VRQ and the divergent thinking scores were consistently higher in the 'informal' schools than in the 'formal' schools. Haddon and Lytton (1971), following up the majority of these children some four years later and retesting them with the same tests, found that children who had attended the 'informal' primary schools continued to perform significantly more highly on the divergent thinking tests than the children who had attended the 'formal' schools, irrespective of the type of secondary school attended. Their use of the technique of multiple regression again illustrates its elegance and power. Lytton and Cotton (1969) compared fourteen year old pupils from 'formal' and 'informal' secondary schools, again matched for mean VRQ and socio-economic background. There were no significant differences on four of the divergent thinking tests; on the Imaginative Stories Test, there was a significant difference in favour of pupils from the 'informal' schools, but on the last test (Incomplete Circles) the difference was significantly in favour of the pupils from the 'formal' schools. Lytton and Cotton attribute these essentially negative findings to the inappropriateness of the simple labels 'formal' and 'informal' for secondary schools, whose organisation is much more complex than that of primary schools. Cabot (1969), however, did find significant differences on the Uses and Meaning of Words tests in favour of sixth form pupils from two progressive boarding schools, comparing them with pupils from a traditional boys' public school and a mixed comprehensive school, while on IQ, the difference was significant in the other direction.

As part of a major study on the effects of streaming, Barker Lunn (1970) tested a group of 1 800 children at the end of their third and fourth years in the primary school with two parallel tests of divergent thinking scored for fluency, flexibility and originality. Within unstreamed schools, she distinguished two types of teacher: the type 1 teacher was in favour of progressive methods but the type 2 teacher was less in favour of progressive methods and her attitudes resembled those of the typical teacher in a streamed school. The most startling finding was that boys in streamed schools showed a significant drop on all three aspects of divergent thinking between the third and fourth years; in the case of girls in streamed schools, the differences were in the same direction but were not significant. Pupils with type 2 teachers in unstreamed schools also showed the same tendency towards deterioration, but only in the case of girls' originality scores was the drop significant. In contrast, pupils with the type 1 teachers tended to show an improvement in fluency and flexibility scores, although the differences were not significant, but no consistent differences emerged for originality scores. Barker Lunn also showed that, on the basis of scores in the fourth year, type 1 teachers had the highest percentage of pupils among those scoring in the top 20 per cent on a composite divergent thinking test score, while type 2 teachers had the lowest (teachers from streamed schools being intermediate). Conversely, among pupils in the bottom 20 per cent, type 1 teachers had the lowest percentage and type 2 the highest.

Two recent studies have concentrated on differences between 'traditional' and 'modern' methods of mathematics teaching. Gopal Rao, Penfold and Penfold (1970) found that the performance of third and fourth year secondary school pupils following 'modern' courses was significantly superior to that of a group of pupils (comparable in ability) following 'traditional' courses on three divergent thinking tests (Hidden Words, Uses of Objects and Concept Formation); the differences on the other two tests (First and Last Letters and Make-Up Problems) were in the same direction but not significant. Richards and Bolton (1971) compared final year pupils from three primary schools: in School C, mathematics was taught by a discovery approach, in School B by traditional methods and in School A, by an amalgam of both methods. The three schools were matched for IQ and socio-economic status. The performance of School C on the mathematics attainment tests, which ranged from a test of mechanical and problem arithmetic to the recent NFER Intermediate Mathematics Test which stresses understanding of concepts rather than routine calculation, was consistently lower than that of the other two schools, though not always significantly so. Schools A and C tended to score consistently more highly than School B on the divergent thinking tests (Circles, Uses of Objects, Consequences, Pattern Meanings and Make-Up Problems), but only in the case of the Circles tests was the performance of pupils in School C significantly higher than that of the pupils in the other two schools.

These studies have produced fairly consistent findings suggesting that pupils studying under progressive regimes score more highly on tests of divergent thinking than their peers in 'traditional' schools. While this evidence is important in helping to establish the construct validity of the tests, there is a danger that it is educationally meaningless when the concurrent and predictive validity of the test has proved so hard to establish. Similarly, caution must be exercised in interpreting the results of Vernon's cross-cultural research (Vernon, 1967, 1969b), in which he included a battery of divergent thinking tests. In particular, he found that the median fluency score of a small group of maladjusted English boys was 106 and their median originality score 108, compared with a figure of 100 for normal schoolchildren of the same age. Only on two other tests (Incomplete Drawings, separately scored but considered as a test of divergent thinking, and Kohs Blocks) did the maladjusted boys score more than 100 and on all the conventional paper and pencil attainment and general ability tests, their scores were around 90. A group of delinquent boys also showed their highest median scores on the divergent thinking tests, but these did not exceed 100.

Barker Lunn's results suggest that the pupil's interaction with his teacher is of great importance. Among medical students, Joyce and Hudson (1968) also found such an interaction. Four tutors were rated for their convergence/divergence by each other, by themselves, by their students and by an independent observer and a remarkable degree of agreement between these different ratings emerged. It was found that, while the four groups of students each taught by one of the four tutors did not differ in their attainment on the final statistics examination, certain types of student gained better examination results if they were taught by particular teachers. It was not consistently the case, however, that divergent students learned best from divergent teachers nor that convergent students learned best from convergent teachers.

Again in the realm of medicine, Byrne, Freeman and M'Comisky (1970) compared the behaviour of five discussion groups composed of general practitioners and structured according to the divergence or convergence of their members (as assessed by tests) and various of their personality attributes. It was found that the two groups containing divergent individuals produced more new ideas than the convergent and 'all-rounder' groups but that these ideas were not of significantly higher quality (as rated by three independent judges). These groups were also rated higher on 'group interaction' but they showed a greater tendency to splinter. A number of other differences between the groups was also reported. More studies such as this which consider personality attributes alongside divergence and convergence are obviously required.

Factors affecting the reliability of divergent thinking tests

As already indicated, many of the inconclusive findings that emerge from studies using divergent thinking tests may be attributable, at least in part, to deficiencies in the tests themselves. Lack of reliability is one obvious deficiency. Nuttall (1971) obtained test-retest reliability coefficients of between 0·54 and 0·65 for his four tests over an interval of two weeks, and Hudson (1968) obtained a parallel forms coefficient of 0·53 with the Uses Test over an interval of four months. Over four years, Haddon and Lytton (1971) obtained a test-retest coefficient of 0·62 for their battery, but the reliabilities of the two parts (verbal and non-verbal) were somewhat lower (0·55 and 0·50 respectively). Such values, which are comparable to those obtained in a number of other studies, fail to inspire confidence and make the interpretation of low correlations between divergent thinking tests and other measures difficult.

Lack of reliability is not the only problem and, as Hudson (1968) points out, need not worry us unduly if we can establish and replicate valid relationships with criteria external to the tests. Of more concern are the results of a series of small studies in which Hudson (1968) showed that the number of responses elicited on tests of divergent thinking was dependent upon the instructions given, the number and type of examples provided and on the 'target' figure set. The most striking demonstration of these effects emerged when a group of boys were tested with the Uses Test on two occasions. On the second occasion they were asked to impersonate a typical scientist and a typical artist. There was a tendency for those boys originally classified as convergers to be relatively more fluent than divergers in impersonating the scientist, and the reverse occurred for the impersonation of the artist. There was also only a very marginal tendency for those who had been the most fluent under the normal conditions to be the most fluent when impersonating the two characters. Hudson concluded: 'Between them these two studies make it clear that an individual's fluency is not a fixed feature of his mental life' (Hudson, 1968, p. 70).

Corroborative evidence comes from a number of studies else-where in the world. For example, Nicholls (1971) found significant relationship between intelligence and verbal and 'non-verbal' divergent thinking (using the tests of Wallach and Kogan, 1965) when the divergent thinking tests were administered under test-like conditions, but non-significant relationships when the tests were administered under game-like conditions. This finding held for both boys and girls. Vernon (1971), who provides a comprehensive review of the literature in this area, found similar but not quite so marked differences between testing conditions. Elkind, Deblinger and Adler (1970), using Wallach and Kogan's tests, and employing a balanced experimental design, found that the scores of children taken to be tested from an 'uninteresting' task were nearly twice as great as the scores of children taken from an 'interesting' task.

Getzels and Madaus (1969) have suggested that there are so many conflicting findings in the whole field of divergent thinking research largely because 'methods' factors (such as testing conditions and scoring procedures) are playing such a large part. They advocate fullscale multitrait-multimethod investigations (Campbell and Fiske, 1959) to clarify the situation, and the studies discussed in this section would certainly seem to imply that such investigations are overdue. But if Hudson is right that fluency is not a stable ability, no amount of sophisticated research methodology can produce harmony out of conflict.

Some conclusions

To suggest that there are many deficiencies in existing tests of divergent thinking may be rather harsh: an ability, or abilities, that are so unstable are worthy of psychological study in their own right and this very fact may cause us to look again at the extent to which such effects are present in more conventional ability tests (see also Heim, 1970). But in terms of studies of the validity of divergent tests along traditional lines, such deficiencies are of major significance. Hudson's studies suggest that there is no uniform 'practice effect' on such tests and as more and more children come to take divergent thinking tests, greater rather than less conflict in results is likely to emerge. There is therefore an urgent need for more reliable tests whose content is more relevant to the interests and abilities of the groups for whom the tests are designed—the A–C Performance Test of Freeman, M'Comisky and Buttle (1969) would seem to be a step in the right direction. With existing tests, we are forced to accept that the generalisability of conclusions from individual studies is very limited.

The value of divergent thinking tests in fields such as educational and vocational guidance has yet to be demonstrated and past work gives rise to little confidence that it eventually will. The promise of divergent thinking tests seems rather to lie in that uncharted area where cognitive and non-cognitive aspects of the mind overlap—in areas such as cognitive style, problem-solving and motivation.

P. E. Richmond

Science teaching

Science and mathematics have led the way in curriculum reform and the work which has had the greatest effect on the classroom and school laboratory is curriculum development rather than any kind of rigorous investigation. The new courses and new methods which have been suggested have naturally led to comment, much of it personal and based on very limited experience, but some built on controlled observation and experiment. Many of the investigations which have been reported are *post hoc* in that they look at suggestions produced by the various projects, for example the Nuffield Science Teaching Projects (1966, 1967, 1970, 1971) or the work of the Scottish Education Department (1969).

The major curriculum development projects, with the exception of the Science 5/13 Project described below, have not made serious attempts to validate ther recommendations statistically. All, however, have run school trials (Fensham, 1971) in which teachers try out the materials and comment on their suitability. Then comes the presentation of published material to teachers who try out the ideas. This forms a massive validation of the programme. Every teacher works in different conditions. The classes may be of boys, girls or both. Perhaps science has two, three or even nine periods a week, perhaps all the lessons are in a laboratory, perhaps half, perhaps the teacher has had no training in teaching science. The variables are too many to list and all make their own uncontrolled contribution to the acceptance or rejection of all or parts of a course. Yet the total of all the experiences of thousands of teachers throughout the country lets the organisers know just how suitable their recommendations are. It is an effective but inefficient procedure.

The contribution which 'in-service training' makes to the validation of published materials is considerable provided it is seen as a two-way process in which teachers can offer suggestions. Teachers involved in discussions which might influence future versions of published courses are each playing a small part in a research and development activity.

Some of the experiments described below involve university lecturers, specialist researchers, examiners and teachers all working together at a problem. One of the advantages of encouraging unsophisticated research and comment from teachers is that it can make them feel that they have something to contribute to a dialogue with the specialist. We may now be entering a phase in which the insights of the teacher can be married to the skills of the sociologist or psychologist and where the teacher who has seen a problem in his classroom will welcome the skilled observer into his room and value the results which a well designed experiment can supply. This article will interpret the term 'research' in its widest sense, including development, and will report findings of immediate interest to schools rather than those of theoretical or long term interest.

Objectives

An early and significant study 'Practical Work in School Science' set out to distinguish between what teachers claim to be doing in the school laboratory and what they are seen to be doing by their students. Kerr (1963) and a team drawn from university education departments devised an ingenious experiment in which the types of practical work carried out at different levels in school were distinguished and tabulated. Then teachers listed the purposes of practical work as they saw them and first year university students were asked to look back on their sixth form courses to list the purposes as *they* saw them. The team found that the teachers thought the most important reasons for doing practical work were: to encourage accurate observation, to promote scientific ways of thinking and to provide an opportunity to find out facts and principles by investigation. But few of the science students had noticed the finding-out element or that they had been led towards a scientific way of thinking and behaving. The inquiry team thought that a much more deliberate and direct attempt should be made to teach for these ends through practical work and that no aspect of science education was more urgently in need of attention.

Soon afterwards, Bloom's Taxonomy of Educational Objectives (1956) became well known in this country. It became available just as interest in objectives was growing fast. The 'cognitive domain' of objectives has since formed a useful framework on which many (too many?) experiments have been built. The 'affective domain' is more difficult to handle and has been much less used. A contributor to discussion at a recent Association for Science Education Conference thought that the 1960s had been the decade of the cognitive domain and that the 1970s will be the decade of the affective domain. He may well be right but it is likely that we shall lean less heavily on Bloom for our affective objectives. Hudson (1969) described procedures to be adopted in devising tests with given objectives. He listed questions and drew up detailed specifications for them by means of a grid with columns headed recall, comprehension, application, analysis and eval- uation, synthesis (after Bloom). His article described statistical analyses but he could only make generalised suggestions including one with which we shall become familiar in a later section '. . . it would appear that the most valid and reliable examinations are likely to be com- posite in nature'. Hockey and Neale (1968) have produced tests in physics, chemistry and biology firmly based on Bloom's objectives. They are complete but are not yet generally available as they are being used in further research. Hoare and Revans (1969) link objectives with programmed learning but again their results, based on a class of 69 students taking 1st MB or BDS exams, are indicative of possibilities rather than conclusive.

In general, small research investigations into educational problems go on side by side with, or after, the large curriculum development projects. The exception in science is the Nuffield/Schools Council Science 5/13 Project. This has been planned and executed with the constant advice of a full time evaluator, Wynne Harlen. Dr Harlen has great insight into the possibilities of school science and an ability to write in a clear, interesting and stimulating way. The booklet she has written for the Project, 'With Objectives in Mind' (Schools Council, 1972b) is a model for anyone wishing to enlist the support of teachers in changing classroom practice for sound and explicit reasons. The booklet starts with a central objective of all scientific activity at junior level: developing an enquiring mind and a scientific approach to problems. Around this are clustered eight more objectives: observing, exploring and ordering observations, developing basic concepts, posing questions and devising experiments or investigations to answer them, acquiring and applying knowledge and manipulative skills, communicating, interpreting findings critically, appreciating patterns and relationships, developing interests, attitudes and aesthetic awareness. Nearly twenty different booklets for teachers and children are now available from the project and it is noteworthy that the later ones display most clearly the objectives, now given in detailed and concrete behavioural terms. In the Project's second Newsletter however (Science 5/13, 1971) it is made very clear that '. . . written objectives, whatever they might be, must never get between teachers and children: there is no substitute for a teacher's sensitive understanding of a child, nor for a child's feeling of that understanding being there.' The careful definition of objectives in the light of the different stages of children's development is itself valid research and has prepared the ground for much more. Once all the publications are readily available and in widespread use we can expect to see changes in practice, attitudes and capacities which may be susceptible to investigation in statistical terms.

Scotland must not be neglected when reporting research in science teaching, for the Scottish Education Department has financed research in several universities and colleges of education, notably Stirling and Glasgow. Many of the experiments are in their early stages and results are not available, but Johnstone has worked with a number of collaborators on themes relating to pupils' views of certain topics in school chemistry. One report which has been published (Johnstone, Morrison and Sharp, 1971/2) is concerned with a single objective of teaching: understanding various topics in chemistry. Pupils were asked to grade various topics in the syllabus as 'easy to grasp', 'difficult to grasp' or 'never grasped'. The result is a pragmatic evaluation of how understanding appears to change from one topic to another. For the sensitive teacher of chemistry who can safeguard all the less obvious objectives of his teaching the information might be useful but there is as yet no attempt to generalise the findings or to explain them in terms of any psychological theories.

Evaluating courses

Expenditure on the Nuffield Science Teaching Projects has run into millions of pounds, yet the proportion explicitly devoted to evaluation or research in any technical sense is virtually zero. The earlier projects did not lend themselves to rigorous appraisal partly because their objectives were not defined in any measurable terms and partly because of the changes which started to occur as soon as they were published. Changes arise at Project Headquarters, through considerations of the Examining Boards, and perhaps most of all at school level. As courses are taken up, so they may be adapted, improved or changed beyond recognition. The Combined Science Project has arisen from the original three O-level courses which, a mere five years after publication, are being seriously challenged by the 'integrated science' approach (Richmond, 1971).

In this situation the evaluator's task is a difficult one indeed. He is trying to measure qualities in an ever-changing scene. Wiseman and Pidgeon (1970) insist that the hard, 'scientific' line of the psychometrist must be softened if he is to take part in curriculum evaluation. He must recognise that the drive and enthusiasm of the innovator at any level is precious and must not be damaged or destroyed. On the other hand the curriculum developer needs to define his aims and his processes clearly enough for his proposals to be evaluated in meaningful terms. Project organisers treat feedback from schools in diverse, idiosyncratic ways (Fensham 1971), ignoring the findings of sociologists and psychologists. The neglect of any theories of curriculum development (Skilbeck, 1971) is serious. Intuitive, empirical work on the curriculum needs to nourish theory building and then, in its turn, to use the increased understanding that any worthwhile theory will provide. (See also the chapter in this volume by Stenhouse.)

Outside the major projects there have been a number of studies in the field of curriculum evaluation and there are signs that the later Nuffield/Schools Council Projects, in particular Science 5/13 (Schools Council, 1972a) and Integrated Science are building on more theoretical foundations. In 1965 Whitfield (Kerr and Eggleston, 1969) devised a teaching scheme using a logical, rational approach to chemistry in contradistinction to one stressing the memorisation of empirical facts. Whitfield's work at Leicester reflected the 'behavioural objectives' approach which characterises much of the work of the Research Unit for Assessment and Curriculum Studies in the School of Education of the University. He discovered the complexity of the issues involved in the evaluation of curricula and notes five specific issues worthy of further consideration:

1 the need for precision in stating behavioural objectives;
2 the different statistical demands which curriculum evaluation makes as compared with routine ranking or selection of individuals;
3 the dilemma that large numbers of objectives are difficult to handle statistically yet small numbers lack precision (he suggests using about eight);
4 sampling errors can be substantial. Groups rather than individuals are being considered and the comparatively small number of groups can easily be unrepresentative of the population;
5 having gained information by objective techniques, subjective value judgements are usually invoked when making subsequent recommendations.

Attitudes

It was the Dainton Committee (Council for Scientific Policy, 1968) which highlighted the 'swing from science' in the sixth forms of our schools. Aspects of the Dainton Report have been dealt with by Butcher (1969) and also in a contribution (Pont, 1970) to Volume 2 of *Educational Research in Britain*. Since that article was prepared, however, the Swann Report (Committee on Manpower Resources, 1968) has underlined Dainton's fears and forecast a spiralling downwards of our science teaching as relatively fewer well qualified science teachers enter the schools to encourage pupils to take up courses and careers in engineering or science. More information was clearly needed and we have seen considerable weight of research resources thrown into investigations of pupils' choices and the factors determining them. The Dainton proposals aimed to restore the place of science and technology in the educational system and to increase society's appreciation and understanding of the scientist and technologist. The Reports caused teachers and research workers to look more closely at the genesis and growth of attitudes towards science. Powerful and well tried methods are now available for determining attitudes and several important studies have been undertaken.

The most important in the long term may be the International Association for the Evaluation of Educational Achievement's Study of Science. An international committee, chaired by an ex-HMI, Dr L. C. Comber, is asking some of the difficult and fundamental questions about the teaching of science. Is liking of science related to the use of investigatory methods or more traditional teaching styles? Is understanding of science increased when students work on their own to discover certain principles? Is there a difference in achievement between those who have worked largely from a textbook or in the laboratory? Does this experience influence subsequent choices of specialisation? It is likely that the UK will provide a fruitful area for investigating these questions for, in Lockard's lists (1970), only the USA has more science teaching projects completed or in progress and the variety of provision for secondary education in Britain is probably second to none.

The IEA project has found that there is sufficient common ground in the content of the science courses of different countries for common questionnaires and tests to be useable. The bulk of the testing is now completed and the data is being processed. The findings should be of major significance for, as IEA Newsletter No. 2 (1971) states 'To reach some justifiable conclusions about these questions, which lie at the heart of science education, on an international scale, would be a major contribution to education.'

Responsibility for IEA work in this country rests with the National Foundation for Educational Research. This organisation has also prepared a Science Attitude Questionnaire (Skurnik and Jeffs, 1971). It has been designed to reveal attitudes on five factors: science interest, social implications of science, learning activities, science teachers and schools. It may be compared with the American Test of Understanding Science (Cooley and Klopfer, 1961) which aims to test understanding 1) about the scientific enterprise; 2) about scientists; and 3) about the methods and aims of science. This is not an attitude test as such but looks at similar themes to the Science Attitude Questionnaire via questions aiming to test understanding. Being well constructed and reliable the NFER test is likely to be widely used in the near future.

The English curriculum development projects have grown out of the voluntary work of members of the Association for Science Education. The contribution of the ASE to changes in school science has been so far-reaching that no article purporting to discuss research and development in school science can ignore it. Yet it was not until 1967 that the ASE decided to create a committee (Bryant, 1968) whose function was 'to look ahead and to examine and initiate projects of a research nature'. The Committee very soon decided to promote work into the attitudes of pupils towards science. Selmes (1969) reports that children find chemistry more enjoyable and less difficult than physics but that attitudes towards biology are variable. In the process he produces a wonderful schoolboy picture of a scientist which can be compared with that of Hudson (1966). Ashton and Meredith (1969) looked at answers, given in an actual A-level general studies examination, to a question asking why pupils thought that the number of students wishing to study arts and social sciences at universities is increasing more rapidly than the number wishing to study the natural sciences. They too reveal a picture of the scientist but a less attractive one than Selmes.' Schoolboys themselves attribute the 'swing from science' to 1) the difficulty of the subject; 2) the lack of opportunity in science for self-expression; and 3) the boredom of lessons particularly in the lower part of the school.

In addition to studies of attitudes the ASE Research Committee has been deeply involved in questions of units and nomenclature. The report on the use of SI Units in Schools (ASE, 1969) has been well received and promises to be definitive with teachers, textbook writers and examining boards. The Working Party studying Chemical Nomenclature is finding its task more controversial and, at the time of writing, has not yet produced agreed recommendations. Several working parties are looking into other questions such as the contact of schools with industry, the integration of science student teachers into school science departments and the teaching of science in London comprehensive schools.

Returning to the question of attitudes, many small-scale experiments have been reported. Laughton and Wilkinson (1968, 1970) report two experiments with boys and girls in Nuffield and non-Nuffield schools. They point to the importance of the inculcation of correct attitudes during the first three years of a GCE course, before specialisation begins. They provide evidence that in some cases attitudes towards science deteriorate during that period. By factor analysis, Ormerod (1971) has gone further along the same line and has found that by the third year (thirteen–fourteen), attitudes to science as a school subject and also to the social implications of science have already emerged as separate factors among the more able half of the English school population. He finds a strong relationship between girls' scores on the 'social implications' items and their choice of science subjects for further study—a relationship which is missing for the boys. In a number of fields pronounced differences between boys and girls are being reported and it would seem desirable for research workers to consider the sexes separately whenever possible.

For several years Hutchings (1963, 1966, 1969) has been interested in factors governing choices in school and is currently engaged on a major study of thirteen year olds. His team is investigating: the nature and range of pupils' expectations, attitudes and interests with special reference to science and technology, the influence on these expectations and on their choices of subjects of such factors as type of school, economic and social background, attitudes of teachers and parents and the range of pupils' attainment and ability.

Of immediate and very practical interest is Hoare and Yeaman's work in the Dundee University Chemistry Department 'Identifying and interviewing science students at risk of failure' (1971). Having an immediate job to do Hoare and Yeaman applied their intimate knowledge of their students and asked 165 of them to agree or disagree with 60 statements covering work habits, motivation, adequacy and personality. Their first aim was a simple one: to help students at risk of failure. Although they found that an academic test given in November or December was a better predictor of subsequent failure than their questionnaires and interviews, nevertheless their procedures did establish scales of 'work habits', 'motivation' and 'adequacy' and they found that, in most cases, the questionnaire revealed at least one weakness which might have been a cause of failure. They found that motivation was all-important and 'viewed with interest and approbation' the appointment of student counsellors at Aberdeen and the Open University.

The work on attitudes tends to be empirical and uncoordinated. Much remains to be published and there is insufficient evidence to date on which to base any confident recommendations or conclusions. There has been no attempt to set up theoretical models of a social, psychological or philosophical nature from which predictions could be made.

Examinations

The question of examinations and the assessment of children and students is of perennial interest to teachers. Results and techniques lend themselves to easy definition and quantification. Research workers and teachers find that they have a common interest and a common language. It is not surprising that reports of work on examinations loom large, especially in the literature of organisations catering for science teachers.

Two distinct though related themes can be distinguished: multiple choice techniques and a consideration of objectives (this linked with the possibility of teacher assessment of their pupils).

Jenning and Leisten (1965) complained that 'there appear to have been no comparative studies of chemistry examinations and little discussion of them in the journals of science education', adding their opinion that 'our experience with objective questions leads us to suggest that they would be ideal in large public examinations such as the GCE'. They did not have long to wait, for the chemists were already preparing their Nuffield O-level papers (Mathews, 1967) which, from the start, included a one hour objective test of seventy questions. Early reports about them were inconclusive and pleaded that judgement should be postponed until 'after some years when an assessment of the long-term effect on the pupils and the curriculum can be made'. Statistical evidence relating to this examination has not yet been released but Hill and Woods (1969) and Oliver and Roberts (1969) have supplied some related evidence. The former recommend true-false chemistry questions both for routine class testing and for internal examinations. Oliver and Roberts carried out a small-scale investigation of the achievements of first year secondary pupils of mixed ability following a Nuffield chemistry course. Using a carefully constructed multiple-choice test they came to the conclusion that Nuffield Stage I material 'can be purposefully assessed by means of a suitable multiple choice examination'.

Nuffield O-level physics examiners at first rejected the idea of multiple-choice questions only to introduce them in 1970. Boulind's account (1968) of early Nuffield O-level examinations is descriptive and rejects the possibilities offered by multiple choice examinations. No account of the reasons for the recent change is available. A-level physics however has benefited from a series of investigations. Scott (1966) looked at practical tests and found that 'the time and effort spent on the practical examinations in their present form are not justified by the results obtained'. Thomson (1966) looked into ways of assessing competence in physics using theory papers. His study compared the performances of sixth formers on conventional A-level papers and on Educational Testing Service papers from Princeton, USA. The latter were of about A-level standard but were, of course, intended to assess young people who had followed quite different physics courses. Thus the question of multiple choice or conventional essay type examinations was not easy to answer directly. The Institute of Physics investigation did however have the benefit, lacking in so many of the reported experiments, of qualified statistical advice from the outset. A stratified sample of boys', girls' and mixed schools from six DES categories of school was used; 600 pupils were involved and correlations were calculated in a variety of ways between the results of conventional A-level physics, the ETS Advanced Placement Examination Part I (44 multiple choice questions) and Part II (problem solving and descriptive work) and teachers' assessments. The correlation between the two A-level papers was 0·72, other correlations are shown in tables 1 and 2.

TABLE I

(1)	(2)	(3)
A level (total)	ETS (I+II)	0·61, 0·63
A level (theory)	ETS (I+II)	0·65
A level (theory)	ETS I	0·56
A level (theory)	ETS II	0·57
A level (theory)	ETS II*	0·60
ETS I	ETS II	0·52, 0·56
ETS I	ETS II*	0·59, 0·58

Column (3) gives the correlation coefficients between the items in (1) and those in (2).

* Refers to marks scaled to take account of different marking standards of examiners.

TABLE 2

(1)	(2)	(3)
Teachers' Assessment		
all headings	A level (total)	0·67
a only	A level (total)	0·66
b only	A level (total)	0·61
a+b only	A level (theory)	0·67
a+b only	ETS I	0·52
all headings	ETS II	0·45
a+b only	ETS II*	0·53

Column (3) gives the correlation coefficients between the items in (1) and those in (2).

The assessments are (a) of factual knowledge; (b) of real understanding of physics.

Consideration of these correlations led Thomson to conclude 'If one believes that the teacher is the best judge of his pupils' abilities, this could mean that the A-level examination is a better measuring instrument than the ETS tests. A more plausible explanation however is that the teachers' assessments were strongly coloured by . . . the mock A-level results', and that '. . . teachers were more successful in predicting the relative order of merit of their own pupils than at estimating their absolute level of attainment'. Nevertheless the work demonstrated that multiple choice examining is a worthwhile method at this level and that one great benefit arising from its introduction would be the increased attention which examiners would have to give to precisely what skills and abilities they were trying to measure.

The Journal of Biological Education also duly considers examinations. In the first volume, Cooper and Foy (1967), consider various procedures and also recommend that objectives be specified at the outset. A well documented study two years later (Stenhouse, 1969), shows a healthy scepticism of basing examinations exclusively on Bloom's cognitive domain (1956), recommending that an 'all-factor' effect be considered.

To date the various sciences seem to be conforming to their school image in the mathematical content of their investigations: physicists use statistics, chemists quote figures and biologists describe systems and procedures. A general booklet produced by the Joint Matriculation Board (1970) provides an interesting and informative illustration of evolving examination techniques as they reflect and determine new procedures in school. All in all the literature on the use of multiple choice questions illustrates the potential power of the technique in GCE science subjects in a persuasive rather than a rigorous way.

At a lower level, notably the Certificate in Secondary Education, the Schools Council, since its formation in 1964, has taken considerable interest in examining in general and in examining science subjects in particular. Its Examinations Bulletins serve to inform teachers about techniques of assessment and, at the same time, to report related investigations. The Schools Council disclaims responsibility for actions taken on its reports saying (1971) 'It will, of course, be understood that the Council's policy in relation to techniques of examining is no more than to undertake experimental work and to make the results generally available. It is for the teachers and examining boards to evaluate the results themselves and to decide what use to make of items in the examinations for which they are responsible'.

Examinations Bulletin No. 8 (1965) aimed to explore ways of examining science which would reflect and tend to encourage good teaching practice and summarised its experiments in the following table:

TABLE 3

	First phase (1963)	Second phase (1964)
Scientific thinking paper	Set and marked centrally	Set centrally and marked by one teacher in each area
Facts and principles paper	Omitted	Set and marked in schools and externally moderated
Practical paper	Taken by one-fifth of the candidates and marked centrally	Taken by all, set centrally and marked by one teacher in each area
Teachers' assessments	Assessment of scientific ability in five equal categories No mark awarded	Order of merit for course work (including oral). Mark by scaling procedure
Number of pupils taking trial	655	935
Number of schools	30	36
Statistical analysis	Reliability of markers (one paper) Difficulty of questions (one paper)	Comprehensive treatment including an item analysis

The scientific thinking paper was designed to test a candidate's ability to suggest hypotheses in explanation of data and to devise experiments to test hypotheses. Item analysis revealed clearly the difficulties candidates for CSE science had in applying scientific method and also how difficult it is to set questions which are pitched at an elementary level, are discriminating and yet test scientific thinking. The authors, on the basis of their investigation, made a number of positive suggestions for future action, including the setting up of question banks, further experimentation with the form of questions and with marking schemes since '. . . certain elements in scientific thinking questions do not appear to lend themselves easily to objective marking'. The practical questions raised more questions than they answered and were followed by another Examinations Bulletin, No. 19 entitled CSE Practical Work in Science (1969). This paper is however discursive and does not attempt any theoretical study of the issues raised. The same is true of Bulletin 15 (1967) where marks were given for exercises, experiments, problems and monthly tests but no serious attempt was made to assess the reliability or validity of the tests used.

Some subjects such as English and foreign languages have a well defined oral content. Science and mathematics would seem to depend far more on experiments, calculations and written work. It is nevertheless quite possible for a boy or girl to be able to act in a perfectly sound scientific manner yet not to be able to express his activities and his knowledge clearly on paper. If a pupil can talk meaningfully about scientific matters he deserves some credit. This is probably most true of those who will not go on to higher education but will leave school early, perhaps to go into industry. Examinations Bulletin No. 21 (Schools Council, 1971) looked into the possibility of examining chemistry by means of a highly structured interview. The validity of the assessments made was to be judged in terms of the candidates' performance on traditionally accepted forms of chemistry assessment. The investigators also started where a teacher usually has to begin; with the syllabus of an examining board. Twelve examiners worked in pairs; eight parallel tests were prepared each containing five questions all involving work with chemicals and apparatus. The correlation between oral marks and overall CSE chemistry marks was 0·62. This was considered to be satisfactory and was in sharp contrast to the rank order correlation of 0·26 between gradings of pupils by members of the pairs of examiners working on general impressions.

The work, initiated by the Nottingham University Department of Education with the support of the East Midland Regional Examinations Board and the cooperation of teachers, is a good example of an investigation supported, but not restricted, by statistics and which provides information offering immediate and useful guidance to the schools. Figures are quoted whenever possible; opinions and advice are given on the basis of both objective and subjective observations. One has confidence in the conclusions of the project, that valid and reliable oral examining in science is possible and could usefully serve as a method of CSE assessment, especially for Modes 2 and 3; or as an instrument of external moderation. Pupils liked the technique, they did not seem unduly nervous and the 'backwash' effect could well be beneficial.

A matter of constant concern to all interested in education from parents to university selectors is the comparability of standards among different examining boards. In 1965 Eggleston (1965) reviewed assessment procedures in secondary school science as used by eight CSE Boards. Every examiner has in the back of his mind the objectives of the science teaching which he is attempting to assess. Eggleston stressed that these objectives must be brought into the forefront of the examiner's mind and that generalised objectives must be analysed to a point at which precise behaviours emerge. The observations included in the 1965 review blossomed into a book 'Studies in Assessment' prepared by Eggleston and Kerr (1969). The book includes one study of assessment in history, three of competence in science and one of a new approach to science teaching: at CSE level, in A-level biology, of special studies in science and of the outcomes of a new approach to organic chemistry.

Two of the studies reflected the rising interest in teacher assessment of their own pupils. Kelly, in 'Assessing Practical Ability in Nuffield A-level Biology' asked his teachers to consider three 'operational divisions' which display sound practical ability: procedure, recording and handling results. It is rare to find a group of teachers committed to following a syllabus to the letter, let alone accepting the constraints of a particular teaching approach. Kelly was leader of the A-level Biology Project and had a group of volunteers who, in order to try out the ideas, agreed to do just that. It is probably only in the pre-publication stages of curriculum development that teachers in England can be persuaded to disclaim their right to shape their programmes to their own pupils', and their own, capacities and interests. Kelly had an unusual opportunity to hold one or two of the most important teaching variables constant and to attempt to assess practical ability in a controlled way. He asked groups of teachers to assess 1) by selected practical exercises in operationally limited categories; 2) by marking practical tests set externally; and 3) by grading the overall term's work. Method 1) was difficult to apply because the weighting of procedure, recording and handling results varied between exercises and was difficult to define. In method 2) attempts to make the test objective caused many short questions to be included with a consequent devaluing of broader and more important aims. Despite difficulties with very large or very small classes, the problems of validity and reliability and the reluctance of some teachers to assess their own pupils, Kelly found that '. . . an overall assessment [by the teacher] would seem to be a better means of reflecting the aims' and that '. . . an overall assessment procedure is comparable in accuracy to a series of practical tests.'

Eggleston and Newbould's study 'Assessing Attainment in Science at CSE level' found that teachers were willing and able 1) to identify situations in their lessons in which behaviourally defined demands were made on the pupils; and 2) to grade pupils' performances on suitable scales. A *written* test in physics gave a correlation of $r=0.45$ with teachers' assessments and demonstrated the feasibility of the use of a written test in moderating and in judging the performance of teachers as assessors. Another of the studies, by D. H. Fox, acknowledges the fact that most Colleges of Education ask their students to write a 'special study' in science. Two methods of assessing the reports were compared: 1) impression marking; and 2) structural assessment from criteria based on Bloom's Taxonomy (1956). He found greater agreement among five lecturers when giving an overall impression than when using the structured assessment. Fox's results however involve only five assessors and twenty eight studies in one college. Replication should not be difficult and is needed before much weight is given to the findings.

Work at Leicester and the reports of the Schools Council give no final answers. They do however provide a convincing body of evidence that teachers from a wide range of environments can help to make valid judgements about testing methods and can assess their pupils in a controlled and satisfactory way. Problems of moderation and communication are not insuperable and no evidence has arisen that results assessed by Mode 3 techniques will necessarily be any less valid than those of Modes 1 and 2.

This section has been a long one and it does the work which has been reported less than justice to label it all 'examinations'. In fact, in the process of looking at assessment techniques important issues are raised which reflect back upon the teaching in school. If a teacher assesses his own pupils he can be free to design unique programmes for them. If he is compelled to look at the objectives of the examination he must perforce consider the objectives of his teaching.

Educational technology

Ten years ago, hopes were high on both sides of the Atlantic that teaching machines and programmed learning would revolutionise teaching and learning in the armed services, industries and schools. Supporters of Skinner's linear technique claimed theoretical support for their methods. Advocates of Crowder's branching techniques were sure that they worked. Experiments were set up to test whether programmes could teach effectively and under what conditions. Science and mathematics were often used in early experiments and programmes because it was believed that they are factual and proceed in a sequential way. The latest available list of programmes in print (Cavanagh and Jones, 1969) puts mathematics at the head with 572 entries (29 per cent) but follows it with engineering 199 (10 per cent) and English language 117 (6 per cent). The scientific entries are spread amongst several categories but even so their comparatively small numbers reflect today's realisation that the study of science involves complex skills and attitudes which are as difficult to pin down as those of most school subjects. Exponents of programmed learning are now less confident. Children do not react like animals. Too many linear programmes are depressingly dull. Branching programmes begin to look more and more like ordinary books and teaching machines have not proliferated.

Centres such as the Institute for Educational Technology at the University of Surrey do not feel constrained to follow any doctrinaire systems but survey the needs of students and the techniques available, adapting the latter to suit the former. Hills (1971a and b), describes a systems approach to learning which '. . . covers the whole process from the definition of a problem, the specification of basic objectives, the selection of a course of action, down to the final evaluation of the success of the system'. Attempting to strengthen undergraduates' understanding of a topic in electricity he took into account:

1 the motivation of the student;
2 the student's state of pre-knowledge before the course;
3 the problems that the student encountered during the course;
4 the nature of the material to be learnt and the media and methods available.

A conventional lecture technique was used for the main part of the course but self-tests could direct a student to a range of supplementary materials: books, programmes, tape recordings with notes (including a recording of the lecture itself) and tape/slide presentations. Hills does not yet support (with figures) his convictions that the methods work, neither does he consider the Hawthorne effect. Nevertheless it is clear that the remedial opportunities offered were welcomed by the students and led to increased understanding. Elton and his colleagues have described many facets of their work with undergraduates (1970a and b; 1971a and b; Bould and O'Connell, 1970) including an account of the effectiveness of a whole range of what they call '. . . prototypes for components of a teaching and learning system'.

At one time computer-aided instruction seemed to hold much promise. It still does, but at what cost? Unfinished work at Leeds University may yield more optimistic expectations but Elton (1971), basing his conclusions on work in the USA (Commission on College Physics, 1970), and funds available in England doubts whether it will be viable in this decade or the next. At Thomas Bennett School in Crawley, however, Reid and Booth (1969) have carried out a modest experiment on computer *monitored* instruction. The work was essentially a trial of an independent learning approach to the teaching of biology. Pupils were tested in conversational mode by a computer. In the process the mechanics and logistics of using a computer terminal in school, connected to a computer miles away, were examined. They had their fair share of technical trouble and their findings relating to the learning which was being tested by the computer were inconclusive. The results were encouraging enough for them to want to continue and they decided that '. . . independent learning is clearly a useful approach for the teaching of some topics . . . in future, when choosing the best method for tackling a topic, teachers will have the option of using individual learning as an alternative to the various types of class-based methods available.' The computer was a valuable aid, pupils easily mastered the technique of using the terminal and the demands of the computer seemed to improve spelling and the care taken in presenting answers! This work formed part of the Nuffield 'Resources for Learning Project'. One of the leaders (Taylor, 1971) has published an important book connected with the project but a full account has yet to appear in print.

Other work in the sciences relating to programming and new media techniques is well scattered through the literature. It does not offer confident answers to any theoretical questions but describes some of the many interesting methods available to science teachers today. Television and other audio-visual methods have been considered by Goodier (1969), Barrington (1969), Glynn (1969) Troth and Lloyd (1968), Pallant (1968), Talbot (1968), Leith *et al.* (1969) and many others. Not a single writer considers that his method is useless. Few give any details of objective evaluation of their results. Invariably the approach is found to have some (ill-defined) value and 'can form a useful part of a teaching-learning environment'.

In the past, financial support for educational research in Britain has been minimal. There has been some improvement over the past few years and important investigations have begun. To mention a few there is the IEA Study of Science, a Science Teaching Methods Project and, in Glasgow, an extensive research programme on new style chemistry syllabuses. The investigations are all being carried out by skilled researchers and should produce well defined results. At the same time descriptive, personal accounts will doubtless continue to make an important contribution to knowledge and to practice.

This chapter has not aimed to cover all areas of research relating to science teaching. It has concentrated on recent work which is of direct significance to practising science teachers. Curriculum Bulletin No. 3 (Schools Council, 1970) has surveyed many findings of a psychological nature and Pont (1970) has given an account, inter alia, of creativity, the 'swing from science' and certain aspects of technology in school. The bibliographies of these two publications and the one below scarcely overlap and, together, they offer an extensive overview of completed research in science education in Britain.

Lawrence Stenhouse

The Humanities Curriculum Project

Introduction

The Humanities Curriculum Project was set up in June 1967 under the joint sponsorship of the Schools Council and the Nuffield Foundation for a three year term. It was located in Philippa Fawcett College of Education in south London and administration was handled by the ILEA.

From June until September 1967, I worked alone. Project staff were appointed from September and were initially four in number. A schools officer was appointed from Easter 1968. A supplementary budget for film research was granted by the Schools Council to cover the period to August 1970, and a film research officer was appointed from July 1968. During 1968 two other members were added to the project team and for a short time a research librarian was also employed. For the greater part of the two years 1968–70 the main project had a staff of eight and for a time of nine.

This represented a substantial investment on the part of the sponsors and it was clearly important to evaluate the work done. An evaluation unit was set up in 1968 under the direction of Mr Barry MacDonald and was given an additional budget. Although this unit was ultimately my responsibility as director (for purposes of administration), it seemed important also to ensure its academic independence. The evaluation unit built up to a staff of four.

In 1970 the original three year offer of accommodation in Philippa Fawcett ran out. The project and evaluation project were, however, extended for a further two years. The project team now shrank to four. Its task was to complete materials but also more importantly to organise dissemination of the project and training support. The evaluation unit continued at full strength. For the sessions 1970 to 1972 the project was moved to the University of East Anglia.

It will be clear from the above that we are concerned here with a research and development project executed by a fairly large team. My own responsibilities were general administration, overall control of experimental design, relations with outside bodies ('boundary defence') and an editorial responsibility for one theme.

I have written about the administration of the project for two reasons. Both education and educational research are arts of the possible: work must be related to the resources available. Also it is important to make it clear that in writing this article I am writing about other people's work as well as my own—but from the point of view of one accepting overall responsibility for the design of the research.

Basic premises

The basic premises of the project are at two levels: it embodies a view of curriculum research, and it is founded on substantive premises in a particular curricular field.

The responsibilities of curriculum research are particularly heavy both because it is based upon substantial investment and because it is action research significant for the well-being of pupils. It is research which should be subject to social policy. This involves us in a paradox from the outset. Those who take part in research need to be driven by curiosity about the possible development of ideas in which they believe. Yet these ideas must not be personal and idiosyncratic, but disciplined by a relation to social policy. The personal interest must be legitimised by reference to social needs. Curriculum research exists to make aspirations into practical possibilities and the aspirations should be those of a substantial number of teachers and educationists. Since education is an area of debate, however, these aspirations will inevitably be those of one section or party in this debate. In a decentralised system such as ours, then, the function of curriculum research is to make alternatives practicable.

Any one research, however, can probably only explore one alternative. Ideally, perhaps, curriculum projects should be paired, each of the pair exploring the consequences of contradictory premises advocated in educational debate. This is seldom possible. Failing this, the best safeguard is to attempt to assimilate curriculum research to the generally accepted canons of social science research. This means an attempt to make work in curriculum speculative rather than evangelical and cumulative rather than *ad hoc*. This is a position difficult to hold for two reasons. First, curriculum is so much a branch of policy that it is difficult consistently to avoid moving from the speculative to the evangelical, especially in the face of a public which expects advocacy and sees the renunciation of the evangelical as a flight from responsibility. Second, the field is so underdeveloped that it is difficult to hold to social science canons: because there is no integrated and developed theory of curriculum innovation, hypotheses have to be derived from case study in an effort to build theory rather than being deduced from theory and used to test it. Moreover, action research can never be undividedly oriented towards theory. Such difficulties are not overcome by failing to face them.

The following procedure was adopted:

1 Select a cogent general educational policy statement in the curricular field in question.
2 By relating its logical implications to the realities of the classroom, produce the outline of a teaching strategy consistent with the aim and feasible in practice.
3 Attempt to develop the strategy, testing its logical consistency in discussion and its feasibility in experimental schools.
4 Make case studies of experimental schools to generate hypotheses regarding the problems and effects to be expected in implementing the curriculum in a wider range of schools.
5 Use this case study experience to design dissemination procedures which will attempt to meet the anticipated problems.
6 Monitor the effects in dissemination both by case study and by measurement.

1), 2), 3) and 5) were the concern of the project; 4) and 6) of the evaluation unit.

It goes without saying that a programme of this kind is too ambitious to be fulfilled in a single project. Many approximations will be needed before procedures are refined. The first step, therefore, was to adopt a policy position.

The point of departure of the project was a passage in Schools Council Working Paper No. 2 (1965) referring to work in the Humanities:

'The problem is to give every man some access to a complex cultural inheritance, some hold on his personal life and on his relationships with the various communities to which he belongs, some extension of his understanding of, and sensitivity towards, other human beings. The aim is to forward understanding, discrimination and judgement in the human field—it will involve reliable factual knowledge, where this is appropriate, direct experience, imaginative experience, some appreciation of the dilemmas of the human condition, of the rough hewn nature of many of our institutions, and some rational thought about them.' (para. 60.)

It seemed that there would be few teachers who would not assent to this aspiration as a desirable one for the new school leaver, few who would be able to come near to seeing their way to implementing it in practice and therefore few who would not dismiss it as unrealistic. Here then was an aspiration which seemed impracticable. And it is the task of curriculum research to give such aspirations a practicable expression. Two further passages in the working paper hinted at the problems.

'All of this may seem to some teachers like a programme for people who have both the mental ability and maturity beyond the reach of most who will leave at the age of sixteen. The Council, however, thinks it is important *not* to assume that this is so, but rather to probe by experiment in the classroom how far ordinary pupils can in fact be taken. The fact is that nothing can prevent the formation of ideas and attitudes about human nature and conduct.' (para. 61.)

and

'But adult procedures in the classrooms . . . will not be successful if a different kind of relationship between teacher and pupil obtains in the corridor or in extracurricular activity. If the teacher emphasises, in the classroom, his common humanity with the pupils, and his common uncertainty in the face of many problems, the pupils will not take kindly to being demoted to the status of children in other relationships within the same institution. Indeed, they may write off the classroom relationship as a 'soft-sell'. (para. 97.)

These statements seemed of great significance. First, they challenged the divisive Newsom assumption that the school leaver was to be seen as a special case by emphasising the common humanity of teacher and pupil and challenging us to treat the leaver as simply a young adult. (In doing so it challenged my own thinking since I had written a book (Stenhouse, 1967) which only imperfectly freed itself from divisive assumptions of this sort.) Second, it suggested that the whole pattern of relationships and of authority in schools would have to be rethought to achieve such a programme. If this were so, a curriculum which faced this demand would have a significance far beyond its own place on the timetable. It would provide a laboratory experience in which teachers could work out a new view of their task and their relationships with pupils. In order to translate this prospect into any kind of practical reality it was necessary to analyse the statements quoted in order to redefine them in operational terms.

An extremely difficult problem, probably inadequately solved, was to produce a statement of aim. The aims of the project must first of all be separated from those of the curriculum. The aim of the project was to make it possible for teachers to develop their work in the direction of the aspirations contained in these basic statements. This meant a continuous development of insight on the part of the team about teacher problems and needs. The function of a teaching aim was briefly to describe the direction of classroom work in order to influence the 'set' of the teacher in the classroom. Such an aim is a summary task definition.

In fact the formulation of a statement of teaching aim was an attempt to produce a simplified statement which summarised the insights of the team into the logic of the teaching. The formulation changed and developed. And the central team itself did not have a blanket consensus.

The aim finally adopted for the Project handbook (1970) was as follows: 'to develop an understanding of social situations and human acts and of the controversial value issues which they raise'. It was intended that this should imply an application of the perspectives of social science, history, the arts and religious thinking to the understanding of human issues. Such understanding should take account of the need to attempt objectivity on the one hand and to tap imaginative sympathy on the other. And it was believed that the crucial problem in handling human issues was controversiality.

The Project also stated five major premises:

1 that controversial issues should be handled in the classroom with adolescents;
2 that the teacher should accept the need to submit his teaching in controversial areas to the criterion of neutrality at this stage of

education, i.e. that he should regard it as part of his responsibility not to promote his own view;

3 that the mode of enquiry in controversial areas should have discussion, rather than instruction, as its core;

4 that the discussion should protect divergence of view among participants, rather than attempt to achieve consensus;

5 that the teacher as chairman of the discussion should have responsibility for quality and standards in learning.

In following this pattern of defining aim and premises, we were attempting to express the normative aspect inseparable from curriculum design in terms which exposed it as a controlled variable in the experiment. It was hoped that those who did not accept the premises would still be able to profit from the Project's work.

For example, if—as happens—a discussion group becomes concerned with action rather than understanding, then the fourth premise does not hold. Consensus and consequently compromise is required if a group is to agree action. This is true even in simulation: a group planning a new orphanage as part of its study of the family becomes an action group.

The overall task of the project was to discover a teaching strategy which would implement these premises in the classroom, to report this strategy, and to support teachers who wished to develop it with training and if necessary with materials.

The experimental framework

In order to follow the experimental design intended it was necessary to enlist teachers as experimental colleagues. We wished to cast the schools with which we worked in the role of teachers, the central team in the role of learners.

Accordingly we recruited thirty two experimental schools which were to work with the central team during the sessions 1968–9 and 1969–70. We saw these not as trial schools, but as development schools. Thus, though we wanted a variety of school settings, we were not concerned with sampling in a statistical sense. At this stage our concern was with producing a prototype rather than with generalising. Some generalisation would of course be possible, but there was no real possibility of sound generalisation from the thirty two schools which developed the strategy in close contact with the central team to the experience of the second generation of schools which might adopt the work.

Our plan therefore was as follows. In summer 1968 we would hold induction conferences for all our experimental schools. By that time we needed to have an outline teaching strategy. We would present to the schools the premises on which we were working, assuming that since they had expressed an interest in joining the Project, they would provisionally accept them. Then we would present our outline of the problems which would be encountered. Finally, by ourselves chairing discussions we would indicate how far we had got in understanding the role demanded of the teacher if he were to develop this kind of work. For us the premises were a constant controlled variable: our diagnoses of problems and suggestions of method were hypotheses to be tested in schools. They can be treated here only in summary.

We visualised an enquiry into human issues conducted in schools in order to increase the understanding of students in accordance with the aim. Such an enquiry would, we assumed, involve research on the part of pupils, written work, visits, improvised drama, art work and so forth. These we took to be the stock in trade of teachers. The novelty came from the fact that the enquiry dealt with controversial issues and the students were young adults in their last two years of school who needed to be hardened off into independence before leaving.

Given the authority position of the teacher, this seemed to imply that the central classroom activity should be discussion rather than instruction. Our premises cast the teacher as chairman of a discussion in a neutral role. This role needed to be worked out in terms of classroom methods.

The fact that the medium of learning was discussion rather than instruction together with the neutral role of the chairman threw into relief the problem of giving a discussion group access to information. It seemed that the best way to do this was to provide them with documentary evidence. Given the pressure on teachers, it seemed advisable for the central team to help them by supplying materials.

The experimental schools were asked to test and develop hypotheses about teaching method and to test and if possible contribute to the materials offered by the central team. Curriculum was seen as a content—method bundle.

Some difficulties encountered

Broadly, the strategy adopted did pay dividends, but it was by no means uniformly successful. We got enough data to pursue our work, but much less than we might have hoped. This was largely due to a series of communication problems which affected both our relations with experimental schools and to an even greater extent the way the work was seen outside the experiment. These problems are worth noting.

1 The attempt to conduct curriculum development on social science lines was not expected and therefore not perceived. This took us by surprise and we therefore failed to stress it sufficiently. In retrospect, the situation is clear. Most British curriculum development had been based upon subject specialists with a mission to reform teaching in their fields. Because humanities was not a 'subject' the situation was rather different. Two leading members of the team, myself and the director of evaluation, were 'educationists'. I had a primary interest in curriculum, the director of evaluation in the sociology of schools and in measurement. Our qualifications were in education and psychology. It was natural for us to think in terms of research design. We did not fully appreciate how difficult it would be to induct our experimental schools into experimental assumptions. Thus we found ourselves struggling to maintain the position of experimentalists rather than educational prophets.

2 We underestimated the authority of national projects backed by the Schools Council and the ambivalent attitude they may generate. We saw the project as testing hypotheses: many of the teachers with whom we worked saw either themselves or us as on trial. Often instead of using their judgement to inform us, teachers allowed what were intended by us as tentative hypotheses to overrule their judgement. Some experimental feedback was distorted by this attitude. It might be designed to reassure us, to challenge us or merely to protect the teacher concerned. In the end, this has partly been overcome, but it has been a formidable problem.

3 Expectations existed concerning what we would be attempting

and it was difficult to overcome them. We had taken an anti-Newsom line: but we were assimilated to Newsom thinking. We had stressed knowledge and understanding but we were expected to be non-intellectual. 'Humanities' as a term was often taken to mean integrated studies: we had interpreted it as a 'human issues programme' and though this could be used as a core for integrated studies, in most of our schools a subject structure was maintained. We saw ourselves as providing support for a particular development whose place in the school should be determined by policy decisions at school level and should vary from school to school: it was often assumed that we should have an answer to questions about the total curriculum—or even that we wished humanities to take over the leavers' curriculum.

4 We were concerned with long term development and particularly with teacher development: we were often perceived as attempting an instant and easy solution to problems.

5 The problem we were tackling and the way it was tackled did not make a direct contribution to problems of discipline and control. In some ways it made these problems more acute. It opened them up instead of containing them, and this ran counter to the hopes of many teachers.

There were a number of other difficulties of this sort. In short, we found ourselves trying to redefine the role in which we were cast by precedents.

Neutrality

One of our greatest problems has been with the concept of neutrality of the teacher; and this probably deserves further discussion.

The initial premise on which the idea of neutrality was based was political. I assume that education is in the classic sense a branch of politics, and I distinguish between a personal ethic and a professional ethic. In most societies the school has two functions which may be called education and socialisation. Education is concerned with the transmission of knowledge and understanding in the sense which supports Jacques Barzun's concept of intellect. Socialisation is concerned with the transmission of the values and folkways of a society or a sub-group in society on the basis of social consensus rather than on the basis of philosophical justification. Whether socialisation in this sense is desirable or an irrational residue is a matter of debate; I shall only argue here that in society as we know it, it is inevitable.

In respect of the social values and folkways our society is pluralist. For example, an Indian child, a Jamaican child, an English child and a Welsh child will have differing values and folkways as will a middle class and a working class child. By adolescence pupils cannot but be aware of this divergence in society. And though there are limits to any society's capacity to tolerate divergence, we in our society favour wide limits.

In this situation, the school appears to have a choice of strategies in facing controversial issues. It may decide that the school should adopt one position in the controversy and ask all teachers to promote it. There is a political problem in enlisting social support outside the school for the line taken by the school. There is a problem inside the school, because some teachers will be asked to commit themselves to a systematic hypocrisy. A second possible position is that the teacher give his own sincerely held point of view. There would be no objection to this if the profession were ready and able to protect teachers who expressed views of any kind and if the authority of the teacher were so slender that his views could be treated equally with those of pupils—or parents. Neither of these conditions seems to hold.

Two positions seem politically possible for the teacher. He can act as devil's advocate, advancing views in which he may or may not believe for the sake of argument, or he can attempt to maintain his neutrality in the face of controversial issues. The first of these was rejected (though fairly popular in America) as involving insincerity on the part of the teacher. The second was adopted. Thus, the teacher, it is suggested, should stand for and promote 'educational values', but in controversial areas he should adopt the criterion of neutrality.

Two points should be made about this. First, that neutrality is not achievable. It is a criterion by which one criticises one's own teaching and should be shared with the students. Second, there appears to be a disparity between a theoretical conception of the issue and practice. Arguing from theory people appear to assume that a typical breach of neutrality would be a statement of faith on the part of the teacher. In observed practice teachers generally breach neutrality in quite a different way. These quotations will illustrate this: 'Do you think it right that workers should be able to blackmail the country by striking?'; 'Wouldn't you all agree that this at least is a case of police brutality?'; 'Do you *really* believe that, John?'

It may well be that the word has been misleading. Impartiality might have been better, though we have come to use impartiality to mean the impartial treatment of students rather than neutrality on issues.

The position I have outlined above is basically a political one. In pedagogical terms it really means a recognition that before students leave school they should learn to subject social values to criticism in the light of educational values. That is, they should come to see that the tools of thinking which the school offers them can be used to criticise social and personal positions. At the same time these tools are not likely to produce consensus: rather they will provide procedures for handling divergence in ways that will be conducive to understanding. This is the essence of reflective teaching and learning.

In practice the issue of neutrality became complicated and more than political. It became apparent that the authority of the teacher was much more powerful than we had understood. Thus breach of neutrality could be opposed on epistemological grounds: it often appeared to transmit to the students the idea that issues could be settled on authority rather than on rational grounds. Moreover, teachers attempting to implement the role of neutral chairman threw much more responsibility on to their pupils and the pupils response to this raised standards of work. At the same time, the role muted the teacher's capacity to transmit low expectations to the pupils. There appeared to be a correlation between acceptance of neutrality as a criterion and quality of work. In particular, breach of neutrality appeared to affect adversely students' capacity to face high reading levels in the material.

Thus, the neutrality variable proved much more significant than we expected. As a result it became more and more difficult to track its relationship to dependent variables and thus less possible than we had intended for teachers who did not accept neutrality to use our work.

Objectives

Almost as controversial as our position on neutrality was our decision not to use objectives in our work.

When the Project was set up (and even now), a particular model for research design in curriculum was dominant. This was an output model, based on objectives.

The procedure suggested was as follows. A general statement of aim should be analysed into objectives—I prefer intended learning outcomes—which should be behavioural in the sense that they specified changes in student behaviour (in the psychological sense of that term) which it was intended that the curriculum should bring about. A curriculum should then be constructed and tested, so far as possible by measuring instruments, for its success in teaching the objectives.

This design was not adopted in the Project.

I have written elsewhere (Stenhouse, 1964, 1968, 1970–1, 1971) of my reservations concerning the objectives model. A detailed discussion would be inappropriate here, but some reservations are worth listing:

1 Objectives tend to be *ad hoc* substitutes for hypotheses. They do not lead to cumulative theory. Hypotheses are therefore generally preferable.

2 The use of objectives assumes a capacity to predict the results of curricula which is not justified by empirical work.

3 Consequently, statements of objectives tend to be oversimplified and self-fulfilling.

4 A centrally designed curriculum development tested by reference to objectives formulated by the central team in detail must imply teacher-proofing. Our curriculum assumed divergent interpretation of a general aim by teachers.

5 The use of objectives tends to make curriculum instrumental and to distort the intrinsic value of content and process. It leads to the concept of an exercise.

6 There are epistemological objections to the idea that all knowledge and understanding can be expressed in terms of specifiable student behaviours.

7 It may be appropriate for the students following a course to have objectives of their own which are to a certain extent divergent.

8 In an exploratory development which enters little charted areas, there is a need to approach the problem of effects speculatively, and in particular to aim at generating hypotheses from case studies.

9 A curriculum may have important effects on teachers and on schools as institutions, not simply on student performance.

For these and other reasons we adopted a process rather than an output model. Given an aim couched in terms of knowledge and understanding (and perhaps also advanced and complex skills), it is possible to devise a teaching process and teaching materials which are consistent with that aim. In this case the aim is analysed into learning process or input, rather than into i.l.o.s or output.

This procedure allows a gradual exploration of the logic and structure of a subject area, both during a curriculum project and by teachers developing a project's work. Instead of i.l.o.s the input model deals with effects which are hypothesised from case studies of practical situations. It aims to produce a curricular specification which describes a range of possible learning outcomes and relates them to their causes. The style of its formulation is: 'If you follow these procedures with these materials with this type of pupil, in this school setting, the effects will tend to be X.'

The problem with the input or process model is its complexity. Among its strengths are that it is amenable to the hypothico-deductive method and hence gives greater promise of a cumulative science of curriculum; it avoids the philosophically dubious position that all knowledge can be expressed as learned behaviours; it allows of students' having divergent objectives within the same curriculum; and it attempts to face the complexity of the classroom.

The experiment in schools

Between October 1967 and January 1968 the trial collection on war was prepared so that it could be printed by Easter. Over 4 000 documents were assembled, from which a collection of just over 200 was selected. A punched card system was used for access to the archive collection.

The first collection was produced in a 'Jackdaw' format. That is, each pupil had a folder of materials for each sub-topic. It was printed in the project. On the basis of feed-back from schools the later collections were restructured: each teacher pack contained a single copy of every document in the collection. A class pack contained twenty copies of each document. Audio-tapes were made by the project team. Later collections were sent out to a printer. As experience built up, the archive collection tended to become smaller in relation to the pack.

In summer 1968 three five day residential conferences were run to induct the teams of teachers from the thirty two experimental schools. The teachers were introduced to the materials, the nature of the experiment was put to them, groups worked in discussion with team members chairing, and there was a general discussion.

During the session 1968–9 the schools worked on collections on war, education and the family. Feed-back on materials was by question-naire supported by interviews with the schools officer or other team members when they visited schools. Information was sought on cover-age of the collection, accessibility of the material to the students (readability and sophistication of ideas), and the extent to which materials provoked or supported discussion. Most schools used only a small proportion of materials (as was intended) so that feed-back on any one piece was not extensive. It was also frequently contradictory, particularly as to readability. Collections were radically re-edited as a result of experience in schools: often only half the trial pack survived. New materials could not be tested in schools because of publication dates.

The most controversial aspect of the packs as they emerged was the high reading level. Both schools and project team remain divided on this issue.

One view in the team is that since the method and attitudes implied by the project are difficult of achievement, it would have been better not to face teachers with so great a reading problem and hence with motivational difficulties. The other view is that the method and attitude are inseparably linked to an assault on reading levels. Certainly, there is evidence that schools taking a purist line on method find reading problems present much less difficulty. In particular they shift from a view that documents must be understood before they are discussed to a view that discussion is a means to understanding. They also value students' capacity to get the gist of a document.

Throughout the sessions 1968 to 1970 the procedure for testing materials was much the same.

In order to develop methodology, we asked teachers to send us tapes of discussion. These were selected by the teachers. Recording conditions were often bad and many tapes were virtually inaudible. Nevertheless, we had enough to work on, and some of the tapes were quite striking in their novelty.

At our second teachers' conferences at Easter, 1969, we presented our work on the tapes as a series of propositions or injunctions to chairmen, and we asked teachers to test these during the second year. We were also able to play tapes to them.

THE HUMANITIES CURRICULUM PROJECT

As a result of experience following this, we concluded that we had made two errors. The expression of the methodology as injunctions was wrong. First, generalisations did not hold. Teacher judgement was at all times necessary. Second, since injunctions were statements, they were treated as instructions to teachers rather than hypotheses. Accordingly, when we published our project handbook we distinguished major variables in discussion and suggested that teachers train themselves by examining tapes of their own teaching in the light of these variables. This analysis required to be related to their own aims.

I believe that this procedure is a profitable one. Basically, we have attempted an operational role definition for the teacher by relating moves on the part of a chairman to the aims of teaching (logic) and to responses on the part of the group (social dynamics). I have no doubt that our work here has a very wide application both in its method and in its substantive findings.

One of the most interesting results of our experiment in schools was our discovery of a very large number of variables in success and failure (as judged by teachers themselves). Organisation, choice of team, social structure of the school and so forth were clearly crucial. This remains true in dissemination. In some cases, for example, we have whole local authority areas in which virtually all schools report success and satisfaction; others in which virtually all schools report failure and dissatisfaction.

This is particularly important since it suggests on analysis that the actual curriculum involved is a much less significant variable in curriculum innovation than might have been thought (particularly since our findings are confirmed by other work); and this points to the possibility of a theory of curriculum innovation which could be cumulative.

Evaluation of the project

The evaluation unit of the Humanities Project differs distinctly in role from those of many other projects. In the first place, the evaluation of teaching materials was in this project taken to be part of the task of the development team. Secondly, the project offered the evaluator no behavioural objectives. It was anticipated that the greater part of the evaluator's work would be in case-studying schools and indeed the title under which MacDonald was appointed was Schools Study

Officer. It was expected that he would study the work of the Project, provide feed-back to the central team about the progress of the experiment in schools, and design a suitable evaluation programme for implementation in 1970–2 when the Project went into dissemination.

Writing of the situation in which he was placed (MacDonald, in press), our evaluation officer explained his problems. 'In this "non-objectives" approach there is no ready-made niche for the evaluator. He must await events, see what happens, trace the different ways in which the work unfolds and try to link patterns of effects to patterns of teaching. *Outcome* and *process* both demand his attention. A particular problem is *which* effects to study. In an evaluation programme, it's no use providing answers to questions that no-one is asking.' Since it was likely that the crucial effects would depend in part upon the actions and communications of the Project team, it was necessary to study their *input*, and since it was likely that the effects would vary from school to school, it was necessary to study *context*.

The initial aim of the evaluator was so to describe the work of the project that it was made accessible to public and professional judgement.

During the first year he concentrated on trying to establish what was happening in schools and on gathering data and generating hypotheses which might help to explain the widely differing experiences and effects reported. This was tackled by broad survey work which generated institutional profiles of schools and by intensive case studies of a small sample. The case study work went on into the second year of the experiment. In a brief outline of his work, MacDonald illustrates the type of proposition he was exploring with the following examples:

1 Human behaviour in educational settings is susceptible to a wide range of variable influences. This is a commonplace yet in curriculum evaluation it is sometimes assumed that what is intended to happen is what actually happens, and that what happens varies little from setting to setting.

2 The impact of an innovation is not a set of discrete effects, but an organically related pattern of acts and consequences. To understand fully a single act one must locate it functionally within that pattern. It follows from this proposition that innovations have many more unanticipated consequences than is normally assumed in development and evaluation designs.

3 No two schools are so alike in their circumstances that prescrip-

tions of curricular action can adequately supplant the judgement of the people in them. Historical/evolutionary differences alone make the innovation 'gap' a variable which has significance for decision-making.

4 The goals and purposes of the programme developers are not necessarily shared by its users. We have seen the Project used variously as a political resource in an existing power struggle between staff factions, as a way of increasing the effectiveness of a custodial pattern of pupil control, and as a means of garnishing the image of institutions which covet the wrapping, but not the merchandise of innovation. The latter gives rise to the phenomenon of innovation without change.

Looking back on MacDonald's work and on conversations with him, I see a significant pattern. He was presented with a project lacking a specification of objectives. Objectives constitute a selection of hypotheses according to hopes. Lack of objectives thrusts on the evaluator of a complex action research with vast numbers of variables the task of selecting hypotheses. The first position, that of the 'descriptive' evaluator, was soon discarded. Instead, it was decided to collect questions asked by decision-makers—the Schools Council, LEAs, heads, teachers, Project team, etc.—and to try to answer them. But deeper study of schools showed that decision-makers often asked the wrong questions or—perhaps better—failed to ask questions which were *in the view of the evaluator* highly significant. MacDonald struggled with the problem of justifying his own judgements of significance and in a crucial series of dialogues with the Project team and with American scholars began to develop propositions which reached towards generalisation and distinguished significant variables. At this point, the exercise ceases to be one of evaluation in the sense measuring against criteria and becomes an attempt to understand innovation through the teasing out of variables and their relation to generalisations. This is what the Germans call 'accompanying research'. Its purpose is seen by the evaluator at this stage as 'that of feeding the judgement of decision-makers by promoting understanding of the considerations that bear upon curricular action'.

The evaluation unit has recently defined its task as follows:

1 To ascertain the effects of the Project, document the circumstances in which they occur, and present this information in a

form which will help educational decision-makers to evaluate the likely consequences of adopting the programme.

2 To describe the present situation and operations of the schools we study so that decision-makers can understand more fully what it is they are trying to change.

3 To describe the work of the Project team in terms which will help the sponsors and planners of such ventures to weigh the value of this form of investment, and to determine more precisely the frame-work of support, guidance and control which are appropriate.

4 To make a contribution to evaluation theory by articulating our problems clearly, recording our experience, and perhaps most importantly, by publicising our errors.

5 To contribute to the understanding of the problems of curriculum innovation generally.

MacDonald comments:

'Not everyone would agree that all of these are defensible objectives for an evaluation unit set up to study one project. I would argue firstly that objectives are in part a function of opportunities, and secondly that, at a time when curriculum development is becoming increasingly the concern of a number of new and relatively inexperienced agencies, there is a need for those involved in the field to contribute what they can towards an understanding of the problems of change.'

The sessions 1970–1 and 1971–2 are the crucial ones for the evaluation unit. During these sessions they are able to study the continuing work in the thirty two experimental schools and also the progress of the 600 or so schools which initially bought materials. Their design for this study contains clinical, psychometric and sociological elements; and they are using two overlapping school samples, one large and one small. The small sample will be studied in detail and the insights gained will be used to interpret results from the large sample.

The programme of tasks is as follows:

1 *In the large sample of schools* (c. 100)
   a) Gathering input, contextual and implementation data by questionnaire.

b) Gathering judgement data from teachers and pupils.

c) Objective measurement of pupil change. (We have, at the beginning of this year, carried out pre-tests of pupils on twenty-one objective tests which represent the combined judgement of teachers, pupils, the central team and ourselves, of likely dimensions of pupil change. This is a massive operation, but will be justified if it can help us establish pupil effects and lead to the employment next year of a small but accurate test battery.)

d) Tracing variations in teaching practice through the use of specially devised multiple-choice feedback instruments which require minimal effort by the teacher and monitored by pupils.

e) Documenting the effect on the school by means of semi-structured teacher diaries.

2   *In a small sample of schools* (c. 12)

a) Case-studies of patterns of decision-making, communication, training and support in local areas.

b) Case-studies of individual schools within these areas.

c) Study of the dynamics of discussion by audiotape, videotape and observation.

Reports of results from the evaluation study are likely to reach publication from the early summer of 1973 onwards.

Denis Lawton

Language, social class and the curriculum

Introduction

One of the features of educational discussion during the 1960s was the attention paid to language as a factor in educational achievement. This trend was due in part to belated recognition of the importance of such psychologists as Vygotsky and Luria, and also to the sociological theories of Bernstein. In 1968 an attempt was made (Lawton, 1968) to review the relevant sociological and psychological research which might throw some light on one kind of educational under-achieving. The result was a partial diagnosis of the learning difficulties experienced by some children in schools, especially the difficulties associated with language and communication. It is not the intention of this paper, therefore, to analyse this research once again, but to trace more recent developments, especially those which have had some influence on curricula and teaching methods in the UK. Since 1968 a number of highly technical and specialised contributions have been made which would sharpen the theoretical diagnosis referred to above. I will not attempt to summarise these, but will review critically the various solutions to the problem which have been suggested. Some of the theoretical advances have been clearly reported in the series of books edited by Basil Bernstein: Brandis and Henderson (1970), in Turner and Mohan (1970), and in Bernstein (1970); other useful discussions will be found in Williams (1970). More recently Bernstein himself has provided a comprehensive review of the theoretical and empirical contributions of his Sociological Research Unit in *Class, Codes and Control I* (1971).

In addition, relevant linguistic research has been reported by Wilkinson (1969 and 1971). But what is also needed is some kind of statement—even if it has to be an interim statement—about what teachers and schools can do towards solving the problem. One of the features of the late 60s and early 70s has been a tendency to move away from 'pure' research to 'action'. For example, Fantini and Weinstein (1968) have suggested that: 'unfortunately, descriptions about the nature of the disadvantaged learner are well ahead of instructional prescriptions that are appropriate. Our concern is with the development of such prescriptive technology functionally linked to descriptive theory.' This paper will report on research of this kind—even where the results are inconclusive or not even evaluated statistically.

Before reviewing these projects and ideas, a brief restatement of the psychological and sociological positions might be helpful if only to clear up some misconceptions which seem to have arisen. The Russian psychologists were responsible for refocusing our attention on to the relation between language and thought. Luria, Vygotsky and others of the school hold a dynamic, not a static view of language—that is they maintain that language is not simply the outward manifestation of inner thinking, but that it shapes, makes possible and even produces some kinds of thought. This implies that the more we know about an individual's or a group's language the more we can deduce about thought. The other way in which the Russians see language dynamically is in the self-regulating function of language: as we internalise language we internalise 'society'; Luria has shown, for example, that children internalise language in such a way as to become self-regulating systems rather than the passive responders to stimuli suggested by Skinner and some of his behaviourist colleagues. Thus language is the uniquely human attribute which enables us to learn, think creatively and change socially—very different from animals without language, who are relatively more dominated by instinct.

The interest of sociologists in language is closely related to the Russian psychological view that man becomes human largely by means of his self-regulating system of language. In sociological terms this means that children are socialised largely by means of language, and also that human beings acquire the capacity for rebellion (or, less dramatically, for change) by means of language: language not only helps us to understand *why* things are as they are, but it also enables us to see what *might* be. Thus one's view of reality is closely bound up with language: the language we have acquired has *some* influence on how we see the world (even if the Whorfian hypothesis is not totally acceptable), and how we *use* language is closely related to social structure. One of Bernstein's major contributions was to illustrate a connection between social structure, language use and 'educability'. His theory has been greatly misunderstood and misinterpreted in this respect, however: he was not, I believe, suggesting that working class language is inferior to middle class language and that therefore working class children are less educable; he was demonstrating that if middle class children acquire the kind of oral expression classified as elaborated code this will give them an advantage in formal educational contexts as education is at present organised. But the sociological interest in language is much wider than this: how people use language is related to social structure, occupation, community and group relations; how people think is related to their use of language.

Language and Education

What has the above discussion of language and thought to do with educational practice? We cannot begin to deal adequately with that question without examining the social structure and in particular the class structure and its relation to education. Working class people have traditionally had little part to play in the power structure; they have not used language to any great extent in their jobs and they have not needed to use language to persuade or coerce their fellows. That does *not* mean that language is unimportant in working class culture; simply that its uses are concentrated on certain functions.

On the other hand, schools are in origin middle class institutions; the attitudes and values transmitted are largely middle class and the language of transmission is also largely middle class. It is therefore not surprising that pupils whose home background has already equipped them with the appropriate kind of oral facility will find less difficulty in adapting to the demands of teachers in the schools.

The differences between middle class and working class pupils in this kind of adaptability are so great that some educationists, such as Bantock (1968) have used them to support an argument against universal education which exaggerated the value of universal literacy. Some writers have refused to take such views as Bantock's seriously, but this is possibly a grave mistake. One of the most interesting features of educational debate in recent years has been the attempt of Professor Bantock (1971) to suggest an alternative kind of popular education, following but modifying the view expressed originally by D. H. Lawrence that the working classes should not be taught to read and write. This is an élitist point of view, but Bantock does show that he has respect for non-literate culture, whereas some other educationists have no qualms about showing clearly that they despise it.

In contrast there are many varieties of educational philosophy which seem to agree that although the *means* of achieving success may be different the goals of education must be the same for all pupils. Hirst (1969), White (1969) and Stenhouse (1968) have all in very different ways expressed the view that we must now be concerned with the education of the whole population rather than providing élite education for a few and mass instruction for the rest. Although the above writings might not be included under 'research' in the usual sense, I have referred to them because they are important in their own right and also because they have coincided with a move towards the kind of research which blurs the distinction between ideas and empirical data, between theory and practice. For example, the Humanities Curriculum Project, directed by Lawrence Stenhouse (see chapter 9 of this book for a detailed description), takes as its guiding brief the following extract from the Schools Council Working Paper No. 2: 'The problem is to give every man some access to a complex cultural inheritance, some hold on his personal life and on his relationships with the various communities to which he belongs, some extension of his understanding of, and sensitivity towards, other human beings. The aim is to forward understanding, discrimination and judgement in the human field.'

Thus the debate is a very sharp one, and it is very difficult to see how the issue can be resolved simply by the kind of evidence that has traditionally been demanded. The other kind of development which has taken place is a sharpening of the dispute about the nature of 'deprivation' in an educational context. On the one hand there has been a tendency to counter arguments about 'inequality of opportunity' by suggesting that some kind of inequality is inevitable unless the family as an institution were abolished—i.e. that the question of inequality or deprivation is a relative one; this may have provided some support for those who seek an excuse for not attempting to eliminate poverty or inequality however gross. On the other hand the Schools Council Research and Development Project in Compensatory Education (1968, 1969) (University of Swansea) has collected information about over sixty American projects, partly to review methods of identifying 'deprivation'. One result of this survey was to cast grave doubt on the usefulness of the Plowden concept of deprived or 'priority' areas, and to focus instead on individual children in need— and their needs were found to be extremely diverse and to be caused by a wide variety of factors.

At the same time there has been a growing awareness that the whole idea of 'compensatory education' is at worst an insult and at best muddled thinking. Bernstein (1970) writes: 'I find the term "compensatory education" a curious one for a number of reasons. I do not understand how we can talk about offering compensatory education to children who in the first place have not, as yet, been offered an adequate educational environment. The Newsom Report showed that 79 per cent of all secondary modern schools in slum and problem areas were materially grossly inadequate, and the holding power of these schools over the teachers was horrifyingly low.

'. . . The concept "compensatory education" serves to direct attention away from the internal organisation and the educational context of the school, and focus our attention on the families and the children. The concept compensatory education implies something is lacking in the family and so in the child . . .'. In the same essay Bernstein has pointed out exactly how research into language can be interpreted in a distorted way: 'It might, and has been said, that my research, through focusing upon the sub-culture and forms of familial socialisation, has also distracted attention away from the conditions and context of learning in school. The focus upon usage of language sometimes led people to divorce the use of language from the sub-stratum of cultural meanings which are initially responsible for the language use. The concept restricted code has been equated with "linguistic deprivation", or even the non-verbal child' (Bernstein, 1970).

This paper rejects ideas such as 'the culturally disadvantaged' child in need of 'compensatory education', and asks instead 'in what ways is the school system failing some of the children who in the past were regarded as slow learners, etc.?' The research (broadly interpreted) relevant to this question will be considered under three sub-headings:

1 organisation of schools,
2 content and methods of teaching,
3 teachers' attitudes and behaviour.

1 Organisation of schools

(a) *The community school.* One significant change of attitude towards the problem of developing and extending children's language within the school situation that has occurred since 1968 has been the tendency to think of the pupils' background and community in more positive terms. In the 1950s and early 1960s the most common idea of a comprehensive school was one in which there would be a good 'social mix': if necessary, pupils should be deliberately brought in from outside the neighbourhood in order to ensure that a mixture of social classes was achieved within the school. More recently, however, the idea has developed that a good primary school or comprehensive secondary school can exist no matter what the area in which it is situated. Thus the task of the school is to take advantage of the particular culture, including the language, of the particular catchment area irrespective of the social class composition. Various discussions of how best to take advantage of the community school idea are contained in papers such as those by Betty (1967, 1969), Corbett (1969a), Eggington (1969), Rowe (1971), as well as the action research described by Midwinter (1969) which will be discussed in detail later.

> 'A community school . . . is not merely a school that welcomes in the parents or is open in the evening for father to do a bit of fretwork. It is a thoroughgoing device to identify school and community in every aspect of the life of each for the better health of both. In a world where, it is often said, the individual is lost against the grey, anonymous and faceless backcloth of society, there is possibly here a hope for the regeneration and rejuvenation of wholesome and dynamic community life' (Midwinter, 1969).

Most of these publications are not concerned with promoting language development as such, but rather in considering the kind of school organisation which will best take advantage of pupils' existing linguistic skills and encourage them to extend their powers of communication, whilst in no ways devaluing their own cultural background.

(b) *Streaming and grouping.* Although there is no research work which looks directly at the effect of streaming on the linguistic development of various groups of children, the evidence so far referred to would seem to indicate that, if children are rigidly grouped by ability, those children who are classified as of lower ability or least able would normally be handicapped by this aspect of school organisation. This would seem to be supported indirectly by such research as the NFER survey conducted by Barker-Lunn (1970). In addition the unintended consequences of streaming have been illustrated by Hargreaves (1967) who showed that children in the lowest stream of a secondary modern school developed a delinquescent sub-culture with values quite opposite to those which were being aimed at by the teachers. Hargreaves does not specifically mention the part played by language in this process, nor the effect of such an organisation on children's linguistic development; nevertheless it would seem clear that in a streamed situation such as he describes there will be little likelihood of the less able children developing intellectually and linguistically in the way that educationists would hope for. (See also the discussion of Hargreaves' work in the chapter by Hoyle.) Thus the general tendency in recent years has been for both secondary schools and primary schools to move away from rigid streaming to more flexible forms of organisation. One such example of flexibility has been analysed by Freeman (1969) in his discussion of team teaching. Freeman has described how in recent years it has become much more common for schools to operate with three different kinds of inter-dependent groupings: large groups with over 100 pupils and one teacher, smaller groups of twelve to fifteen pupils with one teacher, and finally either small tutorial groups of two or three pupils or even a one to one teacher–pupil ratio. This kind of fluidity meets the need which I pointed out in 1968 when I suggested that in a one pupil to one teacher situation, pupils whose language was normally limited to the restricted code were capable of elaborated code responses provided that the stimulus and context were appropriate.

(c) *Other aspects of school organisation.* It may be necessary at this stage to dispel the easy optimism of some who appear to believe that all problems—including linguistic—will disappear with unstreaming. It is much more likely that the relation between school and pupils' achievement is a much more subtle one and that the whole philosophy of a school is involved: Clegg and Megson (1968), for example, suggest that: 'Many rules are a bad sign. . . . Far more important than any rules are the attitudes and values by which a school is run.' The whole question of authority and school organisation is involved:

'If a school, taking a lead from the head, parades its authority, the weaker pupils are likely to suffer. The signs are well enough known: if teachers raise their voices, if children are only allowed to speak when they have one hand in the air, if there is much caning and much berating of children, if the head communicates with the staff by written minutes, if he is not easily accessible to them, if he is un-welcome in the staff room, if his pupils are frightened of him, if he uses selected prefects to perform duties rather than an elected council to discharge responsibilities, the likelihood is that the school lacks the mutual respect and affection between teachers and taught which alone results in true education. Some schools mistake the shadow of education for its substance . . .' (Clegg and Megson, 1968).

2 Content and methods

The best known example of attempted changes in the content and methods of education for children previously labelled 'disadvantaged' has been the follow-up of the Plowden Report (1967) suggestion that there should be educational Priority Areas. In 1968 five areas were chosen for EPA action research projects (two districts of Liverpool, Deptford, Denaby in West Riding, Balsall Heath in Birmingham, and Dundee). £75 000 was granted to establish suitable developmental patterns for educational priority areas. Each of these pilot schemes is developing its own programme according to the particular problems and needs of the area. Perhaps the best documented of these five is the Liverpool project directed by Dr Eric Midwinter. Midwinter argues that the purpose of a project such as his is not to provide an escape route from the slum but to strengthen the community in it. The idea of a community school, referred to above, is basic to his research design. Midwinter has been quoted as saying that he wants his project to produce 'visible examples of successful practice; action is the best research'. The action research relating to primary schools has produced one project related to the curriculum and another related to home and community. Both of these projects are designed not only to promote more effective communication within the schools but also to en-courage parents to participate and communicate as part of a school structure. Evaluation is difficult since Midwinter claims that research can destroy the action, and he has therefore rejected the idea of 'before and after' tests of achievement with the usual control group set-up.

Nevertheless there are reports from teachers and outside observers that a great deal of progress is being made (Midwinter, 1969, 1970; Pulham, 1970; Corbett, 1969b).

The Deptford project, directed by Charles Betty, appears to be concentrating on making use of College of Education students to achieve greater child-teacher interaction communication. In Birmingham the emphasis is on home-school relationships; Dundee researchers are working through playgroups; Denaby also has playgroups as well as a social education centre. None of these projects has yet been evaluated but all of them have been criticised: in particular Professor J. B. Mays in Liverpool has objected that 'we cannot eliminate an endemic disease by making some of the patients more comfortable' (quoted in Corbett, 1969b). Clearly there are limits to what changes in social conditions can be produced by education, and ultimately perhaps we will see some social reform as well as Educational Priority Areas. But meanwhile the efforts being made must be observed carefully to estimate how far they are in accord with the theoretical research and diagnoses that have been carried out.

Not all programmes have been of the 'action research' kind, however. Whilst admitting the considerable difficulties of running an 'intervention programme' simultaneously with fundamental research, two psychologists in Professor Bernstein's Sociological Research Unit have recorded in detail a programme of 'Talk Reform' developed for schools in East London (Gahagan and Gahagan, 1970). This is the first programme of its kind in England which has been taught in a controlled situation and which has been systematically evaluated. The results of the programme certainly justify further experimental study, and much of the programme could be introduced into normal infant school teaching. No attempt will be made here to summarise the content of the intervention programme or the evaluation procedures: the book itself is very short and should be read by all who are concerned with this problem. American intervention programmes have been reviewed by Blank (1970) and Cazden (1970).

For older pupils—in secondary schools—some of the Schools Council and Nuffield Curriculum Development work is of direct relevance. The Humanities Curriculum Project, the Keele Integrated Studies Project, the Moral Education Project, Nuffield Secondary Science and Nuffield Resources for Learning have all been concerned with the need to think of the linguistic abilities and potentialities of the pupils.

The tendency to see language not simply as a problem for English teachers but as a problem for all teachers, and the whole curriculum 'not as a subject to be taught but as an approach to learning' owes a great deal to the London Association for the Teaching of English and its attempts to develop 'A Language Policy Across the Curriculum' (see the Discussion Document of that title introduced by Harold Rosen in Barnes, 1969).

3 Teachers' attitudes and behaviour

Perhaps the most significant factor in encouraging greater achievement by working class pupils has not yet been mentioned: the attitude of (middle class) teachers towards them. This is, of course, related both to the organisation of schools and to the content and methods of teaching —the best possible organisation and the perfect curriculum would be of no value without teachers who could communicate in such a situation. In a community school, if it is to be at all meaningful, we must have teachers who respect and value the community and culture from which the pupils come. This may seem obvious but it is often neglected and there is very little empirical research to support this point. Shumsky's work (1968) does however relate the whole question of teacher-style to teacher effectiveness. Shumsky suggests that a classroom climate in which the learner is more active, more of an individual and is encouraged to innovate is the most effective one. This is partly a question of teacher–pupil verbal inter-change and an active role for the pupil, but also the whole question of the teacher possessing positive attitudes towards the pupil and reasonably high expectations of him are also clearly very important. A large number of studies of teacher effectiveness and teachers' verbal styles have been reviewed in Biddle and Ellena (1964) and more recently by Flanders (1970).

My own work (1968) might be interpreted as suggesting not only the importance of an organisational pattern which facilitated occasional one to one pupil–teacher interaction, but also the fact that the level of performance a teacher expects from a pupil is an important factor in what performance is actually produced by him; this finding has been confirmed by Heider et al. (1968) and Williams and Naremore (1969). More general reviews of teachers' expectations and pupil performance have been summarised by Pidgeon (1970).

Another very important aspect of teachers' attitudes towards pupils is their attitude towards pupils' dialects: there is evidence (Williams, 1970) that some teachers adopt a punitive stance towards pupils whose speech they perceive as sub-standard. There is, of course, no linguistic justification for such judgements (Labov, 1970), but real damage is caused by teachers who feel that pupils' language must be suppressed and replaced by standard English. A great deal of progress would be possible if teachers thought in terms of appropriate and in-appropriate language according to context rather than of 'right' and 'wrong' language; in that case language development in schools would be seen as an extension of linguistic facility into a variety of contexts rather than a simple question of competence in vocabulary and grammar.

Much of the above research might well be interpreted as suggesting that a perfectly organised school with an excellent curriculum could still fail if teachers lacked the appropriate sensitivity and skills in making relationships with pupils. Undoubtedly this was one motive behind the Newsom recommendation that teachers should have sociology in-cluded in their educational studies. But it would be surprising if a limited knowledge of sociological theory produced any dramatic changes in teachers' classroom behaviour. As well as a knowledge of sub-cultural differences, teachers need to develop inter-personal and communication skills. To some extent these can only be acquired by practice—especially when teachers can later review their own perform-ance; but even practice in micro-teaching situations needs to be structured by some kind of theoretical framework. In the USA a great deal of work has been reported: Flanders (1970), Bellack *et al.* (1966); in the UK very interesting insights have been provided by Barnes (1969, 1971). Barnes (1969) examined in detail the pupil–teacher verbal inter-action during a variety of tape-recorded lessons (first year secondary school), and has suggested (Barnes, 1971) a model which might guide the training and re-training of teachers, having found that pupils were generally 'passive recipients of instruction, their role being mainly confined to indicating by short answers that they could rehearse what had previously been taught'. Barnes clearly thinks that such a role is incompatible with modern educational theory and that it is probably related to the teachers' role behaviour. His model of language and classroom learning may provide a very useful means of encouraging teachers to modify their role and their classroom style.

Summary

1 The idea of 'language deficit' has gradually yielded to the idea of 'language difference'.

2 The concept of 'compensatory education' is of very doubtful validity and distracts attention from real educational and social problems.

3 Language is closely related to 'context of situation', and therefore to questions of school organisation and grouping.

4 Language in education should be seen as an integral part of curriculum reform.

5 Teachers' attitudes and behaviour are crucial factors in pupils' linguistic behaviour and learning; teacher effectiveness can be seen largely in terms of verbal interaction.

6 Teacher education needs to be more concerned with language as a means of learning and with the dynamics of classroom communication.

7 More empirical work is needed—a useful model and suggestions for research have been put forward by Barnes (1971).

Conclusions

'The notion of verbal deprivation is a part of the modern mythology of educational psychology, typical of the unfounded notions which tend to expand rapidly in our educational system. In past decades linguists have been as guilty as others in promoting such intellectual fashions at the expense of both teachers and children. But the myth of verbal deprivation is particularly dangerous, because it diverts attention from real defects of our educational system to imaginary defects of the child' (Labov, 1970).

Labov was referring to the controversy about American negro children, but the same message might be applied to the language of working class pupils. Perhaps the clearest lesson to emerge from most of the above research is that we need to look for causes of educational failure *not* in a child's background (or a whole group's environment) but in the school itself, the curriculum and teachers' attitudes.

Elizabeth M. Anderson and Simon H. Haskell

Handicapped children

Handicapped children: Common problems

The general title of 'handicapped children' has been retained for this chapter, not because any attempt is made to cover the whole range of disabling physical, social, intellectual and emotional conditions which may constitute handicaps but rather in recognition of the fact that many educational needs are common to most categories of handicapped children and that research in any one field of special education may be of relevance to others. Particularly as regards the provision of services for the handicapped, there is a need for researchers to take into account the prevalence of handicapping conditions as a whole, and the extent to which they overlap. The last section will, therefore, be concerned with research which relates to handicapping conditions in general; the concept of multiple handicap and the provision of educational services for the handicapped will also be singled out for discussion.

The categorisation of handicaps

Awareness of the general needs of handicapped children does not imply that categorisation of handicaps is unimportant. As is pointed out in the report of a working party on children with special needs (Younghusband *et al.*, 1970), 'delineating a category helps to focus attention on it, and promotes the provision of the necessary resources. Reformulating categories from time to time in the light of experience and research is more than changing labels: it involves a re-thinking of the nature of special educational needs.'

The existing categories of handicapped children laid down in 1954 (HMSO 45) are 1) blind; 2) partially sighted; 3) deaf; 4) partially hearing; 5) ESN; 6) epileptic; 7) maladjusted; 8) physically handicapped; 9) speech defects; 10) delicate. Younghusband *et al.* suggested that these should be changed to 1) visual handicap; 2) hearing impairment; 3) physical handicap; 4) speech and language disorder; 5) specific learning disorder; 6) intellectual handicap; 7) emotional handicap; 8) severe personality disorder; 9) severe environmental handicap; 10) severe multi-handicap. While not all would agree in detail with the proposed reformulations, they reflect the principle that categorisation should be viewed not so much as a categorisation of handicaps or of children, but rather as a categorisation of special needs.

Since earlier volumes of *Educational Research in Britain* have included substantial accounts of research into maladjustment, backwardness and retardation, reading difficulties and environmental handicaps, we decided to concentrate on three of the remaining groups, 1) children with physical handicaps; 2) intellectually handicapped children; and 3) children with specific learning disorders. The first of these includes two major sub-groups, *a*) motor-handicapped children (in particular those with congenital abnormalities); and *b*) those with neurological abnormalities (the emphasis being on cerebral palsy, epilepsy and spina bifida). The intellectually handicapped group includes those children in ordinary or ESN schools, or what were training centres, whose primary difficulty is intellectual retardation. At present the third group of children with 'specific learning difficulties' does not constitute a recognised category, but the growing awareness of their problems suggests this will not be long in coming. Autistic children have been included as a sub-group here since the work of Hermelin and O'Connor (1970) in particular suggests that it is specific cognitive defects which account for the syndrome.

The extent of handicap in Britain

This introduction would be incomplete without an attempt to indicate the extent of handicapping conditions in children in Britain. In the 1964/5 surveys of nine to eleven year old children on the Isle of Wight (Rutter, Tizard and Whitmore, 1970) approximately one child in six was found to have a chronic or recurrent handicap. Four principal types of handicap were included: 1) intellectual retardation 2·6 per cent (IQ of 70 or less); 2) educational backwardness 7·9 per cent (this comprised mainly reading backwardness which was defined as a reading accuracy or comprehension age of at least 28 months below the level predicted on the basis of each child's short WISC IQ); 3) psychiatric disorder 5·4 per cent; 4) physical handicap 5·5 per cent. The authors suggest these figures should be taken as 'minimal' prevalence estimates for handicapping conditions.

Our aim in this chapter has, therefore, been to look firstly at research concerned with three particular groups of children—the physically handicapped; the intellectually handicapped; and those with specific learning disorders, and secondly to discuss research with more general implications. Most of the research under discussion has been carried out since 1963.

Physically handicapped children

I MOTOR-HANDICAPPED CHILDREN

Apart from the large national studies which have already been mentioned in earlier volumes, the main recent research investigations with this group have concerned children with thalidomide deformities.

In volume 2 a preliminary report was given of the pilot study being carried out in Scotland of the educational needs of these children and the results have now been published (Kellmer-Pringle and Fiddes, 1970). The intention was to include all thalidomide children in Scotland, but 26 per cent of the parents were unwilling to participate and only 80 children aged $4\frac{1}{2}$–$8\frac{1}{2}$ years were included. The key question of the study was whether this group were receiving 'the most suitable education to enable them to develop their assets to the fullest extent possible'.

The writers found that although most of the children were severely handicapped 'more than half concerned could well hold their own in ordinary day primary schools', only about a third needing special schooling. They felt that three in four of the children in the study were receiving suitable education; of the others, eight special school children needed a more stimulating environment, transfer to ordinary schools being recommended, while about six children in ordinary schools needed a less demanding or more specialised curriculum.

The authors also looked back at pre-school experiences and forward to adolescence. They concluded that pre-school education was clearly beneficial to this group and that 'it would be desirable to extend similar facilities to all the handicapped', while they thought adolescence 'would bring new and serious problems which should be anticipated now by setting up a psychological counselling service both for parents and children'.

In England a follow-up study of the functional abilities at home and at school of 119 children who had received training at Roehampton Children's Prosthetic Unit, and who had two or more limbs deficient, has been made (Robertson, personal communication). Apart from their limb deficiencies, half the children had one or more additional disabilities, 62 per cent having other skeletal disabilities, 32 per cent eye defects, 21 per cent hearing defects and 15 per cent defects of the cardiovascular system, so that overall they comprised a very severely handicapped group. Miss Robertson looked in particular at 1) the extent and nature of the difficulties at home and at school which might contribute to a child's failure to make satisfactory progress in independence; and 2) how this was affected by the wearing of prostheses. Most of the children were in primary schools, 69 per cent being in ordinary schools and 31 per cent in special schools, and 91 per cent of the class teachers questioned felt the placement had been appropriate. Half of the children needed some help in school: often this help was minimal and only nine auxiliary helpers were employed specifically to help the handicapped children. Poor mobility was felt to be a greater barrier to classroom integration than the child's need for help in personal matters, and children with severe bilateral lower limb deficiencies had greater difficulty in making normal relationships. Despite this, the handicapped children were very well accepted. Children with similar disabilities tended to achieve greater independence in activities of daily living if they were at ordinary schools rather than special schools, but fewer children in ordinary schools participated in group activities.

A serious lack of liaison exists between teachers and para-medical staff, and teachers and parents: 'Most of the parents seemed unaware of what their children did at school and had often not even met the class teacher let alone passed on information about special equipment.' Suggestions sent to the school were usually put into practice but, after a year, especially when the child moved into another class, his special requirements might be overlooked.

2 CHILDREN WITH NEUROLOGICAL ABNORMALITIES

The other major group of 'physically handicapped' children comprises those with neurological abnormalities. In this section we are concerned in particular with children handicapped by cerebral palsy, epilepsy and spina bifida.

Cerebral palsy (CP). There is a limited but growing amount of research concerning cerebral palsied children. Such studies can be divided into two broad categories: firstly surveys of the medical and clinical aspects of this condition, and secondly experimental and predictive studies of the effects of neurological abnormalities and environmental influences upon perceptual, social, language and motor skills, and also on scholastic attainments. Several authors emphasise the greater susceptibility of the young neurologically impaired child to inadequate environmental experiences, compared with the 'non-brain-damaged' physically handicapped child.

Survey findings of incidence and prevalence rates of CP vary, these differences being explicable either in terms of differing diagnostic criteria and terminology used by clinicians, or the suitability of sampling techniques. Among the studies reporting on the prevalence of CP in Britain, the most reliable was that carried out on the Isle of Wight (Rutter *et al.*, 1971). Children in the following clinical categories were excluded: transient motor disorder, degenerative diseases of the brain, brain damage caused by abnormalities of the spinal cord, the exceptionally clumsy and uncoordinated, as well as the 'minimally brain injured', and each child's neurological status was ascertained after a systematic clinical examination. On the basis of a smaller number of cases the authors reported that 4·6 per 1 000 children in the ten to twelve year age group were CP, a rate higher than that reported in other surveys. However, in a larger survey of 11 865 five to fourteen year olds, a rate of 2·9 per 1 000 was established.

A survey which has influenced provision for CP children was that conducted under the auspices of the Carnegie UK Trust. Their findings were published in 1964 and an innovative model school for children with mixed handicaps was set up afterwards. The team carried out systematic studied of CP children in Glasgow, Sheffield and Shropshire. They found that over two thirds of the children in all three centres studied had multiple handicaps and one third were emotionally disturbed, and nearly 80 per cent of the children were not making social contacts with normal peers. It was felt that one third of the children could have been helped if treatment had been available, and in 28 per cent of the cases referrals were unjustifiably delayed. Nearly 25 per cent of the children were not receiving adequate attention. A number of specific recommendations were made for each region. Another important enquiry of a rather different kind was carried out by Hewett (1970) in the East Midlands. Of the 125 school age spastic children in her sample, 26 were having no education or day care while 37 per cent were not provided for in any way by the LAs. Only 10 per cent of the two to four year olds were being provided with pre-school care or training. Twenty-six per cent of the school-age children attended ordinary schools and Hewett found that in general teachers and LEAS were prepared to be helpful and flexible. Only 11 per cent went to special day schools while 30 per cent had home teaching. It was felt that 'the provision of residential care for severely mentally and physically handicapped children was not adequate to meet demand.'

Other surveys have been concerned with the educational and intellectual abilities of CP children. Bowley (1967) followed up 96 educable CPs who had attended the Cheyne Walk Spastic Centre before the age of seven years. Only 15 pupils had been transferred to ordinary schools; two thirds of the group were maintaining satisfactory educational progress and only a very small number were 'maladjusted'.

At the other end of the intellectual range Garfield and Shakespeare (1964) reported on their findings with the severely subnormal CPS. Ninety two children between three and fifteen years were rated on a scale developed by the authors to assess social, locomotor and sensory motor development. Comparisons were made with Piaget's stages of growth in normal children. They found that some maturational development occurred but that generally the children remained very retarded and highly dependent on nursing staff. The authors felt that the children required systematic training in social skills to enable them to lead more independent lives.

Where experimental studies are concerned, the perceptual and visuo-motor disorders of CP children have traditionally attracted considerable attention among research psychologists and have been usefully summarised by Abercrombie (1964). In a number of papers Abercrombie (1960, 1963, 1964) herself has argued that the difficulties of CPs, particularly spastics, in copying simple line figures have their origin in disordered movement, especially oculo-motor defects. She has made the useful distinction between visuo-perceptual and visuo-motor or constructional difficulties. In a series of experiments in which the eye movements of normal and CP children were compared she hypothesised

that a child with such disorders as a squint is 'working on noisy channels; half the time he is getting information from other parts of the
visual field than his targets' (Connolly, 1970). Squinting, according to
Abercrombie, handicaps visuo-perceptual development. This hypothesis was examined by Haskell and Hughes (1965) who compared 30
non CP children with varying degrees of squint (using similar orthoptic
and intellectual criteria as in the Abercrombie study). The authors
failed to confirm that squinters were poorer on the WISC, though
there was a tendency for alternating squinters to be more handicapped
than children with uniocular squints. On a larger sample of normal
children with alternating and uniocular squints, Haskell (1972a) failed
to confirm that alternating vision proved a handicap to educational
attainment on visuo-perceptual and visuo-motor performance.

Wedell (1960a, 1960b, 1961) examined the perceptual ability of CPs
in a series of systematic experiments. In the first study (Wedell, 1960a)
the perceptual ability of four matched groups of CP children (athetoid
and spastics with bilateral, left sided and right sided motor defect) were
compared with each other on a number of tests which included matching cards, light tracing, copying models with bricks, placing parts of a
face in appropriate places, and assembling the parts of a manikin. This
experiment was designed with exceptional care and the data analysis
was thorough. Two unusual findings emerged; that right hemiplegics
showed an absence of perceptual impairment and errors of reversal or
rotation often reported in studies, and that specific forms of perceptual
impairment were not found in CP subjects as a group. When he followed up (Wedell, 1961) thirty six of the children in the 1960 sample
the superior performance of the right over the left hemiplegics was
maintained over a two and a half year interval.

Tyson (1964) investigated tactile perceptual disability in CPs using
a shape matching test in which children were required to select the
correct shape by touch alone. Of the fifteen CP children tested, eight
showed weakness in tactile shape recognition and in comparison with
the 'non-brain damaged group' the difference was significant.

Connolly's experimental studies of the motor behaviour of CP
children marks an important development in this area. His concern to
modify aberrant motor behaviour has practical appeal to both teachers
and therapists. Connolly (1970) asks whether damage to the motor
system in CPs is irrevocable or whether there is remaining plasticity and
scope for training. He hypothesises that the unskilled motor perform-

ance of cps is due to 'inadequate kinesthetic feedback' so that difficulties in monitoring their performance arise. cp children, he argues, encounter difficulty in selecting and interpreting the relevant cues in the neuro-muscular system creating 'signal noise' (in information theory terms) and in extracting 'signal' from 'noise'.

Connolly (1968) carried out an experiment in training more accurate hand movements in hemiplegics using operant conditioning techniques. The apparatus is an interesting 'toy' consisting of a clown's face mounted in a frame. The child is required to touch the clown's nose and control of accurate movement is exercised through reinforcement such as the extinguishing of nose light, or eyes lighting up. The clown also encourages the child with a 'Well done', or Smarties are dispensed.

Connolly and his associates have demonstrated the feasibility of rapidly shaping crude motor responses of cp children to much finer ones, the results being fairly long lasting. He points out that 'if motor responses can be brought under control by applying feedback in another modality (visual) then it might be possible to shift the control to the kinesthetic/proprioceptive system by suitable training pro-cedures'. In other words he raises the exciting possibility of training one modality by another.

Educational studies are few and far between; the few existing studies of the impairment of arithmetical skills in cps have been reviewed by Haskell (1967). The author carried out an experiment in which a group of twenty one cp children aged nine to sixteen years were instructed for thirteen weeks in the four basic rules of arithmetic through teaching machines. A similar matched group was taught by conventional methods. No significant differences in achievement between the groups were noted but such differences as there were favoured pro-grammed instruction. Success in arithmetic was also found to correlate highly with spatial and non-verbal items of tests (Haskell, 1972b).

Phillips and White (1964) compared twenty three cp children whose motor disability occurred very early with thirty two ph children without congenital brain damage, both groups being carefully matched for age and motor disability. Reading and even more so, arithmetic attainment was significantly lower in the cp group.

Spina bifida The increasing numbers of spina bifida children surviving infancy have presented a wide variety of administrative, educational and social problems. Unfortunately the quality of the research on the medical side has not been paralleled on the educational side, with the exception of a very small number of studies and investigations into the intellectual development of the children. These have been generally confined to the use of global 'norm-referenced' IQ tests, or to the obtaining of a development quotient on the Griffiths Scale, the result often being presented without any indication of the age of the subjects or of the test used. The position is changing slowly, especially as psychologists and educationalists are coming to realise that many spina bifida children, in particular those with hydrocephalus, have learning difficulties about which little is yet known.

A series of epidemiological surveys make clear the wide variation in the incidence of the disorder. Laurence (1966) gave a figure of four per 1 000 for the mining area of Glamorgan, estimating the national average as about half this: Henderson (1968) thought it probably 'less than two per 1 000' while Spain (1970) suggests (for the GLC area) about 1·5 per 1 000. There is general agreement that roughly 50 per cent will survive to school age. Lorber (1971) in a major survey of children treated at Sheffield states that 42 per cent of the children in his first series (born 1959/63) survived to two years, while 62 per cent in his second series (born 1967/68) did so. There can now be no doubt that children with spina bifida cystica will comprise a very significant proportion of all physically handicapped children. Forrester (1967), looking at the whole population of motor handicapped children in Wigan and parts of Lancashire felt 'the incidence could easily equal that of cerebral palsy' while Henderson (1968) in discussing the changing pattern of disabilities in Britain also singled out this group for comment.

Frequently these children have associated hydrocephalus: in Lorber's group of children born in 1967/68 63 per cent had hydrocephalus to the extent that insertion of a drainage valve was required, a further 21 per cent had mild hydrocephalus with no shunt and only 4 per cent were without hydrocephalus. Lorber has also grouped the 1959/63 group into five categories, taking into account severity of handicap and IQ. He found that 3 per cent of surviving children had no physical handicap; 15 per cent had a moderate handicap; 49 per cent had a severe handicap (lack of sphincter control and extensive paralysis) combined with an IQ of 80+; 21 per cent had a severe handicap and an IQ in the range 61–79, while 12 per cent had 'extreme' handicaps and IQs below 60.

A study specifically concerned with the assessment of the educational needs of the children was that of Burns (1967) who carried out a full-scale investigation of the physical defects and mental capacity of all children born in Liverpool between 1960 and 1963 with encephalocele and meningocele. Again there was a clear indication that the bulk of the children with myelomeningocele and hydrocephalus fell into the IQ range 70–90. Burns thought that approximately 33 per cent would be suitable for ordinary schools, 54 per cent would need special schooling and 9 per cent were unsuitable for education.

Interesting work on the abilities and attainments of spina bifida children is being done by Tew at the Welsh National School of Medicine. Two studies of current interest are, firstly, that of Laurence and Tew (1967) who have been carrying out a follow-up study of the 65 spina bifida survivors born in South Wales between 1956 and 1962. The children are now aged nine to fifteen years; each is being given the WISC and the Bender Gestalt and tests of reading, spelling, arithmetic and the Bristol Social Adjustment Guide, and teachers and parents are being sent questionnaires.

The other group Tew (personal communication, 1971) is studying is a group of 59 children born between 1964 and 1966. At five and a half years old each child is tested on the WPPSI, Developmental Test of Visual Perception, Reynell Scale and Vineland Scale and the teachers complete a questionnaire on attainment, while at seven years reading, spelling and arithmetic tests are given. A Bristol Social Adjustment Guide is completed by the class teacher and also a questionnaire on concentration span, language, etc. The relationship between severity of handicap and disturbed behaviour in the sibs is also being explored and findings should be available in mid-1973.

Another major study is being carried out by Spain (1969, 1970) in the Greater London Council area. This study is designed to provide information on which the planning of special educational services can be based. It has three main aspects: 1) first, a prevalence study was made of all cases of spina bifida under the age of sixteen living within the Greater London Council area. Over 600 cases have been traced and details about handicaps, schooling and operative treatment collected; 2) second, an incidence study was carried out which suggested a rate of 1·5 per 1 000. This would produce about two hundred children with spina bifida or anencephaly in the GLC area each year of whom probably about ninety to one hundred will survive to school age. Spain suggests that 50–60 per cent of these will require places in schools for the physically handicapped at least at the primary level; 3) third, Spain is carrying out a follow-up study of children born with spina bifida between April 1967 and March 1969. One hundred and sixty one children were assessed at about one year old on the Griffiths Scale. Spain estimated that about 26 per cent of the true spina bifida group were reasonably normal in all respects at this age, a further 56 per cent were normal apart from locomotor and bladder functions and 18 per cent were below normal in most functions, including at least 6 per cent who were severely subnormal. As a group, children with hydrocephalus and a valve did poorly on tests involving hand-eye coordination, this deficit being even more noticeable in two to three year olds who scored poorly on tasks such as bead-threading, use of a pencil or building a tower of bricks. Spain thought this 'consistent finding' unlikely to be due entirely to visual defects and that it 'may imply some kind of cortical or brain-stem damage, specifically affecting the finer hand movements or perception of shapes which would have important implications for the teaching of such children'.

Of particular interest are the studies recently carried out at Hull University and the Hull Royal Infirmary by Miller and Sethi (1971a, 1971b). During 1969–70 they carried out a series of experiments designed to look at spatial and motor deficits in children who had had infantile hydrocephalus. Their subjects were sixteen hydrocephalics (with or without spina bifida) most of whom were in special PH schools and who had IQs of 70 to 100. Controls (matched for CA and sex) were neurologically normal children in ordinary schools. Experiments I–II (Miller and Sethi, 1971a) were concerned with the perception of visuo-spatial relationships. Results on the Bender Gestalt and Frostig Tests suggested that children with hydrocephalus have extremely poor visuo-spatial perception. There was also a special difficulty in figure-ground discrimination and this was confirmed even when poor motor coordination and verbal coding were controlled for. Experiment III showed that the figure-background difficulty was not an artifact of stimulus complexity and that hydrocephalics were much less able than normals to ignore irrelevant background material.

In the fourth experiment (Miller and Sethi, 1971b) the authors attempted to extend the findings on vision to the tactile modality. They found that, unlike subnormals, hydrocephalics were specifically impaired in the perception of tactile stimuli. They also hypothesised that the stretching of the corpus callosum which has been reported to occur in hydrocephalics might result in an attenuated form of the disturbances found in 'split brain' subjects and might explain the mild degree of dyspraxia seen in the child, and their results appear to offer some evidence for this.

Finally the authors looked at impairments in motor behaviour (Miller, 1971, personal communication). They showed firstly that hydrocephalic children were 'grossly impaired' in manual speed as compared with normals, and secondly that this impairment was truly a motor difficulty and not due to a slower decision-making process.

The experimental approach these studies embody should stimulate research of a much needed kind, and the results do confirm the existence in these children of specific deficits which have hereto only been implied by clinical observations.

As Tizard (1968) points out, the findings from a now sizeable number of studies 'indicate that substantial numbers of educable children with meningomyelocele survive to school age and adolescence. . . . The great need is to provide adequate services.' While children with spina bifida comprise quite a diverse group as regards both intellectual development and severity of handicap, the largest sub-group will probably comprise children in the IQ range 70–90 (that is of 'borderline' educational normality), most of whom will have arrested hydrocephalus and will suffer from a lack of sphincter control and limited mobility: many will probably also have rather specific cognitive impairments. Placement decisions will therefore be difficult, particularly as local authorities vary enormously in the range of facilities they offer both within and outside the ordinary school system.

Epilepsy There have been very few research studies concerned directly with the special educational treatment of children with epilepsy. Generally, interest has been focused upon surveys of its incidence and prevalence. The incidence of this disorder in children is differently estimated by various authors, owing partly to the differing criteria used by clinicians and partly to the immense difficulty in establishing the extent to which some transient forms of epilepsy, like petit mal, occur. A summary of the surveys carried out during 1946–60 given in the report of the Principal School Medical Officer (HMSO, 1962) shows variations in estimates from 0·62 to 7·4 per thousand in the five to fourteen school age population.

The College of General Practitioners survey (1960) indicated that 5 per 1 000 in all age groups were affected with epilepsy. A decade later the 10 w study established that in ten to twelve year old children (Rutter et al., 1970a) epilepsy occurred in 8·9 per 1 000 children in this age group. The authors distinguished between those with epilepsy and other 'complicating' conditions like CP and those in whom fits occurred over the past year, as well as those on a regular course of drugs. The prevalence of 'uncomplicated epilepsy in children was 6·4 per 1 000'. Those with fits over the last year accounted for 4·9 per 1 000, and 4·0 per 1 000 were on drugs. The vast majority of children with epilepsy, particularly those with uncomplicated neurological disorders, attend ordinary schools.

Attempts to observe the selective effects of various clinical forms of epilepsy like temporal lobe epilepsy or petit mal on cognitive functioning and educational achievement form the basis of enquiries reported here. Ounsted et al. (1963) reported that some children with petit mal epilepsy suffered from 'retrograde amnesia'.

Temporal lobe epilepsy, the commonest form of focal epileptic discharges, has been studied by Ounsted and his colleagues (Ounsted et al., 1966) in one of the most systematic studies of its kind. The authors considered the manner in which this form of epilepsy affected intellectual development and also examined the interaction between epilepsy and environmental conditions at home and school. One hundred children below the age of sixteen years were selected from a larger clinic population of nearly 1 000 patients. All the children were examined on a battery of tests including neurological, ophthalmological, speech and psychometric measures. The following clinical groups within the sample were compared:

a) children with acquired brain damage and with chronic signs of cerebral insult;
b) those without anatomical insults, but one or more episodes of status epilepticus;
c) those without status or gross insult to the brain.

The findings on intellectual tests lay in the expected direction. Children in the first two groups obtained similar verbal and performance scores as measured on the WISC. Children without a history of status epilepticus or severe brain damage had a mean IQ of 104·7 and performance score of 105·4 and their mean IQs were significantly higher than that of either group a) or b).

The authors hypothesise that it is the early occurrence of status epilepticus or acute insults in children and not necessarily temporal lobe epilepsy which affects intellectual ability when 'early structures of learning' are being laid down.

Rutter et al. (1970b) carried out an interesting clinical study of a group of 138 children between the ages of nine and eleven years with uncomplicated and complicated epilepsy, this being the original sample identified in the Isle of Wight survey (children with complicated epilepsy were those who suffered from other forms of brain disorder which were associated with structural abnormality of the brain, mainly cerebral palsy, and whose epilepsy was presumably secondary to the basic brain disorder). The IQ distribution, as measured on the WISC, was normal (mean score 102). Children with lesions below the brain stem had a mean IQ of 107 compared with the mean IQs of 78 and 74 of those with complicated epilepsy and other brain disorders, respectively. Most children with complicated epilepsy had significantly discrepant scores between their verbal and performance scores on the WISC. Only half the children with epilepsy were reading adequately, whilst 18 per cent were at least two years retarded in their reading comprehension as measured on the Neale analysis of reading ability. Over 40 per cent of children above the age of eight with complicated epilepsy were retarded by at least two years in their reading, whereas in the random control group only 6·8 per cent were retarded. When intelligence was partialled out, children with uncomplicated epilepsy and of normal intelligence still showed specific reading handicaps. Absence from school was an inadequate explanation, as children with physical handicaps but without brain damage, missing as much schooling, showed a much lower rate of reading retardation. It was suggested that poor reading is in part due to the direct effects of brain dysfunction in children. The authors also found that the rate of psychiatric disorder in epileptics (34·3 per cent) was five times that in the general population.

The educational performance of 118 children with uncomplicated epilepsy was examined by Bagley (1970). The children (74 boys and 44 girls with a mean chronological age of 12·6 years and WISC IQ of 99·2) were consecutive referrals to a teaching hospital. Bagley looked at social, psychological and medical factors likely to influence educational performance. On a behaviour questionnaire (Rutter, 1967a) completed by teachers, 40 per cent of the children were identified as presenting serious psychiatric symptoms. While reading retardation was associated with psychiatric disorder, arithmetical retardation was associated with epilepsy.

Mentally handicapped

I EDUCATIONALLY SUBNORMAL CHILDREN (ESN)

The volume and diversity of experimental work carried out with ESN children has been considerably less than in the field of the severely subnormal (SSN).

In an earlier volume Lovell (1968) has reviewed studies on educational backwardness over the period 1962–6 and Chazan (1967) has also reported on a number of research studies on ESN children in England and Wales. Only subsequent studies are considered here.

One of the newer developments in the assessment of learning difficulties in intellectual backwardness has been based on the work of Gedye (Gedye and Wedgwood, 1966) who used an automated testing/recording device to investigate learning problems in head injury of geriatric patients. Davies and Needham (personal communication, 1971) used an apparatus which allowed a subject to 'learn' how to use the machine and then took him through a series of tasks using different strategies for each of four problems to be solved. The performance of the child is automatically recorded by linking the machine to a teletypewriter and the analysis carried out on a general purpose digital computer.

The study in question was a pilot one, and work is continuing on this project, but the preliminary results indicated that the subnormal child's poorer performance is 'non-transitory and is related to poor reading and comprehension and behaviour difficulty'. The authors recommend that further work be carried out to confirm the diagnostic value of apparatus and to deploy strategically the limited time of educational psychologists. Profile analysis of children's performance is also recommended to teachers planning remedial programmes.

The language of ESN children is another major subject of enquiry.

Graham (personal communication, 1970) carried out a four-fold study
of language deficits including:

a) examination of the nature of language deficits;
b) development of diagnostic measure of language deficiencies;
c) development of language programmes;
d) development of evaluation instruments.

Graham looked at failures in terms of lack of structural knowledge
and functional weaknesses, and hypothesised that poor language skills
in ESN children arose from deficiencies in short term memory (STM).
A variety of tests measuring STM were devised and applied, and measures of cognitive abilities and neurological and behavioural characteristics obtained, 90 pupils aged three and a half to seven years from
nursery, primary and ESN schools taking part.

The main finding was that language deficiencies in ESN children
were associated with poor STM, and the STM is a good guide to estimating language adequacy. The hypothesis that defects in STM storage
leads to disordered encoding and decoding of continuous speech was
confirmed.

The attainments of children in ESN schools and the remedial departments of ordinary schools were compared by Ascher (1970 and
personal communication 1971) as regards progress in reading and
arithmetic and attitudes towards teachers. Overall, children in normal
schools progressed more rapidly in both reading and arithmetic.

Other studies such as those of Chazan (1964, 1965) and Williams
(1966) suggest that ESN children are often multiply handicapped.
Chazan noted that over a third of ESN children in South Wales were
maladjusted, and Williams that the greater proportion came from
social classes IV and V. A number of studies reviewed by Chazan
(1967) confirm that ESN special school children often have additional
physical, sensory, social and emotional problems.

A comparatively new area of research in the field of educational
subnormality concerns the contribution which programmed instruction can make, and one particularly interesting current project is that
being carried out at the Programmed Learning Research Unit, Jordanhill College of Education (Hodge, personal communication) into the
application of structured materials and equipment to the educational
needs of handicapped children.

The aims of this study are:

   a) to evaluate the effectiveness of programmed materials for teaching handicapped children in reading, oral and writing skills,
   number and social skills;
   b) to assess the relative effectiveness of different methods of presenting programmes for different types of handicaps;
   c) to examine the attitudes of children with specific handicaps to the
   use of programmes, teaching machines and equipment.

The children concerned include i) mentally handicapped children in the
IQ range 50–70; ii) the physically handicapped including both those
with neurological and motor handicaps; iii) deaf and partially hearing
children.

   Areas of particular interest to the research staff are:

   i)   definition of the specific learning problems associated with each
        type of handicap;
   ii) definition of learning objectives within each class of handicap in
        terms of reading, oral, writing, number and social skills, and the
        order of priorities;
   iii) diagnostic tests and procedures for obtaining specific learning
        capabilities and needs;
   iv) decision structures to enable teachers to decide what materials
        can be used to remedy learning difficulties after these have been
        accurately diagnosed.

A survey has already been conducted into the needs and problems
of 1 333 children in twelve secondary special schools in Glasgow, the
majority of whom were mentally handicapped with a mean IQ of 68.
The authors criticise the type of tests used to assess these pupils, especially the global type tests such as the Stanford-Binet and wisc which
provide little information to teachers either about specific learning
difficulties or about the kind of remedial treatment necessary.

   Serious problems also existed concerning the materials used, including:

   a) lack of materials designed specifically for use by handicapped
   pupils;
   b) their relevance to the needs of secondary mentally handicapped
   pupils about to leave school;
   c) the interest level of the materials;
   d) their structure and grading;

e) absence of materials constructed to encourage and facilitate self-study and self-assessment;

f) absence of a resources centre in Glasgow where teachers could have access to new materials, equipment and test instruments and where evaluation of their effectiveness with handicapped pupils could be undertaken.

In the light of these findings the unit is now undertaking or planning projects in the following areas:

   i) definition of objectives in special schools' curricula in terms of the social skills required by children on leaving school;

  ii) development of devices for presenting materials to children with different categories and degrees of handicaps;

 iii) development of a resources centre for special schools;

 iv) development of materials designed specifically for special schools;

  v) evaluation of commercially and teacher-produced materials.

2 SEVERELY SUBNORMAL CHILDREN (SSN)

In April 1971 responsibility for the SN and SSN in England and Wales was transferred from the health authorities to education, psychologists having been particularly articulate in challenging the neglectful educational provision and concern for subnormal children, and in demonstrating in convincing ways that subnormal children were worthy of being 'educated'.

A number of surveys were carried out to establish the prevalence or mental subnormality in selected areas of England and Wales (Clarke and Clarke, 1965; Tizard, 1964; Kushlick, 1964, 1965; Birch *et al*, 1970) and these investigations helped pinpoint the nature and extent of gaps in financial and human resources available for such children especially in the large mental subnormality hospitals. The Scott report (Ministry of Health, 1962) was a landmark in that it drew attention to the lamentable situation in subnormality hospitals and showed that 82 per cent of the teachers in hospital schools were unqualified. Three years later the British Psychological Society set up a working party to examine among other things the characteristics of facilities for children in subnormality hospitals. The main findings of this survey were reported by Mittler and Woodward (1966). The working party surveyed admissions to seventeen hospitals and looked at the IQ assessment and physical and behavioural characteristics of 403 children under the age of sixteen and at educational facilities.

The main findings showed that 75 per cent were classified as SSN and 25 per cent had one or more additional disorders of motor or sensory function, or of behaviour. Whilst the number of qualified staff in this group of hospitals exceeded that of the national average for such schools, the educational facilities were exceedingly poor. Only 13 per cent of the staff were qualified teachers and there was no indication that the more intelligent children were being taught by them. Only 9 out of the 403 children had been transferred to ordinary schools. The suitability of subnormality hospitals as educational establishments was challenged yet again, especially because of the chronic shortage of qualified staff, and the 'isolation of these institutions from the mainstream of education' remained. Cogent arguments were advanced for the abandonment of the artificial divisions between children regarded as likely or unlikely to benefit from education in normal or special schools.

The belief that rapid educational benefits will result from a change in nomenclature and administrative reorganisation is unjustified. Substantial differences in trained teacher personnel, between Junior Training Centres and subnormality hospitals and special schools, still exist. Nonetheless the authorities are aware of these inadequacies and plans for the rapid expansion of teacher training facilities have been initiated.

In the area of psychological research much valuable work is being done and it is only possible to report here a few of the extensive investigations into such aspects of learning problems of the SSN as learning strategies, cognitive styles, language, social and motor skills, problem solving, concept formation, attentional defects, to name but a few.

Excellent reviews of experimental studies on learning processes in severely subnormal children exist (O'Connor and Hermelin, 1963; Clarke and Clarke, 1965; O'Connor and Hermelin, 1971), O'Connor and Hermelin emphasising that it is '. . . deficits in acquisition rather than poor perception, or transfer ability' which characterise the learning ability of SSNs.

Bryant (1967) has carried out a series of careful experiments in an endeavour to study the relevant features of a task and the learning strategies used by SSN children. An account of his investigations into the language and learning skills of SSNs and normal children appears in a recent volume edited by Richards (1970).

Bryant designed a series of six experiments using imbecile and normal children as subjects. The subjects were required to solve a new task using different materials, having learned a conceptual strategy on the initial learning task. The effects of negative or positive learning, and its facilitation through language, were considered, and also whether familiarity of stimulus material, length of learning period, type of material, reward and so on enhance learning. Bryant (1967) observed that in simple colour sorting discrimination tasks normals and subnormals use different learning strategies. Subnormals, according to Bryant, learn the two responses independently whilst normals do not use this strategy.

There had been some controversy as to the role of language in mediating learning. Bryant (1964) has demonstrated that in some situations the use of language 'for some subnormals is profitable' while in others 'it is harmful'. O'Connor and Hermelin (1963) argue that it is not the language ability of retarded subjects which is affected but rather their inability and lack of opportunity to use language effectively. Luria's work, on the other hand, suggests that learning can be greatly enhanced when accompanied by verbal training (Luria, 1961). Luria and his associates have shown that SSN children were helped when verbal instructions accompanied single actions like squeezing a rubber bulb, and that learning through the 'second signal system' (with the help of speech), whilst more difficult, is necessary for the intellectually handicapped because the child can control his motor behaviour by his own verbal responses.

Another area in which SSN children were considered to be superior to normals was in stereognostic recognition. Mackay and MacMillan (1968) replicated the study by Hermelin and O'Connor (1961) in which it was noted that imbecile children were better on a tactual exploration recognition task than were normals of equivalent mental age. Using normal children and adults SSN matched for MA, they compared performance in stereognostic recognition of familiar material where verbal coding may have been used. Both groups obtained higher scores on familiar material, but normals were superior on recognition of familiar objects whilst SSN performed better on unfamiliar material. It was hypothesised that the stereognostic ability in SSN was unaffected by cerebral damage.

Interest in the conceptualising ability of ssn children is well represented in a series of experiments carried out by Clarke, Clarke and
Cooper (1971). The authors described two recent series of experiments
in the first of which normal and retarded children of varying ages were
required to categorise, rather than match, response cards against
stimulus cards, following a period of training. In the second series
normal and retarded children, undergraduates and retarded adults,
recalled lists of categorisable words. The overall aims were to establish
whether the ability to categorise can be learned and improved through
training on different tasks and materials, and how far the nature of the
training determines that ability. Results did establish the relationship
between training and transfer and suggested that, in experimental
conditions at least, a high degree of transfer can be achieved immediately and sustained as a result of complex rather than difficult category
training, especially when subjects are aware of the possibilities and the
need for categorisation. The authors also came down in favour of the
importance of motivational rather than attentional features in learning
and felt that the value of early learning could be reduced in the absence
of long term reinforcement.

The desire to translate the results of research findings into instructional techniques has long been the concern of several psychologists
working in the field of subnormality. This need is being met at the
Hester Atrian Research Centre (HARC) whose work is described by its
Director, Dr. Mittler, in another chapter of this book. Much of the
experimental work on cognitive functioning is similar to that carried
out in psychology departments of universities. There is, however, an
emphasis on the application of research for the practitioner, and investigations are often set outside laboratory setting. It is the hope of the
HARC that collaborative research by teachers and psychologists will
lead to the development of suitable remedial programmes. One such
joint research programme was undertaken at the University of Newcastle upon Tyne by Arnot, Gorton and Simpson (1967). The investigation was concerned with ways in which teachers could stimulate
the development of language of young mentally handicapped children.
Forty teachers and classes using different approaches and a smaller
number of classes acting as controls participated in this study. The
vocabulary, language structure and use of language of 260 children in
the experiment and 105 in the control groups between the ages of
five and thirteen were investigated. Teachers carried out the pre- and

post-testing programmes as well as devising their own language stimulation scheme, with the assistance and advice of research workers from the University. The programme was carried out over four terms and the results showed that children in the experimental group made greater gains than those who did not receive help. It was shown that the particular methods used in the schools were unimportant and that a knowledge of the language development of children was a crucial factor in determining successful stimulation.

3 CHILDREN WITH SPECIFIC LEARNING DIFFICULTIES

Terminology Much confusion still exists about the terminology used to describe those children who do not have known organic neurological abnormalities and who do not fit into any of the existing categories of handicap but whose performance in certain areas indicates the existence of specific disorders. They have been described as having 'minimal' or 'diffuse' brain damage or dysfuntcion, as suffering from specific cognitive defects, or specific learning disorders, or showing maturational lag or developmental difficulties or, according to the behaviour shown, they are labelled as 'hyperkinetic', 'dyslexic', or simply 'clumsy'. As Bortner (1968) points out, 'the diagnostic and administrative label of "minimal brain damage" has been extended to embrace a huge spectrum of disorders ranging from relatively circumscribed specific disorders in motor, sensory and behavioural organisation to profound disturbances in behaviour and intellect.'

Some of this confusion can be avoided if the suggestions made by Rutter (1967b) are adopted. He felt that the term 'brain damage' was best used as a general one to include a number of different syndromes which all result from some kind of impaired functioning of the brain and that these could be divided into two broad groups. The first would include definite abnormalities of function, in particular cerebral palsy and epilepsy; these have been discussed earlier. The second would include disorders where there are limits or delays in the development of normal functions, the main ones listed by Rutter being retardation of speech development, severe clumsiness, reading retardation and the hyperkinetic syndrome.

All these syndromes except the last could be included under the definition given by Kirk (1962) of a specific learning disability as referring to 'retardation, disorder or delayed development in one or more of the processes of speech, language, reading, spelling, writing or arithmetic, resulting from a possible cerebral dysfunction and from emotional or behavioural disturbance and not from mental retardation, sensory deprivation or cultural or instructional factors'.

This is clearly a wide area, some of which, especially reading disorders, has been covered in earlier volumes, and in this section only a few studies are considered.

SPECIFIC LEARNING DISORDERS

Children with specific learning disorders are likely to be found in ordinary schools and may be very difficult to detect. Francis-Williams (1970) investigated the identification of such children at the pre-school stage. In her study forty four children of normal intelligence aged three to four years, who had been noted at birth as having minor neurological dysfunction, were compared with sixty three normal controls on a battery of tests, as well as rating scales of concentration, independence and capacity for cooperation. The results showed that the children with neurological dysfunction were significantly poorer in language development, ability to copy forms, conceptualising and development of the self concept than the controls, and that their test results showed wider variability. They were also significantly more dependent, had poorer concentration and were less cooperative. Francis-Williams concluded that the following 'should be regarded as signals that a child at three to five years is showing dysfunction or deviant development which produces specific learning difficulties in school:

1 lack of clarity in speech or failure to use language as a symbolic process and to integrate its use into the performance of other learning tasks;
2 difficulties in visuo-spatial performance;
3 clumsiness or awkwardness of movement, difficulties of praxis, delayed sense of body image;
4 more than normal distractability and limited attention span'.

She discusses ways in which such children can be helped before they start formal school and at school itself, referring in particular to the work of Tyson (1963).

Bowley (1969) attempted to detect the incidence of minimal cerebral dysfunction in ordinary junior schools and to plan suitable remedial methods. Her study included 2 280 children in the IQ range of 80–113. 1·49 per cent of the children had disabilities in reading and writing, language development or manual dexterity which retarded educational progress. All were retarded in language and many had marked weaknesses in visual and auditory memory as tested on the ITPA. On the evidence of the psychological assessment and of the neurological examination Bowley concluded that although delayed language development, late talking, limited vocabulary and poor auditory or visual memory and sequencing were the most evident simple causes of reading retardation, other factors suggested minimal cerebral dysfunction affecting speech development, motor control, manual dexterity and perception. A remedial programme based on programmed teaching, speech therapy and occupational therapy produced, after a year, 'quite a dramatic improvement in reading and in the child's general attitude'.

Other studies have concentrated more on specific areas of difficulty, for example visuo-motor skills, that is, those requiring movement under visual control, visuo-motor disorders sometimes appearing in children whose spatial abilities are unimpaired. While their existence in subjects with neurological abnormalities has long been known (Abercrombie, 1964; Abercrombie et al., 1964; Wedell, 1964, 1968), recent research suggests they may exist to a significant degree in apparently 'normal' children.

Brenner, Gillman, Zangwill and Farrell (1967) investigated the extent of this disorder in 810 Cambridgeshire school children aged eight to nine years. All but one of the children with visuo-motor disabilities were identified by screening procedures designed to provide normative data on the range of visuo-motor skills in children of this age. Thirty one children (3·8 per cent) had visuo-motor test scores two standard deviations or more below the mean. Fourteen of the more severely affected children and fourteen controls were observed for three years; while only two of the handicapped children made satisfactory progress in school, only two of the control group did not.

The authors felt that 'when these disorders are present without obvious neurological signs, the children affected seldom receive the understanding and sympathy which might be thought their due. Such children are often accused of laziness or misbehaviour or suspected of being mentally dull. In spite of mounting problems at school, none had been referred to the educational psychologist or to the child guidance clinic.'

Although a general review of recent work on dyslexia has not been included in this chapter (but see also the chapter by Goodacre), one major study which must be mentioned here is that of Ingram *et al.* (1970) who looked at language development and educational attainment in two groups consisting of 82 healthy intelligent pre-school children from social classes I and II with slow speech development and a control group of 138 children. The major findings were that:

1 Children with slow speech development in social classes I and II read and spell at a significantly poorer level after two years' formal schooling than do their normal peers.
2 They were not at a similar disadvantage in arithmetic.
3 For them the Goodenough Draw-A-Man IQ was a better predictor of reading performance at age seven than the Stanford-Binet, the opposite being true for normals.
4 They showed other developmental lags, including visual-recognition and audiophonic difficulties in reading and visuo-motor inadequacies in copying designs.
5 Reading failure seemed to arise from disability which was 'constitutional' in origin.
6 They showed no evidence of organic neurological abnormalities.

The authors feel that their study provides much needed scientific evidence for the authenticity of the concept of specific dyslexia even in children of superior intelligence without brain damage.

Findings in other studies, especially those of Lovell and his associates, are comparable. Lovell and Gorton (1968) in their study of some differences between backward and normal readers of average intelligence found an association between reading ability and tests of audio-visual integration and motor performance and concluded that in some ordinary reading failures neurological dysfunction played a part, while Warrington (1967) found in a sample of children referred to a neurological clinic that a significantly larger number had much lower verbal than performance scores on the WISC. Reading disability was associated with uneven abilities generally, but verbal impairment appeared to be the commonest difficulty.

As mentioned earlier, categorisation is not so important for placement purposes as for drawing attention to certain difficulties so that a thorough diagnostic assessment can be made and special remedial teaching arranged. The comments of Wedell (1968) about perceptuo-motor disorders are equally applicable to other neuro-developmental disorders: it is their early detection which is important since 'often a surprisingly small amount of help in building up one or another of the skills will enable the mildly handicapped child to maintain progress'. It is equally important for the teacher to notice when such help is insufficient, so that more extensive diagnosis and more intensive remedial help can be provided.

AUTISM

Since there is still a lack of agreement about the aetiology of this disorder we feel it is necessary to discuss these children as a separate group. Research here has taken three main forms, epidemiological studies, clinical research and experimental studies.

Lotter (1966) investigated the prevalence of the autistic syndrome in Middlesex among eight to ten year olds and obtained the figure of 2·3 per 10 000. This was based on the number of children firmly diagnosed as autistic and a figure of 4·1 per 10 000 is thought to be more likely, which is very similar to that of 4 per 9 000 suggested by Rutter (1967c). The studies also agreed in showing a clear predominance of boys over girls.

From the clinical point of view, certain behavioural characteristics are generally regarded as typical of the syndrome. Rutter (1966) includes 'aloneness and insistence on sameness; an inability to form adequate social relationships and to tolerate change; absent or abnormal speech development; stereotyped and manneristic behaviour; abnormal responses to sensory stimuli, especially auditory ones; cognitive retardation of varying degree; an inability to play and a restricted and repetitive behaviour repertoire.' In concluding a survey of research on theories of autism, Rutter (1968) has also pointed out where earlier views on autism have been proved wrong. 'Contrary to earlier views, infantile autism is not anything to do with schizophrenia, and is not primarily a disorder of social relationships. The presence of mental subnormality is not sufficient to account for autism and it seems unlikely that psychogenic and faulty conditioning mechanisms are primary factors in its aetiology.'

A number of follow-up studies of autistic children have by now been carried out, which Rutter (1966) reviews. In only about 15 per cent of the cases do educational and social progress approach normality. Rutter and Lockyer (1967) and Rutter, Greenfield and Lockyer (1967) have themselves re-examined sixty three autistic children who first attended the Maudsley Hospital between 1950 and 1958 after a period of five to fifteen years. For most children the onset of the disorder was in early infancy. An important feature of their study was that systematic comparisons were made between autistic children and those with other psychiatric disorders, so that the clinical characteristics specific to autism could be distinguished. They found no single symptoms which did not occur in children with other psychiatric disorders, and only two characteristics, abnormal relationships with other children and retarded language development, were present in all the autistic group.

Rutter *et al.* (1968) suggest that the primary disorder is one of language, especially the comprehension of sounds. When the pattern of cognitive abilities was examined, scores on all tests involving verbal concepts, abstract thought or symbolisation were poor, in contrast to relatively good performance on puzzle-type tests such as the block design and object assembly sub-tests of the wisc. Although many autistic children are also mentally subnormal, Rutter found that even on standard IQ tests between a quarter and a third of them had scores within the normal range. Rutter has also been carrying out a five-year research project at the Maudsley Hospital, supported by the Department of Education and Science and the Gulbenkian Foundation, into the effect of various teaching programmes on autistic children.

Although a number of small scale experimental studies have been carried out, such as those by Hutt *et al.* (1965), who looked at arousal as judged by EEG and other behavioural indicators, and also at social responses under different conditions, the main body of experimental work has been carried out by Hermelin and O'Connor (1970) between 1963 and 1968. Their subjects were drawn from a large, somewhat heterogeneous, group of seventy seven subjects, and from a more homogeneous one of twenty seven children aged six to sixteen who lived at home and attended a special school.

Wing (1967) compared this small group on a number of measures with mongol, aphasic and deaf-blind children. He looked at auditory perception and speech, motor control, visual perception and related functions, behaviour problems, and finally at deficits in non-verbal skills and interests; he found that autistic children had abnormal scores on all measures, except those of non-verbal skills. Two of his main conclusions were that autistic children had multiple handicaps combining several kinds of problems, each of which might occur alone or in other syndromes, and that the more handicaps a child has, the more severe and widespread are his secondary behaviour problems.

Hermelin and O'Connor's work is best summarised in their book *Psychological Experiments with Autistic Children* (1970); only its general scope can be indicated here. In a group of experiments they look at perception and perceptual deficits and conclude that 'while the perception of difference seems relatively unimpaired in autistic children, attention towards verbal stimuli is not sustained, and few comparisons between such stimuli are made and perhaps consequently the processing and utilization of visually presented data is deficient'. Feedback information from response movements is, however, more readily analysed, that is, 'doing something different to different things provides more information than perceptual input alone'.

Another important finding in this area is that the brief visual inspection time shown by the children was paralleled by a relatively fast adaptation to light at the cortical level. There thus seems to be fairly firm evidence that the children attend to visual stimuli for a briefer period than normal or subnormal controls.

In another group of experiments, language, coding, seriation and recall were examined, and possible deficits in semantics, grammar and phonology investigated. Results suggest that immediate rote memory in autistic children is as good as or better than that of normals of similar mental age, but that the recall capacity of the normals 'improved significantly more when syntactically and meaningfully related material was presented than did that of the autistic children'. The autistic children also showed much stronger recency effects. The authors conclude that coding and categorising processes are deficient and that there may be severe impairment in the grammatical and semantic aspects of language.

When responsiveness to stimuli in different modalities was examined, it was found that the children were relatively unresponsive to both verbal and non-verbal auditory stimuli, as were mongol children: the EEG records, however, suggested a different underlying mechanism. These authors think the EEG studies in general show that 'to talk of a general level of either high or low arousal in autistic children is too simplified a view'.

In their summary, the authors mention as important new findings the following characteristics of autistic children:

a) the short visual inspection time;

b) the extensive use of motor cues in preference to visual cues, 'which may indicate an incapacity to classify and interpret visually presented material';

c) impairment in the appreciation of the order of words and in the use of the meaningful and semantic aspects of language.

Overall, they feel that 'the failure of autistic children in the appreciation of order and of meaningful structure in the input must be seen as one of our main conclusions'.

Frith (1970a, 1970b) has re-examined and extended O'Connor and Hermelin's findings. Her experiments were concerned with the reflection of the structure of the input in the output of normal, subnormal and autistic children, and she examines the impairment shown by the autistic group in extracting the relevant features of any visually or auditorily presented material. For example, either a random (e.g. a-b-b-a-b-a) or patterned (a-b-a-b) sequence might be given and recall required. That of normal children was superior when the sequence was patterned, in that they extracted a characteristic feature such as alternation from the sequence and their errors consisted in an exaggeration of such features. Autistic children, however, did no better on patterned than on random sequences and gave incorrect responses in which repetitions were dominant, regardless of whether these had occurred in the given sequence. Frith concludes that autistic children have a general and pathological cognitive disturbance consisting of an impairment in the processing of sequential inputs.

Current issues in the education of handicapped children

THE CONCEPT OF MULTIPLE HANDICAP

In the introductory section the problem of categorisation was discussed, including the reformulation of categories supported by Younghusband *et al.* (1970). A case has also been made by Mittler (1970) for revising the official categories even more radically by replacing them with the 'wider category of learning disorder'. This, he argues, 'would have the advantage of stressing the educational and developmental aspects of the problem as distinct from primarily medical and administrative considerations, and the additional advantage of helping teachers to escape from what may be the excessive specialisation which has resulted from training courses devoted primarily to one handicap'.

Mittler's argument is based on the growing body of evidence about the extent of overlap between handicaps, 'evidence which supports that multi-handicap is the rule rather than the exception'. He is referring not so much to the grosser multihandicaps as to overlap which has hitherto been less obvious. The surveys in Chazan's studies suggested that many ESN children are also maladjusted: various surveys of cerebral palsied children suggest that approximately one half have IQs below 70: the Isle of Wight surveys threw up much information about overlap between handicaps; overall about one in four children who had a handicap of any kind had one or more additional handicaps, and this and other studies stress in particular the relationship between maladjustment and reading difficulties. Research with quite diverse groups (for example autistic, hydrocephalic or language-retarded children) has shown that not one but many rather specific handicaps are often involved.

The implications of this overlap between handicaps have hardly begun to be explored, but any attempts to revise the present categories, to extend or reorganise educational provision for handicapped children and to re-think the training of teachers of both handicapped and 'normal' children must be made in full awareness of the nature and extent of multiple handicap as revealed by recent research.

PLANNING SPECIAL EDUCATIONAL PROVISIONS

Tizard (1971) has singled out four issues 'which appear to be central to the planning and evaluation of special education systems'. These are:

1 The epidemiology of handicapping conditions;
2 The need to evaluate the quality of services;
3 The place of model services or demonstration projects in stimulating change;
4 Large-scale experimental and evaluative trials.

Research in this country has been largely concerned with the first three, in particular with epidemiological studies. These are clearly important in planning, since, if an adequate system of special education is to be designed, the incidence and prevalence of disease or handicapping conditions and the factors leading to change must be known.

As reported in the second volume of *Educational Research in Britain* (Kellmer Pringle, 1970, p. 50), the National Child Development Study (1958 cohort) has stimulated a national study of children with physical and sensory handicaps. Prevalence data have been collected and analysed, and a closer look is now being taken at children with neurological deficits, especially epilepsy, lack of physical coordination or cerebral palsy. Follow-up material will be provided by the 1969 sweep of the whole sample.

The Isle of Wight surveys have already been referred to: there the outstanding finding was that 'handicaps of moderate or severe intensity and of long duration are exceedingly common in the ordinary school population. No system of special schooling can cope with the numbers involved (one child in six or seven), and therefore most responsibility for special educational treatment will fall on the ordinary teacher' (Tizard, 1974).

An important current epidemiological study of handicaps in childhood is being carried out in Bristol by Dent, Ross and Warr (Dinnage, 1970). A register of 9 000 names of handicapped children has been computed from a search of hospital and public health records and from an enquiry in Bristol schools. The register includes children with minor handicaps, psychiatric disorders and severe physical handicaps. The latter are visited at home and the effect of the handicap on family life assessed. Data are being analysed by computer. A clinical and educational sub-study of epileptic children identified through the survey is also being carried out.

Most of the recent major surveys have indicated the need for more special education within ordinary schools. One of the findings of The National Child Development Study (Kellmer Pringle *et al.*, 1966) was that teachers thought 2 per cent of children in their last year of infants' school would have benefited from attendance at a special school because of backwardness or other difficulties. The Isle of Wight surveys confirmed the urgent need to provide part-time special education for ESN pupils in ordinary schools: of 174 children aged nine and ten years who were educationally backward by two SDs or more, only 38 were in full-time attendance at special units, the remainder (6·2 per cent of their age group) being in ordinary schools.

The East Midland study of cerebral palsied children (Hewett, 1970) reported many inadequacies in provision for this group, and the difficulty of obtaining suitable education or day-care being 'a primary source of anxiety' for many parents.

As Tizard (1971) points out, two different problems relating to the issue of where to provide special education are often confused. These are, firstly, the relative merits and drawbacks of different ways of organising special educational treatment and, secondly, questions related to the quality of treatment given in particular establishments.

The first of these problems is of considerable current interest. The NBCC report 'Living with Handicap' (Younghusband et al. 1970) has already referred to the aim of the working party being to look at services for handicapped children with a view to seeing what improvements could be made and what the priorities were. Evidence was collected on medical, social and educational needs and the services of ten LEAS examined in detail. The working party 'welcomed the move towards educating handicapped children in ordinary schools'. While the official policy is that 'no handicapped pupil should be sent to a special school who can be satisfactorily educated in an ordinary school' (Ministry of Education Circular No. 276, 1954), it is only recently that in a few areas real efforts have been made to provide special facilities in ordinary schools as alternatives to special school placement. The question is, of course, a complex one; placement depends not only on degree of disablement but on the child's personality, intelligence and additional handicaps and on the character of the ordinary school. Younghusband et al. also noted that ordinary teachers had too little advice and consultation available.

Two current research studies are concerned mainly with the placement of physically handicapped children in ordinary schools. One is being carried out by the Department of Education and Science (Simpson, personal communication) which in September 1969 sent out a letter to all Principal School Medical Officers in England and Wales enlisting their help in obtaining information about such children. The survey was initiated because it was felt that it would be valuable to have an overall picture of the type and severity of disabilities which can be accepted satisfactorily in ordinary schools, as well as of the specialist services which have been or need to be provided for them. The results of the computer analysis are awaited.

A more detailed three year study is being carried out by one of us (Anderson, personal communication). The aim is to examine in depth issues involved in the integration of physically handicapped children in ordinary primary schools. A variety of measures are being used to look at the academic attainment and social adjustment of 75 PH children with handicaps of varying severity, in ordinary urban and rural schools, with 150 of their non-handicapped classmates matched for age and sex comprising the control group. A smaller group of 25 severely handicapped children, for whom special arrangements have been made in ordinary infant classes (mainly children with spina bifida or cerebral palsy), are also being studied. In all cases headteacher, classteacher and parents are being interviewed. It is hoped that the study will throw light on the factors in the children and the schools that foster successful integration, as well as providing practical information about the sort of arrangements which it is possible and advisable to make for physically handicapped children in ordinary schools. Findings so far suggest that more physically handicapped children could be satisfactorily educated in ordinary schools, provided that LEAs are willing to consider the ordinary school as a serious alternative to special school placement, as is done in Scandinavia (Anderson, 1971). A major caveat, however, concerns children with neurological abnormalities, in particular those with a mild degree of cerebral palsy, whose special problems often go unnoticed. An advisory service for teachers is needed to enable this group to reach their full potential.

RESEARCH NEEDS

Many important issues relating to the education of handicapped children have had to be omitted from this review, as for instance, work related to handicapped school leavers, handicapped adolescents, and the training of teachers.

A major study of the further education, training and employment of handicapped school leavers carried out under the auspices of the NBCC has just been completed. An intensive investigation was made of a selected sample in order to assess the situation over the whole country.

The question of the needs of adolescents was raised by Younghusband *et al.* who noted the 'surprising failure to recognise the acute problem of isolation from their peers that confronts many of the more seriously handicapped adolescents. We think it urgent that (their) needs should receive more systematic study and that greater efforts should be made to meet them as far as possible'. While this is partly a social problem, there is a need to find out much more about the social relationships and the emotional problems of adolescents in the school setting and then for research into ways of meeting them.

The findings already referred to, about the number of children in ordinary schools with special needs, have important implications for the training of ordinary teachers. It would be useful to know the extent to which and means by which the colleges of education are preparing teachers for this responsibility. Complementary to this is the need for research into the type of advisory service which would best meet the needs of teachers with handicapped pupils.

We have reserved to the end what is perhaps the most important issue of all, the question 'What is special about special education?' While paying tribute to the widespread concern and considerable expertise of many special school teachers, Younghusband *et al.* (1970) drew attention to the fact that 'there is little precise evidence about the nature of special education and its results. In a field of education in which so much depends on what teachers can do for their pupils the lack of research comparable to that in the medical fields is disturbing'. While the research reviewed in this chapter is obviously relevant to the educational needs of handicapped children, little of it, with the possible exception of the PI studies, has been concerned with the central and crucial question—what exactly is it about special education that justifies the epithet 'special'. We suggest that it is the answer to this question which still presents the major challenge to researchers in this field.

J. P. Ryan

Maladjustment

It has become almost a tradition to open any discussion of maladjustment with an enquiry into what is meant by the term. This usually leads to the term being discarded and a different one substituted. The new term will not necessarily be an improvement on the old, but will usually be more amenable to the limitations of the speciality within whose framework the discussion takes place.

There is not space here to deal in detail with the alternatives that have been proposed, but since the impact of Rutter and his co-workers (Rutter, Tizard and Whitmore, 1970) will become more widely felt, especially through the use of the Child Behaviour Scales (Rutter, 1967), it is necessary to consider the substitution of their favoured term, 'psychiatric disorder' for the current term, 'maladjustment'. Yule (1968) quotes from the Underwood Report (DES, 1955, p. 22) '. . . a child may be regarded as maladjusted who is developing in ways that have a bad effect upon himself or his fellows and cannot without help be remedied by his parents, teachers and the other adults in ordinary contact with him'. But, noting that both the Underwood Committee and the Scottish Committee (Scottish Education Department, 1964) found it difficult to define maladjustment, Yule goes on to support Rutter's 'psychiatric disorder' terminology. He states the need for 'some classificatory system to facilitate progress in the field of child psychiatry is clearly felt.'

However, the Underwood report, also on page 22, states 'Maladjustment is not a medical term diagnosing a medical condition'. This is the real point at issue. From an educational point of view, there is a broad category of maladjustment. Within this category are found children who are maladjusted with respect to 1) their interpersonal relationships, and some may be suffering from psychiatric disorder; 2) their intra-personal relationships, and many will be psychiatrically

214

disordered. Being in one sub-group will tend to lead to being in the other, and this is one of the main reasons for intervention processes. What is not acceptable from an educational point of view is the equating of maladjustment with psychiatric disorder (see Chazan, 1963). Schools for maladjusted children will tend to contain largely psychiatric cases because these constitute many of the worst problems. Maladjustment remains a vague term in education covering many levels of behaviour and disorder in the same way that the term 'sickness' and 'illness' are used in medicine. It is not intended here to dispute the contention that Rutter's classification will be helpful in child psychiatry, but to re-emphasise the point that the fields of maladjustment and child psychiatry are by no means identical.

It is necessary to define the various behaviours and disorders more closely and to decide whether these come within the category of maladjustment. Rutter (1965) gives a classification of childhood disorders that contains eleven categories including antisocial or conduct disorders, mental subnormality and educational retardation as a primary disorder. It could be argued that none of these three are psychiatric disorders, but from the point of view of the education of maladjusted children, the antisocial or conduct problem child is definitely included, while the other two categories, by themselves are not. The value of Rutter's classification is not that it replaces maladjustment, but that it helps to classify more clearly those disorders that may or may not be considered as coming within the category of maladjustment.

Yule also emphasizes Rutter's view that maladjusted behaviour can be, and often is transient and situational, but the same view was also stated explicitly in 1955 on page 22 of the Underwood Report. One of the problems that needs to be faced in the education of maladjusted children is in deciding which categories involve children who have more or less permanent disorders, or such disorders as to make them ineligible to attend a school for maladjusted children. It is necessary to remember that the function of such schools is to 'effect their personal, social or educational re-adjustment.' For some children the answer might lie elsewhere, such as in special units for the brain damaged.

Detection

From the above it should be evident that the detection of the maladjusted child is really a process whereby children within the categories included in the term 'maladjusted' are identified. This is of exceptional importance when research is considered, and not enough attention has been paid to either the theoretical or the methodological problems involved.

The majority of researches involve the comparison of effects or treatments between an experimental and a control group. If the groups are called 'maladjusted' and 'non-maladjusted' (or by any similar labels) then the degree to which the categories overlap with respect to the conceptual variable of maladjustment as opposed to the criterion variable will confuse and even obscure any relationships or differences. In many cases quite arbitrary splits are made in populations; in others, doubtful measures of maladjustment are correlated against another variable. This leads to such dubious practices, as the total score on the BSAG (Bristol Social Adjustment Guides, Stott, 1966) being correlated for example against sociometric choices, and a statement that maladjustment correlates 0·50 to 0·82 with sociometric choice being produced (Richards, 1967).

Detection of maladjustment has two specific aspects, one related to decision making and the other to quantitative measurement. Decision-making detection is that normally employed in 'clinical' applications, where the investigator has to decide whether or not a child falls into a specific category ('clinical' here does not imply a medical process; it may be an educational one). Even when screening methods are considered, there is a decision as to whether a child is to be investigated further, i.e. is 'screened in' rather than 'screened out'. In research work the decision-making approach is often used, particularly if one of the groups has to meet some criteria of inclusion or exclusion. It should be obvious that it is not sufficient to use a scale to divide a sample into maladjusted *v.* non-maladjusted or high *v.* low anxiety, if these terms are only relative to one another and do not correspond to similarly named categories in the general population. Unfortunately many reported researches appear to commit this error—or at least they fail to make it clear that they do not. But whether inclusion occurs or not will depend upon the criteria, not upon the name of the category. When Angus (1970) was investigating twenty two supposedly autistic children, only one was autistic according to Rimland's Form E-2 Checklist (for parents), but twenty had four or more of Creak's 'signs'. Since Angus was investigating the discrepancy between Rimland's and Hutt's arousal theories, this difference in inclusion by criteria suggested that Rimland and Hutt might be looking at different kinds of children.

More commonly research uses detection methods of a quantitative basis, the aim being to identify the degree of maladjustment. These two aims tend to produce instruments that cannot satisfy both. In particular, if a scale is validated with reference to its discriminating ability, the instrument may be useful and valid at those points which are used in the decision-making process. In effect they become scales with only one interval—the decision-making interval. Scale scores above and below that interval are probably not in equal or systematic intervals, and may not even be in the correct order. There are two situations that can lead to this anomaly—one related to the degree of intercorrelation among items, the other to the 'severity' of the items (i.e. the correlations with the criterion). Stott (1960) uses his Adjustment Guides, any validation of which refers to discriminating ability, as a linear (i.e. quantitative) scale. To compound the error, there are no definitive data available concerning the correlations of the items.

The majority of 'quantitative' or 'objective' measures of maladjustment are obtained from the teachers or parents of children. Studies by Hallworth (1961, 1962) and Morrison et al. (1965) showing a tendency for teachers to rate pupils in specific ways cast some doubt on the objectivity of teacher's ratings. Other than by clinical interviews, little attempt is made to assess maladjustment directly from the child. Methods involving structured or semi-structured observation, as in the London Doll Play Technique (Moore and Ucko, 1961) will remain 'clinical' methods unless their scoring methods can become specified with complete objectivity. The same principle applies to the 'Family Attitude' type test (e.g. Jackson, 1964), which usually involves arguments of considerable circularity to justify the test having any discriminating ability. The data presented to introduce the Family Relations Indicator (Howells and Lickorish, 1963) are not very convincing. A close look at the figures indicates that only 'Punitive Action' and 'Verbally Hostile' can be used with any confidence, and, since the reported results are based on only fifty children, there is plenty of opportunity to 'capitalise on random errors'.

The use of personality tests is not valid unless a strong enough relationship can be demonstrated between the personality variables and levels of adjustment. Gibson (1965) reports a personality test validated against 'three independent criteria of personal adjustment' (teachers' ratings; family data; and the body sway test). Apart from the suitability of these as criteria, Gibson factor analysed data from only 285 boys for a forty two item test. Another example of the dubious practices found is where Mehryar (1967) sought evidence on the validity of the Junior Maudsley Personality Inventory by correlating scores against socio-metric choices and an *ad hoc* 'Guess Who' test. It is difficult to see how validation against unvalidated material can be successful.

The American 'adjustment inventory' approach has been used very infrequently in Britain, though an existing test has been readily avail-able (Rogers, 1961), but some signs are now evident of an interest in the work of Bower (1969). His sociometric measures are perhaps too stereotyped, and the more flexible approach deriving from Moreno (1953) has been used here to investigate adjustment in children. (Dixon, 1967; Rose, 1966; Richards, 1967). The useful guide offered by Evans (1964) provides the basis for more work in this area, although the lack of sophistication in the methods she outlines leads to a good deal of useful information being thrown away.

One technique of investigating the child directly that has been employed here seeks to elucidate the child's self-concept, usually through the methods of the Q-sort (Stephenson, 1953), the semantic differential (Osgood, Suci and Tannenbaum, 1957; Snider and Osgood, 1968), or the repertory grid (Kelly, 1955; Bannister and Mair, 1968; Bannister, 1970). Zahran (1967) found a significant correlation between a positive self-concept and adjustment in adolescents, and, from one theoretical viewpoint, this approach could be very important both for decision making and choosing types of treatment. It is interesting to speculate, however, as to how the apparently useful self-concept approach can be reconciled with the also apparently useful behaviour therapy, since neither camp seems able to tolerate the other.

One major unresolved question, related to the previous section, is that of deciding which 'sub-categories' or 'syndromes' are to be included within the category of 'maladjusted'. Tizard (1968) argues against the creation of syndromes, but he does not make a distinction between maladjustment and child psychiatric disorders. In the latter, syndromes will undoubtedly be identified and 'discovered' as they have always been in medicine; the question is rather whether we want them in maladjustment work, and if we do, how we shall arrive at them. Chazan (1968) implicitly shows that the operational definition of a syndrome is not necessarily constant, although a more thorough investigation of the relevant variables remains to be made.

Incidence

The determination of the incidence of maladjustment is not a problem that can be solved directly. A first requirement is the systemisation of those conditions and disorders which are to be included within the category of maladjustment, followed by studies of the incidence of these conditions and disorders, both in their separate and joint ocurrence.

To be valid an incidence study requires:

1 a satisfactory definition of the disorder;
2 the use of an adequate detection technique;
3 a representative sampling of the population being investigated.

It is maintained here that we have not reached the satisfactory definition stage and cannot progress towards adequate detection methods. However, even without these two steps being attained there may be some justification in attempting to assess incidence, since it could be held that we may never be able to improve our conceptualisation. But few of the studies that have been carried out could be said to be representative of any population except the sample itself. Ryle, Pond and Hamilton (1965) do not even make an analysis in terms of age and yet it is hardly likely that 'patterns of psychological disturbance' will be consistent over the age range from five to twelve years. The impression one gains is of an increasing tendency to rush into print with an analysis of cases referred to child guidance clinics and psychiatric hospital units. The weakness of these studies is threefold.

1 Taken separately, each study does not give enough data to enable comparisons to be made with other studies.
2 Every clinic or unit will have specific factors that influence its referrals, yet no identification of these is usually stated, and there is little evidence that a search is made for such special factors (e.g. tendency to receive the kinds of case one succeeds with).
3 The material is presented 'because it is there'. There is seldom any use of hypotheses leading to a meaningful analysis.

The impression usually given by these studies is unsatisfactory. Important questions arise, but are not investigated, let alone answered.

In most cases the studies contribute nothing of value and yet they continue to be published. A particular example is the report by Graham and Meadows (1967) of psychiatric disorder in the children of West Indian immigrants. As it stands, it tells us virtually nothing, but the inclusion of adequate non-maladjusted control data, plus some sociological background, would have made the data meaningful and the report extremely welcome.

In the current cohort studies (Pringle, Butler and Davie, 1966; Douglas, 1964) there is some hope that a more representative pattern will emerge, particularly in terms of relevant factors in the histories of individual cases. There is need, however, for the longitudinal sample method to be repeated on a cyclic pattern in order to utilise the developing techniques and to check on hypotheses originating in earlier runs of the cycle.

The most promising of cross-sectional studies has been the Isle of Wight survey (Rutter, Tizard and Whitmore, 1970), but the emphasis on medical aspects reduces its value considerably for educational purposes. (See also the chapters by Goodacre and by Anderson and Haskell.) There has been, and undoubtedly will continue to be, considerable 'spin-off' into the educational field. What is required is a similar project with an educational orientation. Studies such as that by Mitchell and Shepherd (1966), using questionnaires, are limited by their inability to control or measure adequately a number of variables that may be important. In fact we are not yet at a position to state what are the important, and what the unimportant variables in such studies.

The difficulties surrounding assessment and incidence are well illustrated in studies relating to children who do not attend school. The child who is a school attendance problem still attracts the attention of researchers, but the conceptual problems remain unsolved. Tyerman (1968) still maintains that many truancy and school phobia cases are basically the same but are evidence of a social class distinction rather than a valid clinical one. Hersov (1960a) maintains that the distinction exists, but the social class imbalance in his sample does not permit his data to contradict Tyerman's assertions. The sample used by Hersov (1960a, 1960b) is probably atypical anyway, since as described elsewhere it contrasts sharply with that of Davidson (1961). Further support for Tyerman's approach is found in the review by Cooper (1966) who emphasises the difficulty in making a meaningful distinction between school phobia and truancy. Hodges (1968) presents data for 'non-attenders' (excluding c.g.c. cases) and the overall picture of much social and emotional disorder would also seem to support Tyerman's views, although Hodges does not analyse her data very well. Although Chazan (1962) supports school phobia as a separate category, his data are not clear. Not only does the lack of controls make his conclusions incomplete, but if lessening of school pressures is effective as a treatment, the theoretical mother-child model of causation, which is a strong part of the phobia approach, is considerably weakened. Much of the support for the school phobia theory comes from psychiatrists and others (e.g. Clyne, 1966; Kahn and Nursten, 1968), working with clinical groups, who do not attempt to compare their clinical population (which is subject to several biases) with matched truant and normal samples. The mere weight of clinical 'phobia' cases does not constitute evidence for a differentiation between them and truants.

A rather more promising approach lies in utilising the data of Regan (1967) who administered the HSPQ and JMPI and a scale of attitudes towards going to school. He found indications of a personality 'type' having a good attitude to schools and that schools tended to cater for that type. Mitchell and Shepherd (1967) investigated children who dislike going to school and found the role of the parent as an enforcer to be important. Both of these studies have reference to the school attendance problem generally, and the solution of the truancy-phobia dispute may lie in utilising this approach to the *whole* problem of school attendance.

Assessment of treatment of the school attendance problem child is difficult. The 'phobia-truant' diagnosis implies a decision as to causation and will probably influence treatment methods. More directly confusing is the fact that most studies are *post hoc*, usually by analysis of records, and that they do not have the built-in control of variables that would assist comparison with other studies (e.g. Warnecke, 1964). This 'analysis of cases handled' can also result in samples too small to be meaningful, e.g. Barker (1968), who states without justification from his data 'that in-patient psychiatric care is a valuable treatment measure in some of the most extreme cases'. Very small samples can be useful if investigated by the single case method, but this implies a carefully designed research.

Development

Again from the viewpoint of an educationalist, the process by which maladjustment occurs in the child is seen as a part of development. To speak of the aetiology of maladjustment permits a facile move into a 'disease theory', whereas we are concerned with aiding adjustment, not with curing disorders. The field is too great to consider many aspects of it here, but some points must be dealt with.

The disentangling of genetic and environmental influences has always been difficult, and tends to yield results only when twin studies are used. The use of this technique in studying maladjustment, however, is of comparatively little practical use because the number of cases encountered is too small to have encompassed most of the behaviours that are relevant. Where some of the disorders or behaviours have been studies in twins, the results have not been clearcut and are usually expressed as probabilities of differences between groups. They can only be applied to individuals with a lower degree of probability.

Stott (1964, 1966a) has shown considerable enthusiasm for a theory of 'multiple congenital impairment' but it is difficult to assess the value of Stott's contribution due to his reliance upon the BSAG as a measure of maladjustment. In addition, he links these theories to those he proposes about delinquency (Stott, 1960), but since his measures of delinquency relate to legal delinquents and not to behavioural delinquents his theoretical structure is made to stand on even more shaky foundations. Contrasted with Stott's ideas are the findings of, for instance, McAllister and Mason (1968) that the delinquent does not generally come out as a different psychological or sociological 'type'. But this whole question needs more of the careful preliminary identification of delinquent acts such as the work carried out by Belson, Millerson and Didcott (1968).

The parental role in the origin of maladjustment is not only generally unclear, but is likely to differ for the several distinct conditions that we might include within the term maladjustment. The seriousness of the disorder cannot be taken as an indication of parental involvement, although it often leads to a search for a particular type of parental personality. At one extreme it has not been possible to see the psychotic child as the result of parental handling, although handling differences between parents of psychotic and parents of mongol children were observed (Pitfield and Oppenheim, 1964). On the whole this supports Creak and Ini (1960), who say of their own work: 'This study hardly supports the view that parental personalities and child-rearing attitudes as seen in our sample are a principal cause of child-hood psychosis.' Where the parent is psychotic, extremely careful studies are needed to disentangle hereditary and environmental effects, but many of the reported studies (e.g. Doniger, 1962) are completely unable to report anything but 'an association' between parent and child variables.

For the majority of those behaviours that might be included as mal-adjusted it is possible to hypothesise some relation to development and child-rearing. When Frank (1965) surveyed this field, he found it extremely difficult to invoke family factors as causes, but he had reservations regarding the finality of his conclusions. The report by Wolff (1961a) on the background of pre-school children attending the Maudsley clinic does suggest that psychiatric disturbances in the parents are over-stressful for such young children, although the contrary hypothesis of the effect of the children upon the parents is not adequately discussed.

Related to parental handling is the effect of separation, which was found by Pringle and Bossio (1960) to be important if accompanied by rejection. Foster children who had been grossly deprived were found by Williams (1961) to have a tendency to remain emotionally handi-capped. Unfortunately both of these studies involved several variables which were not analysed with regard to possible interactions. There are useful collections of research work into foster home care (Dinnage and Pringle, 1967a), residential care (Dinnage and Pringle, 1967b) and adoption (Pringle, 1967) but they tend to be rather uncritical of the methods of the research reported.

Both Brandon (1960) and Wolff (1967) have found that there is no tendency for maladjusted children to have had more obstetric compli-cations surrounding their birth than did controls.

The educational pressure towards nursery schooling was not helped by Douglas and Ross (1965) reporting that children who went to nursery schools or classes were no better, and perhaps worse in their adjustment than non-nursery attenders. While Douglas and Ross do acknowledge the possibility that this may be a reflection of *why* the children were given nursery schooling, rather than a result of it, the fact that this question is not resolved should remind us how unwise we would be to base our actions on assumptions, no matter how well-founded we might *think* these to be.

The overall impressions we gain from these researches relating to development is that on the one hand we know very little about the relationship between influences during development and maladjustment, while on the other hand we make a large number of unsupported. assumptions. This is truly an area where folklore exceeds knowledge.

Maladjustment is often seen as associated with other forms of handicap. There are, however, no comprehensive data relating handicaps to one another; this is true not only for maladjustment. The studies reported are plagued by their lack of representativeness. In most instances the data do not appear to have been collected by any regular sampling procedure.

Some further difficulties involved in such studies can be seen in that by Bowyer, Marshall and Wedell (1963) with severely deaf and partially hearing children. The difficulty of using more well-established tests led them, as it has led others, to employ techniques of doubtful reliability and validity, with consequent problems of interpretation. Fisher (1966) also looked at the social and emotional adjustment of children with impaired hearing in ordinary classes. However, in using the BSAG he avoided some of the problems encountered by Bowyer *et al.*, but by treating the BSAG as an interval scale further problems were created. In fact if Fisher's figures were accepted, not only would 47 per cent of the hearing-impaired have unsatisfactory adjustment, but so would 28 per cent of the 'normal' children—one of the highest estimates that has been reported.

Treatment

In the narrower sense, the treatment of maladjusted children is a medical matter and will not be considered here since so many children ascertained as maladjusted are psychiatrically disordered. But all treatment, even for psychiatric cases, is not medical. Behaviour modification techniques can by no means be regarded solely as medical treatment since they involve the most basic activities of both teachers and parents. Previously educational psychologists have tended to restrict themselves to giving general advice concerning the establishing of desirable behaviour and the elimination of the undesirable. Recent developments in therapeutic treatment, arising more from a psychological background, are having an effect at all levels, from clinical applications in psychiatry to the shaping of behaviour in home and school.

The history of these techniques is fairly long and is well covered in most accounts of them (Rachman, 1962; Eysenck and Rachman, 1965; Beech, 1969; Meyer and Chesser, 1970). Beech gives a good introductory account that pays adequate attention to the problems and limitations of the technique. Bandura (1969) gives a very full account of the theoretical background, and being of American origin, supplements the British works listed. Probably of even more relevance for educationalists, although again American, is the work assembled by Guerney (1969) which gives examples of the use of behaviour modification techniques by teachers, parents and peers. Instances of the use of behavioural techniques in this country can be found in Walton (1961), Kassorla (1968), Nelson and Evans (1968), and McKerracher (1967), the latter using the technique to treat reading difficulties. Since some training courses for educational psychologists and others are including these techniques (Ward, 1971) there should be a considerable expansion of their use in the near future.

For those maladjusted children who have definite psychiatric disorders any intensive treatment should be at least supervised by a child psychiatrist. But the latter should come to realise the help that can be obtained from the teacher, especially in the special school or special class where the teacher, even if not always specially trained, will in most cases be specially interested. It is unrealistic to expect a teacher to have contact with a child for about thirty hours per week and be expected to do nothing. Whatever the teacher does will be treating the child, for good or bad, so that for children with psychiatric disorders, a planned regime, worked out jointly by the psychiatrist, teacher, and preferably also the psychologist can only be an improvement. But it is also unrealistic for the psychiatrist to *advise* the teacher on a one-way basis.

One aspect of treatment that is very closely allied to treatment is placement. At one time the only choice was between residential and day school, but increasing use is being made of smaller special classes, often in or near child guidance clinics, and it is probable that the near future will see more differentiation within the normal school to provide a 'home-based' special education. A feature of these new developments has been the extent to which they have remained educational provisions without the need for medical intervention. This is not to deny the necessity of the child psychiatrist in the cases where children are psychiatrically disordered, but does underline the point that mal-adjustment is not equatable with psychiatric disorder. As yet there appears to be no evaluation of this new approach with its use of informal placements.

The Department of Education and Science has given a guide to-wards purpose-built schools for both residential and day schooling for maladjusted children (DES, 1965). The residential schools are now being sited 'in small towns or on the edge of large towns' as recommended in the Underwood Report (DES, 1955, p. 66). Some of these schools already built here are Hailey Hall, Hertford (the prototype); Moor Top, near Barnsley; The Heath, Colchester; Knowl View, Rochdale; Highfield, Tyldesley; and one now opening at Hartford in Cheshire. Whether residential schooling is of particular value is still an undecided issue to which one subscribes according to one's faith. The study by Petrie (1962) cannot be taken as measuring the effect of the schooling since no control was used to account for the time variable. However, Petrie's assessment showed that improvement did occur over time, which at least allows us to assume that, in the one school studied, the children did not get worse.

The process of special schooling, whether in a special class, unit or school, day or residential, full- or part-time, is also to be considered as a part of treatment. (Wills, 1960; Lennhoff, 1967, 1968, 1969.) What is *done* in the schools is considered below under educational methods, but the overall effect of the schooling upon the maladjustment is more an aspect of treatment. Ives (1963) reports a change to a more positive self-view of children in a special class, but the scope and structure of her study do not permit anything to be derived except suggestions for further investigation.

Prognosis

The whole intervention process that constitutes the education and treatment of maladjusted children is of little value unless 1) it achieves some kind of aimed-for result, and 2) such results do not occur with-out the intervention. The absence of success should be a signal to try new methods, but irrelevance of intervention would demand consider-ation as to whether intervention should in fact occur. While the full

evaluation of intervention is not possible until the problems of conceptualisation and measurement have been solved, there is always a
danger that heavy investment in the earlier stages of the hierarchy of
processes will prevent modification or abandonment of practices
should the follow-up studies indicate the desirability of this.

Because of these problems, two kinds of follow-up studies are
welcome. The first of these involves one or more later checks on the
adjustment of people who have at some time been treated as maladjusted children (e.g. Warren, 1965). It is important in these cases
to include treatment variables, since a follow-up that disregards antecedents is not going to provide useful information.

The second kind of follow-up involves the study of at-risk groups.
McWhinnie's (1967) study of people who were adopted as children is
an example of this. Unfortunately, in her case, the numbers were too
small to give sufficient information regarding adjustment that could be
analysed in any detail.

Wolff (1961b) found that the outcome of cases was noticeably poor.
These were apparently fairly severe cases, and the overall outcome was
heavily affected by cases with either broken homes, or ones in which
there was 'open marital conflict'. The rather poorly presented study by
Balbernie (1966) also indicates the poor results obtainable with children
from unsatisfactory homes, and also points to 'the erratic nature of
casework in the family' (p. 173).

Much of the research done by social workers appears to be on a
rather broad base and is of an exploratory nature (e.g. Philp, 1963). The
recommendations made are also broad-based and seldom relate to the
family with a *specific* problem. It is important in prognostic studies to
attempt to assess the degree of improvement, even on a relatively crude
scale. In his six year follow-up of adolescent psychiatric in-patients,
Warren (1965) does this, and indicates that while there was a considerable improvement between admission and discharge, there was little
overall change from discharge onwards, some cases deteriorating, but
others continuing to improve. When antisocial record was also considered, the number with poorest outcomes almost doubled, but this
was still a significant improvement upon assessment on admission. The
major fault of these studies, from the treatment point of view, is the
lack of any control against which to assess the effects of the intervention.

From the viewpoint of educational treatment, these largely psychiatric prognostications do raise the question as to how much can be done for the more severely psychiatrically handicapped child, especially the one with a poor home background. The very interesting results that Maclay (1967) reports have considerable relevance for the educator. Two of the major findings were:

1 Children who formed good relationships with their peers were less likely to have further psychiatric and/or social problems.
2 Children coming from larger families were more likely to have further psychiatric and/or social problems.

As we should expect, children with psychosomatic disorders showed the best prognosis, while those with organic disease and/or psychosis showed the worst. It was noticeable that the remaining two categories, neurotic and behaviour disorders, which are those most dealt with in schools for maladjusted children, showed about 50 per cent successful prognosis.

Personality

The question of the personality structure of maladjusted children will of course depend upon which children are described as maladjusted. It is a fruitless exercise to measure 'the personality attributes of a group of maladjusted children'. Whether they show typical or atypical patterns will depend upon the composition of the group, and even random sampling from the group is pointless if the group itself is not a representative or a random sample of all maladjusted children. This point has not always been observed. An example of the variation found is the contrasting findings of Hersov (1960b), who finds 54 per cent of his school-phobic children are anxiety cases while only 20 per cent are depressive, and of Davidson (1961) who finds depression in 77 per cent of her cases.

It is of course legitimate to take samples of children with specific disorders, such as enuresis, or school attendance problems (McHale, 1967) and to search for personality variables that distinguish them from children without such problems. But to avoid the contradictions that can occur, as in the Hersov and Davidson studies mentioned above, the samples must be representative. Studies have been made of children involved in burn 'accidents' (Martin, 1970), of children with asthmatic attacks, and of victims in road accidents and in sexual assaults (Burton,

1964, 1968). While not all of these children may be maladjusted, they do fall into unequivocal categories. The studies just cited have tended to lack rigour, but the approach is an encouraging one.

The assessment of those personality traits that are associated with success or failure at school may also be relevant. Research here needs to be carefully done, on an adequate sampling basis, since the analysis of 'presenting' cases, which has a certain amount of superficial appeal, can be very misleading. Thus when Douglas, Ross and Cooper (1967) found no relationship between handedness, attainment and adjustment in their national sample, they were probably correct in ascribing the previous supposed relationship to have arisen through selective referral. Personality traits showing a strong relationship to academic achievement or to response to remedial education can be seen as being of help in assessing the outcome of special educational treatment with maladjusted children. Such variables might also help in deciding how to make the maximum use of special school places.

There are several reports on the relationship between attainment and neuroticism or extraversion. Savage (1966) found that with eight year olds, all correlations of extraversion and neuroticism with IQ and achievement were low. With an older age-range (eleven to fifteen year old boys) Callard and Goodfellow (1962), using the JMPI also obtained low correlations. (See also the chapter by Entwistle and Lomax.)

One of the failings of these researches is the tendency to treat the results rather bluntly. No attempt is made to identify the variables (usually extraversion and neuroticism) more closely, especially with regard to observable behaviour. The test scores are treated as they stand, which is appropriate only if the labels of 'neuroticism' etc. are not attached to them. Savage, for example, is really talking of correlations between scores, not of correlations between the variables that the scores are trying to estimate. In 1960, Thorpe pointed out that scores on neuroticism tests increased in the hospital setting due to a situation effect. There has been no indication that this finding has either been refuted or taken into account.

The multiplication of tests such as the Junior Maudsley Personality Inventory (Furneaux and Gibson, 1961; Gibson, 1967) and the Junior Eysenck Personality Inventory (S. Eysenck, 1965), as well as Gibson's 'improved' scale (Gibson, 1965) indicates that the effort that could go into producing a useful scale in this area is being expended in the production of superfluity.

Educational methods

There has been surprisingly little research in Britain into the efficacy of educational methods with maladjusted children. Since there are two problems, the response of specific personality patterns to specific methods, and the comparison of methods irrespective of the form of the maladjustment, these will be considered separately. There has been more written in the idiom of 'what I did at my school on the North Downs' (e.g. Shaw, 1965) than in that of carefully conducted research. These pioneering efforts should not be disregarded or belittled, but the specificity of situation, the selectivity of children, and the unique genius of the head of the establishment make it impossible to assess the methods used. Like the writings of Freud they are a richer source of further hypotheses than of established fact. One particularly good book in this area is that by Wills (1960), which manages to convey methods rather than just to relate experiences.

The aspects of personality that have been most investigated are: level of anxiety, neuroticism, and extraversion, all expressed as results on standard, usually pencil and paper, tests. There is nothing to indicate that these are the most important aspects of personality with respect to learning. That they are easier to study has perhaps led to their undue emphasis.

Several investigations have been carried out into the relationship between maladjustment and reading failure, and others have related maladjustment to the outcome of remedial work. Although the numbers were small, Sampson (1962) found little if any systematic relationship between reading ability-disability and maladjustment. There is an interesting attempt by Gregory (1965) to relate the BSAG 'categories' to reading failure. Both XC and R were found to be significantly associated with reading failure, but at the five per cent level. Since nine comparisons were made, the one per cent level would have been a more appropriate one to take, since the comparisons were not independent. Gregory offers the interesting argument that since R scores are high for younger poor readers and do not increase with age, they may be linked with the *cause* of the reading failure, whereas XC increases with age and may be an *effect* of the poor reading. The kind of approach used by Gregory is that recommended in the very good review by Sampson (1966), in which she points out that we need to investigate particularly which kinds of maladjustment are involved in reading failure. It had earlier been reported (Boxall, 1963) that high anxiety girls were poor to average in reading, while high anxiety boys read well but low anxiety boys read poorly. But recently Ogden (1971) has found no relationship between anxiety and reading in 11 year old boys. The report by Pringle and Cox (1964) of the influence of the school upon the anxiety level of its pupils also needs to be borne in mind.

It has also been reported by McQuoid (1967) in a study of 1 284 nine to ten year old boys in Northern Ireland, that although general adjustment was related to attainment, there was no systematic relation between most specific personality disorders and attainment. (It is not clear whether what she means by 'maladjustment' is confined to social disorders.) But against this must be placed the report on the National Survey sample (Ross, 1966; Douglas and Ross, 1968), which finds that, in the delinquent child at least, there are both poor attainment and high scores on neuroticism and aggression (see also Yule and Rutter, 1968). The answer may lie in combinations of effects which cannot normally be found in analyses not designed to measure interaction effects. Perhaps future factorial investigations might solve this problem.

When remedial education is considered, maladjustment is often considered to be a related factor. Pringle (1961) found poor present social and emotional development to be associated with poor progress; but Lytton (1967), however, found maladjustment not related to gain, but related to poor hold-up of gains.

Recent investigations into the effects of praise versus blame (or reproof) upon learning, in relation to personality variables, have been indeterminate. In a rather poor study, Rim (1965) investigated the results with extraversion and with high and low neurotic-scoring children. Interactions between extraversion and neuroticism were apparently not considered and the results are therefore inconclusive. Maguire (1966) found no consistent differences between anxiety levels and praise or reproof for rote learning tasks, but praise was consistently better for all anxiety levels. Again a lack of analysis for interactions, also involving extraversion as well as level of aspiration, prevents many possible effects from being ruled out.

Assumptions are sometimes stated or implied that the measured IQ of maladjusted children is an underestimate, due to the maladjustment. This results in some confusion in the evaluation of attainment and remedial gains. While the assumption is probably true for some individuals, there is little evidence of its generality. In fact, Turner, Mathews and Rachman (1967) found no correlation between increase in WISC scores (FS, V or P) and changes in clinical condition. The Verbal score was particularly stable. Over a wide range of maladjustment some relationship might be found, but the available data show that even considerable disorder produces little effect on IQ.

Research methodology

Within the field of maladjustment little or no development of research methods has taken place, nor does it at present appear likely. What is important is the use of research in a field where the nature of the population studied will in some cases require special controls and in others place certain constraints on the statistical analysis employed.

For instance, the study of a specific method of treatment cannot be evaluated against a control group receiving *no* treatment, since a positive result may be due to the fact of *any* treatment rather than the specific treatment. In such cases it is obvious that two control groups are necessary: a non-specific treatment group and a non-treatment group. The absence of such controls is a noticeable feature of work in this field, even in medical studies, where normally one would expect recognition of the placebo effect.

The kinds of data used require that special care be taken with the kinds of statistical analyses used. Applying a neuroticism scale within a school for maladjusted children will produce a distribution which, while deviating considerably from the normal, is nevertheless amenable to such statistical treatment as product-moment correlations. But if the same scale in a normal school produces a J-curved distribution it cannot be treated by the same statistical methods. Violations of this sort are common in the literature.

Another shortcoming in the methodology is the sketchiness of the measures taken or the analysis applied, or both. In some cases this may be due to an unwillingness to subject children or parents to excessive investigation, but in others, especially with regard to the statistical analysis, this does not apply. In one very poor study (Jackson, 1968) it was said 'The numbers are too small for any definite conclusions to be drawn, but the data suggest . . .' No analysis was attempted by Jackson, but a chi square test of her data against a theoretical rectangular distribution of ages (the relevant variable) gives P = ·60 approximately. How can one say that these data suggest anything? When the amount of data available for analysis are limited, a thorough analysis would be expected, but the impression is often given that the researcher has shortened his analysis to enable him to rush into print.

The opposite fault of wringing a pound of statistics from an ounce of data is also found, particularly amongst researchers reported in theses. Some instances of this 'Inland Revenue' approach can be vindicated. Chazan (1965) made a total of forty-seven comparisons between two groups of n = 30. This 'oversquare' analysis is acceptable in searching for areas to be further studied, but the 'results' obtained can have no positive statistical worth. In the study by Jackson (1968) reported above, twenty-one points (=variables) were studied for only forty children. Data matrices like these are commonly out of proportion in reported studies, in some cases with the number of variables actually exceeding the number of children. A nodding acquaintance with probability theory should show researchers (especially students) that this situation would make nonsense of statements about the significance of the interrelationships between the variables.

As indicated with reference to the study of reading failure by Gregory (1965), there is also a failure to recognise the relationship between the level of significance adopted and the number of non-independent applications of a statistical test. Even with data permitting the independent application of tests, the meaning of an isolated significant result amid many non-significant ones is difficult to assess. One of the major faults in research in maladjustment and the child psychiatry is, as stated earlier, the analysis of data 'because it is there' without any hypotheses to direct the investigation, and without the collection of supplementary, confirmatory or comparative data. Far too many of the researches surveyed were so fragmentary as to be virtually worthless.

Perhaps the greatest research weakness of all is the weak design of the investigation. In most cases almost no effort appears to have been spent in devising an adequate, let alone a thorough-going model that is conceptually related to the problem and its variables. Very few investigations for instance make use of factorial analysis of variance, with the result that the interaction of variables is not even considered. Inspection of the trends in some of the reported data suggests strongly that interaction does often occur unnoticed, but in these cases there are seldom sufficient data presented for an observer to carry out an analysis 'from the side-line'.

It has not been the intention here to deal with infantile autism, since not only is there some doubt as to whether this disorder would be classified as maladjusted, but there are already good reviews of what has been and is being done (Wing, 1966; Rutter, 1968; Mittler, 1968). It is necessary however to point to the research being done by the Cambridge group (Hermelin and O'Connor, 1965; O'Connor and Hermelin, 1968) as an example of the tightly conceived experimental work that is both possible and fruitful with disordered children.

Conclusions

This review has been very critical of most of the research reported that might have a bearing on the maladjusted child. It was not intended merely to be critical, but the inadequacy of the research created the need for criticism. A feature of the last ten years has been that we have found answers to few, if any, problems. There will always be some educational flat-earthers who will stick to their beliefs in the face of all evidence, but one feels wont to sympathise with them if the evidence offered is as weak as the major part of what we have seen. Much of the failure to produce acceptable results appears to be due to two major factors. The first of these is the lack of training in research methods, or lack of proper research advice, for those carrying out many investi-gations. In most cases where the study has been carried out by someone with a background in medicine, social work or teaching, the absence of research training is understandable, but where a psychologist is in-volved, some research expertise would be expected. It may occur that the lack of research training typical of, for instance, psychiatrists may be overcome by a team approach, but this is only true if some *influential* member of the team is competent in research. In a few of these studies, conducted with a competent research adviser, it appears that a more senior member of the 'team' has dictated the form of the study. The second factor leading to sub-standard research has un-doubtedly been that this poor material so often gets published. Apart from the unnecessary additions made to the 'flood of print', misleading conclusions derived from poor research continue to bedevil the field, strengthening false arguments and wrong leads.

It has already been maintained that the impetus behind many small researches is the availability of the; data. While this is an understandable reason, it should not be a sufficient reason. 'Interesting' results that are either dubious or invalid are only interesting to those who know no better. If data are available it is only worth analysing if the analysis will be worthwhile. This may seem obvious to the point of tautology but is disregarded by a large number of 'researchers'.

Future research into maladjustment, if it is to be worthwhile, must get away from the analysis of 'available data', derived from inadequate and unrepresentative samples, and turn towards well-conceived research designs. Moreover these designs must be set within an overall matrix or sequence of logical development within the field. Present trends in training, associated with the realisation that the advent of computers has led to a *lowering* of research expertise at certain levels, give us some hope for the future.

Peter Mittler

Learning processes in the mentally handicapped: the work of the Hester Adrian Research Centre

Background

After decades of neglect, the mentally handicapped are receiving increasing attention from all sides. Educationalists have for some time doubted whether the concept of ineducability was a valid one. Everything clearly depended on the aims and methods of education, and how widely it could be defined. It was also obvious that earlier social policies had for all practical purposes created a deprived minority group, starved of financial and human resources, cut off from the main stream of education, and taught for many years by people without any qualifications whatsoever. Improvements were gradually introduced, new teacher training courses set up and purpose built schools began to replace the huts and church halls in which these children were previously kept occupied. It began to be appreciated that many could be greatly helped by appropriate teaching, and by the provision of properly planned educational facilities and materials. Research on adults had earlier suggested that a low IQ was not necessarily synonymous with inability to learn (Clarke and Clarke, 1965); on the contrary, the lower the intelligence the more necessary it became to plan not only day to day objectives but teaching techniques in fine detail. It is possible that subnormal children do not learn merely by being exposed to a rich and stimulus-enriched environment, liberally provided with opportunities for discovery and 'learning through doing'. Many of our schools already provide such an environment, and though such conditions constitute an essential background, teachers of handicapped children are currently preoccupied with ways of finding a balance between stimulation and structure. The more we learn about childrens' learning difficulties, the more we realise the need for a detailed analysis of the processes and strategies which characterise the thinking of subnormal children in general and of individual handicapped children in particular.

In April 1971 responsibility for the education of mentally handicapped children passed from the Health to the Education authorities, both at national and at local levels. Every child is included, no matter how profound his degree of handicap, whether he is at home and attending a special school, or in long-stay residential care in a hospital or hostel. This reform has for long been urged on successive governments, not because anyone thought that it would produce immediate benefits, but because it seemed to constitute an essential first step towards recognising that these children had educational needs which had not previously been acknowledged (British Psychological Society, 1969). It began to be appreciated that they deserved appropriately trained teachers, with access to educational psychologists, advisers and inspectors, and that they should be brought into the mainstream of educational development and planning.

The establishment of the Hester Adrian Research Centre should be seen in the context of these and other important changes in the development of services for the mentally handicapped. Although it was not set up to address itself to specific educational or other problems, it was the hope of its sponsors that it would launch research programmes which might help to provide both practical and theoretical guidance to those professionally concerned with the mentally handicapped, and with bringing about improvements in the services.

The origins of the Centre go back to the assassination of President Kennedy in 1963. In view of the personal and public interest of the Kennedy family in mental handicap, it was hoped that a British national memorial might take the form of an Institute of Special Education. Although this was not accepted by the Government, the idea of a research institute received increasing support from a number of organisations which resulted in the establishment of a steering committee convened by the National Association for Mental Health, under the chairmanship of Lady Adrian. A fund-raising campaign was launched by NAMH which raised enough money to allow the committee to seek university sponsorship. The University of Manchester agreed to house the Centre, which came into being with my appointment as Director in October, 1968, and began active work a year later. It was named after Lady Adrian as a tribute to her work in bringing it into being.

The Centre is currently financed from three sources. Firstly, it receives £10 000 a year from the Sembal Trust, whose promise of £100 000 over a ten year period made it possible for Lady Adrian's committee to begin discussions with the universities. Secondly, we received a grant of £20 000 a year for two years (1970–2) from the Department of Health and Social Security. This grant is not earmarked for any special project, and is designed to allow the Centre to establish and consolidate its activities. Government support will be provided on a different basis from 1972. Thirdly, we have been able to secure the support of research councils for specific research projects or programmes. In particular, the Social Science Research Council has given us three grants – one to study language problems and two others to examine aspects of attention in learning. The North-West Society for Mentally Handicapped Children have enabled us to launch a project concerned with the application of programming techniques to the study and remediation of visual perceptual skills. A grant from the Leverhulme Trust supports a series of studies concerned with ways in which SSN adults and children classify and categories incoming information.

Staff and projects

The Centre consists of nineteen full time research workers, together with technical and secretarial staff. In addition to the Director, a Senior Lecturer and three lecturers, we have been able to recruit a number of research workers for specific projects. Three research studentships have now been allocated to the Centre; two from SSRC and the other from the Government of Northern Ireland. Eleven research associates and research students are registered for higher degrees. Three doctoral and five master's theses have been completed.

The main emphasis of projects so far has been on the investigation of various aspects of cognitive functioning, with special reference to language, perception, attention, memory and learning. Studies have been carried out on both children and adults, and in schools for the educationally subnormal (ESN) and severely subnormal (SSN). Most of the studies have been carried out in schools and hospitals rather than in the university, though we are now equipped to see children on our own premises if necessary. We also have a mobile laboratory which consists of a caravan divided by a one way screen into an experimental and observation room. This is useful (if not ideal) for the experimenters, and is at least an object of interest and curiosity for our subjects.

It may be useful to list the existing projects and the names of staff working on them, even though such lists are inevitably out of date by the time they are published.

1 Assessment and remediation of language comprehension and production in severely subnormal children (Social Science Research Council grant, 1969–73).

    Peter Mittler, MA, PHD   (Director)

    Dorothy Jeffree, MED, DP ED HAND CHILD   (Senior Research Associate)

    Kevin Wheldall, BA   (Research Associate)

    Paul Berry, MED   (Research Associate)

2 Attentional deficit and learning difficulty in severely subnormal and educationally subnormal children (Social Science Research Council grant, 1969–73).

    James Hogg, BA, PHD   (Senior Lecturer)

    Donald Preddy, BSC   (Research Associate)

    Peter Evans, BSC   (Research Associate)

3 Application of attention theory to training and education of the mentally retarded (Social Science Research Council grant, 1971–3).

    Robert Serpell, BA, DPHIL   (Senior Research Fellow, 1971–2)

    Roslyn Wheldall, BA   (Research Associate, 1972–3)

4 The teaching of class concepts to severely subnormal children and adults (Leverhulme Trust grant, 1970–3).

    Peter Herriot, BA, MED, PHD   (Lecturer)

    Roy McConkey, BSC   (Research Associate, N. Ireland studentship)

    Josephine Green, BA   (Research Associate)

    Barbara Thomas, DTMH   (Research Associate)

*5 Effects of training on the recall of stimulus sequences in severely subnormal and educationally subnormal children.

    Colin Elliott, BA, DEP   (SSRC Senior Research Fellow, 1969–71)

*6 An operant approach to the modification of hyperkinetic behaviour.

    Inger Maier, MA, PHD   (Research Associate, 1969–71)

* Completed projects.

240 LEARNING PROCESSES IN MENTALLY HANDICAPPED

7 The application of behaviour modification techniques to the development of profoundly handicapped non-ambulant children (Department of Education and Science grant, 1972–5).

James Hogg, BA, PHD   (Senior Lecturer)
Thomas Foxen, BSC   (Research Associate)
Robert Remington, BSC   (Research Associate)

8 The application of programmed instruction to severely subnormal children (National Society for Mentally Handicapped Children (North West Region) grant, 1969–73).

Clifford Cunningham, BSC   (Robert Bailey Research Fellow)

9 The assessment and development of work skills in severely subnormal adults (Department of Health and Social Security grant, 1972–7).

Edward Whelan, BA, MSC, PHD   (Lecturer)
Gordon Grant, BSC, MSC   (Research Associate, UMIST, 1970–1)
Eileen Tomlinson, MED   (Research Associate)

It is impossible for one individual to provide an adequate account of the work of his colleagues. What follows therefore is merely an introductory sketch which is intended to direct the reader's attention to certain features of some of the projects. It may be appropriate at this point to refer to some preliminary publications produced by and from the Centre as a whole or by individuals; these are listed in the references to this chapter, and will be quoted as appropriate.

Language studies *(Peter Mittler, Dorothy Jeffree, Kevin Wheldall, Paul Berry)*

It is generally agreed that mentally handicapped children show particularly severe speech and language impairments, and that their language skills are generally far lower than might be expected from a knowledge of their development in other areas, such as social or non-verbal skills. It is not clear whether the problem should be seen as one of underfunctioning, or in terms of certain specific defects. Language can be regarded as made up of a number of skills and abilities, and it is possible that some language difficulties may be of a developmental type, while others may be more typical of defects. This was suggested in one of our studies, using the ITPA (Marinosson, 1970). In certain respects, SSN children seem to follow roughly the same developmental sequence as normal children, but they do so at a very slow rate, and never reach some of the stages attained by normal children around the age of five or six years (Mittler, 1972b). Thus, what starts as a developmental delay while the child is still maturing may end as a defect when the growth process is complete. There is also a risk that development may remain at a particular stage for an unnecessarily long period, partly because the nature of the demands made on the child are not directed towards helping him to reach the next stage of development.

Language studies can be described under a number of headings.

COMPREHENSION (K. Wheldall)

Work is in progress on the development of a sentence comprehension test originally devised with Angela Hobsbaum at Birkbeck College, London. Briefly, the child's task is to identify which of three or four pictures best illustrates a sentence spoken by the experimenter. The sentences vary in depth and grammatical complexity, and include simple kernels, passives, negatives, past and future tenses, comparatives, superlatives, embedded clauses. Each picture illustrates an alternative grammatical interpretation. Thus, in response to the stimulus sentence 'The cat is sleeping', the child is simultaneously shown pictures of a *dog* sleeping (noun varied) and a cat *playing* (verb varied). Similarly, for a harder sentence the stimulus sentence 'The girl is cutting the cake' is illustrated by pictures showing—in addition to the correct referent—a *boy* cutting the cake, a girl *eating* the cake, and a girl cutting a *loaf*.

Information on childrens' performance on this test is now available on 116 normal pre-school children with a mean mental age of about three and a half years (tested by A. Hobsbaum) and 200 SSN children matched for mental age on the English Picture Vocabulary Test. Considering only total scores, the performance of the SSN children was significantly inferior to that of the normal controls even though the subnormal children were of course much older and had correspondingly more exposure to language. This finding confirms existing evidence which suggests that subnormal children show lower levels of language functioning than would be expected on the basis of their overall intellectual or social development, and that their scores are consistent with a substantial degree of underfunctioning.

However, order of difficulty of the various types of sentence was on the whole very similar for the two groups, though subnormals seemed to find particular difficulty in dealing with negatives. Test-retest reliability is acceptably high, and different methods of test administration appear to produce identical results (e.g. machine or booklet, coloured or black and white, easy to hard or random order of difficulty). Detailed error analysis is in progress, together with further experiments on methods of presentation of the material (Mittler and Wheldall, 1971).

EXPRESSION (D. Jeffree)

In addition to studies comparing groups of subjects, such as those reported above, Miss Jeffree has been carrying out intensive studies based on single individuals, or on single subjects with a matched control. In one study (Jeffree, 1971) she systematically varied the nature of the teaching situation and the kind of verbal demands made on the child in order to study the effects of these changes on certain language variables: length of utterance, ratio of nouns to verbs and type token ratio (an index of the number of new words in a given number of total words). She worked with an eight year old mongol child whose overall language level was roughly at a four year level, but whose language abilities as assessed by the Illinois tests varied widely around the mean. The various styles or strategies of teaching were not designed to teach the child any skills which she did not already in some measure possess, but to help her to make fuller use of these abilities. The work shows how the teacher can do much more than help a child merely to 'talk more' or 'use language better', and that these broad aims can be broken down to more specific aims, following a full but simple assess-ment of a child's language functions and skills.

In a second study (Jeffree et al., 1972), an attempt was made to devise a teaching programme which would help to facilitate progress from the single word to the two word utterance stage. Subjects were two four year old mongol boys, carefully matched for verbal ability and general developmental level, one of whom acted as experimental subject and the other as his control. The particular two word structure to be taught was the 'pivot-open' construction described by psycholinguists in which one word is systematically used as a 'pivot' on which a larger 'open' class of words is hung. Thus, the child may use constructions such as '*allgone* daddy, *allgone* drink, *allgone* pussy', etc. In fact, very little is known about the transition from one word to two word utterances in normal children, and the psycholinguistic studies underlying the proposed early grammars postulated by Braine (1963) and McNeill (1966) merely provide a convenient working model. But there is reason to believe that SSN children, and mongols in particular, tend to remain at the one word stage for an unduly long period (Mein, 1961); this may partly be due to the unwitting reinforcement of one word labelling responses by parents and teachers who ask questions demanding only one word responses ('Whats that, what colour is it, etc.). In an earlier study, Jeffree and Cashdan (1971) had reported that mothers of subnormal children tended to fire such questions at their children, in contrast to mothers of normal children of comparable levels of language development.

The study is now in its final stages, but seems to have been reasonably successful. After both boys had first been taught the appropriate use of ten common nouns (from their combined existing repertoire), the experimental child was exposed to structured play situations designed to encourage pivot-open utterances using 'gone' as a pivot with five of the original ten nouns. At the same time the control had virtually the same conditions except that his play was relatively unstructured. The experimental subject generalised the 'gone' construction to the second five words without having been formally taught to do so. Moreover, the control subject began to use 'gone' soon after his own training sessions began. Although the study involved daily teaching sessions of fifteen minutes duration extending over several months, the results did suggest that early two word combinations could be taught. Plans are now under way to design teaching programmes to help children acquire and use other linguistic constructions which appear to be relevant to wider aspects of cognitive functioning.

IMITATION (P. Berry)

The ability to imitate language spoken by others used to be considered as a merely mechanical task not requiring comprehension or thought. More recent studies suggest that this view is an oversimplification, and that at least in those cases where a child has some expressive language at his disposal, the way in which he imitates spoken language may reflect his knowledge of the structure of language. In other words, imitation is related to comprehension.

Mr Paul Berry has now completed the first stage of a research programme designed to clarify the possible use of imitation tasks as part of a language assessment and remediation programme. For assessment purposes, it is essential that the structural complexity of sentences be strictly controlled. In the first experiment, ssn children were presented with sentences illustrating various transformations of a kernel sentence: John is driving the car (kernel); is John driving the car? (question); John isn't driving the car (negative); John is driving Daddy's car (possessive); John, please drive your car! (imperative). Number and nature of errors appeared to be strongly related to sentence type and sentence complexity. Other experiments have examined the relationship between the ability to imitate and understand different types of sentence, and also the effect of semantic and syntactic anomalies on accuracy and speed of imitation (Berry, 1971a, b).

Individual differences in learning and attention (James Hogg, Peter Evans, Donald Preddy)

There is wide agreement in the experimental literature that the severely subnormal have difficulties in information processing generally, and in dealing with incoming information in particular. Disorders or defects of input, as opposed to storage or retrieval, have been reviewed from different points of view by O'Connor and Hermelin (1963), Denny (1964), Baumeister (1968) and Hermelin and O'Connor (1970). Specific theories and models have been proposed by Ellis (1963) and Zeaman and House (1963). Ellis emphasises defects in short term memory associated with short stimulus trace duration, whereas Zeaman and House, on the basis of a series of discrimination learning studies, lay more stress on an attentional model of disorder. They point out that subnormals have particular difficulty in discriminating between the relevant and irrelevant features of a stimulus display, which results in practice not so much in a slow overall rate of learning, as in a long time interval before learning begins in the first place. Once learning does begin, however, the slope of the learning curve may well be parallel to that of subjects who showed evidence of learning on earlier trials in the series.

Previous research has generally involved the use of group designs and comparisons, and paid relatively little attention to individual differences within groups. Conventional experimental design and statistical procedures tend to assign individual differences to the 'error' term, and to regard them as a necessary experimental evil. Few research workers have tried to make a systematic study of individual differences in their own right (Gagné, 1967). This omission is particularly unfortunate in the case of the subnormal who show substantial individual differences clinically, behaviourally and also in their performance on learning tasks (Mittler, 1972a).

Dr Hogg and his associates have been examining individual differences in one aspect of personality—the inhibition-excitation dimension —and have tried to relate such differences to the way in which children attend to and learn a discrimination task which is then followed by stimulus generalisation. The inhibition-excitation dimension has been most extensively studied by Soviet psychologists (Luria, 1963; see also Gray, 1964); these workers have discussed the clinical and learning characteristics of different groups—those showing a predominance of either internal inhibitory or excitatory processes, or a balanced 'equilibriated' group. A teachers' questionnaire has now been developed to try to distinguish 'inhibited' and 'excitable' children on the basis of Luria's clinical descriptions. Items are concerned with qualities of speech (slow or fast), degree of restlessness, susceptibility to distraction, speed of work, etc. Preliminary factorial studies of the questionnaire data have yielded two factors, one apparently concerned with stimulus inhibition (inhibition of extraneous stimuli) and the other with response inhibition (behaviour characterised by restraint of responses).

The behavioural and educational significance of these personality differences derives from the fact that a child in a learning situation has not only to make an appropriate response but also to withhold inappropriate responses. The experimental task chosen in this instance was basically within an operant paradigm. Subjects were trained to press a green light panel (S+), and not to respond to a yellow one (S−). Correct responses were reinforced on predetermined schedules. After training to criterion, generalisation stimuli were introduced. The generalisation series involved both the S+ and S− and a further nine stimuli varying in wavelength.

Preliminary results confirm that there are close relations between the response inhibition personality factor and performance in the learning and generalisation tasks. Firstly, during generalisation tests the excitable children respond more frequently to all the generalisation stimuli presented than do the inhibitable children. Secondly, a significant connection is found between personality and the characteristic way in which the child extinguishes when reinforcement is withdrawn. The excitable child again starts pressing the S— which he has previously learnt to inhibit. The inhibitable child starts to inhibit responding to the S+, thus not approaching the stimulus that originally excited a response. Thirdly, there is a significant connection between personality and inter-signal responses (ISR). Thus, if a child while learning incorrectly presses an S—, it goes off the screen. Some children continue to press, however: the more excitable a child the more he tends to do this.

These results suggest that the excitable child is more sensitive to reward than punishment and hence his greater tendency to respond reflects a search for reward and relative indifference to punishment. The reverse is true for the inhibitable child who prefers not to respond, as this ensures non-punishment even if it excludes the possibility of reward.

Although these findings are still tentative, it may be useful to consider their educational implications, if only at a speculative level.

'Generalised advice about inhibitory deficits in the retarded is clearly going to be inadequate from the teacher's point of view when such marked individual differences exist. For the extremely inhibitable child, for whom failure takes on a completely disruptive significance, and who tends to show limited responding to the environment, any teaching programme must modulate failure in such a way that the child learns what is correct and incorrect without withdrawing. Similarly, responding must be encouraged if the child is to gain maximum experience from his environment. The excitable child's learning, however, is liable to be retarded by the fact that failure lacks significance and that he is over-responsive, in an undiscriminating way, to the environment. Such a child, for adequate learning to begin, must become more sensitive to the consequences of his actions, and must see that success is correlated with discerning the need for differential responses. In such a situation, negative reinforcement needs to be emphatic and unambiguous. Making a response physically harder is sometimes necessary, so that the child does not respond automatically without regard to the observable characteristics of the situation' (Hogg et al., 1971; see also Hogg, 1973).

Applications of attention theory to training and education (Robert Serpell, Roslyn Wheldall)

Dr Serpell is engaged on a research project in which a systematic attempt is being made to adapt an existing body of psychological knowledge towards the teaching of specific tasks to young SSN children. The guiding model is derived from attention theory as applied in the subnormality field by workers such as Zeaman and House (1963) who provided evidence to show that SSN children show special difficulties in assimilating and analysing incoming information, and that their performance in laboratory learning situations shows inappropriate attentional biases, and relatively great sensitivity to certain modes of stimulation.

This sensitivity could lend itself to exploitation in the teaching situation if learning problems could be presented in a form which would initially be likely to attract the attention of SSN children. From this starting point their attention would be drawn by a process of fading to the most relevant features of the task. The particular biases to be exploited in the present research include 1) the tactile or haptic modality, 2) novelty or variability and 3) redundancy.

The content of the educational programme was determined on the basis of priorities selected by teachers and other workers as essential attributes for children leaving schools for the severely subnormal (Marshall, 1967; Herriot and Thomas, 1972). These included sign reading and shop-buying. The sub-tasks chosen for teaching purposes were as follows:

SIGN READING

1 Discrimination of visually similar word-forms in the context of 'real' situations:
  a) PUSH vs PULL (opening doors)
  b) SUGAR vs SALT (preparing food and drink)
  c) HOT vs COLD (taps)
2 Recognition of familiar words in the context of selecting packaged items for purchase in self-service shops:
SUGAR, SALT, FLOUR, BUTTER, MARGARINE.
3 Understanding price labels.

SHOP-BUYING

1 Discrimination of money quantities in exchange for goods:
1 vs 20, 2 vs 40, 4 vs 5 etc. (in ½p units) in exchange for corresponding quantities of sweets.
2 Perception of value of higher order units of currency in similar contexts.

The system used for fading can be illustrated by reference to the sign-reading programme. Letters which differentiate between two words are first isolated, and their most salient differences incorporated into the teaching programme. Thus, the most critical letters for PUSH and PULL are SH vs LL; similarly UGR and LT are critical for SUGAR and SALT. In the case of HOT and COLD the common feature is at the centre and the discrimination can therefore be started with emphasis on the contour of the whole words. Thus HOT is introduced as a short rectangular figure and COLD as a longer oblong with rounded ends.

From this analysis each pair of words was reduced to a pair of simple geometric shapes, and a nine step programme devised to fade these pairs into criterial word forms. The specific contribution of attention theory to the design of this experiment lies in a controlled comparison between two methods of highlighting the differences between the discriminanda: haptic information and compounded visual stimulation. In the haptic condition, tactile cues are built into the door handle which the child necessarily grasps when opening the door; similarly the child must touch the haptic cues built into the hot and cold taps and into the handles of the perspex boxes containing salt and sugar. As the programme proceeds, the haptic component is gradually faded out by reducing the third dimension. In the compounded visual stimulation condition, the discriminanda are mounted on panels in such a way that haptic exploration is prevented. Successive visual approximation to words are presented; thus, a pair of scissors fades into stage 1 (V shaped) of PULL and a saucer into stage 1 (O shaped) of PUSH. The visual stimuli are then gradually approximated to words (for illustrations of the programme see Serpell, 1971). In addition to comparing haptic and visual modalities, two types of fading procedure —variable and graded— are being contrasted. Furthermore, the experimental programme described will be compared with a control condition in which the same discriminations will be taught individually by conventional methods such as the Gunzburg Social Education materials, flashcards, word situation cards etc.

At the present stage of the research, the emphasis is primarily on the presentation of a 'real-life' teaching task in a reasonably tight experimental form. The next stage of the research will be concerned with transferring the most viable experimental procedures into classroom practice. This will involve enlisting the cooperation of teachers in incorporating some or all of the experimental procedures into teaching sessions, and making systematic comparisons of their effectiveness.

Memory and organisation processes (Peter Herriot, Josephine Green and Roy McConkey)

Dr Herriot and his associates have been conducting a series of experiments designed to clarify the kinds of strategies and processes that might be involved in dealing with incoming information. His experiments use the technique of free recall. This involves presenting subjects with an array of items which the subject is asked to recall immediately they have been removed. Subjects are shown a slide containing pictures of several objects arranged randomly. The procedure is repeated over several trials, each time with a different arrangement. The important feature lies not in how many items are recalled, but the order in which the items are named. If two items are repeatedly recalled together, this suggests that the subject is imposing some kind of order or structure on to the material. If the presented items are not in any obvious way related to one another, he is likely to have developed his own idiosyncratic categorisation, even though he may be unaware of it, or be unable to verbalise it. This is known as subjective organisation. On the other hand, the experimenter can make it easier for the subject to categorise by using items which are conceptually related (e.g. two items each belonging to the category of furniture, parts of the body and eating utensils). If the subject then groups items from the same category he is said to be 'clustering'.

A number of experiments have now been completed, and others are in progress. Results obtained so far indicate that both subjective organisation and clustering occur in subnormals and that subjects who 'rehearsed' (i.e. said words out loud on presentation) were poorer at subjective organisation. It was concluded from this work that the positive measures of clustering indicated that subjects could group related items in an hierarchical way, but that the positive measures of subjective organisation indicated only a tendency to rote-learn unrelated items. This was due to the inadequacy of the measure of subjective organisation (Herriot and Cox, 1971). Other experiments tested the possibility that different types of cue would help subjects to categorise, and that such cues would have more effect when given at recall than at presentation (Herriot, 1971). Cues were either verbal (e.g.' for eating with', etc.) or mimed (gesture, showing manipulation of cutlery). Either type of cue appeared to be equally successful, but clustering scores actually deteriorated if both were given simultaneously, possibly because the subjects were being overloaded with information. It also appeared to be more helpful to provide cues during the recall phase rather than at presentation. Furthermore, subjects appeared to improve their clustering scores over a three day period, suggesting that some transfer of training was taking place. Experiments are now under way to test this possibility, and to find ways of assisting transfer. These results apply to non-mongols, but not to mongols matched on mental age. Mongols appeared in these experiments to be incapable of benefiting from cues, and had given indications in the previous experiments of being more apt to use a rote-learning strategy. In the experiments as a whole their scores were variable, and fell into no consistent pattern.

If these results can be generalised to larger populations, they suggest that subnormals do impose some structure and categorisation on incoming material, but that they might be helped to do so to a greater degree by presenting verbal or mimed cues at the recall stage. These findings need to be extended and replicated, but may be of direct practical significance for the teacher. Their ultimate aim includes the establishment of a model of information-processing in the subnormal, now presented in monograph form (Herriot et al., 1973).

Memorising and sequencing skills (Colin Elliott)

Another feature of organisation concerns the ability to appreciate that stimuli follow one another in sequential order. In Herriot's experiments subjects were simultaneously presented with different stimuli; Elliott's studies are particularly concerned with sequential aspects of recall. Previous work has shown that subnormal children are poorer than normal children matched on mental age in tasks involving the recall of sequences of words or pictures. This was also shown in the study using the Illinois Test of Psycholinguistic Abilities (Marinosson, 1970). The aims here are to investigate various experimental measures of recall of stimulus sequences. The child may be presented with sequences of pictures or words, and then asked to reproduce the sequence either in the same or in a different modality. Thus, it is possible to use every combination of two inputs (visual and auditory) with two outputs from the child (visual—motor or vocal). Studies on cross modal coding suggest that SSN children have particular difficulties in integrating auditory and visual input. Time intervals between presentation of the stimulus and start of recall trials will also be varied, since it is possible that recall will be impaired with longer delays, as predicted by Ellis's (1963) theory. It might also be predicted that words and pictures which had been named quickly might be recalled better than those which had been named more slowly. This study is also concerned with personality differences on the experimental tasks.

Behaviour modification (Inger Maier)

Most of the studies described so far have been concerned with the analysis and manipulation of *stimulus* characterised in an effort to identify whether certain types of materials or certain methods of stimulus presentation may facilitate learning. By way of contrast, operant and behaviour modification techniques act directly on the *individual* by introducing a systematic programme of reward schedules in an effort to increase the frequency of certain behaviours or to decrease the frequency of others. A large variety of teaching and training techniques is now available, and an impressive amount of work has been done in the USA in teaching self-help skills such as feeding, dressing and toileting, sometimes to profoundly handicapped people. More complex skills, including language, have also been taught (see Weisberg, 1971, for a recent review; also Bijou and Baer, 1967). These methods are open to criticism on a number of technical or even ethical grounds, though they have been frequently misrepresented or oversimplified in popular accounts. One can argue that enough work has now been done to allow operant techniques to be regarded as an essential part of the training of both psychologists and teachers and others concerned with the education and care of the mentally handicapped. One of the advantages of these methods is that they can be taught in modified form to teachers, nurses and, above all, parents. Unfortunately, behaviour modification techniques have hardly been used in Britain, so are unlikely to be widely used for some time.

Inger Maier (1971) has now completed a study on a group of grossly overactive or hyperkinetic children. All the children were patients in a subnormality hospital, and were severely handicapped. The main aim of her research was to introduce a systematic programme of reinforcement designed to increase the duration and frequency of attending responses to a series of visual stimuli. It was also considered important to establish whether the beneficial effects of a training programme carried out under 'laboratory conditions' could be generalised to other tasks in the testroom, and also in the classroom, and whether the child would be less distractible after training.

Sessions were initially conducted in a stimulus reduced room, empty except for the apparatus. This consisted of an experimental box in which various stimulus materials could be displayed, including toys and a moving film cartoon. The child's preference for all the stimulus materials had been predetermined, in order to ensure that each child was first presented with a toy for which he had already shown a high preference. After a number of baseline sessions, the child was rewarded (with Smarties and social reinforcement in the first instance) for approaching the box and looking at the materials. Whenever he looked away from the box, he was 'reminded' to return to it by a flashing red light and a buzzer, both located on the apparatus. Under these conditions both frequency and duration of attending responses increased to a significant degree. The next stage consisted of extinction trials in which attending behaviour was no longer reinforced. After a number of sessions this resulted in the reappearance of the baseline behaviour, thus showing that experimental control had been achieved. Training sessions were then reintroduced for the lesser preferred objects. When the children had learned to attend to these for sustained periods of time, various distractors were hung near the apparatus. Nevertheless, the effects of training were maintained, not only in this condition but also when tasks were presented without the cues provided by the experimental equipment, and when the environment was changed from the testroom to the child's own classroom. Finally, the children were reassessed some weeks after the end of the training sessions. Some extinction had taken place, but the conditioned behaviour quickly recovered with renewed reinforcement.

This study achieved promising results, particularly in respect of the generalisation data. It underlines the importance of assessing learning outside the experimental situation since generalisation does not necessarily take place spontaneously. The programme emphasises that hyperkinetic behaviour can be modified by reinforcing appropriate behaviour and suggests the importance of introducing classroom control based on operant principles.

Application of behaviour modification techniques to the development of profoundly handicapped non-mabulant children (James Hogg, Tom Foxen)

Very few research studies have so far been devoted to the most severely retarded non-ambulant individuals. Many children of this type are cared for in special care units, attached to the new special schools, and have thus become the responsibility of the education authorities who have also assumed control of schools in subnormality hospitals. The needs of these children are difficult to estimate, but there is little doubt that many of them are grossly understimulated, and spend much of their time lying immobile in cots or on mattresses with very little to do.

Some impetus to work in this neglected field is provided by studies of normal infants within the first year of life. Work on newborn and very young babies has established that they are capable of more advanced skills and abilities than had previously been realised; in particular, they appear to be able to make fairly complex discriminations both in the auditory and the visual modality, and to respond by changes of heart rate to quite small changes in the quantity and quality of stimulation (Fantz, 1967; Friedlander, 1970). Very few ssn children are functioning at a neonatal level of development, although they still tend to be described as 'vegetative'. At the very least it should be possible to provide a systematic approach to the assessment of different aspects of their development.

The present condition of most non-ambulant retarded individuals reflects not only a severely impaired central nervous system but also an extremely impoverished environment. Because they initiate very little activity themselves, they tend to receive little or no interaction from their caretakers. Furthermore, their needs are attended to on a non-contingent basis—i.e. they are fed and attended to regardless of

E.R.B. 3—9*

their own behaviour, and this rarely receives reinforcement adequate to maintain or develop it. Such stimulation as they do receive also tends to be unsystematic and arbitrary, in so far as it is unrelated to any plan to help the child to acquire a target behaviour, such as feeding.

Dr Hogg and Mr Foxen have begun the first stages of a study of a ward of non-ambulant children in a subnormality hospital. The aim of the study essentially involves training children in fundamental behaviours required for relatively more complex skills. It is therefore necessary to begin by an evaluation on a time sampling basis of all the behaviours emitted by the child in a 'free' situation; this will be followed by specific testing of basic perceptual and motor skills, using modifications of scales for normal infants. Each child will then be assessed in respect of the skills required for the development of a more complex behaviour; for example, the work of White *et al.* (1964), on the evolution of visually directed reaching is of particular relevance for this population. Operant and shaping techniques will be used to help the child to extend his behaviour repertoire. Such training will only be of value if nursing staff can become involved and can help to bring about changes in ward organisation which will lead to a more individually orientated treatment regime.

Application of programming principles to the study of visual perceptual skills (C. C. Cunningham)

'Perception' may be a reasonably useful shorthand term, but, in common with other global constructs such as 'intelligence', 'learning' and 'memory' it needs to be subjected to a closer analysis in order to identify and isolate at least some of the specific skills and abilities that seem to be involved. It is of little use to say that a child has 'perceptual difficulties' merely on the basis of impressionistic evidence of difficulties in drawing or holding a pencil. Psychologists and teachers need more detailed diagnostic assessments on which to base possible programmes of remediation.

Mr Cunningham's research is addressed to the problem of assessing aspects of visual perceptual functioning in mentally handicapped children. In addition, he is concerned with the application of certain principles derived from programmed learning in an effort to help children to increase and extend perceptual skills. The research also involves the use of a particular teaching machine—the Teddington

Touch Tutor (Cleary and Packham, 1968), though the initial emphasis lies more on the preparation of carefully written programmes than on the use of the machine itself. Both are components of the same system, but it is not always remembered that a teaching machine is only as good as its programmes permit it to be (Cunningham, 1971).

For purposes of the present research, perception is considered as a group of specific skills, which may well be related to one another, but which can nevertheless be separately identified and assessed; where necessary specific perceptual deficits can be remediated or compensated. The particular discriminations which have so far been studied include the following: real objects; familiar shapes (including regular and irregular, open or closed etc.); abstract shapes; colour; rotation and distance. The child's basic task is essentially 'matching to sample', first on specially prepared and individually administered cards, and later on the teaching machine. Matching to sample involves the child in looking at an exemplar and then matching it by pointing at one of three panels immediately below. For example, he might be shown a picture of an apple and have to select another apple from the panels underneath; at the beginning of training he might only be shown the apple while the two 'distracting' panels are left blank. During the course of training the blank panels are gradually 'faded in', so that the child is being systematically trained to attend to relevant aspects and to ignore irrelevant ones. The majority of ssn children who were over five years old and not in special care classrooms could be trained to match to sample.

Those who failed generally did so because they did not make an attending response to the exemplar. Many children, whilst demonstrating their ability to match to sample, consistently failed on specific items or dimensions. This appeared to be caused by their attending and responding to the most salient rather than the relevant characteristic and thus adopting inappropriate strategies for responding.

One of the aims of the research is to throw more light on the kind of strategies adopted by children in perceptual tasks of this nature, and to try and devise a graded teaching programme to help them to overcome or compensate for such difficulties. For example, work is now under way to determine whether children show consistent preferences for either shape or colour, and then to devise specific programmes to teach them to change their preferences and hence their attentional response.

Assessment and development of work skills (Edward Whelan)

Although most of the Centre's work is currently concerned with children, one project which commenced over a year ago was specifically designed with the needs of adults in mind. It has to be remembered that the normal procedure is for SSN children to leave special schools at the age of 16, at a time when their performance on a wide variety of psychological tests corresponds to a level between five and six years (Marshall, 1967). Thus, they are leaving school at roughly the stage of mental development which has been reached by the normal child starting infant school for the first time. Most of them enter Adult Training Centres which have now become the responsibility of social services departments. Very little is known about the aims and activities of ATCs, though it is clear that the majority have progressed from merely 'occupying' trainees to providing some form of industrial therapy. However, relatively few ATCs provide further education of a more formal nature (including reading or number work), though many try to arrange for social education along lines developed by Gunzburg (1968).

Dr Whelan's project is partly concerned with the assessment and training of work skills. Earlier work by psychologists had shown that adult imbeciles were capable of learning surprisingly complex motor and manual tasks, provided that appropriate principles of training were followed, and ample time provided (Clarke and Clarke, 1965). It was also shown that initial learning on a task bore little relationship to the level that could be achieved after training, and that IQ was a poor predictor of how well or how quickly a trainee would learn a manual task.

Dr Whelan has devised a comprehensive test battery consisting of sixteen tasks involving sensory and motor proficiency, coordination and decision-making. These included tests of kinesthetic and tactile functioning, eye-hand and eye-foot coordination, finger dexterity, manual strength and coordination and reaction time on a variety of tasks. These have now been administered to a large number of trainees. A parallel aim of the research is to carry out an analysis of the exact nature of the work tasks currently available in the ATC, using a pre-determined motion time system, MTM-2, which is widely used in industry. The complexity of the work tasks is then related to the skills of the trainee as revealed by the assessment tests. By providing training on a series of graded tasks, it is hoped to discover those job elements which prove particularly difficult, and also to evaluate the predictive validity of the test battery by relating the test profile to actual job performance. Regular administration of a specially designed set of *Industrial Behaviour Rating Scales* facilitates the identification of those other aspects of performance and inter-personal behaviour which would be incorporated to a potential employer. A longitudinal study in this area, incorporating the factor analytic findings of other research workers, provides the basis for a detailed rehabilitative programme currently being developed.

The project calls for the closest cooperation between ATC training staff and the research team; preliminary results are encouraging, suggesting that further training requirements can be usefully specified for the individual trainee so that his skills can be consolidated and developed, and his progress continuously monitored by staff. This should prevent a limited and static view of the abilities of trainees (Whelan, 1971, 1973).

General activities

In addition to specific research projects, individuals or groups of individuals in the Centre have taken part in a number of activities which are briefly described below.

SUBJECT PANEL

The Subject Panel contains basic information on almost all SSN children in the new special schools within a thirty five mile radius of Manchester. Each of the schools was visited, and the staff instructed in the administration of a simple vocabulary recognition test (English Picture Vocabulary Test) which is scored in HARC to provide a rough estimate of mental age. Data on approximately 1 500 children is now available which enables us to select children with known characteristics for specific experiments—e.g. mongols with a mental age between three and four. Information is also available on other test results and on special clinical or behavioural characteristics of the child. The information obtained has been coded, and computer programmes written for data retrieval. This will make it possible to carry out limited longitudinal as well as cross-sectional studies of a large sample of SSN subjects which should be of general interest as a survey investigation as well as of use as a subject panel.

NATIONAL TEACHERS' PANEL

A National teachers' panel has been recruited with the assistance of the National Association of Teachers of the Mentally Handicapped, and their journal *Teaching and Training*. This now consists of over 100 teachers in special schools, adult training centres and hospital schools who have expressed their willingness to help the Centre by answering questionnaires, administering experimental versions of rating scales and other tests, and providing information on curriculum content and needs. This has proved a most useful source of information at national level, and has also relieved pressure on teachers in the north west.

TEACHERS' WORKSHOP

A teachers' workshop consisting of approximately twelve teachers in local special schools met weekly at the HARC under the direction of Dr Herriot and Mrs Thomas. The aim of these workshops was to discuss existing teaching materials and methods and to develop new systematic approaches. A programmed workbook to teach communication and language skills has been prepared, and is being experimentally introduced in a number of schools.

PARENTS' WORKSHOP

In association with the North West Society for Mentally Handicapped Children, workshops for parents of young SSN children were begun in January 1971, organised by Mr Cunningham and Miss Jeffree, and involving other staff and tutors. The workshop aims to help parents to assess the developmental level of their own child, and then to plan a series of games and activities designed to facilitate mental and physical growth. Specially adapted child development charts were prepared for this purpose, and discussed in detail in tutorial groups containing about ten parents each. The course aimed to provide practical and relevant help to parents, and was not primarily designed as a research project, but we hope to learn at first hand about problems arising from the enlistment of parents as 'therapists' with a view to devising a more controlled investigation at a later stage. A preliminary report on the first workshop is available (Cunningham and Jeffree, 1971). Two other workshops have been completed.

HARC BEHAVIOUR RATING SCALE

Work began in October 1969 on the construction of a behaviour rating scale, designed to be completed by teachers. This scale is intended to assess a wide range of behaviour which can be observed in the classroom. A pilot version has been completed, and a preliminary study of its reliability carried out on children in special schools with the help of a national sample of teachers.

EXCITATION-INHIBITION SCALE

Preliminary work has been completed on a scale designed to assess the degree of excitation or inhibition shown by children in special schools. This scale arises directly from Dr Hogg's work on attention, but may prove of wider relevance as an indication of personality factors and their relationship to learning. It is being used in a number of projects in an effort to elucidate the possible role of personality factors in cognitive functioning (Hogg *et al.*, 1971).

Conclusions

Research into the learning processes of the mentally handicapped presents particular difficulties and problems. Some traditional ideas about research design and statistical evaluation necessarily come under critical scrutiny when applied to populations showing such heterogeneity and variance. The validity of group matching and control groups is a case in point. Each research project, and each new experiment forces the research worker to ask himself what it is that he is hoping to discover, whether the means that he is using are appropriate and relevant, and whether his techniques can be used by others. A research programme designed in advance for the benefit of a grant application may need to be modified in the light of findings emerging from experiments. Techniques and models which have proved useful when applied to animals, normal children or students do not always transfer well to the subnormal child, whose interest and motivation need to be engaged before he will take part. Nevertheless, it is important to adapt and apply information from the fields of experimental, educational and developmental psychology, since these provide a body of knowledge which has so far not been productively exploited by people concerned with the education of mentally handicapped children.

Above all, it is important to remember that a research programme cannot be considered complete merely because it is tucked safely into the pages of a learned journal. The research worker must then try to interpret to teachers and other consumers what he has found, and do so in clear and non-technical language. Not all research has practical implications, nor is it necessary that it should have. But it is important to convince teachers of the importance of both basic and applied research, and even to fire some of them with the enthusiasm at least to read and at best to engage in research of their own.

As this chapter was first written in July 1971, some of its contents will necessarily be out of date at the time of publication. Minor revisions of content and bibliography have been carried out at proof stage. Details of current research projects can be obtained from the Centre.

K. M. Miller, B. Hopson and Patricia Hough

Educational and vocational guidance

When a chapter on research in vocational guidance was first considered for inclusion in the second volume of the series *Educational Research in Britain* there was such a dearth of material on the effectiveness of guidance that the chapter was postponed. The situation has improved a little in that considerably more general discussion and development have taken place in the last ten years than occurred before 1960. However, the area is still one where much research is required and in fact rather more research on effectiveness was reported prior to 1951 than has been reported since.

Because of this the present chapter has been planned not only to cover the effectiveness of guidance but also the setting, the definition of the area, the guidance process, guidance techniques and research needs.

Vocational and educational guidance are closely related. However, until very recently, major emphasis, both in research and discussion, has tended to be placed upon the former. Many of the crisis situations with which vocational guidance staff are called upon to deal with are the direct result of the absence of educational guidance at an earlier stage. Both aspects will be dealt with in this chapter.

Guidance setting

Initially vocational guidance in Britain developed in such a way that for most people it was usually associated with the National Institute of Industrial Psychology. That there was a good reason for this has been shown by Alec Rodger in the 1971 C. S. Myers lecture where he traced the development of guidance in the work of the Institute.

In recent years there has been an increase in the number of organisations offering guidance on a fee paying basis. These are either non-profit organisations with a similar basis to NIIP or commercial organisations. Almost all employ psychologists as the principal staff in the guidance team.

The idea that guidance occurred away from school was reinforced by the much later beginning of a government service which was not school based, having the title of employment service rather than guidance service. A study by Aja (1964) investigated the duties of 138 Youth Employment Officers with five years service or less. The investigation lasted ten months and in that time they reported spending 52 per cent of their time in the office, 20 per cent in schools and 3 per cent in factories. The allocation of their duties was 30 per cent given to guidance, placement or reviewing progress, 30 per cent spent on administration and insurance and 20 per cent on travelling. Altogether twenty different functions were identified.

The recent change of title to Careers Advisory Service will, we hope, bring a change in the balance of duties.

There have been several publications dealing with the work, structure and function and future development of the Youth Employment Service. These do consider an increase in the amount of time the officer will spend in schools, as indicated by the headings of sections in one of the main publications—schools, careers work in schools, careers master and the Youth Employment Officer, development of careers work in schools, educational options, careers programmes including conventions and work experience schemes, occupational guidance, timing and conditions of interview and further preparation for starting work such as school leavers' courses. It also envisages an extension of the work outside the school, specific consideration being given to further education, developments in industry, the need to keep in touch with the employers, giving help to employers by providing liaison between them and the schools, the special requirements of groups like the handicapped, the socially unsettled and the migrants. Other contributions on this topic came from Bevan (1967), Bidgood and Gear (1971), Carter (1963, 1966), Galbraith (1967), O'Connor (1971) and Roberts (1970). In his paper Galbraith considered the interrelationship of schools and the youth employment service and described some of the attempts made in one authority to develop guidance teams where both schools and the government service worked together. He saw the main function of such a team as being the maintenance of cumulative records on pupils from the first year onwards and the organisation of careers programmes.

As the Youth Employment Service was the main source of help to actual school leavers, especially those leaving at fifteen or sixteen, it was to be expected that some studies of the consumer perspective would be undertaken. The main study of this type by Jahoda and Chalmers (1963a) involved interviews with students at the beginning and end of their last year at school, during which an interview with a YEO would have taken place.

At the beginning of the year only one in five thought of the YEO as someone with whom they would be likely to talk about jobs before leaving. Even with further indirect probing three in five failed to demonstrate that they had heard of the YEO. Of 140 students interviewed, 85 per cent considered the YEO to have functions of placement only, at the beginning of the year, while 63 per cent held the same view at the end of the year. Seven per cent saw the YEO role as an information giving one, while 22 per cent held this view at the end of the year. While 10 per cent at the beginning saw the YEO in a guidance role, the number grew to 15 per cent by the end of the year. The changes, however, were not simple but complex ones, in that some of those who saw the YEO in a guidance role at the beginning of the year changed to placement or information after the interview. A tentative explanation given by the authors was that the students who changed from seeing the YEO as a guidance person had gained a fuller appreciation of just what guidance could involve from other sources such as TV programmes and therefore became somewhat disillusioned during the year. At the beginning of the year 31 per cent had indicated that they expected the YEO to be one of the avenues helping them to a job and the same percentage held that view at the end of the year.

WITHIN THE SCHOOL

The non-state school, as Daws (1966) points out, has had more opportunity to make the development of the whole child its concern, whereas the local authority school has emphasised scholastic development. The critical factor has been that the parents of pupils in the former type of school have chosen to send their child there and accept the philosophy of the school, whereas no such homogeneity can be assumed in the authority school.

This does not mean that private schools have excelled in vocational and educational guidance, even though careers teachers were recognised earlier and the Public School Appointments Bureau was set up to help boys who had not reached a firm choice of career. One public school employed a qualified psychologist as early as the 1930s. Nor does it mean that no state schools attempted vocational guidance at an early stage. An increasing number of schools during the 1950s had been giving more systematic guidance, but it was only with the introduction of special courses for educational counsellors and careers teachers that official recognition was given. Daws describes the range of counselling functions the school can now be expected to undertake. These are pastoral care, vocational guidance, developmental guidance, personal counselling and parental guidance.

Teachers who become trained as counsellors are expected to be able to work across all areas though with rather less concentration on vocational guidance. What their role will be is determined by the time alloted to them for the job, and the importance attached to it by the headmaster. Several surveys of the functions of educational counsellors trained in the earlier courses have shown that very few were engaged in full-time counselling and some were not officially undertaking any counselling duties (Moore, Fuller and Watts, 1968).

The raising of the school leaving age and the full implementation of a comprehensive system will increase the demand for adequate counselling services within the schools and greater coordination between the school services and the Careers Advisory Service itself. Some attempts have already been made in developing new approaches to this problem: Hatton (1967) describes the introduction of youth tutors in Kent who have the specific aim of helping with the transition of pupils from school to work.

Rowe (1968) described an experiment in counselling in a comprehenseive school where the role of the counsellor was modified to meet the increasing educational needs of the pupils. In that particular school the counsellor was seen as working more on the personal side and rather less on the vocational and educational guidance side. A study in which a more comprehensive series of case studies is reported is that by Moore (1970) in which he describes systems operating in the five large comprehensive schools. Each school had a large degree of common approach though each had specific attributes developed as an interaction of the locality in which the school was situated and the general philosophy of the school administration. One point which came in for considerable discussion was whether the counsellor should be a full-time person or whether the counselling function should be spread over as many of the school staff as possible. One thing that did seem clear was that when it came to vocational guidance, this particular aspect should be concentrated rather more in the hands of a small number of staff who had an opportunity of becoming more specialised in their knowledge of occupational opportunities. This report by Moore is likely to be an influential one for the future development of guidance counselling in comprehensive schools and for that matter in all types of secondary schools.

Another approach to the understanding of the Youth Employment Service has come through studies which endeavour to be specific about what use is actually made of the service itself. Maizels (1965) studied the records for fifteen to eighteen year olds in one London borough over the period 1960–3. Her study showed that it was mainly the secondary modern leavers who used the service and many of the placements were to second and to third jobs. Secondary modern pupils were placed mainly in manual jobs; grammar school and technical leavers placed mainly as apprentices in clerical and non-manual activities. Over half the appointments were to people going to small firms with fewer than 100 employees, while the children finding work without the help of the service were more likely to go into larger firms.

So far the discussion has referred to the secondary school leavers but there is also a degree of service provided for older students in tertiary education. Most tertiary institutions now have counsellors; in some, the counselling function is combined with that of the appointments office, whereas in others it is quite separate. In some colleges of further education there are individual lecturers who have undertaken training in assessment procedures in order to provide educational guidance to the young worker. Also in the government service there are the occupational guidance units which are available to adults desiring assistance in finding or changing jobs (Crinnion, 1967). This service started in 1966 with eleven units, with plans to extend it to twenty-four units by 1967. At the present time some forty units are operating.

Definition of the area

There has been little enough empirical research carried out in vocational guidance, but when one examines the theoretical contributions the position is dismal indeed. There has been increasing discussion of the issues, and it is only because of this that this chapter has a sizeable bibliography. Until Hopson and Hayes' book of readings (1968) and Daws' *A Good Start in Life* (1968a), the last book to be published specifically on vocational guidance in the UK was *The Case for Vocational Guidance* by Angus Macrae in 1934.

The Hopson and Hayes book contained no British theoretical contributions for the simple reason that none existed. Since then, sociologists have become interested in the problems of occupational choice and vocational behaviour. Considerable discussion can be found of a piece-meal variety into the aims of vocational guidance (Fuller and Juniper, 1967; Gill, 1967; Rayner and Atcherly, 1967; Taylor, 1968) but generally speaking, both researchers and practitioners appear content to rely on relatively undiluted American theory.

Daws (1968c) provides a guide to the development of guidance services in this country along with his views on the redefined aims of guidance necessitated by social, educational and technological change. The booklet, *Careers Guidance in Schools* (1965), distributed by the DES defined very broadly what it meant by careers guidance, and this has been defined rather more specifically by Hayes and Hopson (1972).

It is immediately apparent that some confusion is caused by an overlapping of descriptive titles: terms like careers guidance, careers education, career development, vocational guidance, vocational counselling, counselling, etc. are often used interchangeably. In spite of the confusion, however, one can distinguish amongst the writings mentioned certain themes that have developed through the 1960s in relation to 'vocational guidance':

1 there has been a movement away from thinking about the purpose of vocational guidance as simply involving helping someone to find a satisfying job, towards, on the one hand, the broader concept of helping the individual to decide upon the style of life that he wishes to lead, and on the other, the more specific purpose of teaching decision-making skills. The latter is seen as a necessary prerequisite for coping with accelerating social change (Daws, 1967);

2 increasing emphasis on guidance as a developmental process rather than as a crisis-orientated one;

3 a distinct movement towards a more non-directive emphasis and less advice-giving;

4 the realisation that in practice there is no real distinction between educational and vocational guidance;

5 a growing away from the concept of vocational guidance as something that is given to school leavers as an extra-mural facility of the school, towards the notion of its being central to the educational process, demanding curriculum time and special teacher training (Daws, 1969–70, 1972);

6 this broadening of the concept of vocational guidance has led naturally to the demand for this to be an essential part of every young person's education, including the examination streams, sixth formers, the educationally subnormal, the physically handicapped, the below-average child and the immigrants (Hartop, 1966; Montgomery, 1967; Pimblett, 1967; Shouksmith and Taylor, 1964; Wallis, 1969; Wilson, 1964);

7 vocational guidance is seen as applicable not only to school leavers, but to anyone at any stage in his educational or occupational activities as needed. This is witnessed by the setting-up of Occuptional Guidance Units in 1968, and the growth of 'careers counselling' schemes in industry (Avent, 1964; Palmer, 1965; Hopson, 1973);

8 there has been some controversy about the overall social and economic justification for vocational guidance, with the most clamorous voices raised on the side of a client-centred approach rather than a guidance system related to manpower (and womanpower) needs (Cotgrove, 1962; Hayes, 1969);

Although there is much argument over the actual purposes of vocational guidance and its related terms some clarification can be found in the literature (Jackson and Juniper, 1971). Guidance is the more general term which includes functions like:

1 helping the individual to discover information about his abilities, interests, needs, ambitions;

2 providing him with information about the world of work, education, and perhaps even society in general;

3 orientating him well in advance of any decision-making to the need for it and of the helping agencies available;

4 counselling defined variously (Bolger, 1970; Caspan, 1968;

Lytton and Craft, 1968; Schools Council, 1967) but with the common thread of helping the client understand himself and to provide him with the support necessary for him to develop career plans and solutions to his personal problems;

5 a placement service which will enable the individual to implement those plans;

6 a follow-up service to provide further assistance when required.

Counselling has undoubtedly had a major impact in the 1960s on vocational guidance in Britain. Most counsellors when trained are equipped to deal with vocational problems. This has led to concern between careers officers, careers teachers and counsellors, over role conflicts in secondary education (Daws, 1969; Jones, 1969; Locke, 1968; Lytton et al., 1970). This has also stimulated discussion over the subject teacher's responsibility for pastoral care, and there is a growing attitude in secondary school teaching that each teacher has a pastoral role for which he requires some skill in counselling, and that he also has a part to play through his subject teaching in the school's careers programme. This is the sum of how far the concept of vocational guidance has moved away from a talent-matching crisis approach, performed by a local placement specialist, towards a personal growth, developmental model, performed by a team of specialists with some distinct and some overlapping functions, and who are seen as individuals with an educational responsibility. Boreham's model (1967) describing a psycho-dynamic diagnostic approach and treatment of vocational problems, illustrates the move towards viewing vocational guidance as central to mental health issues.

The broader concept of vocational guidance has led to a demand for these services in higher and further education (Barr, 1961; Hankins, 1966; Hughes, 1969; Ryle, 1969) which for the most part have not been met by these institutions.

Considering the research evidence which demonstrates the importance of parents in occupational and educational decision making, there has been a tendency to ignore the role of parents in vocational guidance programmes (Vaughan, 1970). This is regrettable. The fact that guidance counsellors find parents do represent one of their most frustrating problems is no reason for dropping them out of a guidance model.

With the exception of Shimmin (1966) and some sociological work the concepts of work, vocation, occupation, leisure, career, life-style etc., have not been explored. Possibly this is due to the fact that there is an assumption that most people will understand what is being talked about. This is a dangerous assumption as the American arguments over the implications of accepting different definitions of these concepts have shown.

Aspects of the guidance process

OCCUPATIONAL AND EDUCATIONAL CHOICE RESEARCH

Theory In a review of the theoretical approaches to occupational choice, Ginzberg *et al.* (1951) distinguished between the accident, psycho-analytic, and talent-matching theories. Hayes and Hopson (1972) go on to point out how these ignore the role of values, which a comprehensive model would handle, as well as consideration of social and economic factors. In fact much of the theoretical contribution to work on occupational and educational choice in this country is sociological.

Use is made of the concept of the socialisation process. Keil *et al.* (1966) describe the stages by which the young person's vocational development is influenced by previous experience and wider social forces, leading him to develop expectations about work which explain his entry into employment. His consequent 'adjustment' can be expressed as a measure of the satisfaction of his expectations. Musgrave (1967a) distinguishes between primary, secondary and tertiary socialisation to adult life, locating occupational choice in part of the secondary stage of socialisation (i.e. the stage which involves economically productive roles). Within a functionalist framework he relates the individual to the system by means of the concept of economic socialisation. Coulson *et al.* (1967) criticise his standpoint as neglecting the social structure and assuming a high level of role consensus, an argument which Musgrave (1968) later refutes. Chester (1968), in turn, goes on to modify the work of Keil *et al.*, in order to include education in the process. His formulation aims to allow for examination of similar transitions, for example into higher education.

Ford and Box (1967) introduce a variation by using the approach of exchange theory. They argue that it is not necessary to look at the process of acquiring values. They regard values as independent variables which interact with the individual's perception of chances for realising his expectations. Roberts (1968a) goes on to question the role that occupational choice actually plays in the entry to employment. He puts forward an opportunity-structure model of entry in which young people are seen as having a malleable work orientation. Haystead (1971) also takes social structure into account in her view of the processes of choice.

EMPIRICAL RESEARCH

Home and school A variety of studies have looked at the influences of home background and schooling on later educational and vocational choices. Sherlock and Cohen (1966) look at access to dentistry, relating it to Blau's view of occupational choice as a compromise between desired rewards and realities. They claim that the roots of choice are in family background; part of this includes socio-economic level, which Lee (1968) explores in a study of class differentials in educational opportunity.

Most other studies in the area look at both home and school influences. Few use a theoretical framework but tend to investigate the relative importance of family and educational factors in educational and occupational choices. They consider, for example, aspirations in different types of school (Durojaiye, 1969; Roberts, 1968b), effects and implications of the curriculum (Barnard et al., 1967), the role of school staff and others in affecting choices (Hill, 1965).

Higher education Other studies focus on factors affecting career direction in students at college and university (Nisbet and Grant, 1965; Rice, 1964; Swinhoe, 1967). Child and Musgrove (1969), for example, investigate how scientists' attitudes are shaped, while Smithers (1971) looks at students' experience of a sandwich course.

Psychological factors Some researchers look at the factors involved in educational and occupational choice from the point of view of individual differences. They may consider the role of interests, values and achievement drive in the choice process (Meyer et al., 1961; Rowlands, 1961) or they may look at personality types amongst certain occupational fields (Box and Cotgrove, 1966; Davis and Satterly, 1969; Eysenck, 1967; Singh, 1968; Smithers, 1968).

General A further approach to the investigation of occupational choice is taken by those who concentrate on career patterns. Studies have been made following up a group of young people over a period of time (Cohen, 1969; MacDonald *et al.*, 1964; Nelson, 1964; Stern, 1961). Others look at the images developed about particular occupational fields (Clarke, 1968; Coxon, 1967), the sources of information used for choices (Carter, 1962; Veness, 1962), and at attitudes to work in general (Musgrave, 1967b).

TRENDS

Most of the empirical work which has been going on over the last ten years has taken either a sociological *or* a psychological approach to the question of occupational choice. Yet few researchers have based their studies on a theoretical background or tested the concepts suggested. There is a distinct lack of team approach to the study of occupational choice. The combination of the disciplines of psychology, sociology and economics could benefit the field as Butler (1968) suggests. Studies which restrict themselves to consideration of individual or environmental features only, tend to lose valuable data and perspective.

Another trend which has similar implications is that of cross-sectional rather than longitudinal studies. Although the cross-sectional study indicates factors which vary between groups it cannot reveal those whose effects take place only over time, during the process of vocational development. It is perhaps these factors which have greatest relevance for research which could make a contribution to theory.

THE TRANSITION FROM SCHOOL TO WORK AND FURTHER EDUCATION

The transition from school to work is the first major role transition that a young person has to make. This has been considered to be of great importance to the planning of a developmental school guidance programme. A considerable amount of research has been carried out into the adjustment problems of school leavers. Maizels (1970) in her Willesden study provides evidence of the real problems that young people have to face when beginning work. She also shows that the Youth Employment Service is not perceived by the school leaver as being of much assistance, a finding also of Carter's Sheffield study. Palmer (1964) found that although stress existed it might not be as widespread as is sometimes claimed. Approximately two-thirds of her sample of young workers had favourable attitudes towards their jobs.

Veness (1962) provides perhaps the most comprehensive research yet completed into the aspirations and expectations of British secondary school children—for the most part depressingly low and uniform. Most other research has been concerned with these problems plus more detailed enquiries into factors like the nature of apprenticeships (Liepman, 1960; Tonkinson, 1962), the attitudes of young people towards school and job entry (E. A. Allen, 1961; Carter, 1966; Eppel and Eppel, 1953; Paul, 1962; Venables, 1967), the waste of abilities which occurs in the present educational and economic structure (Douglas *et al.*, 1968), the leisure orientations of young people, vital to a broad concept of vocational guidance (Crichton and Jones, 1968; Jephcott, 1967), the experiences of young people at work (Herford, 1964) and the effects of spare-time employment on pupils.

This area is obviously vital to anyone concerned with vocational guidance, and Erikson (1960) goes so far as to suggest that it is the lack of an occupational identity which is the major source of stress in adolescence. If this is so, then the role of 'student' is perhaps even less likely to provide a framework for individual identity than most occupations. Vocational guidance in our institutions for further and higher education is negligible as has been much deplored (Ryle, 1969). Reviews of the research into student wastage and adjustment problems can be found in Gordon Miller book (1970).

OCCUPATIONAL INFORMATION RESEARCH

Only in the past few years have fundamental questions been raised about the role and nature of occupational information within the context of the vocational guidance process. With a recent increase in the amount of careers information on the market, in the forms of literature, films, TV programmes etc., there is a growing awareness of the needs to appraise and select materials for presentation.

ROLE OF OCCUPATIONAL INFORMATION

In 1967, Hayes looked at the part which occupational information can play in a developmental approach to careers guidance. Within a framework of developing concepts about the self, occupational information can be seen as contributing to the evaluation of occupational concepts in relation to the self-concept, in order to help development of appropriate *occupational self-concepts*. He introduced the notion of occupational horizons, the range of which may be influenced by informal factors in the home, school and community, in addition to the formal sources of occupational information.

NATURE OF OCCUPATIONAL INFORMATION

Hayes raised the question of whether occupational information does in fact provide for the individual to relate occupational awareness to the roles he aspires to play in life. Both he and Daws (1970) question the adequacy of occupational information in crystallising occupational self-concepts. They suggest that there are major areas which are neglected: these are the psycho-social aspects of work roles, relating to the identity and life-style which may be associated with particular work situations. Hayes (1970) carried out a study into this question. He found that the psycho-social aspects of work were neglected by the major sources of occupational information in schools; yet they assumed greater importance in relation to purely economic aspects (e.g. pay, tasks, conditions), after work experience. However, a subsequent working paper reveals that awareness of the important dimensions of the work role is not readily transferred to thinking about *other* jobs. This poses a problem for the provision of information to job changers. A further study showed that careers literature in particular neglects the psycho-social aspects of work roles. All these results suggest that the nature of the *content* of occupational information needs reappraisal, whether the medium is written, oral or visual.

PRESENTATION

In addition to the effect of content on the value of occupational information, its presentation can influence the impact it makes. In relation to careers literature, a study found that a number of dimensions of format and lay-out are significant. However attractive information may look, it cannot achieve maximum impact unless it is pitched at a level appropriate to its audience. An ongoing study is investigating the application of a readability measure to careers literature.

USE

Conflicting evidence on the use of various sources of occupational information led Starkey (1970) to investigate whether the influence of parents and peers outweighed that of 'official' sources. His results confirmed the hypothesis, yet indicated that about 50 per cent of his sample had also found information from literature and careers officers useful. The uses and value of different sources of information need more investigation. Watts (1968) suggests, for example, the use of patterns of careers as a guide to students, while Hayes and Hopson (1972) discuss the use of manpower information in the vocational guidance setting. They also cover many possible uses of occupational information in schools.

CONCLUSION

Occupational information is a neglected area of research which demands attention in an information-conscious society. Work investigating ways of collecting and presenting information could be valuable. A start has been made with the Schools Council Career project at Cambridge and a study of the extent of job knowledge held by sixth form boys being conducted by Hatfield Polytechnic and IARC. However many more studies are needed to meet adequately the needs described in this section.

Guidance techniques

With the broadening of the concept of vocational guidance so that it becomes a integral part of the school curriculum, a number of techniques have been developed to help the careers team. Unfortunately, most of these have not been evaluated. The dearth of techniques to provide vocational guidance in the school has meant that new ideas are often immediately implemented without prior evaluation. The

Schools Council has just commenced a three-year programme with the aim of developing materials and techniques for careers education. Initially there are no plans to evaluate them, at least not by any evaluation that an educational researcher would accept.

A wide range of self-assessment techniques exist (AMA, 1970; Barr, 1970; Cattell, 1969; El Shakarwy and Lee, 1965; Hayes and Hopson, 1972; Cavanagh et al., 1962) but only some have been empirically evaluated. The Vocational Guidance Research Unit is producing a teaching programme for self-assessment and life planning based on techniques used for management career development. This will be evaluated.

Occupational visits and work experience themes abound, but we can only discover two empirical studies of these techniques, Hopson (1970), Hopson and Hough (1971).

Counselling is a fashionable term, and much practice which is termed 'counselling' would not fit under any known model. But even where practitioners can define their counselling techniques and objectives, little research has been done to assess how far these objectives are met. Two exceptions are the work done by Shouksmith and Taylor (1964) on the effectiveness of counselling on the achievement of high-ability pupils, and Lawrence's study (1971) assessing the effects of counselling on retarded readers.

Group counselling is increasingly discussed by guidance personnel, but no research has been carried out on this topic, and outside of American contributions, little has been written about it (Williams, 1970).

TECHNIQUES OF PRESENTING OCCUPATIONAL INFORMATION

Current developments include a variety of approaches. These are illustrated by the following examples:

1 Stocks (1971) is developing tests of occupational information. Using a framework of more than forty grouped items (e.g. types of task/contact with people) he is building up profiles of occupations for use in schools.
2 The programmed learning approach is used in a text book for discovering careers which is being developed by K. J. Travers (1971). It is intended to increase pupil-participation in gaining occupational information.

3 Work at the Vocational Guidance Unit (Hopson and Hough, 1971) is focused on a caerers teaching programme which introduces a framework for *evaluating* information about any job and relating it to the self-concept.

Testing

At present very few schools or career advisory offices have staff who are trained in the selection, administration and interpretation of psychological tests. Such research as has been carried out into the use of tests as distinct from the effectiveness of guidance has come mainly from university departments. An experiment in which the contribution of tests was studied was reported by Hopson (1970). He demonstrated that when second and fourth year students were given three tests—general ability, reading and arithmetic—and the test results fed back to them with elementary interpretations a greater realism of self-estimation followed. The control groups, who took the tests but did not receive any feed back, did not change towards greater realism. Hopson indicated that his results were similar to American findings, except that there was no age or maturation difference between the two year groups. It could be that had tests other than ability and achievement been used the maturation effect might have appeared. Information about attitudes, interests and personality are more likely to be differentially appreciated as pupils grow older. One American study not mentioned by Hopson, but of direct relevance to British readers, is that of Goslin (1967) in which both students' and teachers' attitudes to, and knowledge of, tests was studied. The Hopson study also showed that there were no sex differences but that measured intelligence had a bearing on the accuracy of self estimates and the benefit gained from test results.

Another study of the place of tests in the process was reported by Higginbotham and Mountford (1964). This reviewed research prior to 1950 but is still relevant. Experimental groups for whom tests were used differed from the control groups not tested in that they stayed longer in jobs, changed jobs less frequently, were more satisfied with their jobs, appeared more satisfactory employees to their employers and changed more often to a job that had been recommended. A briefer review of the place of tests in the guidance process is that of Rodger and Cavanagh (1964). Rodger has also been involved in an experiment similar to that reported by Higgenbotham and Mountford, but as yet no results are available.

One study (El Shakarwy and Lee, 1965) of a British multi-aptitude test, the Differential Test Battery, showed that the battery, as developed by the author, could for young apprentices in the steel industry be replaced by four new factors. The authors suggested a new type of profile chart for vocational guidance based on the use of the complete battery. Such a suggestion would need to be replicated using the battery with school leavers before any move away from the standard procedures recommended by the test author could be contemplated.

Moore (1970) in his five comprehensive schools found that little if any testing was done. However, in all these schools testing would be introduced if staff and facilities permitted it. All the head teachers recognised the need for training in all guidance and counselling techniques.

Among the main categories of psychological tests those of occupational interests have received most attention recently. Wiegersma and Barr (1960) reviewed the usefulness of such measures and concluded that they provided useful information which should be considered along with other test results. The most comprehensive study so far carried out in Britain is that by Barr (1970) in which he reported an extensive study of changes in interest patterns and also in ability levels with several cohorts in a secondary technical grammar school.

Current approaches to the measurement of occupational interests were reviewed in 1968 when three contributors to a symposium described newer methods of measuring occupational interest (Nelson, Carruthers, Kilcross, 1968).

Nelson reported on the effectiveness of the first British Interest Blank. The main finding in the study was that school leavers who took jobs in line with their main field of interest were more likely to stay longer at the job and be slightly more satisfied with it. Carruthers described work with a new occupational values test with university students, while Kilcross reported on the development of an occupational guide for use with secondary pupils.

At a more sophisticated level, psychometricians have been active in suggesting ways for assessing similarities between an individual's test score pattern and that of an occupational group (Cattell, 1969; Tatsuoka and Cattell, 1970). Using such methods as they have suggested is usually easier when a computer is available. However, for the individual guidance officer short cut nomographs are available for some of the techniques.

The most widely used technique in guidance is the interview, yet very little research has been done on it. One study looked at the characteristics of trainee interviewers in the Youth Employment Service (Cavanagh *et al.*, 1962). A problem immediately encountered was that of defining the criteria for a good interviewer. Having decided upon suitable criteria, the differences between high and low rated interviewers were analysed. The group rated highly spoke less, asked more questions, discussed home and school more. Those who spoke so little as to be deemed reticent were not rated highly. The study also showed that verbal intelligence was not an indication of interview performance, though there was a positive relation between strong persuasive and literary interests and high performance on the interview.

RECORD CARDS

While not necessarily seen as a technique, the record card occupies a salient place in recent writing about guidance and counselling (Moore, 1970). The first study devoted entirely to the topic during the period covered by this review was that of Walker (1950). The usefulness of information from secondary modern school records alone for predicting vocational suitability has been reported by Eyre (1966). The importance of subjective and personality information was demonstrated but an overall assessment of performance in a school year was suggested as a possible best indicator. While agreeing that record cards can be useful, we would emphasise the need for recording comprehensive information and training staff in the appropriate methods of observing and recording.

Effectiveness of guidance

In assessing the effectiveness of guidance, short term, intermediate and long term criteria can be applied. Only one study, recently completed, has used long term criteria (Faruddin, 1971). This was a follow up of 200 cases seen by a single careers advisor at NIIP thirty years before. Of the 144 who were traced and completed a short questionnaire, 104 filled in a second more searching questionnaire. A smaller sub-sample was interviewed. Approximately 60 per cent of those seen were in an occupation of the type recommended, a fact found to be related more to the attitude of the individual to vocational guidance than to the satisfaction with the job. Interests were related to type of job recommended and to that being followed thirty years later, though basic dispositional factors seemed more stable than expressed interests. Faruddin concluded that vocational recommendations at the end of a short consultation can be useful for up to thirty years.

Another study using intermediate criteria was also based on NIIP data (Lancashire, 1971). This was confined to groups of subjects who had been advised to follow either of two closely related fields, solicitor or chartered accountant. The sample of 146 had been guided between 1958 and 1961 when they were aged between fifteen and twenty two. Just over half were interviewed. The study was concerned both with the advisors and the advised. People pursuing careers in the line with the recommendations were those who had been strongly recommended to follow that career. The group not pursuing the career suggested, but still following a professional career, had not been strongly recommended to pursue law or accountancy and had had other careers in mind at the time of the guidance. About half of those not pursuing a professional career of any sort, had at the time of guidance been considering law or accountancy. At the time of the follow-up interview they were either strongly ambitious in the career they had chosen or had no long term plans at all. None of the groups differed in academic achievement or test scores. From the advisors' point of view the investigators found that the staff had been systematically trained in a common approach to testing, interviewing and interpretation of results and tended to make similar recommendations to people having similar characteristics. However, there were differences between the advisors which were associated with their theoretical standpoint and personality. A similar study is now being carried out on a group of engineers.

Most other studies have used short term criteria, though in one (Douglas, 1972) further follow up is planned. In this investigation vocational guidance was not the central aim but came naturally in the longitudinal study of a cohort of children born in a particular week in 1946. Information was collected between the fifteenth and the eighteenth birthdays of young people who had taken tests just prior to turning fifteen.

That part of the report concerned with guidance supplied by the

YEO showed that fifteen year old school leavers who were not interviewed at school by the YEO were more likely to leave their first job
before eighteen. Other results are listed below:

1 Within the small group of boys who seemed most likely to have
difficulty settling at work those who were interviewed at school
by the YEO had fewer changes of job.

2 Survey members who started work in a job that was neither of
the type nor at the level recommended by the YEO were twice
as likely to leave the first job within six months, as were those
in jobs where both type and level were as recommended.

3 Boys and, particularly, girls who started work in a job of the
type they had chosen before leaving school, rather than in the
one recommended by the YEO, were more likely to leave within
6 months.

4 If only one aspect of the work (i.e. type or level) was as recommended, girls were more likely to leave within 6 months if
they got a job of a different type and boys if they got a job at a
different level.

5 Half the boys who got a job at a level below that recommended
by the YEO left it within 6 months.

6 Boys and girls whose first job was not at the level recommended
by the YEO and who had changed jobs before 18, moved towards
the level of work recommended by the YEO.

7 If the YEO simply endorsed the job choice made by the child
before leaving school, the young worker was less likely to go
back for further guidance after starting work than if the YEO
had suggested a different type of job.

The study also showed that the job nominated at fifteen was related
to the job first entered, thus giving further support to the point made
by Chown (1958) and Jahoda (1962), that attitudes, once formed, are
difficult to modify.

As the Douglas study is the only one based on a large (5 000)
representative sample, the implications of the findings are all the more
to be heeded. These were that guidance should start earlier, that more
time should be spent with children more likely to be a risk in the labour
market and that there was a need for help at the time young school
leavers change their first job. Allan (1961) obtained information from
2 024 young men, mainly apprentices, about the advice they had been

given on leaving school. 35 per cent felt they had not been helped enough; 23 per cent were not satisfied with their job; 39 per cent said they had received most help from the family, and found the YEO the second most useful agent; 29 per cent said that no information had been given them about further educational opportunities whilst they were at school.

The impression left by the YEO in interview was investigated by Jahoda and Chalmers (1963a). The majority of the sample had seen the interview as an information-giving session, and at least half could remember no discussion of jobs other than the one they had had in mind to begin with. Recommendations could be distorted to accord with the leavers' own wishes. Some recommendations were of a reversal type when the YEO was seen to encourage the secondary choice rather than the primary one. This happened rather more for girls than for boys. A smaller percentage of the recommendations were novel ones. When the completely new suggestion was at the same level as the type of job the individual had been considering, there was some chance that both boys and girls would act upon it. When boys were offered an alternative which was at a lower level than they had in mind, none accepted the alternative, though a few girls did so. Several other studies come into the same category as those already described, in particular the review of twenty five years work, using tests in guidance by Smith (1951) and some of the studies by Stott (1952) and Handyside and Stott (1958). An unpublished study by Headen and Miller investigated short term satisfactions with guidance. The sample consisted of the first 100 guidance clients of the Independent Assessment and Research Centre. Of the forty five who returned the questionnaire, only two reported not having had satisfaction from the information they received. Headen placed particular emphasis on the adult cases who were by then working in particular jobs and related satisfaction with job to satisfaction with guidance received.

Another type of follow up is that reported by Avent (1967) who tried to trace 200 participants in careers courses attended ten years earlier. Of the fifty eight who replied, the answers to the four critical questions produced rather varied information. Only nine felt that the careers course confirmed their choice of career; twenty four did not. Three had changed their choice of career as a result of the course; thirty five had not. Twenty nine would recommend present employers to offer careers courses to sixth formers as a means of helping them make up their minds. Interestingly enough most of the respondents saw the type of course as useful though they disclaimed influence on themselves. Other studies of courses such as Link courses and work experience situations are currently being carried out.

Another study (Wymer and Bowell, 1971), typical of several, is not a real follow-up study but is one which relates information about abilities with educational outcomes. The test of general ability correlated very highly with course results and was seen as a useful method of advising students as to their likelihood of passing particular courses.

Vocational guidance workers are constantly seeking supplementary information which would help them in determining advice to give. One study which contributes to this particular aspect is that by Brown (1971) who studied the factors which influenced occupational choice in a sample of men and women graduates. He had 900 new graduates complete a questionnaire and interviewed about ninety of them. He also used a measure of occupational interests. He found that about 20 per cent of these graduates had come to university with a firm choice, and another 20 per cent had made a decision by the end of the first year. Many of them reported lack of help or information at school and also dissatisfaction with employers' literature and interviews. The appointment service was seen as a helpful source of information but not as a source of guidance. Before coming to university they were most likely to be influenced by the subject matter and other people. While at university, people and personal factors accounted for 60 per cent of the influence on choice, institutional factors about 30 per cent and general information about 10 per cent. This is another study which does highlight the need for better information at the school stage. Brown concluded by suggesting that appointment services should increase their counselling function, and since then some have done so. Others (Lock, 1951; Stott, 1950; M. B. Vernon, 1965; P. E. Vernon, 1965) have drawn attention to the difficulties of defining success in vocational guidance and classifying individuals accordingly.

Stott reports a study in which this problem was looked at, and describes some of the reasons why clients may appear to be unsuccessful in that they have not followed recommendations given by vocational guidance consultants, or successful in that they have done well in a job which did not appear at the time of the consultation to be one which would have been appropriate. Stott found that very often people came into an unexpected category but on examination of their records the final choice is not incompatible with information which was available at the time.

Research needs

In 1951 Rodger and Lock discussed current needs in vocational guidance. It is a sad reflection that, twenty years later, many of these research needs do not appear to have been dealt with: most of them are as current today as they were then. They saw the needs as

1) better criteria of occupational success leading to a body of classified job information based on a careful analysis of jobs in terms of psychological qualities;
2) development of reporting techniques and better training in guidance interviewing;
3) more valid and reliable psychological tests, both of abilities, aptitudes and personality and interests. Lock, in talking about tests, emphasised a point often overlooked, namely that a map of the mind based on factor analysis is of little use to a vocational guidance officer. Objective measure of motivation were seen as a most important need;
4) widely based and extensive validating studies.

One of the limitations to the use of results is the failure of vocational guidance officers to record case notes systematically. He saw the need for each case to have evidence summarised and an explicit statement for an individual of an ordered hypothesis or hypotheses and a clearly recorded prediction or set of predictions. Research in the design of case records therefore had high priority.

Some of these areas have been tackled. We now have additional and better tests, but as yet very little information about their effectiveness in vocational guidance work. The Central Youth Employment Executive is developing a series of tests for use by careers' officers and will, it is hoped, be able to set up appropriate validity studies.

Certainly inverview training in the Youth Employment Service has been very extensively developed in the period under review but there still seems a need for more systematic theory in training for educational counsellors and careers teachers.

We still await the body of information about jobs and their various criteria of success. This is in part due to the near impossibility of obtaining long term criteria in an era of rapid technological change and job obsolescence added to, and accelerated by, the perennial problem of personal change. Perhaps it would be more meaningful to concentrate on developing operational short term criteria of vocational success. However, vocational success is not the only criterion for evaluating the success of guidance. With the increasing occurrence in some secondary schools of courses on vocational information and career choice, progress must be limited until there is a much bigger body of knowledge about jobs, particularly in psychological terms.

With vocational guidance seen increasingly as a process appropriate to any age or reference group, there is an urgent need to examine and evaluate the general applicability of both techniques and theoretical orientations to the problems of school leavers, students, adults, physically handicapped and other special groups.

Vocational guidance is thought of by many contemporary writers as a process which has as one of its aims the promotion of decision-making skills. However, there is next to no research, either American or British, which has investigated the effectiveness of different decision-making strategies or of the teaching techniques by which these might be conveyed.

Points discussed in this section, together with others raised in the preceding sections, clearly indicate the need for more research in the whole field of educational and vocational guidance.

W. van der Eyken

Further education

Educational research in Britain suffers, comparatively, from a lack of resources. The United States of America devotes 0·3 per cent of its overall education budget to research; in Sweden the figure is 0·17 per cent; and in England and Wales as low as 0·12 per cent. In hard cash, this means that the research-sponsoring agencies, from the Department of Education and Science to the Social Science Research Council and the independent foundations, allocate some £2 million a year to this area, of which by far the greatest amount, nearly half, is devoted to curricular studies. (See also the detailed discussion of such allocations in the chapter by Taylor.)

Within the broad sweep of educational research, further education has a minor role, despite the fact that it is the area which, together with teacher training, has enjoyed the greatest growth in recent years. Woodhall and Ward (1972) has suggested that if one regards further education as a *sector* of the education system, then current research projects within it represent only 5·3 per cent of all projects sponsored in the two years 1968–70, commanding 3·8 per cent of the total research resources made available in that period. If, on the other hand, one considers further education as no more than a *category* of activity, then in these two years there were only fourteen projects, some 2·3 per cent of the total, costing in all £63 000 or 1·7 per cent of the global research resources for this period. Michaels (1971) has shown that the distribution is not only small, but uneven, and Cole and van der Eyken (1971) have tried to indicate some of the reasons inherent in the field of further education for this apparent imbalance.

One of the problems that immediately becomes obvious is that of definition. 'Further education', unlike almost every other sector of the educational spectrum, is not definable in terms of its institutions, its courses, or its clientele. It is, in fact, not a generic term at all, but a collective one; attempts at definition therefore end by becoming so global in their span as to include virtually all educational activities beyond primary schooling. It involves many different modes of study —full-time, part-time, sandwich courses, day and block release and evening study— and a broad age range, dealing with both a hierarchy and a range of studies which themselves interlock to provide a three-dimensional model whose complexity remains largely uncharted. Although it lies somewhat outside the scope of this chapter, the study by Smith (1970) into the costs of further education throws interesting light on the workings of this complex system.

Attention has, however, been given to the mechanisms whereby students enter various levels of further education, and, more recently, studies by Phillips (1969), Barnard and McCreath (1970), McCreath (1971), Askham (1968), Douglas (1968) and Susie Barry (1971) have sought to elucidate decision-making processes for secondary school pupils and, in particular, for sixth formers, with their concomitant effects on further education. Barnard and McCreath, for example, showed in a sample of 8 765 fifth formers, 5 728 lower sixth formers and 4 998 upper sixth formers, how the demands of university entry requirements shaped the curricula and the realistic academic options of pupils in the schools. Douglas's classic longitudinal study of 5 000 babies born in one week in March 1946 has already demonstrated the effects of socio-economic forces operating on the schools system and on people who do not satisfy the requirements of the system. Phillips studied the options available to pupils at different levels of grammar school and related them to faculty choice at university entrance, including a comparison with other European countries. Askham and Barry carried out broad surveys of sixth form aspirations, and in both cases tried to gauge the extent towards which sixth formers were informed of opportunities in further education—which, given the evidence of Barnard and McCreath, was depressingly small and, over a gap of four years, showed no signs of improving. It will remain for subsequent volumes of the Douglas survey to provide data on the actual movement of students from the schools to the FE system. In particular, we are remarkably ignorant of the characteristics of those who do *not* enter further education, and of comparisons in the subsequent career patterns of those taking vocational courses and others not doing so. Recent studies at the London School of Economics by Maglan and Layard (1970) and Layard, Sargan, Ager and Jones (1971), suggest, inter alia, that the public return on an investment in City and Guilds technicians' courses is not very high (about eight per cent per annum) but, as these calculations will vary considerably from industry to industry, it remains to be seen whether the students entering further education establishments are themselves a sub-élite chosen, largely by industry, for preferential treatment in terms of day and block-release, and whether, if this is the case, they enjoy a continued priority within industry during their subsequent working lives.

Selection

In any case Lee (1966, 1968) and Lee and Hordley (1970) have suggested that the concept of further education as an 'alternative route' needs considerable revision. They point out that at any given time the extent of working class opportunities in the 'alternative route' will depend on the effect of at least three largely independent factors. First in importance is the rate of participation by working class children in technical classes. Secondly, one should examine the transition rates of these children at each 'hurdle' in the system. Finally, there is the acceptability of a given educational qualification as a way of entering employment at a given level. It ought to be pointed out that we are here referring to the technical education aspect of FE, involving day-release in either an apprenticeship or traineeship arrangement, and, since Heywood (1969; 1971) has already dealt with the field of engineering education in an earlier volume of the present series, I shall concentrate on the 'education of craftsmen and technicians' aspect, while recognising that it covers only a sector—albeit a large and important sector—of the total field.

Lee and Hordley (1970) compare the findings of Cotgrove (1958) with more recent data from the Crowther and Robbins reports to come to the conclusion that opportunities for working class children via technician education have increased in recent years. They also suggest that the transition rate for working class children through the 'hurdles' of the system is broadly the same as for other groups, and finally, they voice the belief that educational qualifications are becoming more important to industry. Compared with the pre-war situation, this is almost certainly the case, though in an earlier paper by Lee (1966) he drew attention to the fact that this increase in opportunity has not gone very far and that, rather than indicating a trend, it may simply be a step function arising out of the relative expansion of white collar and technical jobs as compared with manual work. Has opportunity really increased, or is it just a case that manual jobs have declined in industry? Certainly, Lee indicated the doubt on this issue when he commented in an earlier discussion (1966) that 'the complaint of those now engaged in vocational education is usually of the widespread failure of industry to recognise the qualifications they confer'.

The evidence for these statements is, as Lee and Hordley have repeatedly emphasised, sketchy. A study carried out by the Brunel University Further Education Group within two local technical colleges provided the following social breakdown among first-year craft and technician day-release students. They are compared with data from the 1966 Census drawn from a 10 per cent sample of the relevant local authority:

	Two college sample	1966 Census
Professional	4·6	5·8
Intermediate	15·9	14·0
Non-manual skilled	18·9	22·8
Manual skilled	41·4	35·2
Partly skilled	8·5	14·3
Unskilled	3·0	7·4
Armed Forces	1·0	0·5

This local bias towards the 'skilled worker' category in this study (N = 573) is, of course, no reflection on the colleges, but simply mirrors the selection processes of industry which releases these students to the FE sector. (Incidentally, recent work by Lee seems to indicate that this 'skilled worker' bias could be a *general* feature.) But all these studies, including the evidence considered by Lee, emphasise that there is no data which allows us to be sanguine about the extent towards which industrial selection and the awarding of apprenticeships is mitigating class differentials. There is increasing discussion in industrial training circles for the need for selection 'techniques', despite evidence that the selection methods we at present command have very little predictive value when related to factory floor or works ratings. This rather dogmatic statement needs amendment and qualification, for Roger Shipton's study (1968) did, for example, indicate that there was *some* relationship between industrial assessment and some of the Birkbeck tests, though it may be that the tests themselves are 'job-specific' rather than being generally applicable throughout industry. Vickery (1969), working within the specialised Darlington textile industry with a largely female work force, has given a clear picture of the problems that face the employer in trying to select manpower. 'Selection is based on the interview, the medical check-up and the general remarks of the school report. Up to now we have not found any dexterity test that gives a sufficiently accurate correlation to justify it.' Pendlebury and Hardman (1967), working with engineering craft apprentices at Rolls Royce, found that interview ratings had no predictive value either for success on the factory floor or at the local college, and that a battery of intelligence, spatial and numerical ability tests failed to predict success during works training. Their suggestion, that headmasters' ratings might prove more successful than either of these two other choices as predictors, might if accepted have the effect of broadening class differentials within industrial occupations, if for no other reason than the result of the 'culture clash', to use Lawton's (1970) phrase, the effects of which are chronicled in the Douglas surveys. Other evidence, however (Grimes, 1969; Mary Barry, 1969) suggests that even headmasters' reports give low or negligible correlations with works assessments, and Ross (1962) has similarly reported a lack of any significant relationship between boys' hobbies and their practical assessment on the factory floor. McMahon (1962) and Montgomery (1962) showed that among apprentices at Ferranti's there were high correlations between technical theory qualifications and supervisors' ratings, but non-significant correlations between these theoretical qualifications and factory ratings. These findings have been corroborated by Chappel (1967), who found that previous academic attainment at school was the most valuable general guide to selecting apprentices for trade school, but that this prediction could be improved slightly by adding to it the combined scores of two tests in mathematics and mechanical reasoning. She also stressed the major difficulty of this type of study—finding a reliable criterion of work performance.

This lack of significant correlation between test performance and industrial rating has not, however, created any noticeable lessening in the amount of selection testing carried out in industry. Maizels (1970) reported that among sixty-five employers, selection, in three cases out of five, involved some form of written test, despite the fact that in specifying their requirements for the job, employers made rather more frequent references to personal attributes such as appearance, temperament, character and health than to any academic qualifications, practical abilities or special aptitudes. The analysis of the qualifications specified for apprentices showed certain striking contrasts in the relative frequency with which certain requirements were specified. Educational qualifications, particularly up to 'O' levels, and mechanical aptitude and ability were much more frequently stressed by the larger than the smaller firms, which, if anything, tended to emphasise personal attributes and qualities or, as in the case of some firms, to make no specific demand whatever. It may be the case, however, that even among large firms demanding quite specific academic qualifications and mental abilities, works ratings in practice are based more on these personal characteristics, and that this accounts, for example, for the lack of correlation in studies such as those of Grimes and Barry. When, however, an attempt was made by Bates (1969) to look at aspects of the personality, interests and motivation of aircraft apprentices which might be relevant for selection and training, the result was disappointing. On the two Eysenck personality dimensions, there appeared to be no practical significant difference between any of the aero sub-groups, a finding similar to that of van der Eyken (1971) for first-year technical college students. Bates was able to compare his aero apprentices with a group of ex-apprentices and a further group of under-twenty ones in his study on job aspirations, and, again, his main conclusion was that the groups were rather similar in their traits. He did express surprise, however, at the finding that current aero apprentices seemed to want more security from their jobs than the two other groups tested. Bates considers that a group under training would express less concern with security than the other groups, but it seems at least equally likely that the anxiety associated with training, and the possibility of being either dismissed or down-graded within a highly selected group of apprentices, would be present even without the added pressures of adolescence that are always associated with this particular sector of education and training.

On a list of 102 hobbies, activities and interests, Bates could find no more than small differences between his sub-groups within the aero industry. It may be, of course, that significant differences do exist between apprentices in different industries or between apprentices and non-apprentices so that the major variance was already removed from Bates' sample, but his somewhat rueful comment that 'at our present stage of knowledge such devices as personality tests, job aspiration questionnaires and interest check-lists are unlikely to prove of value as aids to the selection and training of apprentices' does seem justified.

It was for this reason that work within the Brunel Further Education Group has recently turned to the exploration of new methods which might have an application in this sphere. In particular, work is now going on in the possible use of a Level of Aspiration measure, based on the concepts first formulated by Kurt Lewin and his collaborators at the University of Berlin in the thirties.

This search for measures which will predict successful industrial performance is important, even if the present situation has not produced any very positive lead, at a time when industrial training boards are preparing and introducing new curricula into the FE sector, for it may transpire that, in fact, knowledge content is rather less relevant to the factory floor than behavioural characteristics and that, for instance, the role of what is broadly described as general or liberal studies, holds an ultimately more important role for industry than the current vocational aspects of the FE courses (Cowell and Entwistle, 1972). Once again, research into further education is handicapped by the lack of job evaluation studies carried out on the shop floor, and the assumptions inherent within the system about industrial needs and student requirements. But see, on this, Lee, 1972 and the data now being gathered by the Engineering Industry Training Board, 1971.

Equally, we have little evidence that college selection for courses is effective. Williams and Boreham (1971) have recently shown that CSE results, in general, are poor predictors of college performance. There is an interesting, though highly specific, example in the case of the School of Electronic Engineering, REME (1968), which has the task of selecting candidates for a technician course in the army equivalent to Part I of the CGLI 49 technician certificate. On REME's own selection procedures, 117 recruits were entered for the course, and of these 86 passed out as trained technicians, giving a failure rate of 26·5 per cent. If the minimum selection requirement had been 2 GCE O-levels, regardless of subject, only 53 of the 117 recruits would have been chosen, and the failure rate would have been 22·6 per cent, giving a trained output of 41. If GCE O-levels in mathematics and physics had been demanded, only 19 recruits out of the 117 would have been selected, the failure rate would have been 21 per cent and the output 15 trained men. If four GCE O-levels, including mathematics and physics, had been insisted upon, only 16 of the original 117 would have been chosen, the failure rate would then have been 25 per cent and the output only 12 trained technicians. This selection requirement would have reduced the input to 13·7 per cent and the output to 14 per cent of what it actually was.

Placement

The REME example represents a special case of an institution with sharply defined objectives and the freedom to make its own selection specifications away from national considerations, yet it underlines the point that the assumptions inherent in the FE system, coupled with the arbitrary nature of industrial selection, provide checks as well as opportunities for ability. It is a commonly known fact that the power of colleges to re-allocate students to courses other than those recommended by employers is limited. The reasons for this are not that industry is inherently opposed to the educational progress of its employees, but that the nature of the firm often governs the levels of manpower which can be employed. A young man whose abilities allow him to take an Ordinary National Certificate is of no use to a local firm which needs craftsmen. Hence a considerable degree of overlap of ability occurs within the technical colleges themselves, and the question of 'placement', as Ethel Venables (1960, 1961) has called it, remains an intractable one.

In a study carried out by the Brunel Further Education Group, van der Eyken (1971) tested 571 craft, technician, and ONC first-year students in two local technical colleges. To find out the possible extent of mis-placement within these two colleges, all four cognitive test scores (AH4 verbal and non-verbal, English and mathematics) were included in a multivariate discriminant analysis which tried to group subjects in terms of their overall performance on these tests, on the assumption that the tests were good predictors of college academic success. (A more recent study within BOAC by Gibson (1971) suggests no significant correlation between AH4 and college success.) The subsequent result showed that as many as 27 per cent of craft students in one college and 16 per cent in another college should, on this assumption, have been on technician courses, while 23 per cent of technicians in one college and 12 per cent in another college should have been on craft courses. Incidentally, this study also threw some light on the variation in selection levels between different sectors of industry, for included in the sample was a sub-sample of apprentices from the aero industry, selected on a national basis from a very large application list.

The main airline corporations take great care over their selection procedures and the high technological content of the job and the necessity for ensuring great technical competence within the hangars and workshops has created standards which are unlike those of other industries, while retaining the nomenclature of normal industrial categories. So it was shown that the mean scores on cognitive tests achieved by aero apprentices were more akin to the test performance of ONC students in the construction or other industries. The aero industry has been conscious of this mis-match itself, and a study by Cannon (1969) into the attitudes and aspirations of a sample of aero apprentices, indicated that job expectations following training were not being met among the sample. Cannon himself postulated four reasons: that the firm was over-selecting, that it was over-training, that training creates expectations higher than can be realised in actual work conditions, and finally, that the organisation and evaluation of work itself limits the apprentice's potential.

Wastage

Industrial factors of this kind are a contributory factor to the single most dominant characteristic of day release into further education—wastage. The Crowther Report (1960) illustrated the very high drop-out rates prevailing on national certificate courses within FE. A study carried out by the Northern Counties Technical Examinations Council (Morrison, A. T., no date) suggested that changes made in the structure of these courses since Crowther reported, and contained in the Ministry of Education's White Paper (1961), had certainly improved matters. The average proportion awarded on ONC in the last three years of the superseded scheme was 48·9 per cent, the annual figures being 1962—50·9 per cent; 1963—46·5 per cent; and 1964—49·4 per cent. The proportion who were successful in the new scheme in 1965 was 64·6 per cent, which indicates that the rather sterner selection procedures introduced after Crowther did have an effect on subsequent success rates. Such figures are, however, misleading, for this same investigation indicated that there was something like a 16 per cent drop-out in the first year of the progression from the first to the second year of the General course, and that only two per cent of students enrolling for the four-year cycle of two G course stages and two ONC stages actually managed to complete the cycle in the minimum

time. Because of the built-in facility to repeat years in further education, longitudinal studies require lengthy periods of follow-up if they
are to measure the actual 'success' rate of courses, and with the recent
spate of change within FE, such studies may tend to be of only historical
interest. 'Repeating years', with its associated failure, must contribute
to the subsequent high failure rate within FE. These, if only we could
obtain them, would prove a more telling measure of the effectiveness
or a course than exam success rates. Pollock's interesting study in
Scotland (1970) on wastage in national certificate courses there provides
evidence that this is the case. In this study, carried out by the Scottish
Council for Research in Education, 1 210 students enrolled in the first
year of the ONC in September 1966 have been followed up. Although
at the time of writing the results were not yet completely analysed,
Pollock found that only a handful of students who failed in the first
year of their course gained an ONC in the two subsequent years. 'This
implies that the vast majority have either given up the course completely
or, if continuing in study, have failed at least once more.' He goes on to
suggest that if this is indeed the case, the first-year success in such a
course may well be crucial.

Another example of the attribution that occurs throughout the
length of FE courses of a day-release kind can be found in van der
Eyken's study (1971) in which a cohort of craft and technician students
was followed up for two years. The relevant data is given in the following table:

Progress of day-release students in a local tech. over two years

	Craft	Technician
Initial intake	111	26
No. passing internal exam at end of first year	97 % pass = 87·4	20 % pass = 77
No. enrolled and completing second year of course	60	18
No. passing Pt. 1 external exam at end of second year	36 % pass = 60	15 % pass = 83·3

Though it makes no allowances for possible 're-entry' into other
colleges (for this, see below), the data indicates that, while examination
passes are at a respectable level, at the end of two years the original
craft intake was reduced by two-thirds, and the technician intake very

nearly halved, largely through students 'dropping out' at the end of the first year.

Lipshitz (1971b) has looked at the overall wastage rates in the first year of craft courses in a number of technical colleges, and suggested that the drop-out rate can vary from virtually nothing to nearly fifty per cent, most of it occurring within the first term of the academic year.

Despite the provocative suggestion from Vaizey (1971) that 'wastage' may have a positive virtue in cost terms as far as undergraduate courses are concerned, FE wastage would appear to be wasteful in both institutional and personal terms. To find out more about the factors influencing such wastage, Lipshitz (1971a) carried out a pilot study within the Brunel Further Education Group in which samples of 'drop-outs' and 'stayers' from first year courses in a single technical college were compared, on the basis of depth interviews with the boys and background information gleaned from their firms, their former schools and college. As one would surmise, the industrial base proved to be one of the major influences. Industry not only hires, it also fires. And with firing, there goes the apprenticeship, day-release and industrial training. Industry creates the system that either supports an apprentice in his studies, or denies him support. It either encourages or it discourages, sometimes at great human cost, as Venables (1972) has dramatically demonstrated.

The pilot study also indicated, however, that some of the drop-outs were simply younger than those staying on at college, that the decisions they made about leaving school and subsequent employment were possibly inappropriate reactions attributable to parental pressures or parental indifference, and that many of the drop-outs were described by the school teachers as 'restless' or 'unable to concentrate'. Inevitably, the results of this study pointed once again to the lack of proper counselling and vocational guidance provided by the schools (Miller, 1970, makes much the same point), though the question has to be asked whether any system of counselling could prevent some youngsters from entering employment unsuited to their particular abilities or temperaments. The study also gave an indication, however, that dropping out, far from being in some way an act of social deviance, may in fact be a very positive act with benefits to the individual if he subsequently 'drops in' to another industry, or another apprenticeship. *Dropping* out does not necessarily mean *opting* out and indeed the whole question of wastage is considerably more complex than simple statistics will allow. To understand the phenomenon, and its converse, 'staying on', we need to know a great deal more about the characteristics of day-release students in further education.

Student characteristics

Both Venables (1967) and Moore (1969) have indicated some of the characteristics of day-release apprentices at technical colleges. They have both pointed to the fact that these boys—and we are, of course, talking only about boys, for girls have yet to be accepted by the engineering and construction industries—come largely from secondary modern and comprehensive schools, and suffer from what Venables described as a linguistic barrier. In van der Eyken's study of two colleges (1971) it was notable that mean scores in an English test differed significantly between craft, technician and ONC groups. Venables quotes one young apprentice as saying: 'When you're a working-class lad like me and you come to a college like this it takes a bit o' time before you understand what folks are saying. You've nearly got to learn another language.' This is notably so in many cases, and it has important implications for teaching. (See also the chapter by Lawton for a more detailed discussion of this point.) Bearing in mind that 28 000 of the 41 000 teachers in FE are untrained, and often recruited straight from industry, according to Roberts and Cantor (1971), there are likely, on the face of it, to be problems of communication, and this gives special point to the nature and presentation of liberal studies within the colleges.

A characteristic which many teachers have noted, but which only recently became the subject of research, is in the area of the students' mathematical ability, 'mathematics' in this context probably being better described as 'calculations'. Teachers often complain that FE students are weak at calculations, but it was only recently that Ruth Rees (1972, 1973), in the Brunel Further Education Group, analysed the results of 10 000 City of Guilds craft and technician examination papers and found that, throughout the sample, there existed not only areas of specific weakness, but also an overall tendency for students to avoid calculation questions if it was possible to do so. On the basis of this analysis, a calculations test was constructed and given in six technical colleges to 1 000 students, covering craft, technician and

ONC levels. At the same time, teachers of these classes were asked to predict their students' performance on the test. Two major points have arisen as the result of this work. In the first place, it has been found that there are common areas of difficulty which run through the entire apprentice sample, irrespective of the level of course, as well as suggestive evidence that each group has its own specific area of weakness. Secondly, when the responses from the teachers were analysed, it was seen that for technician students, teachers tended to predict very much higher performance than was in fact achieved, and this may be an indication that FE teachers are making assumptions about previous school experience which are not borne out.

Another major issue arises out of this study: given that candidates will avoid calculation questions in examinations if they can, their freedom to do so, and their subsequent chances of success, depend on the extent to which examining boards 'load' their papers with calculation questions, or make specific demands to answer at least some questions of this type. In 1970 there was wide discrepancy between the boards on this point. More recent evidence suggests that they have become aware of this issue.

A more intractable problem for study is the motivation of day-release students, and here questions of industrial support, the age of the student, family background, academic achievement and all the variables associated with adolescence come together to create a confused pattern. Some of the data in the wastage study by Lipshitz suggest that this group of young people has an inability to accept the strategy of deferred rewards inherent in industrial apprenticeships, and in so far as this characteristic is common to adolescents as a whole, there may be a discrepancy between the strategies employed by the education system and by industry and the needs and demands of young people unable to appreciate their long-term goals. A recently completed three-year study by Weir (1971) for the Scottish Council for Research in Education makes the point that attitudes to FE are shaped more by the course than by the college or the year of the course. 'Each course seems to attract entrants of a different type,' comments Weir, suggesting once again that the industrial selection and subsequent support, coupled with the degree to which FE is integrated with industrial training and subsequent promotion and job satisfaction, is probably one of the prime factors affecting success on college courses. Weir puts it this way: 'It is apparent that the way an industry organises its training, the opportunities for promotion which exist within that industry and the student's perceptions of further education's relevance to his industry and his prospects are of importance to each course group.' He found, for example, that in courses such as catering or electrical installation work, where the majority of students saw no conflict between colleges and their jobs and ambitions, more favourable attitudes prevailed about FE than in other courses, like joinery or mechanical engineering, where students perceived a gulf between the 'real' tasks of work and the 'unreal' world of the college.

As already mentioned, Weir's study also indicated that, to the students, the least popular subjects in technical colleges were liberal studies, science and calculations, and although he was not able to probe the reasons for these choices, we can guess that they are associated with 'relevance' and 'difficulty', and in the case of calculations, offers some support for the findings of Rees (1972).

Weir's study provides a great deal of data on students' attitudes to technical colleges, and about the general view among students that colleges do not provide enough facilities for day-release students. Although it is obviously difficult for colleges to cater in terms of common rooms, club facilities and extra-curricular work for boys who appear only once a week, and who then have a very full day of study to complete, there is also the fact that college finances are based on student hours, and that this system sometimes emphasises the importance of full-time students in the college to the detriment of the day-release students.

What emerges in many of these studies is an indication that the characteristics of the technical college itself have, as far as day-release students are concerned, only a marginal effect on the performance and motivation of students. The education system has only a tenuous hold over them. Their attendance on one day a week is an ancillary exercise to the four days spent in industry. It is at work, with its sense of urgency and of realism, that the real battles are fought.

At the same time, the philosophy and organisation of the college itself can, as Weir's data seemed to suggest, have an effect. Yet surprisingly, given the great advances in organisational studies in recent years, the technical college as an organisation has scarcely been studied at all, and it is only in the last two years that studies, such as those of Charlton, Dent and Scammels (1972) and Tipton (1972, 1973) have begun to throw light on how such complex and often very large institutions organise themselves. A research project currently being conducted within the Further Education Group at Brunel University aims to thrown light on how such organisation affects the actual educational priorities within a college.

Where do these studies take us? In the first place, it must be pointed out that some of the most interesting and potentially profitable studies are still at an early stage, but are likely to increase our knowledge of this substantially in the next year or two. In particular, a very large monitoring study of the new City and Guilds 500 Engineering Craft Studies course, being carried out by Susie Barry in the Brunel Further Education Group, and involving 33 colleges, 600 teachers and some 3 500 students throughout the UK, should produce a detailed picture of the factors affecting student success in colleges, as well as indicating some of the major educational and industrial variables operating in colleges situated in different localities, and in different social, industrial and geographic areas. This study will also give an indication of the ways in which new curricula are introduced into technical colleges, and of the problems associated with innovations of this kind. Other studies within the Brunel Further Education Group in mathematics, learning strategies, Level of Aspiration tests and a pilot study analysing the administrative structure of a local college, together with a continuing programme of work in this area being conducted by the Scottish Council for Research in Education and some of the studies mentioned by Cole and van der Eyken (1971), ought, during the next two or three years, to add considerably to our overall understanding of the nature of further education, as far as it affects day-release students.

But is this enough? More importantly, are empirical studies of this kind really doing more than mapping the surface of the problem? Given the lack of resources described at the beginning of this chapter, it would be more profitable both for our overall understanding and for the technical colleges themselves if more local studies could be conducted within the colleges by the staff. To this end, the Brunel Further Education Group has recently launched an Association which aims to promote collaborative research with FE colleges (including Polytechnics) in which each member carried out its own study within its own institution as part of an agreed project. The aim is not merely to encourage colleges to pursue research immediately relevant to their own decision-making process, but to enable such studies to be compared and hence collated. It has the additional merit of providing a 'workshop' for educational research in an area desperately short of trained and skilled researchers, and hence of providing a form of staff development.

If this tentative start can be developed, and more colleges can be encouraged to undertake initially small, but rewarding, projects, it will not only stimulate teachers to consider research a satisfying and rewarding occupation, but may also create more posts for research workers within FE and, in so doing, provide what is now notably missing—a proper career structure for the educational researcher.

Donald Lomax

Teacher education

It may be argued that the chief purpose of research into the education
of teachers is to improve the programmes of teacher preparation which
are provided in university departments and colleges of education. In
recent time, however, more stress has been placed on increasing the
numbers of students in training than on improving the processes by
which they are educated. As by the end of this century it seems likely
that we shall need half a million teachers to satisfy the needs of the ten
million children who will then be in our schools (Wilson, 1969), it
seems probable that questions concerning the demand for and supply
of efficient teachers will continually require consideration. The realisation that we are unlikely to have enough good teachers within the
foreseeable future has led to the conclusion that we must make the best
use of our limited resources, and must seriously question the efficiency
of our present programmes of teacher education.

These programmes have been developed mainly during the last
seventy years, on the basis of an increased knowledge of general
psychological principles, an inadequate understanding gained from the
practical experience of teachers, and the growth of studies in the social
sciences and philosophy (Smith, 1971). Those who have been involved
in research into teacher education have therefore found it necessary to
seek greater understanding of teaching behaviour and greater knowledge of its influence on pupil learning. At the present time we may be
only cautiously optimistic, for the attainment of such knowledge and
understanding would still leave us with the task of modifying our
institutions and their teacher education courses—a task which Othanel
Smith has likened to that of rebuilding vehicles while they are in motion.
Unfortunately, until relatively recent times, there has been little
rigorous British research into teacher education, and although American
studies may now be counted by the thousand (Barr, 1929, 1948; Barr

et al., 1952, 1961; Gage, 1963; Biddle and Ellena, 1964; Smith, 1969), it remains true that we still have a serious lack of dependable knowledge upon which to base our training procedures. It is the purpose of this chapter, within the limited space available, to review some aspects of British research to suggest problems for future investigations.

It is not unusual in reviews of this kind to start by explaining the great difficulties facing the author who attempts to impose a classification upon the varied assortment of recent studies. Here we shall adopt a systems approach (Astin, 1964; Oxtoby, 1967; Taylor, 1969b; Cohen, 1973), in which we shall direct our attention towards contextual variables, input variables, process variables and output variables, although the assignment of studies to these headings will often be somewhat arbitrary. Most of the studies discussed will be of British origin, but occasional reference will be made to work in the United States, Canada, Australia, France and Norway.

Contextual variables

As Taylor (1969a) has pointed out, it is hardly possible to understand the present problems and achievements of colleges and departments of education without some knowledge of their development during the last one hundred and thirty years. The development of colleges as institutions of higher education offering professional courses of study has been traced by Ross (1973), who has analysed the voluntary tradition, the local authority contribution and the unresolved dichotomy between professional and general education. The Area Training Organisation has evolved as a way of drawing together the various agents which claim to have a measure of control over teacher education. The creation and development of the ATOs has been described by Turner (1973) in a penetrating analysis of their structure, difficulties and aspirations. Studies of the historical development of university departments of education from the early 1840s to the present day have been provided by Tuck (1973a, 1973b) in papers which contain an abundance of fascinating detail. Interesting comparisons between the English and Scottish traditions of teacher education have been made possible by a lucid account of developments north of the border in a paper by Scotland (1973).

One of the important characteristics of the teaching profession is its size (Vaizey, 1969). The fact that teachers are such a large group means that numerically they resemble other occupational groups such as shop assistants or nurses rather than the smaller exclusive professional groups. Etzioni (1969) classifies teaching in the same category as nursing and social work, and regards these as 'semi-professions' whose members are trained within a relatively short period and thus acquire a less specialised body of knowledge. Hence they have lower status and weaker authority than other smaller professional groups. The characteristics of the teaching profession have also been analysed by Sir Ronald Gould (1973) in a vigorous study outlining the progress which the profession has made during the last one hundred years. His conclusion is that teaching is a profession which performs a definite social service. In future, he believes, it will demand of its members rigorous study of the theory and practice of education.

A major contextual variable which has had profound effects upon the development of teacher education is society's demand for well-educated teachers (Taylor, 1969a, 1969b). This demand may be interpreted as a function of the national birthrate, the population age distribution, and the stage of technological development which a country has achieved. Taylor also outlined the effects of these influences on teacher supply and has discussed the desirability of a more structurally differentiated teaching force.

A further source of useful information for researchers is provided by the statistics of education which the Department of Education and Science produces annually. These reports include detailed analyses of the costs of various sectors of the system and thus produce useful data for both the educationalist and the economist. In theory, economics should provide a useful paradigm for rational decision-making about teacher education, but as Drake (1973) points out, little is known about costs and benefits of training in any occupation. Although it is possible to analyse the publicly borne costs of teacher education, or the relationship between teacher education and the labour market, other aspects of the current situation—such as the task of measuring private and social rates of return on teacher education—present severe difficulties which indicate the need for cautious planning and serious research efforts.

Input variables

Under this heading we shall consider a variety of student teacher characteristics. Again studies will by necessity be somewhat arbitrarily grouped under such sub-headings as teachers' social origins, reasons for occupational choice, examination qualifications, intellectual abilities, personality characteristics, attitudes and motivation. Some of the studies reported could easily be included under several of these headings.

THE SOCIAL ORIGINS OF TEACHERS

Floud and Scott (1961) have argued that the principal social characteristics of the teaching profession in England and Wales are largely to be explained by the rapidity of its growth during periods of expansion initiated by the passing of the Education Acts of 1870, 1902 and 1944. There seems to be little doubt that this growth created opportunities for social advancement which the children of working-class parents found attractive. Floud and Scott report the results of a study undertaken in 1955 in which a randomly selected, stratified sample of teachers were approached by means of a postal questionnaire which included questions concerning the social origins of teachers and their personal histories. A final total of 8 516 completed schedules was established as representative of the total population from which the sample was drawn. By comparing recruitment figures for the profession in pre-war and post-war periods, they were able to identify interesting changes in the social origins of teachers during the last half century. The authors concluded that there had been 'a breaking down of "caste" lines between the different types of school', and that there was 'more resemblance than hitherto in the background of the teachers in them'. But they also concluded that the largest group of teachers in all schools was drawn from non-manual family backgrounds.

The Robbins Report (1963) provided more recent statistics on the social class background of teachers. In 1961–62 54 per cent of the student teachers who entered colleges of education in England and Wales were drawn from middle-class backgrounds and 23 per cent from upper-working-class backgrounds. Not surprisingly 92 per cent of these student teachers were the products of selective secondary schools and had almost all remained at school until the age of eighteen. Lomax (1971), reporting a detailed study made at a large northern college of education almost a decade later, produced similar results. He found that only 10 per cent of the students in his sample had fathers who were engaged in semi-skilled or unskilled work, whilst almost 40 per cent had fathers who were in professional or managerial positions. As a relatively small percentage of working class children are successful in the selective school system, it is hardly surprising that teachers should tend to be drawn from middle class or upper working class groups. Little and Westergaard (1964) reporting on the trend of class differentials in educational opportunity in England and Wales, pointed out that in the eleven to thirteen year-old group, the child from a professional background had nine times as much chance of entering a grammar school as the child of an unskilled manual worker. At the age of seventeen the child from the professional home had thirty times as much chance of still being at school. They also found wide sex differences in opportunity; the daughter of a manual worker had approximately only one chance in five hundred of entering a university.

There has been an accumulation of evidence to suggest that one of the factors closely associated with the child's academic achievement at school is the parental attitude towards education. When the Plowden Committee (1967) interviewed a sample of primary school children's parents, they discovered that manual workers experienced greater difficulty in communicating with teachers than did parents working in non-manual occupations. If working class people find it difficult to approach teachers, it would seem reasonable to suggest that teachers might make greater effort to reach understandings with these parents. Cohen (1967), however, reported that neither student teachers nor headmasters revealed much interest in the possibility of extending the teacher's role beyond the classroom. In view of the difficulties in establishing systems of communication between parents and teachers, it would seem that there are likely to be unfortunate opportunities for mutual misunderstanding to develop. Musgrove and Taylor (1965) produced evidence to support these fears. In order to investigate the way in which teachers perceived their roles, to discover the teachers' perceptions of parental views, and to ascertain parental viewpoints, questionnaires were administered to 237 parents and 470 teachers. The results of the enquiry suggested that teachers had a narrow perception of their role, attaching most importance to academic instruction and moral training, whilst regarding social training as lying outside the realm of their responsibilities. It seemed that parents agreed with this order of priorities, but the teachers under-estimated the importance which parents attached to moral training, being convinced that parents were more concerned with the teachers' part in securing the social advancement of their children. Further evidence of the importance of parental attitudes was provided by Sandford, Couper and Griffin

(1955) in their study of social class influences in higher education. In a sample of ninety seven students drawn from a college of science, they found that whilst thirty seven had received active encouragement from their parents to pursue their studies, only five had experienced parental opposition. The college had a larger proportion of working class students than would usually be found at a provincial university and few of the parents had experienced further education. The inability of the parents to give educational and vocational guidance may have produced a lack of confidence in career choice found amongst these students. In a study conducted at a college of education, Lomax (1969) was unable to find a single student who had experienced opposition to plans for continuing studies at the tertiary level. It seemed likely that potential working-class recruits to the teaching profession who had experienced parental opposition to their career plans, had found this obstruction insurmountable.

Evidence of other influences of family background was provided by the work of Smelser and Stewart (1968) in their investigation of the links between birth order and college attendance. They found that even in small families birth order (as well as the sex of the children) significantly influenced educational opportunity.

Although disadvantages in home background thus appear to be formidable obstacles, which many potential working class teachers may fail to surmount, there is some evidence that those who do proceed to the tertiary level of education experience relatively low rates of academic failure as a possible consequence of being such a highly selected group (Marris, 1964).

As the teaching profession is so much larger than other more exclusive professional groups, it is perhaps inevitable that its members should on the whole be of 'modest social class origin' (Leggatt, 1970). There would, however, be important implications if the pattern of recruitment were to change. It might, for example, be somewhat ironic if at a time when increasing numbers of working class children are staying longer at school, the proportion of teachers recruited from this class should show a tendency to decline (Kelsall and Kelsall, 1969).

OCCUPATIONAL CHOICE

In the study of any occupational group it may be important to understand the factors which persuade applicants to seek admittance to it.

In past years it has been usual to regard teachers as people having a sense of vocation. Bambridge (1970), however, refers to Altman's (1970) 'inescapable conclusion ... that any pretension today that teaching is a vocation is quite false' and goes on to argue that although students are drawn into teaching in a diversity of ways, they are often attracted by the 'regularity' which the profession offers. Whether students have a sense of vocation or not, one might expect their own school experience to have produced interests which would influence their choice of career. Butcher and Pont (1968) reported a study in Scotland in which 1 100 secondary school pupils rated fifteen careers on six criteria. Although boys and girls differed in their interests, they agreed quite closely on the usefulness and prestige of various careers. Girls placed teaching first in their rank order of job preference, whilst boys placed it fifth. In the earlier study Evans (1952) had found that pupils who had the greatest liking for school were themselves most attracted towards a teaching career, whilst Morrison and McIntyre (1969) also commented on the considerable influence that serving teachers may have on recruitment to their profession. When Evans (1957) investigated the interests of an older group of students (graduates preparing to teach in grammar schools), she found that correlations between interest scores and practical teaching marks were almost all insignificant and was led to comment that 'over-enthusiastic students should be regarded with suspicion'. Morris (1969), however, in a study of the sixth form and college entrance, found pupils claiming that the prospect of 'interesting work' was an important reason underlying their decision to continue their studies. Other studies (Bewsher, 1966; Derricott, 1968) suggest that it is an interest in people which makes the teaching profession an attraction for many students, while Clark (1968) reports that students who have no desire to teach have little liking for children. In a study of college of education students Raby (1970) also found that the dominant student career motive was the desire to work with children. Less happily, it seemed that 40 per cent of the chosen sample had believed, whilst still at school, that no other alternative careers were open to them. Lomax (1971) pointed out that 'so few students had career plans, and so few had any knowledge of other jobs that it seemed very likely that the process of drift, which had carried them to the college, would probably carry them back into schools and perhaps leave them there becalmed'.

The results of an interesting French study have been reported by

Corruble (1971). It is suggested that the recruitment and training of teachers might be improved if more account were taken of the motivations underlying career choice. The subjects in this investigation were 240 French pupil teachers, who were asked to assess their motives on fifteen scales. Among the principal findings, Corruble reported that teaching was chosen as a career because it appeared to be a safe and sheltered profession, and that the urge to look after the young was often tied to a search for security that was not entirely healthy. The investigator suggests that it is legitimate to inquire into the psychological processes which underlie the liking for authority over young persons. In a recent British study (Ashley *et al.*, 1970), the reasons students gave for entering the profession were factor-analysed. The investigation revealed that different student groups placed different emphasis on three teaching roles which might be conceptualised as: the teacher as educator, the teacher as worker and the teacher as person. An interesting review of this work has been written by Rolls and Goble (1971). Another study of college sub-cultures has been made by Mayfield (1972) who used the Clark-Trow typology (1966) to investigate the characteristics of groups whose role orientations are defined as either collegiate, vocational, academic or non-conformist.

Although the foregoing studies are provocative, we are forced to recognise that occupational choice is a complex process which is unlikely to be fully understood in terms of the data supplied by the blunt research instruments which are at present at our disposal (Butler, 1968; Cohen, 1973). Yet colleges of education have invariably attached importance in their selection procedures to the reasons applicants give for choosing their career. Individual colleges often select students according to their own particular criteria and may place differing emphases on career motivations. Within the system as a whole, however, the strength of the student's desire to teach has less meaning as a variable upon which selection might be based, for virtually all applicants obtain places somewhere within the network of colleges. It seems likely that some students in colleges of education are only there because they cannot obtain university places. The Robbins Report revealed that 85 per cent of college students who had originally hoped to gain admittance to universities, still wished that they had been able to achieve this ambition. Disappointed university rejects are able to continue their academic studies in college, but it is possible that they may have limited interest in vocational aspects of their courses (Rolls and Goble, 1971).

The notion of 'commitment' which we seek to impart to our future teachers by virtue of our concept of 'education' has been penetratingly analysed by Aspin (1972).

EXAMINATION QUALIFICATIONS

In recent years an increasingly larger number of students, holding at least minimum entrance qualifications, have been unable to secure university places. The increase in the number of rejected university candidates has resulted in a steady flow into the colleges of education of young people seeking some other avenue of educational advancement. In terms of attainment, as measured by the General Certificate of Education A-Level examination, the universities have always had first choice of the available talent. The investigation conducted by Land (1960) in a representative sample of colleges in England and Wales, revealed that only 13 per cent of the students had three A-level passes. Similar figures were produced by the Robbins Report (1963), and in 1970 the Central Register and Clearing House analysis showed that still only 13 per cent of the annual intake of college students had three A-level passes. However, if a wider view of A-level performance is taken, it becomes clear that the entrance qualifications of college students have steadily improved. During the period between 1955 and 1970 the number of college entrants having two or more A-levels rose from a little under 20 per cent of the intake to almost 40 per cent, while the number of students having one A-level also approximately doubled. At the present time the majority of university students hold three good passes in the GCE A-level examination.

Discussions about the predictive value of these examination results have continued over a number of years, often in the absence of adequate supporting evidence. Summarising the available evidence from the university sector Butcher (1968) concluded that, on the whole, positive significant correlation between A-level results and performance in university examinations had usually been found. He added, however, that A-level results could not be regarded as an adequate means of selection unless they were supported by other evidence. Although GCE results have been of only limited value as predictors of student performance in colleges of education in the past, it seems likely that they may be regarded as increasingly important as the number of students studying for the BEd degree grows. In a college sample in which 57 per cent of the students had two or more A-level passes, Lomax (1969) found that these examination results were good predictors of subsequent academic performance. As more students have turned their attention towards the BEd degree, researchers have started to study the differences existing between students following BEd courses and students studying for the teacher's certificate. The appearance of 'two classes' of student within colleges has disappointed and saddened many college staff. However, studies such as that by Gallop (1970) have drawn attention to group differences of this kind. In addition to pointing to the expected superiority of the BEd student in terms of A-level attainment, Gallop draws attention to other interesting differences, such as the fact that the degree students are more oriented towards a career in secondary schools, and attach greater importance to their academic subject interests.

Some recent evidence of the limited predictive value of GCE examinations has been provided by Brown (1971) working at the New University of Ulster. A group of students who would normally have taken certificate courses in colleges of education have been admitted to university courses. These students are regarded as full members of the university, use the same academic and social facilities, take the same range and number of course units, and are assessed in the same way as degree students. This particular group of students was selected on the basis of headteachers' reports, interview appraisals, performance on the AH4 intelligence test and GCE A-level grades. Equal weight was given to each of these criteria. The typical degree students were selected only on the basis of A-level grades. At the end of the first year the examination results of the experimental group were compared with those of first year honours students. The experimental group had fewer high scores but also had a lower failure rate. Brown concludes that a wider range of students can successfully study university courses than has hitherto been considered possible. Only four out of the sixty members of the experimental group had A-level grades of three Cs, whereas two hundred and eight out of four hundred and sixteen honours degree students had these grades or better. On the basis of these first year examination results 37 per cent of the experimental group was transferred to degree programmes. It seems, therefore, that a considerable number of students in colleges of education may have the ability to take advantage of the kind of opportunity being offered by the New University of Ulster. It is important to remember, however, that there are wide intercollegiate differences in ability between student bodies (Simons, 1965 and 1968). These differences would have to be considered in planning the future extension of educational opportunity.

It has been usual in many countries to employ various measures of academic performance to select students for courses of teacher training. These may be appropriate procedures if our main intention is to select students who will gain academic success at college. It is possible, however, that this concentration on academic potential may lead us to neglect talents of equal importance to the teacher. Were we to take a wider view of human values, we might try to select students who would be capable of making an important contribution to later community life far beyond the college classroom (Richards *et al.*, 1967).

INTELLECTUAL ABILITIES

As British students are such a highly selected group it is hardly surprising that they obtain intelligence scores which are well above the mean for the general population. It is also hardly surprising that teachers in training tend to be of lower ability level than those preparing to enter more exclusive professions, for many colleges have, at best, only a second choice of the available talent. Within the body of teachers in training there is, however, such a wide ability range that differences exist between various sub-groups. Students training for service in secondary schools, for example, usually gain higher scores on intelligence tests than those training for the primary sector, who often have greater interest in children.

One of the most extensive investigations testifying to the intellectual superiority of university students over college students was that of Dickson *et al.* (1965), who reported a large scale cross cultural study. This research, which was sponsored by the University of Toledo, Ohio, produced interesting comparisons between student teachers in the United Kingdom and their counterparts in the United States. One of a large number of findings was that British student teachers scored higher than American trainees on intelligence and verbal comprehension tests. An analysis of the British sample revealed that university postgraduate certificate students obtained significantly higher scores than the college of education students on most of the intelligence tests used in the enquiry.

The intelligence of students has seemed to have such obvious importance that various tests of ability have been included in many of the test batteries employed by researchers. Much of the work done with groups already selected on the basis of previous academic attainment has suggested that with such populations it is of relatively minor significance. Lomax (1969), however, in a study of student teachers, used a battery of intelligence measures, which included an individually administered instrument, the Wechsler Adult Intelligence Scale, and several group tests including the AH5 and the Cattell Culture Fair Test. The pattern of significant correlations obtained between the test scores and fourteen criteria of student performance suggested that further detailed analysis of these relationships might be worthwhile. On many occasions in the past there has been a tendency to add a single measure of intelligence to a test battery and then to proceed to discuss the results as if there were no other mental abilities to be considered. Eysenck (1947) pointed out, over twenty years ago, that the literature already contained over a thousand published papers in this area, and that most of the correlations which had been obtained were too low to be of use in prediction. He advocated the use of several measures of ability, arguing that a single measure gave too narrow a description.

PERSONALITY CHARACTERISTICS

Because it seems probable that the personality of the teacher is a significant variable in the classroom the personal qualities of the teacher have always merited attention, and have been subjected to considerable research. Amongst the thousands of studies of this kind in the United States, that of Ryans (1960) provides an example of the large scale kind of study which is seldom possible in Britain, involving 6 000 teachers, 1 700 schools and 100 separate researchers. The small scale studies usually conducted in Britain have been quite numerous but have generally provided contradictory findings. Thus although there has always been strong support for the view that the real determinants of success in teaching are qualities of personality, character and temperament, from a reading of the literature it is difficult to reach conclusions about which of these characteristics is important, and one is forced to recognise the truth in Vernon's (1953) much quoted comment that 'teachers are as diverse in their psychological traits as any other occupational group' making it 'fallacious to talk of the teaching personality as something distinct and consistent'.

It has been common practice during the last few years to include such well known objective tests as the Cattell Sixteen Personality Factor Questionnaire, the Maudsley Personality Inventory, the Eysenck Personality Inventory or the Minnesota Multiphasic Personality Inventory in test batteries, and to administer these to samples of students drawn from colleges of education or university departments of education. The performance criteria used in these studies are usually academic examination results or teaching practice marks. Not surprisingly in view of the limitations placed on these studies by the sampling procedures employed and the sometimes unrecognised criterion problem, not to mention the limitations of the tests themselves, their findings are either unhelpful or pedestrian. If it is true, however, as Smith (1971) has claimed, that 'every item of hard knowledge springs out of a slush pile of data and interpretations heaped up by adventures that left the main questions unanswered', then there may be grounds for optimism. Recently a number of studies have made use of well-known objective personality tests, e.g. Solomon, 1967; Pervin, 1967; Morgan, 1969; Lomax, 1969; Marsland, 1969; Ainslie, 1969; Gurney, 1970. (See also the chapter by Entwistle in the present book.) Studies in this group which have sought to link the major personality dimensions of introversion-extraversion and neuroticism-stability to teacher performance have produced inconsistent findings. Where the Sixteen Personality Factor Questionnaire has been used, virtually all of the sixteen factors have appeared to be in some way significant somewhere in somebody's results. Some researchers unfortunately ignore the advice of the 16 PF test producers and use only one form of the test, which leads one to suspect the reliability and validity of their findings. Even if past studies are given credit for helping to clear a little of the ground for future researchers, it must be recognised that we know very little about the relationships between personality characteristics and teacher effectiveness.

ATTITUDES

One of the most ambitious projects in this area was initiated by McLeish (1969), who investigated student attitudes in ten colleges of education which had a combined annual intake of over 1 600 students. A large battery of tests, designed as measures of certain basic personality dimensions—educational, social and political attitudes—was administered to 1 671 students upon entry to the colleges. Two or three years later 1 478 of these students were retested. As the ten colleges as a whole could be regarded as a miniature social system having input and output, the research aimed to discover the results of the 'processing' which the students had experienced during their years within the system. 'The general hypothesis underlying the investigation was that the ten different colleges, established in a variety of urban or rural environments, providing different educational regimes, operated to produce different, measurable effects not only in the standards of academic achievement of students but also on their attitudes and possibly on their value systems as well'.

The preliminary analyses revealed that:

1) very experienced teachers on one year courses changed little in their attitudes. They gained information, acquired some insights and skills but retained their personal beliefs and opinions;
2) mature students on two year courses changed in certain areas. In religious affiliation, for example, there was change in the direction of non-commitment; there was no change, however, in basic personality structure or in personal values;
3) students who were on three year courses changed surprisingly in some unexpected ways, and yet failed to change in other ways which might have been expected.

Although no changes took place in basic personal values, significant changes were located in the areas of educational and social opinions. It seemed that in many respects the students had tended to become more like their college lecturers. The most interesting results of the study were, however, concerned with the influence of the college environment. 'The actual changes in students, which were a movement towards a secular and radical humanism and naturalism, and away from a narrow and social conservatism, were related to college environment in terms of their "quality" and "religiosity". There was a direct relationship between the educational quality of the environment and the amount of change that took place in the students.' Since these preliminary results were published, further analyses of the two and half million items of information that were available have been carried out at the University of Alberta. In his recent report, McLeish (1973) attempts to relate the nature of the environments to the 'outputs' and discusses the physical, social and psychological characteristics of colleges with reference to the basic changes which occur in students over the period of their courses.

In an earlier study on a smaller scale Shipman (1965) used such instruments as attitude scales, questionnaires and interviews to investigate a college of education culture, and succeeded in discovering attitude differences between various student groups. In a later paper Shipman (1967) reported that during their first six months in service the attitudes of new teachers become very like those of most of their new colleagues. The influence of their former college lecturers seemed therefore to have been essentially of a temporary nature. Most investigations of this kind have produced similar results, suggesting that although the attitudes of students may change during their years at college, their early contact with the real world of teaching promotes further changes in reverse direction.

A seminal contribution to the study of the structure of teachers' attitudes was that of Oliver (1953) who sought to relate educational philosophies to psychological categories. The study was carried forward by the work of Thompson (1957), Butcher (1959) and Oliver and Butcher (1962), who identified three relatively independent dimensions which they named naturalism, tendermindedness and radicalism. In a subsequent study of student teachers and inservice teachers, Butcher (1965) reported that the students were significantly more radical, naturalistic and tenderminded in their attitudes than the practising teachers. Further analyses suggested that these tendencies were reversed as the young teacher gained experience in schools. McIntyre and Morrison (1967) replicated the work of Butcher in making a comparison of English and Scottish students. They confirmed that students obtained increased scores in tendermindedness, naturalism and radicalism during their vocational training. In another paper Morrison and McIntyre (1967) report the results of an experiment in which 100 teachers were retested with the Manchester scales at the end of their first year in teaching. They found that although the educational opinions of teachers had changed during their college courses, these changes were reversed during the first year in their jobs.

A relatively recent development in attempts to measure teacher attitudes has been the increasing use of semantic differential techniques. Kitchen (1965) used the semantic differential technique to investigate five areas of interest; attitudes to the teaching profession, to training, to the self, to teachers as people and to abstract values. A factor analysis of the results revealed a contrast between the attitudes of first and third year students. First year students tended to associate college with the personal attainment of maturity, while third year student attitudes reflected much more concern with responsibilities to their chosen profession. Manion (1970) used similar techniques to study attitude changes occurring in a sample of first year college of education students. He found that some student criticisms were traceable to the emphasis placed by the college staff on a belief that the fostering of 'right' attitudes and dispositions towards children was more important than the transmitting of knowledge of intellectual skills. The major finding to emerge from the study was that the students' frame of reference was 'external to the college'. The students' interests and values tended not to coincide with those of the college.

An instrument which has been used in a number of studies of teacher attitudes, despite its shortcomings, is the Minnesota Teacher Attitude Inventory, which was designed to assess the liberalism of teacher-pupil attitudes. Herbert and Turnbull (1963) used the test as part of a battery which they administered to 232 students and found that it correlated with student performance in educational studies. Like other British researchers, however, they did not find the instruments entirely satisfactory for use with British populations and recommended the rewording of various test items. Evans (1966) repeated this criticism and also noted that the American norms were not applicable in Britain. Unfortunately it is fairly easy for subjects to perceive the ideas on which the test is based, with the result that 'faking' of responses is relatively easy. A modified version of the MTAI, was used in an interesting, large scale, cross-cultural comparative study of student teachers in Dickson *et al.* (1965) and Dickson and Wiersma (1966), and revealed no significant differences between British and American students.

TEACHER ROLES

Although much has been written about teacher roles, few studies have centred on the relationship between the student's professional education and the in-service roles which he must fill. A useful survey of studies of the teacher's role has been made by Westwood (1967a and 1967b) who suggests that teacher training should be regarded as the period when the student develops his concept of the mature teacher's behaviour. In studies written from different viewpoints, Grace (1967) has discussed the changing role of the teacher and Camplin (1970) the development of a professional self-image in student teachers. Two other recent works may be of particular interest to women teachers. Case (1968) has examined the attitudes and interests of mature married women and young single women, firstly in colleges of education and secondly in their first teaching posts, whilst Jenkins (1971) has studied the role conceptions of students in a women's specialist college and in four mixed colleges of education.

MOTIVATION AND ACHIEVEMENT

As part of a study designed to examine the relationships between personality, study methods and academic performance, Entwistle and Entwistle (1970) administered a questionnaire relating to academic motivation to 139 university students and 118 college students. The analysis of the data suggested that tests of personality, motivation and study methods might be used in guidance programmes in attempts to reduce student wastage. Earlier efforts to devise tests of academic achievement motivation for use with secondary school children (Buxton, 1966; Entwistle, 1968) had met with some success. Entwistle developed a twenty four item self-rating inventory to assess academic motivation. The scores obtained by children on the inventory were found to correlate more closely with school attainment than with reasoning ability. A further implication of this study was that academic motivation, as measured by the Aberdeen instrument, was not closely related to social class. Entwistle et al. (1971), carried out a further study of the relationship between motivation, study methods and academic performance using as subjects 898 university students, 562 college of education students and 190 students chosen from colleges of technology and polytechnics. One of the interesting findings was that the motivation and study method scales might be useful in improving the accuracy of prediction based only on GCE A-level results. (See also Entwistle's chapter in the present book.)

Interesting work is being carried out at the present time in the School of Education at the Hebrew University of Jerusalem, Israel, by Leah Adar who is studying learning motivation and student types.

Adar has analysed four 'sources' of motivation to determine under which conditions each of them will operate as an actual motivating force, and has examined the characteristics of four 'types' of student who correspond to the four motivational dispositions. At the University of Bradford, Cohen and Boothroyd (1972) have employed anglicised versions of need-achievement scales, developed by Mehrabian (1968, 1969), for separate use with female and male students, and have studied differences in need-achievement level between 'committed' and 'non-committed' student teachers. Cohen and Reid (1972) have conducted a parallel investigation of matched groups of Certificate of Education and BEd, degree students.

The process of teacher education

Relatively little research has been undertaken in Britain into the organisation of colleges and departments of education or into the effects of such organisation upon learning. Thus we know little about many problems associated with the development of curricula and teaching methods within these institutions, and even less about the subtle influences which their environments exert.

ENVIRONMENTS FOR LEARNING

McLeish (1969, 1973) carried out a large scale investigation in ten different colleges of education in the Cambridge Institute area, using techniques inspired by the work of Pace and Stern in the United States.

'It was anticipated that as different colleges provide different levels of intellectual stimulation, so they can be expected to generate a specific ethos or "climate", an affective and conative atmosphere as characteristic of the college as the intellectual and academic aspirations and pretensions. This "climate", as well as differences in the teaching methods used were expected to influence students in their attitudes to knowledge, to teaching as a profession and to their own development as persons.'

A comprehensive battery of measures brought together under the title of 'The Cambridge Survey of Educational Opinions' was administered to most of the students in an annual intake to the colleges and was readministered to the group as their courses neared completion. It was hoped that the research would illuminate the relationship between changes in students and the characteristics of the environment within which they worked. The subsequent analyses of the results produced some interesting findings, only a few of which may be briefly mentioned here.

1) It proved to be possible to categorise college environments on the basis of data provided by the inventories used in the study.

2) An individual's reaction to a college environment was linked with previous experience, group morale, social and political ideals, and individual personality characteristics. Students as a whole, however, agreed about the major criteria to be considered in evaluating a college.

3) Ten factors of the environments of the colleges and four output factors were discovered. The environment factors were: co-educational/maturity, school orientation of the training programme, teacher-training of staff, masculinity-femininity of staff, student cohesiveness, democratic structure of the institution, science versus humanities emphasis in the curriculum, academic subjects versus practical subjects emphasis in the curriculum, institutional maturity, and institutional responsiveness to 'social utility' demand. The output measures discovered were: radical humanist outlook, educational permissiveness attitude, academic achievement, and a general 'change' factor.

4) Two aspects of the college environments were related to changes in students. There was a direct relationship between the general excellence of the college environment and the degree of 'swing' towards radical humanism. It also seemed that non-commitment to religion and a radicalism in social and political views were related to environments which were academically favourable and religiously liberal.

An interesting longitudinal study of the professional socialisation of student teachers is being conducted by Marsland (1969) in a large mixed college. The research aims to discover the strength and source of a variety of factors which influence student attitudes and conceptions of the teacher's role. Other studies of various environmental influences on student performance have been provided by Shipman

(1965) and Otley (1966), whilst an insightful analysis of methods of assessing the impacts which colleges make upon their students has been provided by Feldman (1970). The fundamental changes in the structure of administration in colleges of education in England and Wales during the 1960s, which may have had important associations with the changing patterns of impact upon students, have been reviewed by Collier (1973a). After discussing the dominant values of the English tradition of teacher training, which Taylor (1969a) has described as those of a 'social and literary romanticism', Collier examines the inevitable tensions existing between values which focus on positive relationships within a community, and those which focus on a rigorous impersonal discipline of the mind. In discussing the structure of authority, he maintains that the three forms of power, which Etzioni (1961) distinguished in his study of complex organisations, are to be seen at work in colleges of education. 'Coercive' power which depends on the use or threat of force is manifested in the power which the college governors have to expel a student or to compel him to withdraw as a result of inadequate academic performance. 'Utilitarian' power, which depends on the use of economic rewards or penalties, is made manifest in degrees and certificates which when awarded qualify the recipient for certain occupations and salaries. 'Normative' power, which is that exercised by an idolised party leader or a loved teacher, may be recognised at work in the efforts an institution makes to ensure that its students develop a genuine attachment towards it or its staff.

THE CURRICULUM

It seems unlikely that all the objectives, which are so vital to a modern teaching profession, can be achieved within the initial period of training. However, if we were to regard these objectives as the basis for a distinctive, professional education, then initial training, the probationary year and in-service education could be seen as an 'on-going continuum'. An interesting analysis of the problems associated with the probationary year has been written by Taylor and Dale (1973). The research of Cane (1969) for the National Foundation for Educational Research gives us a picture of the sort of in-service curriculum that the teachers believe they require, and Sir Henry Wood (1970) has stressed the need for all parties—tutors, employers and

teachers—to be involved in decisions made on the curriculum. Whatever decision-making processes are utilised they seem certain to be
vitiated by the absence of well planned, rigorous research. The implications of some new ideas on curriculum development have been
discussed by Rudd (1973), who has reported recent research involving
groups of teachers, who devised courses for early-leaving secondary
pupils through group work in local centres. The major achievements
of the research were improved planning, growth of feeling for group
work and greatly improved professional confidence.

TEACHING PRACTICE

Although practical experience of teaching within the school setting has
always constituted an essential element in courses of teacher training,
there is unfortunately a serious paucity of research upon which to base
future teacher education procedures. Indeed Tibble (1966), in discussing practical teaching, pointed out that—'We have not engaged in
any serious evaluation of the purposes and methods used in this branch
of our work ... In general it is fair to say that in practical work
training we took over a set of procedures from the Board of Education
when it gave up its responsibility for running the Certificate Courses,
and we have continued these largely unchanged to the present day.'

Cope (1970, 1973) has reviewed the reasons for our failure to modify
in any fundamental fashion, the provision for practice teaching, and
has discussed her own research carried out during the period 1965–1971.
The findings of these studies have been discussed in two recent reports
(Cope, 1971a, 1971b). This research into school practice was undertaken in two stages. The first stage was a small-scale two year enquiry
which involved two colleges, four LEAs and thirty-five schools. The
second stage involved a 'school supervised' practice, which operated
between a college and its teaching practice schools. In an effort to
develop the liaison between college and schools, and to increase the
teachers' sense of participation, small scale innovation was introduced.
'Both stages of the research provided ample evidence of the problems
of maintaining an adequate liaison between the colleges and the colla-
borating schools' (Cope, 1973). Cope believes that at a time when a
reappraisal of teacher training is under way, there is a temptation to
simplify the process by proposing the handing over of responsibility
for teaching practice to the schools. This she believes to be a dangerous

arrangement, which might lead to the creation of a dichotomy between theory and practice. The outcome would then be that 'the colleges, cut off from their work in the field, will retreat into irresponsibility, and the schools, engaged in a self-perpetuating activity, will sink into complacency.' It therefore seems that, if variety of practice supervision is to be ensured, and if students are to be equipped for present professional competence and future professional growth, the expertise of both schools and colleges will be required (Cope, 1973).

During the last decade a number of innovations have been introduced into teaching practice situations by various colleges and departments. Caspari and Eggleston (1965) reported an interesting investigation at the Leicester School of Education. In this research some of the techniques employed by social workers were introduced into the training programme. At the University of Bristol, Hannam, Smyth and Stephenson (1971) have described the experiences students encountered in meetings with adolescent pupils in less structured situations outside school. Richardson (1967), again at Bristol, has used group study techniques with students in attempts to further their understanding of the processes of group interaction. Griffiths and Moore (1967) have analysed data provided by the headteachers of schools used by a college for teaching practice. Their analysis made it clear that both the headteachers and their staffs lacked the skills of trained supervisors. No school had ever held a staff meeting to discuss teaching practice which was a matter meriting only minimal amounts of concern. Derrick (1971) reported a study in which a sample of students from two colleges of education selected some personal qualities which they considered necessary for success in their practice schools and colleges. Practice schools were associated with fewer problems than the colleges. Derrick believes that 'colleges might look at student problems more perceptively than they do'.

One of the more interesting recent developments in teacher education is the introduction of 'micro-teaching' techniques. A great deal of work on this process has been done in the United States at Stanford University. Micro teaching is characterised by a systematic simplification of the complexities of the normal teaching situation, feedback on performance, and replanned repetition of the teaching episode. Allen and Ryans (1969) have produced a comprehensive study of micro-teaching techniques. In Britain interesting work is under way at the New University of Ulster and at the University of Sterling.

TEACHING METHODS

Prevailing methods of teaching in colleges of education have been discussed by Collier (1973b). In his comprehensive paper Collier reviews current developments in lecture and seminar techniques, closed circuit television and programmed instruction. He considers that the most striking features of these developments are the growth of student-centred methods and the increased use of audio-visual techniques. Collier argues that the

> 'technical developments of the last two decades have created a new situation in the educational world in which a vastly greater range of teaching methods has become available than has ever been possible before ... It has become urgent for the academic communities of the colleges to embark on the arduous and indeed soul-searching process of making explicit their aims and objectives, and ordering their priorities; and on the equally difficult and refractory task of assessing the effectiveness of their courses for achieving the declared aims and objectives ... The over-riding questions of defining objectives and evaluating courses raise in an acute form the general problem of innovation: how is a college staff to re-create itself as a consciously self-evolving academic community?'

The outputs of teacher education

As Taylor (1969b) has pointed out, serious problems face those who seek to investigate the outputs of colleges and departments of education, for the criteria of successful student performance are but poorly conceptualised. It is fair to admit, however, that the criterion problem has frustrated most researchers who have concerned themselves with human performance. In an article written some thirty years ago, Stott (1939) stressed the necessity to refine the concept of occupational success and also to recognise its limited value. Eleven years later, the same writer (Stott, 1950), having sought to define occupational success in terms of five concepts, concluded that the word 'success' now had so many meanings that it had lost its value as a technical term and should be limited to the description of the attainment of self-chosen goals. Davies (1950) agreed that occupational success should be judged from a variety of standpoints, but stressed its emotional basis and took it to refer to a pattern of attitudes built up towards a worker by himself and by those who judged his performance. Reeves (1950) agreed that we do not need to seek unchallengeable criteria of occupational success and felt that it would be useful to find satisfactory criteria for use in a limited context for a limited time. Rodger (1965) believed that it was possible to see four important trends in thinking about the criterion problem. Firstly, there was growing discontent with the way in which the distinction between 'objective' and 'subjective' criteria was often made. He warned that a manifestly subjective assessment does not become objective simply because it is expressed in figures instead of words. Secondly, it was recognised that our criteria vary in importance from time to time and from place to place. Thirdly, there was the understanding that not only must we fit the job to the man and the man to the job, but we must also fit the man to his own expectations and carefully consider the employer's expectations. Finally, Rodger detected a reawakening in the techniques of job analysis. Thompson (1965), like Davies and Reeves, discussed the use of multiple criteria. He went on to point out that a basic weakness of criteria is their static nature which results from measurements being taken of an individual at some moment in time, whereas in real life we deal with a changing individual and changing situations. O'Neil (1965) reported the successful use of multiple criteria in his Australian work and described the way in which factor analysis revealed those criteria which were of little relevance. Vernon (1965) outlined the need for immediate, intermediate and long term criteria. The comments of these occupational psychologists may serve to suggest the serious problems encountered in any study of occupational success. Mitzel (1960) points out that although we have seen more than half a century of research in the field of teacher training, no standards yet exist which are generally agreed to be the criteria of teaching success. He goes on to declare that the task of identifying effective teachers is crucial to teacher education, certification, selection and promotion. Cope (1970), however, argues that 'since total research into teacher education in this country has been so limited, it seems a pity that so much of it has concentrated on selection, evaluation and prediction'. It would be better, she believes, to focus more attention on the objectives and processes of training. 'The brutal fact is', she says, 'that in spite of over 2 000 studies we have no objective criteria of what constitutes teacher competence.' It must be recognised that teacher efficiency is relative. In their presentation of American work in this field, Biddle and Ellena (1964) draw attention to the cultural, social and physical influences which modify a teacher's performance. Most of the criteria currently used to evaluate teacher success have been subjected to vigorous criticism. Earlier in this chapter the criteria for selection for teacher training in Britain were discussed and were found to be less than satisfactory. Sandven (1969) has examined similar problems in Norway. In discussing the difficulty of selecting the people best fitted for careers in teaching, he makes a distinction between the criteria which are applicable at the start of a teacher training career and other criteria which need to be applied at later stages of professional advancement. In his investigation he compared successful and rejected applicants for four year training courses in Norway, where entrance examinations were set at various colleges throughout the country. The findings of the study were that there was a considerable overlap between successful and rejected candidates in terms of examination performance and an even greater overlap between these groups when their performance on other tests of ability was compared. Sandven concluded that little evidence could be found to justify confidence in the criteria being applied in selection procedures.

One of the most ambitious British investigations into teacher success was that of Wiseman and Start (1965), who followed up 248 teachers from one Area Training Organisation as part of a long term study. As might be expected, they found little correlation between the assessments made of students in college and other later criteria of successful professional performance. Other researches have produced similar results. Start (1966) has discussed the problem of interpreting teacher success and the variety of criteria used to assess it. He points to differences in the criter a employed by university education lecturers and headteachers. In a later study Start (1967) followed up 452 students who had been teaching for three years, and again found little connection between the criteria employed in colleges of education and later in-service success. The ways in which headteachers assess the performance of their assistant teachers obviously affects the system of promotion within schools. Start (1968) obtained headteacher's ratings of their assistants on nine measures of teaching competence. His findings were that assistant teachers with personality profiles very similar to, or very different from that of the headteacher usually received higher ratings for social competence and teaching ability. The teachers who received the lowest ratings for teaching had a tougher, self-confident unconventionality which tended to make them more independent of the headteacher.

As Poppleton (1968) has pointed out, we cannot train teachers if we cannot specify the objectives of training. In her paper she described attempts to establish criteria on an empirical basis by the analysis of statements about successful teaching. The assessment form she describes was based on those observable aspects of teaching which were thought by university lecturers and in-service teachers to discriminate between good and bad teachers. The method employed in the investigation had its origin in Flanagan's (1954) Critical Incident Technique, but differed from this earlier work in that it was concerned with broad behavioural tendencies rather than with specific incidents. The results indicated that the university supervisors of teaching practice were mainly concerned with the academic qualities of their students, whereas the schools were equally concerned with the student's ease of manner and warmth of personality. Another example of different groups in teacher education holding different views of successful performance in schools was provided by Sorenson (1967). He analysed the responses of 163 students at the end of an eight week teaching practice and discovered that students and supervisors had markedly different views of what constituted effective teaching behaviour. Shipman (1967) also reported discrepancies between supervisors and their students on teaching methods. An analysis of the schools being used in the teaching practice also revealed that the placement of the student influenced the assessment awarded by the supervisor. Hore (1971) reported the results of an Australian investigation into the relationship existing between the student's attractiveness and the supervisor's assessment on teaching practice. The female students who obtained an 'attractive' rating were also awarded significantly better marks than their less fortunate 'unattractive' contemporaries. In view of the kind of evidence presented above, it is not surprising that in their investigation, Rudd and Wiseman (1962) reported that 590 teachers believed the teaching method courses and the periods of teaching practice had been relatively unsatisfactory experiences during their training courses. Cortis (1968), in a study of 259 students drawn from three colleges of education, reported an apparent dichotomy between the professional and academic criteria of success which were being used. Success in the classroom appeared to be linked with previous teaching experience and naturalistic, tender-minded attitudes to education, whereas academic success seemed to be associated with high verbal ability and tough-minded attitudes to education. In a detailed study of student teachers Lomax (1969) used fourteen criteria of teacher success to provide a broad evaluation of student achievement. No less than 218 predictor variables were found to be associated with the various criteria. It would seem that we should use a much wider range of criteria if we seek to evaluate career success.

A relatively recent development, which may help us to understand more about the classroom situation and thereby help us to modify teacher training processes, is the study of interaction analysis. The term 'interaction analysis' is used to describe systems of categorisation by means of which the processes of human interaction may be described and analysed (Cope, 1973). Although this kind of work has been going on in the United States for many years, British studies are of relatively recent origin. Wragg (1971) has outlined the various studies which are currently in progress in the United Kingdom. The concept of teacher effectiveness and the various research designs employed to investigate it have been discussed by Garner (1973). He reaches the conclusion that the criterion in such studies should take the form of a description of teaching styles. The difficulty is that we have inadequate knowledge of teaching styles and of the effects of different styles on children's learning. One of the most rigorous recent investigations designed to throw light on these problems is that of Duthie (1970), whose study of Scottish Primary Schools attempted to define critical differences between 'traditional' and 'progressive' teaching methods.

The education of teachers ought to be logically determined by the nature of the job which awaits them in the community. The rigorous development of a concept of teaching is therefore a prerequisite for the creation of teacher education processes. Unfortunately we know too little about the relationship between teacher behaviour in the classroom and the changes which occur in children as a consequence of this behaviour. If teacher education programmes are to be demonstrably valid, then we must try to establish relationships between the courses we provide in colleges and departments of education and later criteria of successful performance in the profession. If these criteria of successful professional performance are also to be considered valid, they will need to be associated with the learning of children.

Harriet Greenaway

The work of the Society for Research into Higher Education

Foundation of the Society

The interest in and concern about higher education which led to the appointment in 1961 of the Committee on Higher Education under the chairmanship of Lord Robbins produced also, in 1964, the formation of the Society for Research into Higher Education. The connexion between the Robbins report (1963) and the Society is apparent in paragraph 804 of the report:

> 'The University Grants Committee is paying increased attention to the development of educational research in the universities with particular reference to research into the many aspects of higher education. ... The various agencies concerned in the future machinery of government that we have recommended should work together in developing this research and ensure that there is no avoidable duplication of effort.'

It is this coordination of research into higher education that the Society aims to achieve.

The intense interest generated during the two years when the members of the Robbins Committee were sitting and after the publication of their report resulted in a group of people led by Dr Nicolas Malleson, Director of the Research Unit for Student Problems at the University of London, organising a conference on 'Research into higher education after Robbins'. It was held in London in March 1964 and received support from the Acton Society Trust. A proposal to form a Society for Research into Higher Education was discussed, with the subsequent formation of a Steering Committee. In December 1964 the Society was launched by that committee at a conference in London.

In addressing the conference Lord Fulton, who later became the Society's first President, underlined the reasons why the formation of the Society was so timely. Discussing the change of mood in educational research over the previous few years, he said

'There can be little doubt of the part which the Robbins Committee played in changing it. As its work proceeded, drawing more university interest and cooperation, great areas of ignorance were revealed for all to be aware of; and the report itself provided such light in the dark places of the past that few would regard it as tolerable to be without a continuing scrutiny in the future.'

During the following year the aims and objects of the Society were formulated. These are 'to promote and encourage research into higher education and its related fields'. This wording was made deliberately wide so that the development of the Society would be able to go along whatever lines should prove most suitable at any time. Compilation and dissemination of information on research into higher education was an intention right from the start. The way in which the publications of the Society have tended to concentrate on particular areas is a product of history rather than of rigid policy. It is probably true of many learned societies that like Topsy they 'just growed'. It is apparent when reviewing the first seven years of the SRHE that its development has been considerably affected by the interests and drive of its Governing Council and staff as well as by the general mood and interests of the academic world at large.

How it works and what it does

Most learned societies start as an act of faith. Their growth rate varies but they normally start with a good deal of help being provided by the few people who had the original idea. Time and money spent on them are somehow 'lost' in the normal day's work of those involved. The SRHE is no exception. However, there comes a point (a marginal membership figure of 400 has been quoted) when the amount of time involved becomes too great to lose. Paid staff are necessary and the organisation is really established. In the case of the SRHE this point was reached in September 1965 when the number of members stood at 39 corporate and 300 individual. Mrs Catherine Chandler was the first of the Society's staff and her part in the organisation of the Society in its early days is still noticeable. A year later the first full-time Organising Secretary, Dr Robert Oxtoby, was appointed. When his successor, Mrs Hilary Black, resigned in 1969 the work had expanded so much that two appointments were required to replace her. The Administrator, Miss Harriet Greenaway, and the Publications Officer, Mrs Susan MacIntyre, have found that the work has developed enough for their time to be more than fully occupied.

In January 1966 the Society was registered as a company limited by guarantee and not having a share capital. In December 1966 it was awarded educational charity status. Its management is vested in the hands of a Governing Council elected annually at the AGM, the officers being elected by the Governing Council. The first chairman was Dr Nicolas Malleson, who was succeeded in 1968 by Professor Graeme C. Moodie, and in 1971 by Professor Henry Walton. Sir Eric Ashby succeeded Lord Fulton as President in 1967 and, following his resignation, was in turn succeeded in 1971 by Mr Charles F. Carter. One of the aims of the Governing Council has been to reflect within the Society the breadth of higher education within the United Kingdom. This has not yet been achieved as successfully as it might be in that the membership of the Society and the membership of the Governing Council are over-representative of the university sector. However, a gradual redressing of the balance is taking place as the polytechnics become more settled and research in colleges of education becomes more widespread.

From April 1966 to March 1968 the Society received a grant from the Department of Education and Science of £2 500 a year. The remainder of its income in the early years was derived from membership subscriptions. Since 1967 the Society's work as a small publishing house has blossomed to a state where, by 1970-1, income from sales of publications represented more than 45 per cent of the total income. Compared with many learned societies, the SRHE is in a difficult position, as there is no one discipline from which it can automatically attract members. Increasing membership is a difficult and time-consuming business. In 1966 there were 213 individual and 82 corporate members. By 1971 there were 358 individual, 10 students and 179 corporate members, an increase in five years of 60 per cent of individual and 120 per cent of corporate members. The annual loss of individual members is about 70 so great efforts are needed to retain as well as to attract members. This is a vital part of the work of the

Administrator because, as no government or foundation grant is received at present, the Society can only fulfil its function if it has adequate subscriptions to support it. Compared with many other academic organisations and learned societies its finances are ludicrously small.

Membership falls into three categories, each covering both UK and overseas members: corporate, which can be 'any body corporate or partnership or educational establishment engaged or interested in research into higher education and its related fields'. As already mentioned, universities account for over half the corporate members. Efforts were made in 1970 to attract student unions and, in 1971, polytechnics and colleges of education to enrol, with some success. Individual membership is open to 'any individual engaged or interested in research into higher education and its related fields' with a reduced subscription for students. In April 1971 55 per cent of individual members were in universities, 14·6 per cent in colleges of education, further education, art, commerce or management, 7·3 per cent in polytechnics, colleges of technology or technical colleges; and 7·3 per cent were students or representatives of student unions. 17 per cent of the total individual and student members were overseas.

It is easy to describe what the Society is not and therefore the benefits which its members do not receive. It is less easy to describe what benefits they do receive and why the Society has such an important role. It is not a trade union nor a research institute nor an employment agency nor a provider of funds for impoverished potential researchers. It does, however, act as a channel of communication between many academic organisations throughout the world; it answers research inquiries and puts researchers in touch with others; it abstracts articles and books on higher education research, publishing these abstracts each quarter; it maintains and publishes a register of who is doing what research at which institution; it arranges for research to be discussed in its regional branches and at its annual conference; it has a number of working parties which study different aspects of research, publishing the results of their deliberations; and it publishes original research in monographs. These functions are all important parts of the Society's work which were envisaged from its inception. One role which was in the minds of the original members of the Governing Council but which did not become a reality until 1970 was the way in which the

Society would act as a stimulator of thinking on general subjects such as the conditions in which research workers work and the amount of in-service training which university lecturers receive. It acts not exactly as a pressure group but as a forum through which careful study of these subjects can be coordinated and publicised.

The Society as a publisher

Publications policy is decided by a Publications Committee which was set up in 1969. Its present membership comprises four members of the Governing Council and three cooptions, one of whom is the educational correspondent of a national daily newspaper. The appointment of a Publications Officer in December 1969 formalised the situation which had been developing since 1966, when the first publications appeared. The original intention of the Governing Council was to sponsor the publication of research results and monographs, which would then be published by an established publisher. This idea was shelved, partly because it had proved to be worth-while to have the *Abstracts* and *Register of Research* published by the Society when a quick and reasonably cheap printer had been found. Compared with commercial publishers the SRHE's publication time for publications is remarkably fast.

There has been a gradual change in the way in which manuscripts have been received. At first work was commissioned but now a fairly steady stream of unsolicited manuscripts is received. One of the Society's advantages as a publisher is that it encourages and attracts specialist work, which is normally too long for articles in journals but not of sufficiently general appeal for the normal commercial market. There has been a concentration, on occasions, on particular topics. In view of the amount of academic and general interest in these subjects the Society probably draws attention only to the tip of the iceberg. From 1965–9 there was great interest in student residence and this formed the theme of the second annual conference in December 1965. In his preface to the conference papers Malleson (1966) wrote 'The papers presented here ... demonstrate, more than anything else, the very small scale of current work on what is inevitably a very large problem. It shows the enormous gap between what could and should be done and what is being done.' These words could apply equally to any other aspect of research into higher education and from that time onward the Society has contributed to publicising the work that is being done. Six papers were given on different aspects of research into student residence at the conference in 1965. In December 1967 Marie Clossick's study of the Rayleigh Tower at the University of Essex was published (Clossick, 1967). This was the first research report to be handled by the Society and its sales showed that an organisation which can publish quickly what is both topical and scholarly fills a vacuum highly successfully. Hatch's (1968) discussion of the literature on student residence and Brothers' (1970) paper on findings from the student residence project continued the emphasis given to this subject.

Another constant theme in SRHE publications is teaching methods. The Society's first publication in this area was Beard's *Research into Teaching Methods in Higher Education* (1967), which has become a standard work. In 1966 a working party on teaching methods started its deliberations, which resulted in 1968 in the first of a series of monographs. To date these are: *Objectives in Higher Education* by Beard, Healey and Holloway (1968), *Aims and Techniques of Group Teaching* by Abercrombie (1970), and *Technical Aids to Teaching Higher Education* by Flood Page (1971). The work of working parties in general is discussed later but the working party on teaching methods is the first to have made a significant contribution to published work in its particular field. More monographs are due to be published as a result of its meetings.

Other monographs published by the Society cover a variety of topics, such as selection and academic performance (Abercrombie *et al.*, 1969), while others are rarities in a limited field such as Silver and Teague's bibliography on British universities (1970). In having no rigid policy on topics (within the field of higher education research) the Society provides a useful forum in which discussion is generated and information made available. Through encouraging the publication of research it hopes to augment research in colleges of education and further education.

Conferences, and therefore the papers published afterwards, have fallen into two categories: those with a theme and those without. Early conferences were built on a central theme such as student residence and library services. However, from 1967 to 1970 the annual conference had no central theme, to the delight of some and annoyance of others. From the point of view of providing an interesting conference stimulation can be provided with or without a central idea, but from the point of view of producing an interesting publication a theme is an advantage.

In 1971 it was decided that there was a demand for the publication of short pamphlets, of short life in small editions, which could mainly be printed in the Society's office. These would be research reports or discussions on subjects of topical interest where publication should be achieved very quickly in order to maximise impact. A slightly slow beginning produced the first two pamphlets in this series in July 1971, one being the result of the deliberations of a working party on conditions and careers of research workers, and the other a survey on the training of university teachers commissioned by the Society (Greenaway, 171a).

The two publications which regularly provide information about research into higher education are the *Register of Research into Higher Education* and the *Research into Higher Education Abstracts*. The *Register* is a biennial loose-leaf volume which lists who is doing research on what aspect of higher education in which institution. The Society's intention is that it should describe every relevant research project being undertaken in the UK and as many as possible overseas. Limitations of staff mean that, at present, it is never quite as comprehensive as it might be. A supplement is published after a year to bring entries up to date and to introduce new ones. The first issues of the *Register* were listed in alphabetical order of principal research workers, but the 1970 edition was classified by subject. In that edition there are 24 entries under 'students' background and characteristics', 35 under 'selection and attainment of students,' and 33 under 'teaching and learning situations: training' which show how much more emphasis is given to that type of research than to curriculum (10) or architecture and buildings (4).

Research into Higher Education Abstracts started in 1966 and are published quarterly. Their aim is to include every relevant article or book that has appeared during the quarter, with (so far) a total of about 80 abstracts in each issue. For an organisation with as small a staff as the SRHE it is obviously necessary to rely very heavily on people working in the field to help with abstracting. Over the course of a few years a team of abstractors has been built up and exchange arrangements with a number of journals enable the Society to receive free copies for abstracting purposes. With the increasing specialisation in all subjects today it is not surprising that some subjects receive more coverage than others. The *Abstracts* are classified in the same way as the *Register* which gives easy reference from one to the other.

These two publications form the backbone of the research information service at present provided. The Society's Governing Council hopes that in the future this work can be developed and extended so that a really sound centre of research information will exist. A large number of research inquiries are received each year which would be better answered if there were someone specialising in this side of the work.

Working parties

It will be clear from what has already been said that the SRHE does not itself normally undertake research but that it coordinates what is being done. The Society's various working parties exist to provide meetings in which information can be exchanged and ideas developed. They usually aim to publish the results of their deliberations, normally in the form of the Society's monographs. Apart from small seminars on specific topics, the following subjects have been studied by working parties since 1966: examinations, teaching methods, professional examinations, innovation in higher education, research in specific subjects, conditions and careers of research workers, and colleges of education. The usual form of working is for various members of the group to write papers on their own particular aspect of the subject so that, after a series of meetings, a jointly agreed document is produced. The final work is collated by one person.

The way in which the working parties operate is well summarised by Jahoda (1967) in introducing the papers of the working party on examinations. 'Two years ago the Society for Research into Higher Education established a working party to look into the problem of examinations for the first university degree. About twenty teachers from a dozen institutions of higher education followed the Society's open invitation to its members to participate, and decided to engage in a systematic analysis of the problem.' This systematic analysis brought together a variety of ideas on university examinations including a long survey by Cox, and shorter papers by Ager and Weltman, Ager, Oppenheim *et al.* and Himmelweit (1967). The fact that one complete issue of *Universities Quarterly* (June, 1967) was devoted to the papers of this working party is an indication of the importance both of the subject and the quality of work produced.

Reference has already been made to the working party on teaching methods. This is the longest-standing group, which started in 1966 and is still very active under the chairmanship of Professor W. D. Furneaux. Like the group on examinations its members are drawn from a variety of different institutions. The group does not meet together very frequently but its work is done mainly by the circulation of papers which are discussed at the meetings and eventually published. Furneaux (1968) introduced the series of publications by explaining its origin. 'In the summer of 1966 the SRHE organised a meeting for a small group of its members who had expressed an interest in studying methods of teaching relevant to higher education. Some of them were university teachers, anxious to improve their knowledge of educational theory. Others were research workers engaged in the experimental study of teaching methods, or in such fields as psychology, sociology and linguistics, who welcomed an opportunity to discuss their work with a more heterogeneous collection of interested colleagues than would normally have been easily accessible to them. From this discussion arose the Working Party on Teaching Methods in Higher Education.' So far the subjects covered, and published, are objectives in higher education, group teaching and technical aids to teaching. One of the interesting off-shoots from the work of this group has been the fact that the subjects are of much wider interest than one might have expected. If sales are a reasonable guide to areas of interest Abercrombie's (1970) monograph on group teaching is being used as background information in many industrial training boards, medical practices, and the armed services as well as the whole range of educational establishments. Although the work of this working party is geared to higher education, its findings are of a much wider significance.

The working party on examinations had excluded consideration of university examinations in professional subjects in view of the special and complex roles of the professional institutions in determining examination requirements outside the university. A separate working party on professional examinations was therefore established in 1967 to study professional examinations to final first degree level. Smaller working parties of professionals summarised developments in their own subjects. Reports have been received on accountancy, architecture, dentistry, engineering, librarianship and medicine. These reports deal with:

1) the organisational structure of the profession;
2) the effect of the edicts of the various professional and legal bodies on the educational structure;
3) the objectives of first degree courses and the techniques used to test their attainment;
4) changes and their effects in the overall educational and examination structure; and
5) problems of measurement and possible new techniques.

Comparative study of these reports has been initiated. These enquiries have been factual and have not taken into account the changed pattern of education or the philosophies that are increasingly questioning the pattern of professional education at the undergraduate level.

The subject-monograph working party convened by Flood Page started work in 1970. Its aim is to make teachers in higher education aware of what research has been done in their subject, what is being developed, and what it might be reasonable to attempt. The first subject to be investigated is chemistry, which was chosen because there were more chemists than other people who had expressed an interest in this group and because a reasonable amount of work has been done. This study is still in its initial stages, but it is hoped to be able to produce reports on various different subjects in the course of time.

The working party on innovation in higher education started in 1969 on the initiative, and under the chairmanship, of K. G. Collier. In a note to the SRHE Governing Council he said that there are 'three areas of concern that are shared by all types of institution, in which innovation and investigation seem . . . to be particularly important'. These areas he cited as: 'how to provide appropriate education for a greatly increased student population, amounting to perhaps 30 per cent of the eighteen to twenty-one age-group; how to adapt authority structures in higher education to meet the changing aspirations of contemporary society; and how to encourage the rapid diffusion of constructive innovation in higher education'. After a few meetings it was decided that case studies of different innovations taking place in institutions of higher education would be assembled, each fitting into a set framework of analysis. The subjects to be covered are: the Architectural Education Research Unit at the School of Environmental Studies, University College London; the University Teaching Methods Unit of the Institute of Education, University of London;

the use of new methods in medical education; the Inter-University Biology Project; the construction of new degree courses at Enfield College of Technology; the experimental unit at Goldsmiths College. Papers are currently in production.

The working party on conditions and careers of research workers was born out of a discussion at the Society's AGM in 1969 started by Hatch. As a result of the discussion on the careers and terms of employment of research workers the meeting resolved 'That the attention of the Governing Council be drawn to the problems of lack of security, especially financial security, of people employed in higher education and that a working party be set up to investigate and report'. The working party which resulted included people from various different interested bodies including the Association of University Teachers and the Social Science Research Council. The conclusions reached by the group, chaired by Mrs M. L. J. Abercrombie, were partly that research workers should have more consistent and stable salary scales with status equivalent to other academic staff, and partly that the way in which research into higher education is organised requires longer-term finance and the recognition that different types of research may need different types of structures. The report of the working party (1971) distinguished between 'action research aimed at promoting change' and 'academic research of a conventional kind'. The report was discussed at the annual conference in December 1970 when a number of participants were congratulatory in their comments about the Society's facilitating the production of such a report. In some ways this working party showed the Society moving in a new direction; that of providing a discussion centre on the way in which people active in higher education work rather than what they are working on.

The working party on colleges of education was set up in 1970 as part of the general interest in teacher training. The Governing Council was a little concerned at the university bias within the Society's activities and therefore decided that a group should look at how the Society could achieve a better interchange of ideas between colleges of education and itself. This group, under the chairmanship initially of K. G. Collier and now Alec Gresty, functions more as an action committee than a study group but it is encouraging researchers in colleges of education to submit research work for publication.

The working parties represent a major part of the work which the Society is able to do in coordination of ideas and information. The encouragement given in particular topics has been noticeable most in teaching methods but a significant impact is expected also from other reports.

Regional branches

Regional branches exist in London and the South-East, Midlands, North-East, North-West (in association with the Northern Group for Educational Research), Scotland and Wales. Unsuccessful attempts were once made to launch a branch in the South-West, and tentative approaches have been made towards forming a branch in Northern Ireland. Regional branches have existed since 1966 and provided, in the Society's early days, an excellent way of spreading its influence. The bringing together of academics in the various institutions in an area to discuss the research which each other is undertaking is a fundamental part of the Society's work. Most branches have three or four meetings a year, sometimes on a theme running through the whole series. The format of meetings varies: sometimes they are held in the evening, sometimes afternoon and occasionally all day on Saturday. Some branches normally meet in the same town, as the Midlands branch does in Birmingham; others circulate around the region, as the London and South-East branch does, where meetings were held in Norwich and Guildford in 1970. As with the organisation of the working parties, the way in which regional branches work varies according to the interest, expertise and time available of those who run the branch and those who attend the meetings. Meetings of the branches are organised by members of the Society, each branch having one member who acts as secretary. Some also have fully-fledged committees. There is a representative of each regional branch on the Governing Council so that a flow of information and ideas is maintained between the central organisation and the members in the different regions. A wide range of topics has been discussed in the branches, those in the year 1970–1 including: 'Counselling and academic achievement' (Midlands); 'The transition from school to college of education' (Midlands); 'Teacher training—current trends in Cardiff' (Wales); 'Evaluation of teaching methods in the University of Liverpool' (North-West); 'Higher education—teaching, learning and closed-circuit television' (London and the South-East); 'Research into higher education—a criticism of the present position' (Midlands). Development of regional branches is likely in the future, perhaps with residential conferences or with study groups supplementing those centrally organised.

Conferences

The annual conference in December is the largest single event in the Society's calendar. It is normally attended by about 150 members and their guests and has always been held in London. From the point of view of ease of transport it is a convenient location, but from the point of view of encouraging more involvement in the work of the Society in other parts of the country it has its drawbacks. However, this point has been taken into account when organising conferences on specific subjects, some of which have been held outside London.

Most annual conferences have covered a number of topics, with the exception of that in 1965 which had student residence as its theme. For 1971 a theme was reintroduced and a new format devised. An all-day free-ranging discussion on 'Innovation in higher education' was planned to provoke good audience participation. The organisation of this conference departed from the earlier system—the reading of research papers followed by discussion from the floor. In these earlier conferences some very useful discussion has ensued on subjects such as student residence (1965; Brothers, 1970), the structure of university costs (Carter, 1968), postgraduate research in the humanities (Rudd, 1968), the role of the British university teacher (Halsey, 1969), motivation affecting success and failure at university (Wankowski, 1969), supplementary predictive information for university admission (Drever, 1968; Sainsbury, 1970), an exploration of professional social-isation—the college of education and the teacher's role (Marsland, 1970), educational objectives and student performance within the binary system (Entwistle and Percy, 1971).

Conferences organised on particular topics have perhaps proved more useful than the formal annual ones. In November 1967 a conference was held on research into library services in higher education. This dealt not only with library services and the needs of the user, but with research currently being undertaken (particularly in OSTI and Aslib) and future implications of research (establishment of priorities and the impact of research on libraries and the parent institution). The papers were later published (1968). In the summer of 1968 student unrest exploded, hitting Europe in May. On behalf of the Social Science

Research Council the SRHE organised a three-day residential conference, at very short notice, on 'Unrest in the universities—research implications'. This was held at the University of Sussex in July 1968 and was attended by about eighty specially invited people including some from Europe and the USA. At a time when everyone has a vested interest it is helpful to have independent bodies to bring together the different factions.

The independent position of the Society was also useful in its organisation of a conference on the training of university teachers which was organised jointly with the Association of University Teachers. One representative from each university was invited: about sixty people attended the two day conference in April 1970 at the University of York. One of the results which emerged from the discussions was that there was more training being undertaken in more universities than had previously been realised. Participants at the conference were asked to supply details from their own universities which were then circulated to each vice-chancellor and elsewhere. Following the success of this conference and its subsequent document the SRHE Governing Council commissioned a survey on in-service training of university teachers which was undertaken by the Administrator in the spring of 1971, the results being published by the Society the following July. Even in the year between the York conference and Harriet Greenaway's survey a lot had been achieved. The catalytic effect of the Society's coordinative efforts in York was apparent when one looks at the dates when a number of universities made their policy decisions on training and the implementation of those decisions. The mere fact that this survey was conducted by the Society, having no interest other than a research one, is indicative of the usefulness of a central independent body as well as of the importance of the subject. This particular facet of the Society's work in liaison between institutions of higher education is an interesting development. It is something more than just the provision of an information service or another administrative function: it is a boost to research by providing a basis of information from which the researchers can lead on.

In December 1969 a conference on student wastage was held which was attended by about thirty people who had been at the annual conference the previous day. The organisation of the conference was done by David Armstrong and John Heywood but the conference was sponsored by the Society. The lack of consistent terminology being used by people working on student wastage was discussed, among other things. As a result the Society's Administrator was asked to devise a terminology which could be used by everyone. This was circulated to all members of the Society for their comments prior to publication (Greenaway, 1971b).

International contacts

In the summer of 1969 an International Contacts Committee was set up under the chairmanship of Professor W. R. Niblett with Miss Kay Pole as its secretary. In her note to the Governing Council she explained the reason behind its formation. 'The objective in formalising international contacts is to provide the same service for overseas members as for members in this country; it is not to set up an international market for the exchange of information, desirable as this may be.'

Areas of most interest to members have been chosen as the pilot areas to start with, these being Europe and North America, where the Society has more overseas members. Australia and New Zealand will be the next areas to be involved. The intention of the International Contacts Committee is that information will be obtained from the countries chosen about the research which is being undertaken there. Heads of Departments and institutes have been asked to suggest names of more junior colleagues who will be prepared to act as contacts. By early 1971 twelve contacts in North America and sixteen in Europe had been made. A limited amount of material has been collected, but classification of it into any really useful form is yet to be done. In 1972 the Council of Europe awarded the Society, at the instigation of the International Contacts Committee, a small grant to assist in the compilation of a register of current research throughout Western Europe.

The future

In the seven years of its existence the SRHE has grown to a state where it is regarded by people in social science research as one of the bodies of note. Its inclusion by the SSRC in its list of professional associations and learned societies to be consulted on their common problems in 1970 gave the Society the feeling of being well established. Similarly, the relations with the Department of Education and Science show a sound regard.

The future is full of imponderables. The biggest problem which the Society has to face is how to provide a better research information service. The basis is there. However, the Society's income is so limited that far too much time is spent chasing small amounts of money and cutting out any inessential expenditure, which restricts the amount of time and facilities available for more constructive work. It is somewhat ridiculous that well-qualified staff have to spend their time on too many routine things which should be done by more junior staff. This hinders the Society in providing the level of service which it could and wishes to provide. If there were a research information officer who would deal with abstracting, compilation of the *Register of research* and research inquiries, and would build up a really first class information service the world of higher education could benefit enormously. However, until funds are available (and simply increasing subscriptions and publication prices becomes prohibitive) this will remain a dream. The generosity of the University of London in housing the Society rent free in one of its buildings came to an end in 1972 when these rooms were needed by the University. Luckily, The City University stepped in to provide subsidised accommodation in one of its houses. The present financial system does not allow for expenditure on accommodation at market rate, so funds will have to come from somewhere other than subscriptions and sales if subsidies are to be avoided.

This paints a gloomy picture, but it is frustrating for administrators to have ideas on how the organisation which they administer should develop when the money is not available to support them. On a more constructive note (and these ideas are necessarily a slightly personal view) the work of the regional branches could be expanded. One of the difficulties in any organisation these days is that there is a pebble in the pond effect. So much is done in London that people elsewhere, either in the UK or overseas, can be somewhat left out. In the world of higher education this is a ridiculous state of affairs because there is so much research being carried out in places like Lancaster and Sussex, but because of distance many decisions are taken without as strong a voice being heard from non-Londoners as there might be. Some working parties, but not all by any manner of means, are composed solely of London and home counties members. If the regional branches could have their own working parties much more communication and encouragement of research could take place.

It is the same with the development of international contacts. If the Society is really to act as the channel of communication which it tries to be, it must have more information from more places about what research is being done. One of its most valuable functions is to put researchers in touch with others who are working in the same field. The *Register of research* is an invaluable start, but it is not as comprehensive as it could be.

The Society's work as a publisher has been described earlier. Since the appointment of a Publications Officer, a much more professional approach to publications has been possible and this work is improving all the time. With a narrow immediate market, but a much larger potential market, it is likely that research into higher education, when properly handled, will extend its influence much more. It is quite obvious that with so much research being undertaken policy decisions ought to be influenced by facts. The more widely the results of research are known the more useful that research will have been. Expenditure of public money must reap benefits in terms of savings on unnecessary items when those savings have been prompted by research results. If the work of the Society for Research into Higher Education can help in the influencing of policy by making more facts known, it will well justify its existence. It has made a very good start: the future is wide open and full of exciting possibilities.

Bibliography

British research in education: some aspects of its development

BANTOCK, G. H. (1961) 'Educational Research: A Criticism', *Harvard Educational Review*, **31**, iii, 264–80.

BUTCHER, H. J. (1968) (ed). *Educational Research in Britain 1* London: University of London Press.

BUTLER, R. A. (1952) 'The 1944 Act seen against the pattern of the times', in University of London Institute of Education *Jubilee Lectures*, 39–55.

CAVENAGH, F. A. (1926) Review of Everitt Dean Martin's *Psychology* in *The Forum of Education*, Nov., 237–8.

CLARKE, F. (1943) *The Study of Education in England* London: Oxford University Press.

COLLINGWOOD, R. G. (1939) *An Autobiography* Oxford: Clarendon Press.

CUNNINGHAM, K. S. (1934) *Educational Observations and Reflections* Melbourne: University Press, for Australian Council for Educational Research.

DENT, H. C. (1970) *1870–1970: Century of Growth in English Education* London: Longman.

ELVIN, H. L. (1965) *Education and Contemporary Society* London: Watts.

EVANS, E. G. S. (1963) 'Research in Education', *Education for Teaching*, **60** (February), 15–28 and 68–70.

EVANS, K. M. (1968) *Planning Small-Scale Research* Slough: National Foundation for Educational Research.

FOULDS, G. A. (1954) 'Review of Anne Anastasi's *Psychological Testing*', *British Journal of Psychology*, **45** (November), 311.

HEARNSHAW, L. S. (1964) *A Short History of British Psychology, 1840–1940* London: Methuen.

HIGGINSON, J. H. (1958) 'Sadler's German Studies', *British Journal of Educational Studies*, **6**, 119–27.

HUDSON, L. (1966) *Contrary Imaginations* London: Methuen.

KANDEL, I. L. (1930) 'The philosophy underlying the system of education in the United States', *Educational Yearbook 1929* New York: International Institute of Teachers College, Columbia University, 461–547.

KNIGHT, R. (1951) 'The scientific background to educational change', in Dobinson, C. H. *Education in a Changing World* Oxford: Clarendon Press, 84–104.

London County Council Education Committee (1905), Minutes.

LOVELL, K. and LAWSON, R. S. (1970) *Understanding Research in Education* London: University of London Press.

MCARTHUR, PETER (1903) *To be taken with salt: an essay on teaching one's grandmother to suck eggs* London: Limpus Baker.

MITCHELL, F. W. (1967) *Sir Fred Clarke, Master-Teacher, 1880–1952* London: Longman.

MONROE, W. S. *et al.* (1928) *Ten Years of Educational Research, 1918–1927* Urbana: University of Illinois. Bureau of Educational Research, College of Education Bulletin, No. 42.

MORRIS, B. S. (1955) 'Educational Research in England and Wales', *International Review of Education*, I, 77–98.

NISBET, J. D. and ENTWISTLE, N. J. (1970) *Educational Research Methods* London: University of London Press.

OLIVER, R. A. C. (1946) *Research in Education* London: Allen & Unwin.

PETERS, R. S. and WHITE, J. P. (1969) 'The Philosopher's Contribution to Educational Research', *Educational Philosophy and Theory*, I, ii, 1–15.

PIDGEON, D. A. (1968) 'Educational Research in England' in *The World of Educational Research (Conference Report)* Toronto: Ontario Institute for Studies in Education and the Canadian Council for Research in Education, 101–9.

REEVE, J. R. (1938) 'Education and Social Progress', in Curtis, A. P. *London Head Teachers Association, 1888–1938* London: University of London Press.

RODGER, A. (1946) 'Review of Arthur Traxler's *Techniques of Guidance*' in *Occupational Psychology*, **20** (October), 200.

RUSK, R. R. (1912) *Introduction to Experimental Education* London: Longman.

RUSK, R. R. (1932) *Research in Education* London: University of London Press.

SANDIFORD, P. (1918) *Comparative Education* London: J. M. Dent.

SANTAYANA, G. (1922) *Soliloquies in England* London: Constable.

SUKHIA, S. P., MEHROTRA, P. V. and MEHROTRA, R. N. (1963) *Elements of Educational Research* Bombay: Allied Publishers.

TAYLOR, W. (1966) 'The Sociology of Education' in Tibble, J. W. *The Study of Education* London: Routledge & Kegan Paul, 179–213.

TAYLOR, W. (1969) *Society and the Education of Teachers* London: Faber & Faber.

THOULESS, R. H. (1969) *Map of Educational Research* Slough: National Foundation for Educational Research.

Times Educational Supplement 4 Jan., 1916; 30 Nov., 1916; 12 Sept., 1918; 6 Feb., 1919; 18 Jan., 1947; 23 May, 1952; 6 May, 1960; 27 June, 1969.

WALL, W. D. (1968) 'The Future of Educational Research', in Wall and Husén *Educational Research and Policy-Making* Slough: National Foundation for Educational Research, 5–12.

WARBURTON, F. W. (1962) 'Educational Psychology', in *Annual Review of Psychology*, **13**, 371–414.

WISEMAN, S. (1962) 'The Tools of Research—Men and Machines', *British Journal of Educational Psychology*, **32**, 218–23.

Additional sources

BLACKWELL, A. M. (1950) *A list of researches in education and psychology* Slough: National Foundation for Educational Research.

BURT, C. (1957) 'The Impact of Psychology upon Education', *Yearbook of Education* London: Evans, 163–80.

CANE, B. S. (1967) 'Educational Research in England and Wales', *International Review of Education*, **13**, *ii*, 152–61.

FOSKETT, D. J. (1965) *How to find out: Educational Research* Oxford: Pergamon.

FOSS, B. M. (ed.) (1969) *Psychology in Great Britain*. Supplement to the *Bulletin of the British Psychological Society*, London (especially historical sections, one by L. S. Hearnshaw, two by J. C. Kenna).

KNOX, H. M. (1950) 'The Study of Education in British Universities' *The Universities Review*, **23**, *i*, 34–40.

National Foundation for Educational Research *Annual Reports*.

RIPPLE, R. E. (1968) 'Impressions of Educational Psychology and Research in England', *Educational Psychologist*, **5**, *ii*, 3, 5, 11.

SCHONELL, F. J. (1947–48–49) 'The Development of Educational Research in Great Britain', *British Journal of Educational Psychology*, **17**, *iii*; **18**, *i*, *ii*; **19**, *i*, *ii*, *iii*.

Scottish Council for Research in Education *Annual Reports*.

SELLECK, R. J. W. (1968) *The New Education, 1870–1914* London: Pitman.

WALL, W. D. (1963) 'The contribution of Sir Cyril Burt to Educational Psychology', *Forward Trends*, **7**, *ii*, 39–44.

WISEMAN, S. (1959) 'Trends in educational psychology', *British Journal of Educational Psychology*, **29**, 128–35.

YOUNG, M. (1965) *Innovation and research in education* London: Routledge & Kegan Paul.

Journals

British Journal of Educational Psychology
British Journal of Educational Studies.
British Journal of Psychology.
Educational Research.
Education for Teaching.
Forum of Education.
The Journal of Education.
Scottish Educational Studies.
The Universities Review.

Support for educational research and development

CANE, B. and SCHRODER, C. (1970) *The Teacher and Research* Slough: National Foundation for Educational Research.

CHANAN, G. (ed.) (1972) *Research Forum on Teacher Education* Slough: National Foundation for Educational Research.

Council of Europe (1971) *Survey of Educational Research in Europe* (five volumes) Strasbourg: The Council.

DOUGLAS, J. W. B. (1964) *The Home and the School* London: MacGibbon & Kee.

DOUGLAS, J. W. B. *et al.* (1968) *All our Future* London: Peter Davies.

EIDE, K. (1971) *Educational Research Policy* Paris: Centre for Educational Research and Innovation, OECD (mimeo).

GLASS, D. (ed.) (1954) *Social Mobility in Britain* London: Routledge & Kegan Paul.

HÄRNQVIST, K. (1973) 'Training and career structures of educational research workers', in Taylor, W. (ed.) *Research Perspectives in Education* London: Routledge & Kegan Paul.

HERU (1972) *Report* of the Higher Education Research Unit at the London School of Economics (mimeo).

LEVIEN, R. E. (1971) *National Institute of Education: Preliminary Plan for the proposed Institute*. A report prepared for the Department of Health, Education and Welfare, Santa Monica: Rand Corporation.

National Foundation for Educational Research (1970) *Annual Report* Slough: The Foundation.

PIDGEON, D. and YATES, A. (1957) *Admission to Grammar Schools: The third interim report on the allocation of primary school leavers to courses of secondary education* London: Newnes.

TAYLOR, W. (1972a) 'Retrospect and Prospect in Educational Research', *Educational Research*, **15**, *i*, 3–9.

TAYLOR, W. (1972b) 'Prospects and Problems in Educational Research Co-operation in Europe', *Information Bulletin 1/1972* Strasbourg: Council of Europe.

TAYLOR, W. (ed.) (1973) *Research Perspectives in Education* London: Routledge & Kegan Paul.

TIZARD, J. (1972) 'The Policy of the Educational Research Board', SSRC *Newsletter No. 14* March.

The study of schools as organisations

ANDERSON, J. G. (1969) *Bureaucracy and Education* Baltimore: Johns Hopkins University Press.

BARON, G. and TAYLOR, W. (1969) *Educational Administration and the Social Sciences* London: Athlone Press.

BIDWELL, C. E. (1965) 'The school as a formal organization', in March, J. G. (ed.) *Handbook of Organizations* New York: Rand McNally.

BLAU, P. N. (1964) *Exchange and Power in Social Life* New York: John Wiley.

CARLSON, RICHARD O. (1962) *Executive Succession and Organizational Change* Chicago: Midwest Administration Centre, University of Chicago.

CARLSON, RICHARD O. (1964) 'Environmental constraints and organizational consequences', in Griffiths, D. E. (ed.) *Behavioural Science and Educational Administration* 63rd Yearbook of the National Society for the Study of Education, Chicago: University of Chicago Press.

CHIN, R. (1960) 'Problems and prospects of applied research', in Bennis, W. G., Benne, K. and Chin, R. *The Dynamics of Planned Change* New York: Holt, Rinehart & Winston.

CHRISTIE, T. and GRIFFIN, A. (1970) 'The examination achievements of highly selective schools', *Educ. Res.*, **12**, iii, 202–8.

CHRISTIE, T. and GRIFFIN, A. (1971) 'A reply', *Educ. Res.*, **13**, iii, 242–4.

CICOUREL, A. and KITSUSE, J. I. (1963) *The Educational Decision Makers* New York: Bobbs Merrill.

CLARK, B. R. (1960) *The Open Door College* New York: McGraw Hill.

COHEN, L. (1970) 'School size and headteachers' bureaucratic role conceptions', *Educ. Rev.*, **23**, i, 50–58.

CORWIN, R. G. (1967) 'Education and sociology of complex organizations', in Hansen, D. A. and Gerstl, J. E. (eds) *On Education: Sociological Perspectives* New York: John Wiley.

DAVIES, W. B. (1970) 'On the contribution of organizational analysis to the study of educational institutions', Paper presented to the Annual Conference of the British Sociological Association.

EGGLESTON, S. J. (1967) *The Social Context of the School* London: Routledge & Kegan Paul.

ETZIONI, A. (1961) *A Comparative Analysis of Complex Organisations* New York: Free Press.

FELDMAN, K. A. (1971) 'Some methods for assessing college impacts', *Sociology of Education*, **44**, ii, 133–150.

FORD, J. (1969) *Social Class and the Comprehensive School* London: Routledge & Kegan Paul.

GETZELS, J. W. and GUBA, E. G. (1957) 'Social behaviour and the administrative process', *School Review*, **65**, iv, 423–41.

GETZELS, J. W., LIPHAM, J. M. and CAMPBELL, R. F. (1968) *Educational Administration as a Social Process* New York: Harper Row.

GLASER, B. and STRAUSS, A. (1968) *The Discovery of Grounded Theory* London: Weidenfeld & Nicolson.

GRIFFITHS, DANIEL E. (1959) *Administrative Theory* New York: Appleton-Century-Crofts.

GRIFFITHS, DANIEL E. (1964a) 'On the nature and meaning of theory', in

Griffiths, D. E. (ed.) *Behavioural Science and Educational Administration*, 63rd Yearbook of the National Society for the Study of Education Part II Chicago: University of Chicago Press.

GRIFFITHS, DANIEL E. (1964b) 'Administrative theory and change in organizations', in Miles, M. B. (ed.) *Innovation in Education* New York: Teachers College Press.

GROSS, N. and HERRIOTT, R. E. (1965) *Staff Leadership in the Public Schools* New York: John Wiley.

HALPIN, A. W. (1967) *Administrative Theory in Education* New York: Macmillan.

HANSEN, D. A. (1967) 'The uncomfortable relation of sociology and education', in Hansen, D. A. and Gerstl, J. E. (eds) *On Education: Sociological Perspectives* New York: John Wiley.

HARGREAVES, D. H. (1957) *Social Relations in a Secondary School* London: Routledge & Kegan Paul.

H.M.S.O. (1970) *Public Schools Commission Second Report* London.

HOYLE, E. (1965) 'Organizational analysis in the field of education', *Educ. Res.*, **7**, *ii*, 97–114.

HOYLE, E. (1969) 'Organization theory and educational administration', in Baron, G. and Taylor, W. *Educational Administration and the Social Sciences* London: Athlone Press.

HOYLE, E. (1970) 'Planned organisational change in education', *Research in Education*, **3**, 1–22.

HUGHES, M. (1970) *Secondary School Administration: a Management Approach* Oxford: Pergamon.

JENSEN, G. (1965) *Educational Sociology: an Approach to its Development as a Practical Field of Study* New York: Centre for Applied Research in Education.

KATZ, FRED E. (1964) 'The school as a complex social organization', *Harvard Ed. Rev.*, **34**, *iii*, 428–55.

KALTON, G. (1966) *The Public Schools: a Factual Survey* London: Longman.

KING, R. (1968) 'The formal organisation of the school and pupil involvement', Paper read to the Education Section of the British Sociological Association.

KING, R. (1969) *Values and Involvement in a Grammar School* London: Routledge & Kegan Paul.

KING, R. (1970) 'The social organization of the school', University of Exeter Institute of Education. Mimeo.

LACEY, C. (1970) *Hightown Grammar: The School as a Social System* Manchester: Manchester University Press.

LAMBERT, R. (1968) *The Hothouse Society* London: Weidenfeld & Nicolson.

LAMBERT, R., MILLHAM, S. and BULLOCK, R. (1970) *Manual to the Sociology of the School* London: Weidenfeld & Nicolson.

LITWAK, E. and MEYER, H. J. (1965) Administrative styles and community linkages in Reiss, A. J. (ed.) *Schools in a Changing Society* New York: Free Press.

LITWAK, E. and MEYER, H. J. (1967) 'The school and the family: linking organizations and external primary groups' in Lazarsfeld, P. *et al.* *The Uses of Sociology* New York: Basic Books.

LORTIE, DAN C. (1964) 'Proposals for long-term research on team teaching' in Shaplin, J. S. and Olds, H. *Team Teaching* New York: Harper Row.

LUNN, J. BARKER (1970) *Streaming in the Primary School* Slough: National Foundation for Educational Research.

MOELLER, GERALD H. and CHARTERS, W. W. (1966) 'Relation of bureaucratisation to sense of power amongst teachers', *Admin. Sci. Quart.*, **10**, 444-65.

MOORE, B. M. (1970) *Guidance in Comprehensive Schools: a Study of Five Systems* Slough: National Foundation for Educational Research.

MONKS, G. (1968) *Comprehensive Education in England and Wales* Slough: National Foundation for Educational Research.

MONKS, G. (ed.) (1971) *Comprehensive Education in Action* Slough: National Foundation for Educational Research.

MOUZELIS, N. (1967) *Organisation and Bureaucracy*: London: Routledge & Kegan Paul.

PARSONS, T. (1966) 'Some ingredients of a general theory of organizations', in Halpin, A. W. (ed.) *Administrative Theory in Education* Chicago: University of Chicago Press.

POWER, M. J. *et al.* (1967) 'Delinquent schools?', *New Society*, **10**, 264.

PUNCH, K.F. (1969) 'Bureaucratic structure in schools: towards redefinition and measurement' *Ed. Admin. Quart.*, **5**, ii.

REVANS, R. W. (1965) 'Involvement in school', *New Society*, **6**, 152.

ROBBINS, M. P. and MILLER, J. R. (1969) 'The concept school structure: an enquiry into its validity', *Ed. Admin. Quart.*, **5**, i.

ROSE, GORDON *et al.* (forthcoming) *Counselling and School Social Work.*

ROSENTHAL, R. and JACOBSON, L. (1968) *Pygmalion in the Classroom* New York: Holt, Rinehart, Winston.

SELZNICK, P. (1941) 'Institutional vulnerability in mass society', *Am. J. Soc.*, **56**.

SELZNICK, P. (1957) *Leadership in Administration* Evanston: Harper Row.

TURNER, C. M. (1969) 'An organizational analysis of a secondary modern school', *Soc. Rev.*, **17**, i, 67-86.

WAKEFORD, JOHN (1969) *The Cloistered Elite* London: Macmillan.

YOUNG, MICHAEL (1965) *Innovation and Research in Education* London: Routledge & Kegan Paul.

Child rearing practices

BERNAL, J. and RICHARDS, M. P. M. (1970) 'The effects of bottle and breast feeding on infant development', *J. Psychosom. Res.*, **14**, 247-52.

BERNSTEIN, B. (1965) 'A socio-linguistic approach to social learning', in Gould, J. (ed.) *Penguin Survey of the Social Sciences* Harmondsworth, Middlesex: Penguin Books.

BERNSTEIN, B. (1967) 'Play and the Infant School', *Where*, Supp. 11.

BERNSTEIN, B. and DAVIES, B. (1969) 'Some sociological comments on Plowden', in Peters, R. S. (ed.) *Perspectives on Plowden* London: Routledge & Kegan Paul.

BERNSTEIN, B. and HENDERSON, D. (1969) 'Social class differences in the relevance of language to Socialization', *Sociology*, **3**, 1-20.

BERNSTEIN, B. and YOUNG, D. (1967) 'Social class differences in conceptions of the uses of toys', *Sociology*, **1**, 131-40.

BRONFENBRENNER, U. (1958) 'Socialization and social class through time and space', in Maccoby, E. *et al.* (eds) *Readings in Social Psychology* (3rd edition) London: Methuen.

COOPER, J. E. and MCNEIL, J. (1968) 'A study of houseproud wives', *J. Child Psychol. Psychiat.*, **9**, 173-88.

DOUGLAS, J. W. B. (1964) *The Home and the School* London: MacGibbon & Kee.

DOUGLAS, J. W. B., LAWSON, A., COOPER, J. E. and COOPER, E. (1968) 'Family interaction and the activities of young children', *J. Child Psychol. Psychiat.*, **9**, 157-71.

FRAZER, E. (1959) *Home environment and the School* London: University of London Press.

JACKSON, B. (1968) 'Going through the mill', *The Guardian*, 20 December.

JACKSON, B. and MARSDEN, D. (1962) *Education and the Working Class* London: Routledge & Kegan Paul.

KENT, N. and DAVIS, D. R. (1957) 'Discipline in the home, and intellectual development', *Br. J. med. Psychol.*, **30**, 27-33.

KLEIN, J. (1965) *Samples from English Cultures* (Vol. II) London: Routledge & Kegan Paul.

LAWTON, D. (1968) *Social Class, Language and Education* London: Routledge & Kegan Paul.

LYTTON, H. (1971) 'Observation studies of parent-child interaction: a methodological review', *Child Devel.*, **42**, 651-84.

NEWSON, E. (1967) 'The Pattern of the Family in Modern Society', *Public Health*, **81**, 176-83.

NEWSON, J. and NEWSON, E. (1968) *Four Years Old in an Urban Community* London: Allen & Unwin.

NEWSON, J. and NEWSON, E. (1970) 'Changes in concepts of parenthood', in Elliott, K. (ed.) *The Family and its Future*, London: J. & A. Churchill.

PLOWDEN, LADY B. (1967) 'Children and their Primary Schools', London: HMSO.

PRINGLE, M. K. (1965) *Deprivation and Education* London: Longman.

RAVENETTE, A. T. (1970) 'Culturally handicapped children', in Mittler, P. (ed.) *The Psychological Assessment of Mental and Physical Handicaps* London: Methuen.

ROBERTSON, J. (1965) 'Mother-Infant Interaction from Birth to Twelve

Months: Two Case Studies', in Foss, B. M. (ed.) *Determinants of Infant Behaviour III* London: Methuen.

ROBINSON. W. P. and RACKSTRAW, S. J. (1967) 'Variations in mothers' answers to children's questions, as a function of social class, verbal intelligence test scores and sex', *Sociology*, **1**, 259–76.

SWIFT, D. F. (1964) 'Who passes the 11+?', *New Society*, 5 March.

SWIFT, D. F. (1965) 'Educational psychology, sociology and the environment: a controversy at cross-purposes', *Br. J. Sociol.*, **16**, 334–50.

SWIFT, D. F. (1968) 'Social Class and Educational Adaptation', in Butcher, H. J. (ed.) *Educational Research in Britain 1* London: University of London Press.

THOMPSON, P. (1969) 'Memory and History', SSRC Newsletter no. 6, 16–18.

TIZARD, B. and JOSEPH, A. (1970) 'Cognitive development of young children in residential care: a study of children aged 24 months', *J. Child Psychol. Psychiat.*, **11**, 177–86.

WISEMAN, S. (1964) *Education and Environment* Manchester: Manchester University Press.

YOUNG, M. and MCGEENEY, P. (1968) *Learning Begins at Home* London: Routledge & Kegan Paul.

Reading

ABERNETHY, D. et al. (1967) 'Children's in-school reading in Belfast—a suggestive survey', *Reading*, **1**, iii, 10–18.

ALDERSON, C. (1968) *Magazines Teenagers Read* Oxford: Pergamon Press.

BERG, L. (ed.) (1969) *Nippers* (Groups of graded books for children aged six to nine) Basingstoke, Hants: Macmillan.

BIRNIE, J. R. (1967) 'Inconsistencies in i.t.a. and t.o.—an examination of four popular children's readers', *Reading*, **1**, iii, 19–25.

BIRNIE, J. R. (1968) 'Inconsistencies in i.t.a. and t.o.—a further examination of four popular children's readers', *Reading*, **2**, iii, 13–18.

BIRNIE, J. R. (1970) 'Up the royal road again—in search of inconsistencies in i.t.a.', *Reading*, **4**, 28–32.

BOOKBINDER, G. E. (1970) 'Variations in reading test norms', *Educ. Res.*, **12**, ii, 99–105.

BORMUTH, J. R. (1966) 'Readability—a new approach', *Reading Research Quarterly*, **1**, iii, 79–132.

BUTCHER, H. J. (ed.) (1968) *Educational Research in Britain 1* London: University of London Press.

CARVER, G. (1970 in England) *Word Recognition Test* London: University of London Press.

CASHDAN, A. and PUMFREY, P. D. (1969) 'Some effects of the remedial teaching of reading', *Educ. Res.*, **11**, ii, 138–42.

CASHDAN, A. et al. (1971) 'Children receiving remedial teaching in reading', *Educ. Res.*, **13**, ii, 98–105.

CHAZAN, M. (ed.) (1970) *Reading Readiness* University College of Swansea Faculty of Education.

CLARK, M. (1970) *Reading Difficulties in Schools* Harmondsworth, Middlesex: Penguin Books.

CLARK, M. (1971) '3. Severe Reading Difficulty: A community study', *Br. J. educ. Psychol.*, **41**, i, 14–18.

CLAY, M. M. (1969) 'Reading errors and self-correction behaviour', *Br. J. educ. Psychol.*, **39**, i, 47–56.

COLLINS, J. E. (1961) *The Effects of Remedial Education* University of Birmingham Institute of Education.

Devon Local Education Authority (1970) *Devon Report No. 2: Reading attainments of seven year old Devon pupils: 1969, Devon paper on current issues in education.*

DOWNING, J. (1968) 'The initial teaching alphabet and educationally subnormal children', *Developmental Medicine and Child Neurology*, **10**, 200–5.

DOWNING, J. (1969a) 'i.t.a. and slow learners: A reappraisal', *Educ. Res.*, **11**, iii, 229–31.

DOWNING, J. (1969b) 'The perception of linguistic structure in learning to read', *Br. J. educ. Psychol.*, **39**, iii, 267–71.

DOWNING, J. (1970a) 'Children's concepts of language in learning to read', *Educ. Res.*, **12**, ii, 106–12.

DOWNING, J. (1970b) 'Relevance versus ritual in reading', *Reading*, **4**, ii, 4–12.

DOWNING, J. (1971) 'A review of ten years' research', in Merritt, J. (ed.) *Reading and the Curriculum* London: Ward Lock Educational.

DOWNING, J. and LATHAM, W. (1969) 'A follow-up of children in the first i.t.a. Experiment', *Br. J. educ. Psychol.*, **39**, iii, 303–5.

FARNWORTH, M. (1971) 'A consideration of reading readiness in terms of perceptual maturity', *Forward Trends*, **14**, i, 13–16; also *Forward Trends*, **14**, ii.

FISHER, B. and WILLIAMS, P. (1969) 'The Tell-a-story technique for identifying young children likely to experience reading difficulties', in *Children at Risk*, Occasional Publication no. 2, University College of Swansea Department of Education.

G.A.P. (1965–67) *Reading Comprehension Test* London: Heinemann.

GARSIDE, S. D. (1968) 'Vocabulary and sentence length in two commonly used readers', *Reading*, **2**, ii, 17–23.

GOODACRE, E. J. (1969a) 'Learning how to teach reading—a research note on the findings of a postal survey', in Peters, M. (ed.), *Conference: Professional Preparation of Students for the Teaching of Reading* Cambridge Institute of Education.

GOODACRE, E. J. (1969b) 'Published reading schemes', *Educ. Res.*, **12**, i, 30–5.

GOODACRE, E. J. (1970a) 'Reading research—1969', *Reading*, **4**, i, 23–7.

GOODACRE, E. J. (1970b) 'The concept of reading readiness', in Chazan, M. (ed.), *Reading Readiness* University College of Swansea Faculty of Education.

GOODACRE, E. J. (1971) *Provision for Reading* University of Reading School of Education.

GOODACRE, E. J. and CLARK, M. (1971) 'Initial approaches to teaching reading in Scottish and English schools', *Reading*, **5**, *ii*, 15–21.

GOODMAN, K. (1970) 'Dialect rejection and reading: a response', *Reading Research Quarterly*, **5**, *iv*, 600–3.

HAAS, W. (1969) 'From look-and-say to i.t.a.', *Times Educational Supplement*, 28 November.

HAMMOND, D. (1967) 'Reading attainment in the Primary Schools of Brighton', *Educ. Res.*, **10**, *i*, 57–64.

INGRAMS, T. T. S. (1971) '2. Specific learning difficulties in childhood: A Medical Point of View', *Br. J. educ. Psychol.*, **41**, *i*, 6–13.

Inner London Education Authority (1969) *Literacy Survey: Summary of interim results of the study of pupils reading standards.*

JONES, K. J. (1968) 'Comparing i.t.a. with Colour Story Reading', *Educ. Res.*, **10**, *iii*, 226–34.

KEIR, G. (1970) 'The use of pictures as an aid to reading', *Reading*, **4**, *i*, 6–11.

LATHAM, D. (1971) *Six Reading Schemes: Their Emphasis and their Interchangeability* Cambridge Institute of Education.

LAVENDER, J. (1970) *The Reading Miscues made by a Group of Children of Common Reading Age: A Study in Depth* Cambridge Institute of Education thesis.

LAWRENCE, D. (1971) 'The effects of counselling on retarded readers', *Educ. Res.*, **13**, *ii*, 119–24.

LOVELL, K. and GORTON, A. (1968) 'A study of some differences between backward and normal readers of average intelligence', *Br. J. educ. Psychol.*, **38**, *iii*, 240–8.

MACKAY, D. and THOMPSON, B. (1968) 'Programme in Linguistics and English Teaching, Paper 3', *The Initial Teaching of Reading and Writing* London: Longman.

MCFIE, J. and THOMPSON, J. A. (1970) 'Intellectual abilities of immigrant children', *Br. J. educ. Psychol.*, **40**, *iii*, 348–51.

MERRITT, J. E. (1968) 'Assessment of reading ability: a new range of diagnostic tests?', *Reading*, **2**, *ii*, 8–16.

MERRITT, J. E. (1970) 'The Intermediate skills', in *Reading Skills* (UKRA, Nottingham), London: Ward Lock Educational, 42–65.

MILES, T. R. (1971) '1. More on Dyslexia', *Br. J. educ. Psychol.*, **41**, *i*, 1–5.

MILNE, A. and FYFE, T. W. (1969) 'An attempt to control and assess the teacher variable in reading research', *Reading*, **3**, *i*, 22–7.

MITTLER, P. and WARD, J. (1970) 'The use of the Illinois Test of Psycholinguistic Abilities on British Four-year-old Children: A Normative and Factorial Study', *Br. J. educ. Psychol.*, **40**, *i*, 43–54.

MUNDY, J. H. (1970) 'Language teaching and the young immigrant', *Trends in Education*, **20**, 21–6.

NAIDOO, S. (1971) '4. Specific Development Dyslexia', *Br. J. educ. Psychol.*, **41**, *i*, 19–22.

O'KELLY, E. (1970) 'A method for detecting slow learning Juniors', *Educ. Res.*, **12**, *ii*, 135–9.

PETERS, M. L. (1970) 'Trends in Reading Schemes', *Cambridge Institute of Education Bulletin*, **3**, *ii*, 2–7.

REID, J. F. (1966) 'Learning to think about reading', *Educ. Res.*, **9**, *i*, 56–62.

REID, J. F. (1968) 'Dyslexia: a problem of communication', *Educ. Res.*, **10**, *ii*, 126–33.

REID, J. F. (1970) 'Sentence structure in reading primers', *Research in Education*, **3** (May), 23–37.

RIGLEY, L. (1968) 'Reading disability and the Isle of Wight survey', *Reading*, **2**, *iii*, 3–8.

RUTTER, M. *et al.* (1970) *Education, Health and Behaviour* London: Longman.

SAMPSON, O. C. (1969) 'A study of incentives in remedial teaching', *Reading*, **3**, *i*, 6–10.

SHEARER, E. (1968) 'Physical skills and reading backwardness', *Educ. Res.*, **10**, *iii*, 197–206.

SIMS, N. and WILLIAMS, P. (1969) 'The development of Phonic skills in infant school children—a preliminary study', *Children at Risk*. Occasional Publication 2. University College of Swansea Department of Education, Schools Council Research Project in Compensatory Education.

SOUTHGATE, V. (1971) 'Colour codes compared with i.t.a.', in Merritt, J. E. (ed.) *Reading and the Curriculum* London: Ward Lock Educational, 95–110.

STRICKLAND, R. C. (1962) 'The Language of elementary school children: its relationship to the language of reading textbooks and the quality of reading of selected children', Bloomington, Indiana: *Bulletin of the School of Education, Indiana University*, **38**, *iv*.

THACKRAY, D. V. (1971) 'Readiness for reading with i.t.a. and t.o.—A research report', in Merritt, J. E. (ed.) *Reading and the Curriculum*, London: Ward Lock Educational, 111–24.

UHL, N. and NURSS, J. (1970) 'Socio-economic level styles in solving reading-related tasks', *Reading Research Quarterly* **5**, *iii*, 452–85.

WARBURTON, F. W. and SOUTHGATE, V. (1969) *i.t.a. An Independent Evaluation* London: Murray, and Edinburgh: Chambers.

WARD, J. (1970) 'The factor structure of the Frostig development test of visual perception', *Br. J. educ. Psychol.*, **40**, *i*, 65–7.

WOOSTER, A. O. (1970) 'The evaluation of self as a reader', in *Reading Skills* (UKRA, Nottingham), London: Ward Lock Educational, 107–17.

WRAGG, M. (1968) 'The leisure activities of boys and girls', *Educ. Res.*, **10**, *ii*, 139–44.

YOUNG, D. (1969) *Group Reading Test* London: University of London Press.

Personality and academic attainment

Those marked with an asterisk were used by Warburton in producing the summary shown as Table 2 in the text.

ADCOCK, C. J. (1965) 'A comparison of the concepts of Cattell and Eysenck', *Br. J. educ. Psychol.*, **35**, 90–8.

ALLPORT, G. W. (1963) *Pattern and Growth in Personality* London: Holt, Rinehart & Winston.

ALPERT, R. and HABER, R. N. (1960) 'Anxiety in academic achievement situations', *J. abnorm. soc. Psychol.*, **61**, 207–15.

*ANDERSON, A. W. (1961) 'Personality traits in the reading ability of Western Australian University freshmen', *J. Educ. Res.*, **54**, 234–7.

*BALLHAM, A. (1960) 'The relationship between problem solving in arithmetic and concept attainment, intelligence and personality characteristics', Diploma in Educational Psychology Dissertation, Department of Education, University of Manchester.

*BALLHAM, A. (1965) 'The relationship between personality factors and attainment, intelligence and personality characteristics', M ED thesis, Department of Education, University of Manchester.

*BANKS, J. (1964) 'The relationship between problem solving in arithmetic and concept attainment, intelligence and personality characteristics', M ED thesis, Department of Education, University of Manchester.

*BEECH, F. (1963) 'Investigation into effects of personality factors on progress in English and mathematics in two secondary modern schools', unpublished DASE Dissertation, Department of Education, University of Manchester.

BENNETT, S. N. (1971) 'The relationship of personality and intellectual measures to convergent and divergent school attainment', Paper read at the BPS Education Section Conference at York.

BIRNEY, R. C., BURDICK, H. and TEEVAN, R. C. (1969) *Fear of Failure* New York: Van Nostrand.

BRENNAN, T. and ENTWISTLE, N. J. (1974) 'Predicting academic performance of arts and science students by multivariate classification' (in preparation).

BROWN, G. (1970) 'An investigation into the relationships between performance and neuroticism', *Durham Res. Rev.*, **25**, 483–8.

*BURDICK, L. A. (1963) 'Analysis of sixteen personality factor questionnaire and elementary student teachers at Indiana State College', *College Journal*, 57–9.

BURT, C. (1965) 'Factorial studies of personality and their bearing on the work of the teacher', *Br. J. educ. Psychol.*, **35**, 368–77.

BUTCHER, H. J., AINSWORTH, M. and NESBITT, J. E. (1963) 'Personality Factors and School Achievement—a Comparison of British and American Children', *Br. J. educ. Psychol.*, **33**, 276–85.

*BUTCHER, H. J. and GORSUCH, R. (1960) 'Predicting academic achievement in Junior High School and High School', *I.P.A.T. Information Bull.*, no. 4.

CALLARD, M. P. and GOODFELLOW, C. L.(1962) 'Neuroticism and Extraversion in Schoolboys as measured by the JMPI', *Br. J. educ. Psychol.*, **32**, 241–50.

*CATTELL, R. B. (1960) 'Predicting success in the academic aspects of medical school', *I.P.A.T. Information Bull.*, no. 4.

CATTELL, R. B. (1965) *The Scientific Analysis of Personality* Harmondsworth, Middlesex: Penguin Books.

CATTELL, R. B. and BUTCHER, H. J. (1968) *The Prediction of Achievement and Creativity* New York: Bobbs-Merrill.

*CATTELL, R. B., SEALY, A. P. and SWENEY, A. B. (1966) 'What can personality and motivation source trait measurements add to the prediction of school achievement?', *Br. J. educ. Psychol.*, **36**, 280–95.

*CORTIS, G. (1966) 'The prediction of student performance in colleges of education', MED thesis, Department of Education, University of Manchester.

COWELL, M. D. and ENTWISTLE, N. J. (1971) 'Personality, study attitudes and academic performance in a technical college', *Br. J. educ. Psychol.*, **41**, 85–9.

*DICKENSON, W. (1966) 'The relationship between the abilities, personality traits and performance of students in the first year general courses for engineers in technical colleges', M ED thesis, Department of Education, University of Manchester.

DUCKWORTH, D. and ENTWISTLE, N. J. (1972) 'Intervening variables in the relationship between personality and school attainment'. Unpublished report, Department of Educational Research, University of Lancaster.

ENTWISTLE, N. J. (1967) 'The transition to secondary education: the age of transfer and correlates of academic success in the first year of secondary school', unpublished PH D thesis, Department of Education, University of Aberdeen.

ENTWISTLE, N. J. and BRENNAN, T. (1971) 'The academic performance of students, II—Types of successful students', *Br. J. educ. Psychol.*, **41**, 268–76.

ENTWISTLE, N. J. and CUNNINGHAM, S. (1968) 'Neuroticism and School attainment—a linear relationship?', *Br. J. educ. Psychol.*, **38**, 123–32.

ENTWISTLE, N. J. and ENTWISTLE, D. M. (1970) 'The relationships between personality, study methods and academic performance', *Br. J. educ. Psychol.*, **40**, 132–43.

ENTWISTLE, N. J., NISBET, J. B., ENTWISTLE, D. M. and COWELL, M. D. (1971) 'The academic performance of students. I—Prediction from scales of motivation and study methods', *Brit. J. educ. Psychol.*, **41**, 258–67.

ENTWISTLE, N. J., PERCY, K. A. and NISBET, J. B. (1971) 'Educational objectives and academic performance in higher education', unpublished report, Department of Educational Research, University of Lancaster.

ENTWISTLE, N. J. and WELSH, J. (1969) 'Correlates of school attainment at different ability levels', *Br. J. educ. Psychol.*, **39**, 57–63.

ENTWISTLE, N. J. and WILSON, J. D. (1970) 'Personality, study methods and academic performance', *Univ. Quart.*, **24**, 147–56.

EYSENCK, H. J. (1951) 'Social attitudes questionnaire and scoring key', *Br. J. Psychol.*, **42**, 114–22.

EYSENCK, H. J. (1965) *Fact and Fiction in Psychology* Harmondsworth, Middlesex: Penguin Books.

EYSENCK, H. J. (1972) 'Personality and attainment: an application of psychological principles to educational objectives', *Higher educ.*, **1**, 39–52.

EYSENCK, M. J. and COOKSON, D. (1969) 'Personality in primary school children: 1—Ability and achievement', *Br. J. educ. Psychol.*, **39**, 109–22.

EYSENCK, S. B. G. and EYSENCK, H. J. (1963) 'On the dual nature of extraversion', *Br. J. soc. clin. Psychol.*, **2**, 46–55.

EYSENCK, H. J. and EYSENCK, S. B. G. (1969a) *Personality Structure and Measurement* London: Routledge & Kegan Paul.

EYSENCK, H. J. and EYSENCK, S. B. G. (1969b) '"Psychoticism" in children: a new personality variable', *Res. in Educ.*, **1**, 21–37.

FRASER, B. (1967) 'An investigation into the relationship between personality variables and attainment in a secondary modern school', unpublished dissertation (Diploma in Educational Psychology—Child Guidance), Department of Education, University of Manchester.

FURNEAUX, W. D. (1962) 'The Psychologist and the university', *Univ. Quart.*, **17**, 33–47.

*HALLIWELL, C. (1963) 'The relationship between personality measures and performance in a training college for teachers', PH D thesis, Department of Education, University of Sheffield.

HALLWORTH, H. J. (1961) 'Anxiety in secondary school children', *Br. J. educ. Psychol.*, **31**, 281–91.

*HOLLAND, J. L. (1960) 'The prediction of college grades from personality and aptitude variables', *J. educ. Psychol.*, **50**, 245–54.

*HOLLAND, F. J. (1960) 'Predicting academic success on a general college curriculum', *I.P.A.T. Information Bull.*, no. 4.

HUDSON, L. (1968) *Frames of Mind* London: Methuen.

JOHN, K. (1973) 'Some differences in the personality, attitudes and cognitive styles of students choosing arts or science specialisms in the sixth form and at university', unpublished M SC thesis, Department of Educational Research, University of Lancaster.

JONES, H. GWYNNE- (1960) 'Relationship between personality and scholastic attainment', *Bull. Br. psychol. Soc.*, **40**, 42.

KELVIN, R. P., LUCAS, C. and OJHA, A. (1965) 'The relation between personality, mental health and academic performance of university students', *Br. J. soc. clin. Psychol.*, **4**, 244–53.

*KLINE, P. (1966) 'Extraversion, neuroticism and academic performance among Ghanaian university students', *Br. J. educ. Psychol.*, **36**, 93–4.

KLINE, P. and GALE, A. (1971) 'Extraversion, neuroticism and performance in a psychology examination', *Br. J. educ. Psychol.*, **41**, 90–3.

LAVIN, D. E. (1967) *The Prediction of Academic Performance* New York: John Wiley, Science Editions.

*LOCKE, M. (1958) 'The relationship between academic performance of university students and various cognitive and personality variables', unpublished report.

LUNZER, E. A. (1960) 'Aggressive and withdrawing children in the normal school', *Br. J. educ. Psychol.*, **38**, 119–23.

LYNN, R. and GORDON, I. E. (1961) 'The relation of neuroticism and extraversion to educational attainment', *Br. J. educ. Psychol.*, **31**, 194–203.

*MAYFIELD, A. (1966) 'Personality, sportsmanship and sociometic status in relation to physical ability in technical high school', unpublished report.

MORRISON, A., MACINTYRE, D. and SUTHERLAND, J. (1965) 'Teachers' personality ratings of pupils in Scottish primary schools', *Br. J. educ. Psychol.*, **35**, 306–19.

NISBET, J. D. and ENTWISTLE, N. J. (1969) *The Age of Transfer to Secondary Education* London: University of London Press.

*PORTER, R. B. (1964) 'A comparative investigation of the personality of sixth grade gifted children and a norm group of children', *J. educ. Res.*, **58**, 132–4.

RIDDING, L. W. (1967) 'An investigation of the personality measures associated with over- and under-achievement in English and arithmetic', *Br. J. educ. Psychol.*, **37**, 397–8.

*RUSHTON, J. R. (1966) 'The relationship between personality characteristics and scholastic success in 11-year-old children', *Br. J. educ. Psychol.*, **37**, 397–8.

*RUSHTON, J. R. (1968) 'A longitudinal study of personality characteristics and academic achievement', PH D thesis, Department of Education, University of Manchester.

RUDD, E. (1970) 'Student performance in university assessments in relation to individual characteristics', *Social Science Research Council, Annual Report, 1969–70*, London: HMSO.

RUDD, W. G. A. (1970) *C.S.E.: A Group Study Approach to Research and Development* London: Evans/Methuen Educational.

SAVAGE, R. D. (1962) 'Personality factors and academic performance', *Br. J. educ. Psychol.*, **32**, 251–3.

SAVAGE, R. D. (1966) 'Personality Factors in Academic Attainment in Junior School Children', *Br. J. educ. Psychol.*, **36**, 91–4.

SEDDON, G. M. (1972) 'Eysenckian theory and its relationship to performance on complex tasks'. Paper read to the BPS Education Section Conference at Lancaster.

SHARPLES, D. (1971) 'A longitudinal study of the Personality and the Attainments and Attitudes of Junior School Children', unpublished PH D thesis, University of Bath.

SMITHERS, A. G. and BATCOCK, A. (1970) 'Success and failure among social scientists and health scientists at a technological university', *Br. J. educ. Psychol.*, **40**, 144–53.

*SOLOMONS, E. (1961) 'An investigation into the relationships between personality traits, interests and attainments with particular reference to the difficulty of the task', Diploma in Educational Guidance Dissertation, Department of Education, University of Manchester.

*SOLOMONS, E. (1965) 'Personality factors and attitudes of mature training college students', M ED thesis, Department of Education, University of Manchester.

*STAVELEY, B. (1967) 'The abilities and interests of craft and technical students of mechanical engineering', M ED thesis, Department of Education, University of Manchester.

*VENABLES, E. (1963) 'Social differences among day-release students in relation to their recruitment and examination success', *Br. J. soc. clin. Psychol.*, **3**, 138–52.

VENABLES, E. (1967) *The Young Worker at College—a study at a Local Technical College* London: Faber & Faber.

WANKOWSKI, J. A. (1968) 'Some aspects of motivation in success and failure at university', in *Proceedings of the Fourh Annual Conference for the Society for Research into Higher Education* London: SRHE.

WARBURTON, F. W. (1968a) 'The assessment of personality traits', in Morris, J. F. and Lunzer, E. A., *Development in Learning, Volume 3—Context of Education* London: Staples.

WARBURTON, F. W. (1968b) 'The relationship between personality factors and scholastic attainment', unpublished report, Department of Education, University of Manchester.

*WARBURTON, F. W., BUTCHER, H. J. and FORREST, G. M. (1963) 'Predicting student performance in a university department of education', *Br. J. educ. Psychol.*, **33**, 68–79.

WILSON, J. D. (1971) 'Predicting levels of first year university performance', *Br. J. educ. Psychol.*, **41**, 163–70.

WOOD, R. (1971) 'Personality and attainment: a reanalysis of the "Age of Transfer" data', *Br. J. educ. Psychol.* (unpublished report).

Convergent and divergent thinking

BARKER LUNN, J. C. (1970) *Streaming in the Primary School* Slough: National Foundation for Educational Research.

BURT, C. (1962) 'Critical notice—"Creativity and Intelligence"', *Br. J. educ. Psychol.*, **32**, 292–8.

BUTCHER, H. J. (1968) *Human Intelligence* London: Methuen.

BYRNE, P. S., FREEMAN, J. and M'COMISKY, J. G. (1970) 'General practitioners observed: a study of personality, intellectual factors and group behaviour', *Br. J. med. Educ.*, **4**, 176–84.

CABOT, I. B. (1969) 'Creativity as a function of type of education' in Ash, M. (ed.) *Who Are the Progressives Now?* London: Routledge & Kegan Paul.

CAMERON, L. (1968) 'Intelligence, creativity and the English examination', *Scot. educ. Studies*, **1**, 55–60.

CAMPBELL, D. T. and FISKE, D. W. (1959) 'Convergent and discriminant validation by the multitrait-multimethod matrix', *Psychol. Bull.*, **56**, 81–105.

CATTELL, R. B. and BUTCHER, H. J. (1968) *The Prediction of Achievement and Creativity* Indianapolis: Bobbs-Merrill.

CHILD, D. (1968) 'Convergent and divergent thinking and arts/science', *Abstracts of the British Psychological Society, Education Section Annual Conference, 1968.*

CHILD, D. (1969) 'A comparative study of personality, intelligence and social class in a technological university', *Br. J. educ. Psychol.*, **39**, 40–6.

CHILD, D. and SMITHERS, A. (1971) 'Some cognitive and affective factors in subject choice', *Ris. in Educ.*, **5**, 1–9.

CHILD, D. and SMITHERS, A. (1973) 'A validation of the Joyce-Hudson scale of convergence and divergence', *Br. J. educ. Psychol.*, **43**, 57–61.

CHRISTIE, T. (1970) 'Cognitive bias, university faculty and degree of success', *Abstracts of the British Psychological Society, Education Section Annual Conference, 1970.*

CRONBACH, L. J. (1968) 'Intelligence? Creativity? A parsimonious reinterpretation of the Wallach-Kogan data', *Am. educ. Res. J.*, **5**, 491–512.

CRONBACH, L. J. (1970) *Essentials of Psychological Testing* (3rd ed.) New York: Harper and Row (Harper International Edition).

DACEY, J., MADAUS, G. F. and ALLEN, A. (1969) 'The relationship of creativity and intelligence in Irish adolescents', *Br. J. educ. Psychol.*, **39**, 261–6.

ELKIND, D., DEBLINGER, J. and ADLER, D. (1970) 'Motivation and creativity: the context effect', *Am. educ. Res. J.*, **7**, 351–7.

FEE, F. (1968) 'An alternative to Ward's factor analysis of Wallach and Kogan's "creativity" correlations', *Br. J. educ. Psychol.*, **28**, 319–21.

FREEMAN, J., BUTCHER, H. J. and CHRISTIE, T. (1971) *Creativity* (2nd edition) London: Society for Research into Higher Education.

FREEMAN, J., M'COMISKY, J. G. and BUTTLE, D. (1969) 'Student selection: a comparative study of student entrants to architecture and economics', *Int. J. educ. Sci.*, **3**, 189–97.

GETZELS, J. W. and JACKSON, P. W. (1962) *Creativity and Intelligence* New York: John Wiley.

GETZELS, J. W. and MADAUS, G. F. (1969) 'Creativity', in Ebel, R. L. (ed.) *Encyclopedia of Educational Research* (4th ed.) New York: Macmillan.

GOPAL RAO, G. S., PENFOLD, D. M. and PENFOLD, A. P. (1970) 'Modern and traditional mathematics teaching', *Educ. Res.*, **13**, 61–5.

GUILFORD, J. P. (1950) 'Creativity', *Am. Psychol.*, **5**, 444–54.

GUILFORD, J. P. (1956) 'The structure of intellect', *Psychol. Bull.*, **53**, 267–93.

GUILFORD, J. P. (1959) 'The three faces of intellect', *Am. Psychol.*, **14**, 469–79.

GUILFORD, J. P. (1967) *The Nature of Human Intelligence* New York: McGraw-Hill.

HADDON, F. A. and LYTTON, H. (1968) 'Teaching approach and the development of divergent thinking abilities in primary schools', *Br. J. educ. Psychol.*, **38**, 171–80.

HADDON, F. A. and LYTTON, H. (1971) 'Primary education and divergent thinking abilities—four years on', *Br. J. educ. Psychol.*, **41**, 136–47.

HARGREAVES, H. L. (1927) 'The "faculty" of imagination', *Br. J. Psychol. Monogr.*, **3**.

HARTLEY, J. and BEASLEY, N. (1969) 'Contrary imaginations at Keele', *Univ. Quart.*, **23**, 467–71.

HASAN, P. and BUTCHER, H. J. (1966) 'Creativity and intelligence: a partial replication with Scottish children of Getzels and Jackson's study', *Br. J. Psychol.*, **57**, 129–35.

HEIM, A. W. (1970) *Intelligence and Personality* Harmondsworth, Middlesex: Penguin Books.

HUDSON, L. (1966) *Contrary Imaginations* London: Methuen.

HUDSON, L. (1968) *Frames of Mind* London: Methuen.

JOYCE, C. R. B. and HUDSON, L. (1968) 'Student style and teacher style: an experimental study', *Br. J. med. Educ.*, **2**, 28–32.

LOVELL, K. and SHIELDS, J. B. (1967) 'Some aspects of a study of the gifted child', *Br. J. educ. Psychol.*, **37**, 201–8.

LYTTON, H. and COTTON, A. C. (1969) 'Divergent thinking abilities in secondary schools', *Br. J. educ. Psychol.*, **39**, 188–90.

MACKAY, C. K. and CAMERON, M. B. (1968) 'Cognitive bias in Scottish first-year science and arts undergraduates', *Br. J. educ. Psychol.*, **38**, 315–18.

MCHENRY, R. E. and SHOUKSMITH, G. A. (1970) 'Creativity, visual imagination and suggestibility: their relationship in a group of ten-year-old children', *Br. J. educ. Psychol.*, **40**, 154–60.

MCNEMAR, Q. (1964) 'Lost: our intelligence? Why?', *Am. Psychol.*, **19**, 871–82.

MARSH, R. W. (1964) 'A statistical re-analysis of Getzels and Jackson's data', *Br. J. educ. Psychol.*, **34**, 91–3.

MILLS, J. (1970) 'Convergent/divergent skills and sixth form courses', *Abstracts of the British Psychological Society, Education Section Annual Conference, 1970*.

NICHOLLS, J. G. (1972) 'Some effects of testing procedure on divergent thinking', *Child Devel.*, **42**, 1647–51.

NUTTALL, D. L. (1971) 'Modes of thinking and their measurement', unpublished PHD thesis, University of Cambridge.

PONT, H. B. (1970) 'The arts—science dichotomy', in Butcher, H. J. and Pont, H. B. (eds) *Educational Research in Britain 2* London: University of London Press.

RICHARDS, P. N. and BOLTON, N. (1971) 'Type of mathematics teaching, mathematical ability and divergent thinking in junior school children', *Br. J. educ. Psychol.*, **41**, 32–7.

SHAPIRO, R. J. (1968) 'Creative research scientists', *Psychologia Africana Monogr.*, **4**.

SHOUKSMITH, G. A. (1970) *Intelligence, Creativity and Cognitive Style* London: Batsford.

SULTAN, E. E. (1962) 'A factorial study in the domain of creative thinking', *Br. J. educ. Psychol.*, **32**, 78–82.

TORRANCE, E. P. (1962) *Guiding Creative Talent* Englewood Cliffs, N.J.: Prentice-Hall.

VERNON, P. E. (1964) 'Creativity and intelligence', *Educ. Res.*, **6**, 163–9.

VERNON, P. E. (1967) 'A cross-cultural study of "creativity tests" with 11-year boys', *New Res. in Educ.*, **1**, 135–46.

VERNON, P. E. (1969a) 'Ability factors and environmental influences', in Wolfle, D. (ed.) *The Discovery of Talent* Cambridge, Mass.: Harvard University Press.

VERNON, P. E. (1969b) *Intelligence and Cultural Environment* London: Methuen.

VERNON, P. E. (1971) 'Effects of administration and scoring on divergent thinking tests', *Br. J. educ. Psychol.*, **41**, 245–57.

WALLACH, M. A. and KOGAN, N. (1965) *Modes of Thinking in Young Children* New York: Holt, Rinehart & Winston.

WARBURTON, F. W. (1970) 'The British intelligence scale', in Dockrell, W. B. (ed.) *On Intelligence* London: Methuen.

WARD, J. (1967) 'An oblique factorisation of Wallach and Kogan's "creativity" correlations', *Br. J. educ. Psychol.*, **37**, 380–2.

YAMAMOTO, K. (1965) 'Effect of restriction of range and test unreliability on correlation between measures of intelligence and creative thinking', *Br. J. educ. Psychol.*, **35**, 300–5.

Science teaching

ASHTON, B. G. and MEREDITH, H. M. (1969) 'The attitudes of sixth formers', *School Science Review*, **174**, 15–19.

Association for Science Education (1969) *SI Units, Signs, Symbols and Abbreviations*.

BARRINGTON, H. (1969) 'The effectiveness of teaching science by TV', *Higher Education Journal*, **17** (spring), 26–8.

BLOOM, B. S. (ed.) (1956) *Taxonomy of Educational Objectives: the Classification of Educational Goals: Handbook 1: Cognitive Domain* London: Longman.

BLOOM, B. S. (ed.) (1964) *Taxonomy of Educational Objectives: the Classification of Educational Goals: Handbook 2: Affective Domain* London: Longman.

BOUD, D. J. and O'CONNELL, S. (1970) 'Towards an educational technology of laboratory work', *Visual Education*, December, 12–13.

BOULIND, H. F. (1968) 'Nuffield XI: O-level physics examinations', *School Science Review*, **169** (June), 670–9.

BUTCHER, H. J. (1969) 'An investigation of the swing from science', *Research in Education*, **1** (May), 38–57.

BRYANT, J. J. (1968) 'The new education committees of the A.S.E.', *Education in Science*, **26** (February), 19–20.

CAVANAGH, P. and JONES, C. (eds) (1969) *Yearbook of Educational and Instructional Technology 1969–70* London: Cornmarket Press.

COOPER, B. and FOY, J. M. (1967) 'Examinations in higher education—a review', *J. Biol. Educ.*, **1**, 139–51.

COOLEY, W. W. and KLOPFER, L. E. (1961) *Test on Understanding Science* Princeton Educational Testing Service.

Commission on College Physics (1970) *Report on 'Conference on Computers in Undergraduate Science Education'*, University of Maryland.

Committee on Manpower Resources for Science and Technology: Working Group on Manpower for Scientific Growth (1968) *The Flow into Employment of Scientists, Engineers and Technologists* (Swann Report) London: HMSO Cmnd 3760.

Council for Scientific Policy (1968) *Enquiry into the Flow of Candidates in Science and Technology into Higher Education* (The Dainton Report) London: HMSO Cmnd 3541.

EGGLESTON, J. F. (1965) *A Critical Review of Assessment Procedures in Secondary School Science* University of Leicester.

EGGLESTON, J. F. and KERR, J. F. (1969) *Studies in Assessment* London: English Universities Press.

ELTON, L. R. B. (1970) 'The use of duplicated lecture notes and self-tests in University teaching', *Aspects of Educational Technology*, **4**, 366–73.

ELTON, L. R. B. (1971) 'Educational Technology and the Student Explosion', unpublished talk to the International Conference on Educational Technology.

ELTON, L. R. B. *et al.* (1970 and 71) 'Self teaching', *Visual Education* November 1970, 21; December 1970, 12–13; January 1971, 7, 8; February 1971, 17–19.

ELTON, L. R. B., HILLS, P. J. and O'CONNELL, S. (1971) 'Teaching and learning systems in a University physics course', *Physics Education*, **6** (March), 95–101.

FENSHAM, P. J. (1971) 'The time factor in curriculum development', *Journal Curriculum Studies*, **3**, ii, 179–83.

GLYNN, E. (1969) 'Programmed learning—an organisational problem? Chemistry programmes for the Nuffield A-level project', in Dunn, W. R. *Aspects of Educational Technology*. 2 Dunn, W. R. and Holroyd, C. (eds) 231–9, London: Metheun.

GOODEIR, J. M. (1969) 'An audio-visual approach to science teaching', *Visual Education* (December), 34–7.

HILL, G. C. and WOODS, G. T. (1969) 'Multiple true-false questions', *School Science Review*, **173** (June), 919–22.

HILLS, P. J. (1971a) 'The development of a self-teaching situation involving use of tape/slide presentations', *Visual Education* (January), 7–8.

HILLS, P. J. (1971b) 'Science teaching and educational technology Part II', *School Science Review*, **182** (September), 14–23.

HOARE, D. E. and REVANS, H. M. (1969) 'Measuring attainment of educational objectives in chemistry', *Education in Chemistry*, **6**, 78–80.

HOARE, D. E. and YEAMAN, E. J. (1971) 'Identifying and interviewing science students at risk of failure', *Universities Quarterly*, **5**, iv, 471–83.

HOCKEY, S. W. and NEALE, P. D. (1968) 'The Schools Council science education project', *Education in Science*, **27** (April), 55–6.

HUDSON, B. (1969) 'Measuring attainment in education', *Education in Chemistry*, **6**, 84–7.

HUDSON, L. (1966) *Contrary Imaginations: a Psychological Study of the English Schoolboy* London: Methuen.

HUTCHINGS, D. G. (1963) *Technology and the Sixth Form Boy* Oxford: University of Oxford Institute of Education.

HUTCHINGS, D. (ed.) 1966 *Towards More Creative Science* Oxford: Pergamon Press.

HUTCHINGS, D. (1969) 'Is there a sixth form swing to technology?', *CRAC Journal*, **3**, iii, 3–5.

International Association for the Evaluation of Educational Achievement (1971) *The IEA Study of Science Newsletter No.2* (May), 5–6, Sweden: I.E.A. Bureau.

JENNINGS, K. R. and LEISTON, J. A. (1965) 'True or false? Some thoughts on examination questions', *Education in Chemistry*, **2**, 283–6.

JOHNSTONE, A. H., MORRISON, T. I. and SHARP, D. W. A. (1971/2) *Education in Chemistry*, **8**, 212–13.

Joint Matriculation Board (1970) *Examining in Advanced Level Science Subjects of the GCE* Manchester: the Board.

KERR, J. F. (1963) *Practical Work in School Science* Leicester: University Press.

LAUGHTON, W. H. and WILKINSON, W. J. (1968) 'Pupils' attitudes to science teaching', *Education in Science*, **26** (February), 31–3.

LAUGHTON, W. H. and WILKINSON, W. J. (1970) 'The science opinion poll', *Education in Science*, **37** (April), 25–7.

LEITH, G., AMARIA, RODA P. and WILLIAMS, H. (1969) 'Applications of programmed learning principles to the preparation of TV lessons in elementary science and mathematics', *Programmed Learning and Educational Technology*, **6**, iv, 209–30.

LOCKARD, D. J. (1970) *Seventh report of the International Clearinghouse on Science and Mathematics Curricular Development, 1970* American Association for the Advancement of Science and Science Teaching Centre, University of Maryland.

MATHEWS, J. C. (1967) 'The Nuffield O-level chemistry examinations', *Education in Chemistry*, **4**, 2–10.

Nuffield Foundation Science Teaching Project (1966) *O-level Physics, O-level Chemistry, O-level Biology* London: Longman/Penguin Books.

Nuffield Foundation Science Teaching Project (1967) *Junior Science* London: Collins.

Nuffield Foundation Science Teaching Projects (1970) *Combined Science. A-level Biology, A-level chemistry* London: Longman/Penguin Books.

Nuffield Foundation Science Teaching Project (1971a) *Secondary Science* London: Longman.

Nuffield Foundation Science Teaching Project (1971b) *Integrated Science Bulletin, No. 3* Nuffield Integrated Science Project.

OLIVER, P. H. and ROBERTS, I. F. (1969) 'A test to measure the achievements of first-year secondary pupils of mixed ability following the Nuffield chemistry course', *School Science Review*, **175** (December), 423–33.

ORMEROD, M. B. (1971) 'The social implications factor in attitudes to science', *Br. J. educ. Psychol.*, **41**, Part 3, 335–8.

PALLANT, D. (1968) 'The use of tape-recordings in school biology', *School Science Review* (November), 331–3.

PONT, H. B. (1970) 'The arts-science dichotomy', in Butcher, H. J. and Pont, H. B. (eds) *Educational Research in Britain 2* London: University of London Press.

REID, D. J. and BOOTH, P. (1969) 'The use of individual learning with the Nuffield biology course', *School Science Review*, **172** (March), 493–506.

RICHMOND, P. E. (1971) *New Trends in Integrated Science Teaching* Paris Unesco.

Schools Council (1965) *Examinations Bulletin No. 8: C.S.E. Experimental Examinations: Science* London: HMSO.

Schools Council (1967) *Examinations Bulletin No. 15: Teachers' Experience of School Based Examining: English and Physics* London: HMSO.

Schools Council (1969) *Examinations Bulletin No. 19: C.S.E. Practical Work in Science* London: Evans/Methuen Educational.

Schools Council (1970) *Curriculum Bulletin 3. Changes in School Science Teaching* London: Evans/Methuen Educational.

Schools Council (1971) *Examinations Bulletin No. 21: C.S.E.: an Experiment in the Oral Examining of Chemistry* London: Evans/Methuen Educational.

Schools Council (1972a) *Science 5/13 Series* London: Macdonald Educational.

Schools Council (1972b) *With Objectives in Mind* London: Macdonald Educational.

Science 5/13 (1971) *Newsletter 2. Schools Council Science 5/13 Project*.

SCOTT, D. W. (1966) 'Practical examinations', *Physics Education*, **2** (May), 52–9.

Scottish Education Department (1969) *Curriculum Paper No. 7: Science for General Education* London: HMSO.

SELMES, C. (1969) 'Attitudes to science and scientists: 12/13 year-old pupils', *School Science Review*, **174**, 7–14.

SKILBECK, M. (1971) 'Curriculum development', letters in *Times Educational Supplement*, 20 August.

SKURNIK, L. S. and JEFFS, P. M. (1971) *Science Attitude Questionnaire* Slough: National Foundation for Educational Research.

STENHOUSE, D. (1969) 'An examination of selection pressures in biology', *Journal of the Institute of Biology*, **3**, 221–35.

TALBOT, A. R. (1968) 'An exploratory project in the application of CCTV to the teaching of chemistry and physics', *Visual Education* (January), 21–3.

TAYLOR, L. C. (1971) *Resources for Learning* Harmondsworth, Middlesex: Penguin Books.

THOMPSON, N. (1966) 'An experiment in examining at A-level standard I, II', *Physics Education*, **1**, 107–13, 163–9.

TROTH, D. and LLOYD, H. A. (1968) 'Science for all: an account of the adaptation of the Nuffield Foundation's science courses for all streams in a secondary modern school, using the medium of closed-circuit television', *Visual Education* (May), 33–41.

WISEMAN, S. and PIDGEON, D. (1970) *Curriculum Evaluation* Slough: National Foundation for Educational Research.

The humanities curriculum project

The Humanities Curriculum Project (1970) *The Humanities Project: An Introduction* London: Heinemann Educational Books.

MACDONALD, B. (in press) 'Briefing decision-makers—the evaluation of the Humanities Curriculum Project', *Bulletin of Evaluation Studies* The Schools Council (available at present as a mimeographed paper).

The Schools Council (1965) *Raising the school leaving age: a cooperative programme of research and development* Working paper no. 2, London: HMSO.

STENHOUSE, L. (1964) 'Aims or standards?', *Education for Teaching*, **64**, 15–21.

STENHOUSE, L. (1967) *Culture and Education* (2nd ed. 1971) London: Nelson.

STENHOUSE, L. (1968) 'The Humanities Curriculum Project', *Journal of Curriculum Studies*, **1**, i, 26–33.

STENHOUSE, L. (1970–1) 'Some limitations of the use of objectives in curriculum research and planning', *Paedagogica Europaea*, 73–83.

STENHOUSE, L. (1971) 'The Humanities Curriculum Project: the rationale', *Theory into Practice*, **10**, iii, 154–162.

Language, social class and the curriculum

BANTOCK, G. H. (1968) *Culture, Industrialisation and Education* London: Routledge & Kegan Paul.

BANTOCK, G. H. (1971) 'Towards a theory of popular education', *Times Educational Supplement*, 12.3.71 and 19.3.71.

BARKER-LUNN, J. C. (1970) *Streaming in the Primary School* Slough: National Foundation for Educational Research.

BARNES, D. (1969) *Language, the Learner and the School* Harmondsworth, Middlesex: Penguin Books.

BARNES, D. (1971) 'Language and learning in the classroom', *J. Curric. Stud.*, **3**, i, 27–38.

BELLACK, A. A. *et al.* (1966) *The Language of the Classroom* New York: Teachers College, Columbia University.

BERNSTEIN, B. B. (1970) 'A critique of the concept compensatory education', in Rubenstein, C. and Stoneman, C. (eds) *Education for Democracy* Harmondsworth, Middlesex: Penguin Books.

BERNSTEIN, B. B. (1971) *Class, Codes and Control I* London: Routledge, Kegan & Paul.

BETTY, C. (1967) 'Community school', *Trends in Education*, **6**, April 28–32.

BETTY, C. (1969) 'A community primary school', *Forum*, **11**, ii, 50–1.

BIDDLE, B. J. and ELLENA, W. J. (eds) (1964) *Contemporary Research on Teacher Effectiveness* New York: Holt, Rinehart & Winston.

BLANK, M. (1970) 'Some philosophical influence underlying pre-school intervention for disadvantaged children', in Williams, F. (ed.), *Language and Poverty* London: Markham House Press.

BRANDIS, W. and HENDERSON, D. (1970) *Social Class Language and Communication* London: Routledge & Kegan Paul.

CAZDEN, C. (1970) 'The neglected situation in child language research and education', in Williams, F. (ed.) *Language and Poverty* London: Markham House Press.

CLEGG, A. and MEGSON, B. (1968) *Children in Distress* Harmondsworth, Middlesex: Penguin Books.

CORBETT, A. (1969a) 'Community school', *New Society*, 355, 27.2.69.

CORBETT, A. (1969b) 'Are educational priority areas working?', *New Society*, 372, 13.2.69.

EGGINGTON, D. (1969) 'Community relationships in a primary school', *Educational Development Centre Review*, **3** (June).

FANTINI, M. D. and WEINSTEIN, G. (1968) *The Disadvantaged* New York: Harper & Row.

FLANDERS, N. A. (1970) *Analyzing Teaching Behaviour* Reading, Mass.: Addison-Wesley.

FREEMAN, J. (1969) *Team Teaching in Britain* London: Ward Lock.

GAHAGAN, D. M. and GAHAGAN, G. A. (1970) *Talk Reform* London: Routledge & Kegan Paul.

HARGREAVES, D. (1967) *Social Relations in a Secondary School* London: Routledge & Kegan Paul.

HEIDER, E. R., CAZDEN, C. B. and BROWN, R. (1968) 'Social class differences in the effectiveness and style of children's coding ability', *Project Literacy Report*, 9, Cornell University.

HIRST, P. H. (1969) 'The logic of the curriculum', *J. Curric. Stud.*, **1**, ii, 142–58.

LABOV, W. (1970) 'The logic of non-standard English', in Williams, F. *Language and Poverty* London: Markham House Press.

LAWTON, D. (1968) *Social Class, Language and Education* London: Routledge & Kegan Paul.

MIDWINTER, E. (1969) *Educational Priority Areas: the Philosophical Question*, Occasional Papers 1, The Liverpool Educational Priority Area Project.

MIDWINTER, E. (1970) *Home and School Relations in Educational Priority Areas*, Occasional Papers 4, The Liverpool Educational Priority Area Project.

PASSOW, A. W., GOLDBERG, M. and TANNENBAUM, A. J. (eds) (1967) *Education of the Disadvantaged* New York: Holt, Rinehart & Winston.

PIDGEON, D. A. (1970) *Expectation and Pupil Performance* Slough: National Foundation for Educational Research.

PULHAM, K. (1970) *The Liverpool Educational Priority Area: a Description* The Liverpool Educational Priority Area Project.

ROWE, A. (1970) *The School as a Guidance Community* Feltham: Pearson Press.

Schools Council Research and Development Project in Compensatory Education (1968) *Compensatory Education: An Introduction*, Occasional Publications 1.

Schools Council Research and Development Project in Compensatory Education (1969) *Children at Risk*, Occasional Publications 2.

SHUMSKY, A. (1968) *In Search of Teaching Style* New York: Appleton-Century-Crofts.

STENHOUSE, L. (1968) 'The Humanities Curriculum Project', *J. Curric. Stud.*, 1, i.

TURNER, G. J. and MOHAN, B. A. (1970) *A Linguistic Description and Computor Program for Children's Speech* London: Routledge & Kegan Paul.

WHITE, J. (1969) 'The curriculum mongers', *New Society*, 13, 336.

WILKINSON, A. M. (ed.) (1969) *The State of Language* University of Birmingham.

WILKINSON, A. (1971) *The Foundations of Language* London: Oxford University Press.

WILLIAMS, F. (ed.) (1970) *Language and Poverty* London: Markham House Press.

WILLIAMS, F. and NAREMORE, R. (1969) 'On the functional analysis of social class differences in modes of speech', *Speech Monographs*, 36.

Handicapped children

ABERCROMBIE, M. L. J. (1960) 'Perception and eye movements; some speculations on disorders in cerebral palsy', *Cerebr. Palsy Bull.*, 2, 142–8.

ABERCROMBIE, M. L. J. (1963) 'Visual disorders and cerebral palsy', *Little Club Clinics in Developm. Med.*, 9, 52–8.

ABERCROMBIE, M. L. J. (1964) 'Perceptual and visuo-motor disorders in cerebral palsy', *Little Club Clinics in Developm. Med.*, 11.

ABERCROMBIE, M. L. J., GARDINER, P. A., HANSEN, E., JONCKHEERE, J.,

LINDON, R. L., SOLOMON, G. and TYSON, M. C. (1964) 'Visual, perceptual and visuomotor impairment in physically handicapped children', *Percept. mot. Skills*, **18**, 561–625.

ANDERSON, E. M. (1971) *Making Ordinary Schools Special* London: College of Special Education.

ARNOT, A., GORTON, K. and SIMPSON, P. (1967) 'Investigations into structuring and evaluating situations designed to stimulate the language development of mentally handicapped children', *Funded by Ministry of Health, University of Newcastle-on-Tyne*.

ASCHER, M. (1970) 'Attainments of children in ESN schools and Remedial Departments', *Educ. Res.*, **12**, iii, 213–19.

BAGLEY, C. (1970) 'The educational performance of children with epilepsy', *Brit. J. Ed. Psychol.*, **40**, 82–3.

BIRCH, H. G., RICHARDSON, S. A., BAIRD, D., HOROBIN, G. and ILLSLEY, R. (1970) *Mental Subnormality in the Community: a clinical and epidemiologic study* Baltimore: Williams and Wilkins.

BORTNER, M. (1968) *Evaluation and Education of Children with Brain Damage* Illinois: C. C. Thomas.

BOWLEY, A. H. (1967) 'A follow-up study of 64 children with cerebral palsy', *Develop. Med. Child Neurol.*, **9**, 172–82.

BOWLEY, A. (1969) 'Reading difficulties with minor neurological dysfunction. A study of children in junior schools', *Develop. Med. Child Neurol.*, **11**, 493–503.

BRENNER, M. W., GILLMAN, S., ZANGWILL, O. L. and FARRELL, M. (1967) 'Visuo-motor disability in schoolchildren', *Br. med. J.*, **4**, 259–62.

BRYANT, P. E. (1964) 'Verbalization and flexibility in retarded children', *Proc. of the International Conference on the Scientific Study of Mental Retardation* Copenhagen.

BRYANT, P. E. (1967) 'Verbal labelling and learning strategies in normal and severely subnormal children', *Q. J. exp. Psychol.*, **19**, 155–61.

BURNS, R. (1967) 'The assessment of school placement in children suffering from encephalocele and meningomyelocele in the City of Liverpool' *Devel. Med. Child Neurol.*, Supplement No. 13, 23–9.

BUTCHER, H. J. and PONT, H. B. (eds) (1970) *Educational Research in Britain 2* London: University of London Press.

CHAZAN, M. (1964) 'The incidence and nature of maladjustment among children in schools for the ESN', *Br. J. educ. Psychol.*, **34**, 292–304.

CHAZAN, M. (1965) 'Factors associated with maladjustment in ESN children', *Br. J. educ. Psychol.*, **35**, 277–85.

CHAZAN, M. (1967) 'Recent developments in the understanding and teaching of educationally subnormal children in England and Wales', *Am. J. ment. Defic.*, **72**, 244–52.

CLARKE, A. M. and CLARKE, A. D. B. (1965) *Mental Deficiency: The Changing Outlook* London: Methuen (2nd ed.).

CLARKE, A. M., CLARKE, A. D. B. and COOPER, G. M. (1971) 'The development of a set to perceive categorical relations', in Haywood, H. C. (ed.) *Social-cultural aspects of mental retardation* New York: Appleton Century-Crofts.

CONNOLLY, K. (1968) 'The applications of operant conditioning to the measurement and development of motor skill in children', *Develop. Med. Child Neurol.*, **10**, 697–705.

CONNOLLY, K. (1970) 'Intersensory integration and motor impairment', in Connolly, K. (ed.) *Mechanisms of Motor Skill Development* London: Academic Press.

DENT, N. A., ROSS, E. and WARR, E. E. (1972) 'Epidemiology of handicaps in childhood', in *The Handicapped Child: Research Review Volume 1* London: Longman.

DINNAGE, R. (1970) *The Handicapped Child: Research Review Volume 1* London: Longman.

FRANCIS-WILLIAMS, J. (1970) *Children with Specific Learning Difficulties* Oxford: Pergamon Press.

FRITH, U. (1968) 'Pattern Detection in Normal and Autistic Children', PHD thesis, University of London.

FRITH, U. (1969) 'Emphasis and meaning in recall in normal and autistic children. *Lang. Speech*', **12**, 29–38.

FRITH, U. (1970a) 'Studies in pattern detection in normal and autistic children: 1. Immediate recall of auditory sequences', *J. abnorm. Psychol.*, **76**, 413–20.

FRITH, U. (1970b) 'Studies in pattern detection in normal and autistic children: 2. Reproduction and production of colour sequences', *J. exp. Child Psychol.*, **10**, 120–35.

FORRESTER, R. M. (1967) 'Motor handicap in children: a study of a population in 1965', *Develop. Med. Child Neurol.*, **9**, 22–9.

GARFIELD, A. and SHAKESPEARE, R. (1964) 'A psychological and developmental study of mentally retarded children with cerebral palsy', *Develop. Med. Child Neurol.*, **6**, 485–94.

GEDYE, J. L. and WEDGWOOD, J. (1966) 'Experience in the use of a teaching machine for the assessment of senile mental changes', *Proc. VII Int. Congr. Gerontol.*, Vienna, 205–7.

HASKELL, S. H. and HUGHES, V. A. (1965) 'Some observations on the performance of squinters and non-squinters on the Wechsler Intelligence Scale for Children', *Percept. mot. Skills*, **21**, 107–12.

HASKELL, S. H. (1967) 'Impairment of arithmetic skills in cerebral palsied children and a programmed remedial approach', *J. Spec. Educ.*, **4**, 419–24.

HASKELL, S. H. (1972a) 'Visuo-perceptual, visuo-motor and scholastic skills of alternating and uniocular squinting children', *J. Spec. Educ.*, **6**, i.

HASKELL, S. H. (1972b) *Arithmetical Disabilities in Cerebral Palsied Children: Programmed Instruction a Remedial Approach* Illinois: C. C. Thomas.

HENDERSON, P. (1968) 'Changing patterns of disease and disability in school children in England and Wales', Br. med. J., 2, 239–334.

HERMELIN, B. and O'CONNOR, N. (1961) 'Recognition of shapes by normal and subnormal children', Br. J. Psychol., 52, 281–4.

HERMELIN, B. and O'CONNOR, N. (1970) Psychological Experiments with Autistic Children Oxford: Pergamon Press.

HEWETT, S. (1970) The Family and the Handicapped Child London: Allen & Unwin.

HUTT, S. J., LEE, D. and OUNSTED, C. (1965) 'Digit memory and evoked discharges in four light-sensitive epileptic children', Devel. Med. Child Neurol., 5, 559–71.

HUTT, S. J., HUTT, C., LEE, D. and OUNSTED, C. (1965) 'A behavioural and electro-encephalographic study of autistic children', J. psychiat. Res., 3, 181–98.

INGRAM, T. T. S., MASON, A. W. and BLACKBURN, I. (1970) 'A retrospective study of 82 children with reading disability', Develop. Med. Child Neurol., 12, 271–81.

KELLMER PRINGLE, M. L., (1970) 'The National Bureau for Co-operation in Child Care', in Butcher, H. J. and Pont, H. B. (eds) Educational Research in Britain 2 London: University of London Press.

KELLMER PRINGLE, M. L., BUTLER, N. R. and DAVIE, R. (1966) 11,000 7 year olds London: Longman.

KELLMER PRINGLE, M. L. and FIDDES, D. O. (1970) The Challenge of Thalidomide. A Pilot Study of the Educational Needs of Children in Scotland Affected by the Drug London: NBCC.

KIRK, S. A. (1962) Educating Exceptional Children Boston: Houghton Mifflin.

KUSHLICK, A. (1964) Prevalence of recognised mental subnormality of I.Q. under 50 among children in the South of England, with reference to the demand for places for residential care Paper read to the International Conference on the scientific study of mental retardation: Copenhagen.

KUSHLICK, A. (1965) 'Community services for the mentally subnormal', Proc. of the Royal Society of Medicine, 59, 374–90.

LAURENCE, K. M. (1966) 'The survival of untreated spina bifida cystica', Devel. Med. Child Neurol., 8, Suppl. 11, 10.

LAURENCE, K. M. and TEW, B. J. (1967) 'Follow-up of 65 survivors from 425 cases of spina bifida born in South Wales between 1956 and 1962', Develop. Med. Child Neurol., Suppl. 13, 1–3.

LORBER, J. (1971) 'Results of treatment of myelomeningocele', Develop. Med. Child Neurol., 3, 279–303.

LOTTER, B. (1966) 'Services for a group of autistic children in Middlesex', in Wing, J. K. (ed.) Early Childhood Autism London: Pergamon Press.

LOVELL, K. (1968) 'Backwardness and retardation', in Butcher, H. J. (ed.) Educational Research in Britain 1 London: University of London Press.

LOVELL, K. and GORTON, A. (1968) 'A study of some differences between backward and normal readers of average intelligence', *Br. J. educ. Psychol.*, **38**, 240–8.

LURIA, A. R. (1961) *The Role of Speech in the Regulation of Normal and Abnormal Behaviour* Oxford: Pergamon Press.

MACKAY, C. K. and MACMILLAN, J. (1968) 'A comparison of stereognostic recognition in normal children and severely subnormal adults', *Br. J. Psychol.*, **59**, 443–7.

MILLER, E. and SETHI, L. (1971a) 'The effect of hydrocephalus on perception', *Devel. Med. Child Neurol.*, *Suppl. 25*, 77–81.

MILLER, E. and SETHI, L. (971b) 'Tactile matching in children with hydrocephalus', *Neuropädiatrie*, **3**, 191–4.

Ministry of Education Circular No. 276 (1954) London: HMSO.

Ministry of Health (1962) *Report on the Training of Staff of Training Centres for the Mentally subnormal* London: HMSO.

MITTLER, P. and WOODWARD, M. (1966) 'The education of children in hospitals for the subnormal: a survey of admissions', *Develop. Med. Child Neurol.*, **8**, 16–25.

MITTLER, P. (1970) 'The concept of multiple handicap', in Mittler, P. (ed.) *The Psychological Assessment of Mental and Physical Handicaps* London: Methuen.

O'CONNOR, N. and HERMELIN, B. (1963) *Speech and Thought in Severe Subnormality: An Experimental Study* Oxford: Pergamon Press.

O'CONNOR, N. and HERMELIN, B. (1971) 'Cognitive deficits in children', in 'Cognitive Psychology', *Br. Med. Bull.*, **27**, 227–32.

OUNSTED, C., HUTT, S. J. and LEE, D. (1963) 'The retrograde amnesia of petit mal', *Lancet*, **1**, 671 (letter).

OUNSTED, C., LINDSAY, J. and WARMAN, R. (1966) 'Biological Factors in Temporal Lobe Epilepsy', *Clin. Dev. Med.*, **22**, London: Spastics/Heinemann.

PHILLIPS, C. J. and WHITE, R. R. (1964) 'The prediction of educational progress among cerebral palsied children', *Develop. Med. Child Neurol.*, **6**, 167–74.

RICHARDS, B. W. (1970) *Mental Subnormality: Modern Trends in Research* London: Pitman.

RUTTER, M. (1966) 'Prognosis: psychotic children in adolescence and early adult life', in Wing, J. (ed.) *Childhood Autism: Clinical, Educational and Social Aspects* Oxford: Pergamon.

RUTTER, M., GRAHAM, P. and BIRCH, H. G. (1966) Interrelations between the choreiform syndrome, reading disability, and psychiatric disorder in children of 8–11 years. *Develop. Med. Child Neurol.*, **8**, 149–59.

RUTTER, M. (1967a) 'A children's behaviour questionnaire for completion by teachers. Preliminary findings', *J. Child Psychol. Psychiat.*, **8**, 1–11.

RUTTER, M. (1967b) 'Brain damaged children', *New Education*, **3**, 10–13.

RUTTER, M. (1967c) 'Psychotic disorders in early childhood', in Coppen, A. J. (ed.) Recent developments in schizophrenia *Br. J. Psychiat., Special Publication 1.*

RUTTER, M., GREENFIELD, D. and LOCKYER, L. (1967) 'A 5 to 15 year follow-up study of infantile psychosis', *Br. J. Psychiat.,* 113, 1183–99.

RUTTER, M. and LOCKYER, L. (1967) 'A 5 to 15 year follow-up study of infantile psychosis. I: Description of sample', *Br. J. Psychiat.,* 113, 1169–82.

RUTTER, M. (1968) 'Concepts of Autism', in Mittler, P. (ed.) *Aspects of Autism* London: BPS.

RUTTER, M., TIZARD, J. and WHITMORE, K. (eds) (1970a) *Education, Health and Behaviour* London: Longman.

RUTTER, M., GRAHAM, P. and YULE, W. (1970b) 'A Neuropsychiatric Study in Childhood', *Clin. Dev. Med.,* 35/36, London: Spastics/Heinemann.

SPAIN, B. (1969) 'Estimating the future school population of spina bifida children within London', *G.L.C. Research and Intelligence Unit. Quart. Bull.,* 7, 18–25.

SPAIN, B. (1970) 'Spina bifida survey', *G.L.C. Research and Intelligence Unit. Quart. Bull.,* 12, 5–12.

TIZARD, J. (1964) *Community Services for the Mentally Handicapped* London: Oxford University Press.

TIZARD, J. (1968) 'Children with myelomeningocele: social and educational problems', *Develop. Med. Child Neurol., Suppl. 15,* 1–5.

TIZARD, J. (1971) 'Planning and evaluation of special education', paper given at European Association of Special Education International Conference— Teaching the Handicapped Child, Norköpping, Sweden, 25 July– 2 August.

TIZARD, J. (1974 in press) 'The epidemiology of handicapping conditions of educational concern', in Varma, V. P. (ed.) *Advances in Educational Psychology 2* London: University of London Press.

TYSON, M. (1963) 'Pilot study of remedial visuomotor training', *Special Education,* 52, 22–5.

TYSON, M. (1964) 'Shape matching test', in Abercrombie, M. L. J., Gardiner, P. A. G., Hansen, E., Jonckheere, J., Lindon, R. L., Solomon, G. and Tyson, M. C. 'Visual, perceptual and visuomotor impairments in physically handicapped children', *Percept. mot. Skills Monogr. Suppl. 18,* 595–601.

WARRINGTON, E. K. (1967) 'The incidence of verbal disability associated with reading retardation', *Neuropsychologica,* 5, 178–80.

WEDELL, K. (1960a) 'The visual perception of cerebral palsied children', *J. Child Psychol. Psychiat.,* 1, 215–27.

WEDELL, K. (1960b) 'Variations in perceptual ability among types of cerebral palsy,' *Cerebr. Palsy Bull.,* 2, 149–57.

WEDELL, K. (1961) 'Follow-up study of perceptual ability in children with hemiplegia', in *Hemiplegic Cerebral Palsy in Children and Adults* London: Spastics/Heinemann.

WEDELL, K. (1964) 'Some aspects of perceptual-motor development in young children', in *Learning Problems of the Cerebral-Palsied* London: Spastics.

WEDELL, K. (1968) 'Perceptual-motor difficulties', *Special Education*, **57**, 25–30.

WILLIAMS, P. (1966) 'Some characteristics of ESN children', *Br. J. Psychiat.*, **112**, 79–90.

WING, J. (1967) 'The handicaps of autistic children—results of a pilot study', in Richards, B. W. (ed.) *Proceedings of the Congress of the International Association for the Scientific Study of Mental Deficiency* England: Mick and Jackson.

YOUNGHUSBAND, E., BIRCHALL, D., DAVIE, R. and KELLMER PRINGLE, M. L. (1970) *Living With Handicap* London: NBCC.

Maladjustment

ANGUS, Z. (1970) 'Autonomic and cognitive functions in childhood psychosis', *British Psychological Society Bulletin*, **23**, xxc, 228–9 (abstract).

BALBERNIE, R. (1966) *Residential Work with Children* Oxford: Pergamon Press.

BANDURA, A. (1969) *Principles of Behaviour Modification* New York: Holt, Rinehart & Winston.

BANNISTER, D. (ed.) (1970) *Perspectives in Personal Construct Theory* London: Academic Press.

BANNISTER, D., and MAIR, J. M. M. (1968) *The Evaluation of Personal Constructs* London: Academic Press.

BARKER, P. (1968) 'The in-patient treatment of school refusal', *British Journal of Medical Psychology*, **41**, iv, 381–7.

BEECH, H. R. (1969) *Changing Man's Behaviour* Harmondsworth: Penguin Books.

BELSON, W. A., MILLERSON, G. C. and DIDCOTT, P. J. (1968) *The Development of a Procedure for Eliciting Information from Boys about the Nature and Extent of their Stealing* London: The Survey Research Centre (of the London School of Economics and Political Science). Mimeographed.

BOWER, E. M. (1969) *Early Identification of Emotionally Handicapped Children in School* (2nd ed.) New York: Thomas.

BOWYER, L. R., MARSHALL, A. and WEDELL, K. (1963) 'The relative personality adjustment of severely deaf and partially hearing children', *British Journal of Educational Psychology*, **33**, i, 85–7.

BOXALL, J. (1963) 'Anxiety and retardation in reading', *British Psychological Society Bulletin*, **16**, l, 42 (abstract).

BRANDON, S. (1960) 'An epidemiological study of maladjustment in childhood', unpublished MD thesis, University of Durham.

BURTON, L. (1964) 'Three studies of deviant child development', unpublished doctoral thesis, The Queen's University of Belfast.

BURTON, L. (1968) *Vulnerable Children* London: Routledge & Kegan Paul.

CALLARD, M. P. and GOODFELLOW, C. L. (1962) 'Neuroticism and extraversion in schoolboys as measured by the Junior Maudsley Personality Inventory', *British Journal of Educational Psychology*, **32**, *iii*, 241–50.

CHAZAN, M. (1962) 'School phobia', *British Journal of Educational Psychology*, **32**, *iii*, 209–17.

CHAZAN, M. (1963) 'Maladjusted pupils: Trends in post-war theory and practice', *Educational Research*, **6**, *i*, 29–41.

CHAZAN, M. (1965) 'Factors associated with maladjustment in educationally subnormal children', *British Journal of Educational Psychology*, **35**, *iii*, 277–85.

CHAZAN, M. (1968) 'Inconsequential behaviour in school children', *British Journal of Educational Psychology*, **38**, *i*, 5–7.

CLYNE, M. B. (1966) *Absent: School Refusal as an Expression of Disturbed Family Relationships* London: Tavistock.

COOPER, M. G. (1966) 'School refusal', *Educational Research*, **8**, *ii*, 115–27.

CREAK, M. and INI, S. (1960) 'Families of psychotic children', *Journal of Child Psychology and Psychiatry*, **1**, 156–75.

DAVIDSON, S. (1961) 'School phobia as a manifestation of family disturbance: its structure and treatment', *Journal of Child Psychology and Psychiatry*, **1**, 270–87.

Department of Education and Science (1955) *Report on the Committee on Maladjusted Children* (The Underwood Report) London: HMSO.

Department of Education and Science (1965) *Boarding Schools for Maladjusted Children* (Building Bulletin 27) London: HMSO.

DINNAGE, R. and PRINGLE, M. L. K. (1967a) *Foster Home Care: Facts and Fallacies* London: Longman.

DINNAGE, R. and PRINGLE, M. L. K. (1967b) *Residential Child Care: Facts and Fallacies* London: Longman.

DIXON, E. (1967) 'Personality Traits and Sociometric Status amongst secondary-school Children', unpublished MED thesis, University of Manchester.

DONIGER, C. R. (1962) 'Children whose mothers are in a mental hospital', *Journal of Child Psychology and Psychiatry*, **3**, 165–73.

DOUGLAS, J. W. B. (1964) *The Home and the School* London: MacGibbon & Kee.

DOUGLAS, J. W. B. and ROSS, J. M. (1965) 'The later educational progress and emotional adjustment of children who went to nursery schools or classes', *Educational Research*, **7**, *i*, 73–80.

DOUGLAS, J. W. B. and ROSS, J. M. (1968) 'Adjustment and educational progress', *British Journal of Educational Psychology*, **38**, *i*, 2–4.

DOUGLAS, J. W. B., ROSS, J. M. and COOPER, J. E. (1967) 'The relationship between handedness, attainment and adjustment in a normal sample of school children', *Educational Research*, **9**, *iii*, 223–32.

EVANS, K. M. (1964) 'Sociometry in schools. I. Sociometric techniques', *Edu-*

cational Research, **6**, *i*, 50, 58, and 'II. Applications', *Educational Research*, **6**, *ii*, 121–8.

EYSENCK, H. J. and RACHMAN, S. (1965) *The Causes and Cures of Neurosis* London: Routledge & Kegan Paul.

EYSENCK, S. B. G. (1965) 'A new scale for personality measurement in children', *British Journal of Educational Psychology*, **35**, *iii*, 362–7.

FISHER, B. (1966) 'The social and emotional adjustment of children with impaired hearing attending ordinary classes', *British Journal of Educational Psychology*, **36**, *iii*, 319–21.

FRANK, G. H. (1965) 'The role of the family in the development of psycho-pathology', *Psychological Bulletin*, **64**, *iii*, 191–205.

FURNEAUX, W. D. and GIBSON, H. B. (1961) 'A children's personality inventory designed to measure neuroticism and extraversion', *British Journal of Educational Psychology*, **31**, *ii*, 204–7.

GIBSON, H. B. (1965) 'A new personality test for boys', *British Journal of Educational Psychology*, **35**, *ii*, 244–8.

GIBSON, H. B. (1967) 'Teacher's ratings of schoolboys' behaviour related to patterns of scores on the New Junior Maudsley Inventory', *British Journal of Educational Psychology*, **37**, *iii*, 347–55.

GRAHAM, P. J. and MEADOWS, C. E. (1967) 'Psychiatric disorders in the children of West Indian immigrants', *Journal of Child Psychology and Psychiatry*, **8**, 105–16.

GREGORY, R. E. (1965) 'Unsettledness, maladjustment, and reading failure: A village study', *British Journal of Educational Psychology*, **35**, *i*, 63–8.

GUERNEY, B. G. (ed.) (1969) *Non-professionals as Psychotherapeutic Agents* New York: Holt, Rinehart & Winston.

HALLWORTH, H. J. (1961) 'Teachers' personality ratings of high school pupils', *Journal of Educational Psychology*, **52**, 297–302.

HALLWORTH, H. J. (1962) 'A teachers' perception of his pupils', *Educational Review*, **14**, 124–33.

HERMELIN, B. and O'CONNOR, N. (1965) 'Visual imperception in psychotic children', *British Journal of Psychology*, **56**, *iv*, 455–60.

HERSOV, L. A. (1960a) 'Persistent non-attendance at school', *Journal of Child Psychology and Psychiatry*, **1**, 130–6.

HERSOV, L. A. (1960b) 'Refusal to go to school', *Journal of Child Psychology and Psychiatry*, **1**, 137–45.

HODGES, V. (1968) 'Non-attendance at school', *Educational Research*, **11**, *i*, 58–61.

HOWELLS, J. G. and LICKORISH, J. T. (1963) 'A projective technique for investigating intra-family relationships designed for use with emotionally disturbed children', *British Journal of Educational Psychology*, **33**, *iii*, 286–96.

IVES, D. C. (1963) 'The effects of treatment in a special class in a junior school on retardation and maladjustment with special reference to the concept of self', *British Journal of Educational Psychology*, **33**, *i*, 90–2 (abstract).

JACKSON, L. (1964) 'A study of 200 school-children by means of the Test of Family Attitudes', *British Journal of Psychology*, **55**, *iii*, 333–54.

JACKSON, L. (1968) 'Unsuccessful adoptions: a study of 40 cases who attended a child guidance clinic', *British Journal of Medical Psychology*, **41**, 389–98.

KAHN, J. H. and NURSTEN, J. P. (1968) *Unwillingly to School* (2nd edition) Oxford: Pergamon Press.

KASSORLA, I. (1968) 'Modification of the behaviour of autistic children', *British Psychological Society Bulletin*, **21**, *lxxi*, 97–8.

KELLY, G. A. (1955) *The Psychology of Personal Constructs* New York: Norton.

LENNHOFF, F. G. (1967) *Exceptional Children* (2nd edition) London: Allen & Unwin.

LENNHOFF, F. G. (1968, 1969) *Learning to Live* Shrewsbury: Shotton Hall Publications.

LYTTON, H. (1967) 'Follow-up of an experiment in selection for remedial education', *British Journal of Educational Psychology*, **37**, *i*, 1–9.

MCALLISTER, J. and MASON, A. (1968) 'Types of juvenile delinquents, derived from an analysis of psychological and sociological measures', *British Psychological Society Bulletin*, **21**, *lxxi*, 114 (abstract).

MCHALE, A. (1967) 'An investigation of personality attributes of stammering, enuretic, and school-phobic children', *British Journal of Educational Psychology*, **37**, *iii*, 400–3 (abstract).

MCKERRACHER, D. W. (1967) 'Alleviation of reading difficulties by a simple operant conditioning technique', *Journal of Child Psychology and Psychiatry*, **8**, 51–6.

MACLAY, I. (1967) 'Prognostic factors in child guidance practice', *Journal of Child Psychology and Psychiatry*, **8**, 207–15.

MCQUOID, J. C. (1967) 'Emotional adjustment and backwardness in the primary school child', *British Psychological Society Bulletin*, **20**, *lxvii*, 62–3 (abstract).

MCWHINNIE, A. M. (1967) *Adopted Children: How they Grow Up* London: Routledge & Kegan Paul.

MAGUIRE, U. (1966) 'The effects of anxiety on learning, task performance and level of aspiration in secondary modern school children', *British Journal of Educational Psychology*, **36**, *i*, 109–12.

MARTIN, H. L. (1970) 'Antecedents of burns and scalds in children', *British Journal of Medical Psychology*, **43**, 39–47.

MEHRYAR, A. H. (1967) 'Some evidence of the validity of the Junior Maudsley Personality Inventory', *British Journal of Educational Psychology*, **37**, *iii*, 375–8.

MEYER, V. and CHESSER, E. S. (1970) *Behaviour Therapy in Clinical Psychiatry* Harmondsworth: Penguin Books.

MITCHELL, S. and SHEPHERD, M. (1966) 'A comparative study of children's behaviour at home and at school', *British Journal of Educational Psychology*, **36**, *iii*, 248–54.

MITCHELL, S. and SHEPHERD, M. (1967) 'The child who dislikes going to school', *British Journal of Educational Psychology*, **37**, *i*, 32–40.

MITTLER, P. J. (ed.) (1968) *Aspects of Autism* London: British Psychological Society.

MOORE, T. and UCKO, L. E. (1961) 'Four to six: constructiveness and conflict in meeting doll play problems', *Journal of Child Psychology and Psychiatry*, **2**, 21–47.

MORENO, J. L. (1953) *Who Shall Survive?* New York: Beacon House.

MORRISON, A., MCINTYRE, D. and SUTHERLAND, J. (1965) 'Teachers' personality ratings of pupils in Scottish primary schools', *British Journal of Educational Psychology*, **35**, *iii*, 306–19.

NELSON, R. O. and EVANS, I. A. (1968) 'The combination of learning principles and speech therapy techniques in the treatment of non-communicating children', *Journal of Child Psychology and Psychiatry*, **9**, 111–24.

O'CONNOR, N. and HERMELIN, B. (1967) 'The selective visual attention of psychotic children', *Journal of Child Psychology and Psychiatry*, **8**, 167–79.

OGDEN, J. A. (1971) 'A study of the effects of anxiety upon reading attainment of children', unpublished Diploma Dissertation, University of Manchester.

OSGOOD, C. E., SUCI, G. J. and TANNENBAUM, P. H. (1957) *The Measurement of Meaning* Illinois: University of Illinois Press.

PETRIE, I. R. J. (1962) 'Residential treatment of maladjusted children: A study of some factors related to progress in adjustment', *British Journal of Educational Psychology*, **32**, *i*, 29–37.

PHILP, A. F. (1963) *Family Failure* London: Faber & Faber.

PITFIELD, M. and OPPENHEIM, A. N. (1964) 'Child rearing attitudes of mothers of psychotic children', *Journal of Child Psychology and Psychiatry*, **5**, 51–7.

PRINGLE, M. L. K. (1961) 'The long-term effects of remedial treatment', *Educational Research*, **4**, 62–6.

PRINGLE, M. L. K. (1967) *Adoption—Facts and Fallacies* London: Longman.

PRINGLE, M. L. K. and BOSSIO, V. (1960) 'Early, prolonged separation and emotional maladjustment', *Journal of Child Psychology and Psychiatry*, **1**, 37–48.

PRINGLE, M. L. K., BUTLER, N. R. and DAVIE, R. (1966) *11,000 Seven-year-olds* London: Longman.

PRINGLE, M. L. K. and COX, T. (1964) 'The influence of schooling and sex on test and general anxiety as measured by Sarason's scales', *British Psychological Society Bulletin*, **17**, *liv*, 7A–8A.

RACHMAN, S. (1962) 'Learning theory and child psychology: therapeutic possibilities', *Journal of Child Psychology and Psychiatry*, **3**, 149–63.

REGAN, G. (1967) 'Personality characteristics and attitude to school', *British Journal of Educational Psychology*, **37**, *i*, 127-9.

RICHARDS, H. H. (1967) 'Psychological factors associated with the status of children attending a comprehensive school in Breconshire', *British Journal of Educational Psychology*, **37**, *ii*, 261-2 (abstract).

RIM, Y. (1965) 'Extraversion, neuroticism and the effect of praise or blame', *British Journal of Educational Psychology*, **35**, *iii*, 381-4.

ROGERS, C. R. (1961) *Personal Adjustment Inventory* New York: Association Press.

ROSE, J. I. (1966) 'A sociometric comparison of well-behaved and badly-behaved classes', *British Journal of Educational Psychology*, **36**, *iii*, 331 (abstract).

ROSS, J. M. (1966) 'Delinquency, maladjustment and school attainment', *British Psychological Society Bulletin*, **19**, *lxiii*, A9 (abstract).

RUTTER, M. (1965) 'Classification and categorization in child psychiatry', *Journal of Child Psychology and Psychiatry*, **6**, 71-83.

RUTTER, M. (1967) 'A children's behaviour questionnaire for completion by teachers: preliminary findings', *Journal of Child Psychology and Psychiatry*, **8**, 1-11.

RUTTER, M. (1968) 'Concepts of autism: A review of research', *Journal of Child Psychology and Psychiatry*, **9**, 1-25.

RUTTER, M., TIZARD, J. and WHITMORE, K. (1970) *Education, Health and Behaviour* London: Longman.

RYLE, A., POND, D. A. and HAMILTON, M. (1965) 'The prevalence and patterns of psychological disturbance in children of primary school age', *Journal of Child Psychology and Psychiatry*, **6**, 101-13.

SAMPSON, O. C. (1962) 'Reading skill at eight years in relation to speech and other factors', *British Journal of Educational Psychology*, **32**, *i*, 12-17.

SAMPSON, O. C. (1966) 'Reading and adjustment: A review of the literature', *Educational Research*, **8**, *iii*, 184-90.

SAVAGE, R. D. (1966) 'Personality factors and academic attainment in junior school children', *British Journal of Educational Psychology*, **36**, *i*, 91-2.

Scottish Education Department (1964) *Ascertainment of Maladjusted Children* Edinburgh: HMSO.

SHAW, O. L. (1965) *Maladjusted Boys* London: Allen & Unwin.

SNIDER, J. G. and OSGOOD. C. E. (1968) *Semantic Differential Technique: A Sourcebook* Chicago: Aldine.

STEPHENSON, W. (1953) *The study of behaviour: Q-technique and its methodology* Chicago: University of Chicago Press.

STOTT, D. H. (1960) 'Delinquency, maladjustment and unfavourable ecology', *British Journal of Psychology*, **51**, *ii*, 157-70.

STOTT, D. H. (1964) *Thirty-three Troublesome Children* London: National Children's Home.

STOTT, D. H. (1966a) *Studies of Troublesome Children* London: Tavistock.

STOTT, D. H. (1966b) *The Bristol Social Adjustment Guides* (3rd edition) London: University of London Press.

THORPE, J. G. (1960) 'Neuroticism in children: II: Indentification and measurement of a neuroticism factor', *British Journal of Psychology*, **51**, *ii*, 153–5.

TIZARD, J. (1968) 'Questionnaire measures of maladjustment: A postscript to the symposium', *British Journal of Educational Psychology*, **38**, *i*, 9–13.

TURNER, R. K., MATHEWS, A. and RACHMAN, S. (1967) 'The stability of the W.I.S.C. in a psychiatric group', *British Journal of Educational Psychology*, **37**, *ii*, 194–200.

TYERMAN, M. J. (1968) *Truancy* London: University of London Press.

WALTON, D. (1961) 'Experimental psychology and the treatment of a ticqueur', *Journal of Child Psychology and Psychiatry*, **2**, 148–55.

WARD, J. (1971) 'Modification of deviant classroom behaviour', *British Journal of Educational Psychology*, **41**, *iii*, 304–13.

WARNECKE, R. (1964) 'School phobia and its treatment', *British Journal of Medical Psychology*, **37**, 71–9.

WARREN, W. (1965) 'A study of adolescent psychiatric in-patients and the outcome six or more years later. I. Clinical histories and hospital findings', *Journal of Child Psychology and Psychiatry*, **6**, *i*, 1–17; 'II. The follow-up study', *Ibid.*, *iii/iv*, 141–60.

WILLIAMS, J. M. (1961) 'Children who break down in foster-homes: a psychological study of patterns of personality growth in grossly deprived children', *Journal of Child Psychology and Psychiatry*, **2**, 5–20.

WILLS, D. (1960) *Throw away Thy Rod* London: Gollancz.

WING, J. K. (ed.) (1966) *Early Childhood Autism* Oxford: Pergamon Press.

WOLFF, S. (1961a) 'Social and family background of pre-school children with behaviour disorders attending a child guidance clinic', *Journal of Child Psychology and Psychiatry*, **2**, 260–8.

WOLFF, S. (1961b) 'Symptomatology and outcome of pre-school children with behaviour disorders attending a child guidance clinic', *Journal of Child Psychology and Psychiatry*, **2**, 269–76.

WOLFF, S. (1967) 'The contribution of obstetric complications to the etiology of behaviour disorders in childhood', *Journal of Child Psychology and Psychiatry*, **8**, 57–66.

YULE, W. (1968) 'Identifying Maladjusted Children', paper read to the Association for Special Education, 29th National Bi-annual Conference (mimeographed).

YULE, W. and RUTTER, M. (1968) 'Educational aspects of childhood maladjustment: some epidemiological findings', *British Journal of Educational Psychology*, **38**, *i*, 7–9.

ZAHRAN, H. A. S. (1967) 'The self-concept in the psychological guidance of adolescents', *British Journal of Educational Psychology*, **37**, *ii*, 225–40.

Learning processes in the mentally handicapped: the work of the Hester Adrian Research Centre

BERRY, P. (1971a) 'Imitation of Language in Subnormal Children', unpublished M ED thesis, University of Manchester.

BERRY, P. (1971b) 'Imitation of language in severe subnormality: a psycholinguistic assessment technique', paper presented to the XVIIth International Congress of Applied Psychology, Liege, Belgium, July 1971.

BIJOU, S. W. and BAER, D. M. (1967) 'Operant methods in child behaviour and development', in Bijou, S. W. and Baer, D. M. (eds) *Child Development: Readings in Experimental Analysis* New York: Appleton Century Crofts.

BRAINE, M. D. S. (1963) 'The ontogeny of English phrase structure: the first phase', *Language*, **39**, 1–13.

British Psychological Society (1969) 'The educational needs of mentally handicapped children: memorandum of evidence to the Department of Education and Science and the Department of Health', *Bulletin of the British Psychological Society*, **23**, 39–46.

CLARKE, A. and CLARKE, A. D. B. (eds) (1965) *Mental Deficiency: the Changing Outlook* (2nd edn) London: Methuen.

CLEARY, A. and PACKHAM, D. (1968) 'A teaching system for visual discrimination skills', in Dunn, W. R. and Holroyd, C. (eds) *Aspects of Educational Technology*, **2**, 75–84.

CUNNINGHAM, C. C. (1971) 'The development of software for handicapped children', in Packham, D., Cleary, A. and Mayes, T. *Aspects of Educational Technology* London: Methuen.

DENNY, M. R. (1964) 'Research in learning and performance', in Stevens, H. A. and Heber, R. (eds) *Mental Retardation* Chicago: University of Chicago Press.

ELLIS, N. R. (1963) 'The stimulus trace and behavioral inadequacy', in Ellis, N. R. (ed.) *Handbook of Mental Deficiency* New York: McGraw Hill.

FANTZ, R. L. (1967) 'Visual perception and experience in early infancy: a look at the hidden side of behavior development', in Stevenson, H. W., Hess, E. H. and Rheingold, H. L. (eds) *Early Behavior: Comparative and Developmental Approaches* New York: John Wiley.

FRIEDLANDER, B. Z. (1970) 'Receptive language development in infancy: issues and problems', *Merrill-Palmer Quarterly of Behavior and Development*, **15**, 7–51.

GAGNÉ, R. M. (ed.) (1967) *Learning and Individual Differences* Columbus: Merrill.

GRAY, J. A. (ed.) (1964) *Pavlov's Typology: Recent Theoretical and Experimental Developments from the Laboratory of B.M. Teplov* London: Pergamon.

GUNZBURG, H. C. (1968) *Social Competence and Mental Handicap* London: Bailliere, Tindal and Cox.

HERMELIN, B. and O'CONNOR, N. (1970) *Psychological Experiments with Autistic Children* London: Pergamon.

HERRIOT, P. and COX, ADELINE M. (1971) 'Subjective organisation and clustering in the free recall of subnormal children', *American Journal of Mental Deficiency*, **75**, 702–11.

HERRIOT, P. and THOMAS, BARBARA (1972) 'The expressed objectives of special school and adult training centre staff', *Teaching and Training*, **10**, 96–8.

JEFFREE, D. (1971) 'A language teaching programme for a mongol child', *Forward Trends*, **15**, 33–8.

LURIA, A. R. (1963) *The Mentally Retarded Child* London: Pergamon.

MCNEILL, D. (1966) 'Developmental psycholinguistics', in Smith, F. and Miller, G. A. (eds) *The Genesis of Language* Cambridge, Mass: MIT Press.

MAIER, I. (1971) 'An operant approach to the modification of hyperkinetic behaviour', *Bulletin British Psychological Society*, **24**, 229A.

MARINOSSON, G. (1970) 'A comparative study of normal, educationally subnormal and severely subnormal children on the revised Illinois Test of Psycholinguistic Abilities', unpublished MA thesis, University of Manchester.

MARSHALL, A. (1967) *The Abilities and Attainments of Children Leaving Junior Training Centres* London: National Association for Mental Health.

MEIN, R. (1961) 'A study of the oral vocabularies of severely subnormal patients. II Grammatical analysis of speech samples', *Journal of Mental Deficiency Research*, **5**, 52–9.

MITTLER, P. (1972a) 'New directions in the study of learning deficits', in Clarke, A. D. B. and Lewis, M. M. (eds) *Language, Speech and Thought in the Mentally Retarded* London: Butterworth.

MITTLER, P. (1972) 'Language development and mental handicaps', in Rutter, M. and Martin, J. A. (eds) *The Child with Delayed Speech* London: Spastics Society and Heinemann.

O'CONNOR, N. and HERMELIN, B. (1963) *Speech and Thought in Severe Subnormality* London: Pergamon.

SERPELL, R. (1971) 'Applications of attention theory to the training and education of retarded children and adults', *Progress Report to Social Science Research Council, October 1971* (unpublished).

WEISBERG, P. (1971) 'Operant procedures with the retardate: an overview of laboratory research', in Ellis, N. R. (ed.) *International Review of Research in Mental Retardation* (vol. 5) New York and London: Academic Press.

WHELAN, E. (1971) 'Assessment and development of work skills in retarded adults', Paper presented to *International Seminar of Vocational Rehabilitation of the Mentally Retarded* American Association for Mental Deficiency and U.S. Department of Health Education and Welfare (ed. Loth, J., Jnr.).

WHITE, B. L., CASTLE, P. and HELD, R. (1964) 'Observations on the development of visually directed reaching', *Child Development*, **35**, 349–64.

ZEAMAN, D. and HOUSE, B. (1963) 'The role of attention in retardate discrimination learning', in Ellis, N. R. ed.) *Handbook of Mental Deficiency* New York: McGraw Hill.

Selected publications by HARC staff

1 'The Work of the Hester Adrian Research Centre: A Report for Teachers', (ed. P. Mittler). Monograph Supplement, *Teaching and Training*, **8**, pp. 47 (1970).

'The study of learning processes in the mentally Handicapped' (P. Mittler)
'Testing and teaching language skills' (P. Mittler, D. Jeffree, S. Pickstone)
'Language abilities of normal, ESN and SSN children: a comparative study' (G. Marinosson)
'The use of programmed learning in the teaching of visual perceptual skills' (C. Cunningham)
'Assessment and behavioural modification in the mentally handicapped' (E. Whelan)
'A systematic approach to the treatment of overactive children' (I. Maier)
'The learning of class concepts' (P. Herriot)
'Can the memory of subnormal children be improved?' (C. Elliott)
'Attentional difficulties in learning' (J. Hogg, P. Evans, D. Preddy)
'Learning and the electrical activity of the brain' (J. Tansley)

2 'Hester Adrian Research Centre: Preliminary Report of Research Programmes' unpublished Report, January 1970, pp. 54.

'Introduction' (P. Mittler)
'Assessment and remediation of language comprehension and production in SSN children' (P. Mittler, D. Jeffree, S. Pickstone)
'Attentional deficit and learning difficulty in ESN and SSN children' (J. Hogg, P. Evans, D. Preddy)
'The teaching of class concepts to SSN children' (P. Herriot)
'The use of the EEG for learning in the mentally handicapped' (J. Tansley)
'Application of operant techniques to the investigation and improvement of learning and other behaviour in mentally retarded children with electrophysiological monitoring of responses' (E. Whelan)
'An operant approach to the modification of hyperkinetic behaviour (I. Maier)
'The application of programmed instruction to SSN children' (C. Cunningham)
'Inhibitory deficit and stimulus control in the learning of retardates' (P. Evans)
'Span of attention in SSN and ESN children' (D. Preddy)

'The effect of training on the recall of stimulus sequences in ESN and SSN children' (C. Elliott)
'A comparative study of matched normal, ESN and SSN children on the revised edition of the Illinois Test of Psycholinguistic Abilities' (G. Marinosson)

3 'Learning Disabilities of Severely Subnormal Children', unpublished papers delivered to symposium of the British Psychological Society's Division of Educational and Child Psychology, York, January 1970. pp. 52.

'New directions in the study of learning deficits' (P. Mittler)
'Language in the severely subnormal' (Peter Herriot)
'Functional assessment: operant approaches' (E. Whelan)
'Inhibitory deficit in the retarded child' (J. Hogg)

4 Symposium on the Work of the Hester Adrian Research Centre, delivered to Annual Conference of British Psychological Society, Exeter, April 1971, (unpublished papers, pp. 65)

'Learning deficits in the severely subnormal' (P. Mittler)
'Language comprehension in the severely subnormal' (P. Mittler and K. Wheldall)
'Free recall in the severely subnormal' (P. Herriot and J. Green)
'Inhibitory aspects of learning and behaviour in the SSN and ESN' (J. Hogg, P. Evans and D. Preddy)
'An operant approach to the modification of hyperkinetic behaviour' (I. Maier)

5 'Mental Retardation and Behavioural Research', Institute for Research into Mental Retardation Study Group No. 4, University of Hull, September 1971, to be published by J. & A. Churchill, London and Williams & Wilkins, Baltimore, 1973 (eds. A. D. B. and Ann Clarke). Papers from HARC include:

'Assumptions underlying the use of psychological models in subnormality research' (Peter Herriot)
'Applications of attention theory to teaching in schools for the severely subnormal' (Robert Serpell)
'The application of educational technology to mental retardation' (Clifford Cunningham)
'The teaching of language' (Peter Mittler)

6 'Assessment for learning in the Mentally Handicapped', Ciba Foundation and Institute for Research into Mental Retardation Study Group No. 5, Ciba Foundation, London, December 1971, to be published by J. & A. Churchill, London and Williams & Wilkins, Baltimore, 1973 (ed. P. J. Mittler). Papers include:

'Purposes and principles of assessment' (Peter Mittler)

'Personality assessment of the subnormal as the study of learning processes' (James Hogg)
'Developing work skills: a systematic approach' (Edward Whelan)

7 *A Workshop for Parents of Young Mentally Handicapped Children: Report on an Introductory Course for Parents (January–June 1971).* (C. C. Cunningham, D. Jeffree, with I. Maier, E. Whelan, and P. J. Mittler). Manchester: National Society for Mentally Handicapped Children (North West Region) and Hester Adrian Research Centre.

BERRY, P. (1971a) 'Imitation of Language in Subnormal Children', unpublished MED thesis, University of Manchester.

BERRY, P. (1971b) 'Imitation of language in severe subnormality: a psycholinguistic assessment technique', paper presented to the XVIIth International Congress of Applied Psychology, Liege, Belgium, July 1971.

BERRY, P. (1972) 'The comprehension of possessive and present continuous sentences by normal, ESN and SSN children', *American Journal of mental Deficiency*, **76**, 540–4.

CUNNINGHAM, C. C. (1971) 'The development of software for handicapped children', in Packham, D., Cleary, A. and Mayes, T. *Aspects of Educational Technology* London: Methuen.

CUNNINGHAM, C. C. (1971) 'Learning system for the retarded', *Education*, **138**, 343–5.

CUNNINGHAM, C. C. (1973) 'The application of educational technology to mental retardation', in Clarke, A. and Clarke, A. D. B. (eds) *Mental Retardation and Behavioural Research* London: Churchill Livingstone; Baltimore, Md.: Williams & Wilkins.

HERRIOT, P. (1971) 'Disorders of communication', in Petrie, I. (ed.) *Handicapped Children—their Potential and Fulfilment* Wallasey, Cheshire: Joint Council for the Education of Handicapped Children.

HERRIOT, P. (1972) 'The effect of order of labelling on the subjective organisation and clustering in free recall of severely retarded adults', *American Journal of mental Deficiency*, **76**, 632–8.

HERRIOT, P. (1973) 'Assumptions underlying the use of psychological models in subnormality research', in Clarke, A. and Clarke, A. D. B. (eds) *Mental Retardation and Behavioural Research* London: Churchill Livingstone; Baltimore, Md.: Williams & Wilkins.

HERRIOT, P. and COX, ADELINE M. (1971) 'Subjective organisation and clustering in the free recall of subnormal children', *American Journal of mental Deficiency*, **75**, 702–11.

HERRIOT, P. and GREEN, JOSEPHINE M. (1971) 'Free recall in the severely subnormal', *Bulletin British Psychological Society*, **24**, 228A.

HERRIOT, P., GREEN, J. M. and MCCONKEY, R. (1973) *Organisation and Memory:*

A Review and a Project in Subnormality London: Methuen Studies in Mental
Handicap (in press).

HERRIOT, P. and THOMAS, BARBARA (1972) 'The expressed objectives of special
school and adult training centre staff', *Teaching and Training*, **10**, 96–8.

HOGG, J. (1973a) 'Introduction to behaviour modification', in Thomas, D. T.
(ed.) *Fundamentals in the Education of Mentally Handicapped Children*
London: Routledge & Kegan Paul (in press).

HOGG, J. (1973b) 'Personality assessment of the subnormal as the study of
learning processes', in Mittler, P. (ed.) *Assessment for Learning in the
Mentally Handicapped* London: Churchill Livingstone; Baltimore, Md.:
Williams & Wilkins.

HOGG, J., EVANS, P. L. C. and PREDDY, D. (1971) 'Inhibitory aspects of learning
and behaviour in the SSN and ESN child', *Bulletin British Psychological
Society*, **24**, 228A.

JEFFREE, D. (1971) 'A language teaching programme for a mongol child',
Forward Trends, **15**, 33–8.

JEFFREE, D. (1971) 'Research into language development', *The Team Approach*
London: National Society for the Mentally Handicapped Child.

JEFFREE, D., WHELDALL, K. and MITTLER, P. (1973) 'The facilitation of two
word utterances in two mongol boys', *American Journal of mental Deficiency*
(in press).

MAIER, I. (1971) 'An operant approach to the modification of hyperkinetic
behaviour in severely subnormal children', unpublished PH D thesis,
University of Manchester.

MAIER, I. (1971) 'An operant approach to the modification of hyperkinetic
behaviour', *Bulletin British Psychological Society*, **24**, 229A.

MARINOSSON, G. (1970) 'A comparative study of normal, educationally subnormal and severely subnormal children on the revised Illinois Test of Psycholinguistic Abilities', unpublished MA thesis, University of Manchester.

MITTLER, P. (ed.) (1970) *Psychological Assessment of Mental and Physical Handicaps* London: Methuen.

MITTLER, P. (1971a) 'Language deficits in mentally handicapped children', in
Bryant, P., Mittler, P. and O'Connor, N. (eds) *The Handicapped Child—
Recent Research Findings* London: College of Special Education, *Guide
Lines for Teachers No. 11*, 25–41.

MITTLER, P. (1971b) 'The influence of social class on psycholinguistic abilities:
some implications for special education', *Forward Trends*, **15**, 6–11.

MITTLER, P. (1972a) 'New directions in the study of learning deficits', in
Clarke, A. D. B. and Lewis, M. M. (eds) *Language, Speech and Thought
in the Mentally Retarded* London: Butterworth.

MITTLER, P. (1972b) 'Language development and mental handicaps', in Rutter,
M. and Martin, J. A. (eds) *The Child with Delayed Speech* London: Spastics
Society and Heinemann.

MITTLER, P. (1972c) 'Assessment of language abilities', in Rutter, M. and Martin, J. A. (eds) *The Child with Delayed Speech* London: Spastics Society and Heinemann.

MITTLER, P. (1972d) 'Education of the mentally handicapped', *British Journal of hospital Medicine*, **8**, 155–8.

MITTLER, P. (ed.) (1973) *Assessment for Learning in the Mentally Handicapped* London: Churchill Livingstone; Baltimore, Md.: Williams & Wilkins.

MITTLER, P. (1973) 'Language and communication', in Clarke, A. and Clarke, A. D. B. (eds) *Mental Deficiency: The Changing Outlook* (3rd edition) London: Methuen (in press).

MITTLER, P. and WARD, J. (1970) 'The use of the Illinois Test of Psycholinguistic Abilities on English four year old children: a normative and factorial study', *British Journal of educational Psychology*, **40**, 43–54.

MITTLER, P. and WHELDALL, K. (1971) 'Language comprehension in the severely subnormal', *Bulletin British Psychological Society*, **24**, 227A.

MITTLER, P. and RUTTER, M. (1972) 'Environmental influences on language development', in Rutter, M. and Martin, J. A. (eds) *The Child with Delayed Speech* London: Spastics Society and Heinemann.

SERPELL, R. (1971) 'Applications of attention theory to the training and education of retarded children and adults', *Progress Report to Social Science Research Council, October 1971* (unpublished).

SERPELL, R. (1973) 'Applications of attention theory to teaching in schools for the severely subnormal', in Clarke, A. D. B. (ed.) *Mental Retardation and Behavioural Research* London: Churchill Livingstone; Baltimore, Md.: Williams & Wilkins.

WHELAN, E. (1971) 'Assessment and development of work skills in retarded adults', Paper presented to *International Seminar of Vocational Rehabilitation of the Mentally Retarded* American Association for Mental Deficiency and US Department of Health Education and Welfare (ed. J. Loth, Jnr).

WHELAN, E., MOORES, B., GRANT, G. and CASMAS, S. (1971) 'Mental health and management science', *Advance II*, 39–46.

WHELAN, E., GRANT, G. and MOORES, B. (1972) 'Applications of methods-time measurement in training centres for the mentally handicapped', *AIIE Transactions: Industrial Research and Development* (in press).

WHELAN, E. (1973) 'Developing work skills: a systematic approach', in Mittler P. (ed.) *Assessment for Learning in the Mentally Handicapped* London: Churchill Livingstone; Baltimore, Md.: Williams & Wilkins (in press).

Educational and vocational guidance*

AJA, K. A. (1964) 'A study of the Utilization of Manpower in the Youth Employment Service', PHD thesis, University of London.

* An extended bibliography may be obtained from the authors.

ALLEN, E. A. (1961) 'The attitudes to School and Teachers in a Secondary Modern School', *British Journal of Educational Psychology*, **31**, 106–9.

ALLEN, K. R. (1961) 'Unguided Careers: Towards an Integrated Guidance System', *Technical Education*, **3**, *vi*, 12–14.

ALLEN, K. R. (1961) 'Unguided Careers: 1. The Consumers Assess Vocational Guidance', *Technical Education*, **3**, *v*, 14–15.

Assistant Masters Association and Association of Assistant Mistresses (1970) *Careers Work in Schools* London: Cambridge University Press.

AVENT, C. (1964) 'A Careers Advisory Service for Technical Institutions', *A.T.I. Paper*.

AVENT, C. (1967) 'Careers Courses in Retrospect', *Education*, April, 816–17.

BARNARD, G. A., MCCREATH, M. D. and FREEMAN, J. (1967) *Preliminary report of Project on Factors Influencing Choice on Higher Education* University of Essex.

BARR, F. (1961) 'Student Guidance in Technical Education' *Educational Research*, **3**, 126–38.

BARR, F. (1970) 'A Study in Change in Educational Interests of a group of Secondary School Children', MPHIL thesis, University of London.

BIDGOOD, D. K. and GEAR, B. L. (1971) 'The Careers Office and Its Service', *Bacie Journal*, March, 19–22.

BEVAN, B. (1967) 'How the Youth Employment Service Helps the Under 18s', *Where*, **23**.

BOLGER, A. W. (1970) 'Counselling—an Overview', *Forum*, **13**.

BOREHAM, J. L. (1967) 'The Psycho-Dynamic Diagnosis and Treatment of Vocational Problems', *British Journal of Social and Clinical Psychology*, **6**, *ii*, 150–8.

BOX, S. and COTGROVE, S. (1966) 'Scientific Identity, Occupational Selection and Role Strain', *British Journal of Sociology*, **17**, 20–8.

BROWN, W. G. (1971) 'Making a Choice', *Further Education*, **2**, 105–8.

BUTLER, J. R. (1968) *Occupational Choice: a Review of the Literature* London: D.E.S. Science Policy Studies.

CARTER, M. P. (1962) *Home and School and Work* Oxford: Pergamon Press.

CARTER, M. P. (1963) 'Moral and Social Considerations in the Work of the Youth Employment Officer', *Youth Employment*, **16**, 7–13.

CARTER, M. (1966) *Into Work* Harmondsworth, Middlesex: Penguin Press.

CASPAN, I. (1968) 'Counselling—Definitions and Dilemmas', *The New Era*, **49**, *ix*.

CATTELL, R. B. (1969) 'The profile Similarity Coefficient in Vocational Guidance and Diagnostic Classification', *British Journal of Educational Research*, **39** 131–42.

CAVANAGH, P. et al. (1962) 'Y.E.S. Interviews—A Criterion Problem', *Occupational Psychology*, **36**, *iii*, 132–9.

CHESTER, R. (1968) 'Youth, Education and Work: A Revised Perspective', *Social and Economic Administration*, **2**.

CHILD, D. and MUSGROVE, F. (1969) 'Career Orientations of some University Freshman', *Educational Review*, **21**, *iii*, 209–17.

CHOWN, S. (1958) 'Formation of Occupational Choice among Grammar School Pupils', *Occupational Psychology*, **32**, *iii*, 171–82.

CLARKE, J. H. (1968) 'The Image of the Teacher', *British Journal of Educational Psychology*, **38**, *iii*, 280–5.

COHEN, L. (1969) 'Student Identification with a Profession', *Educational Research*, **12**, *i*, 41–5.

COTGROVE, S. (1962) 'Education and Occupation', *British Journal of Sociology*, **13**, 33–42.

COULSON, M. A., KEIL, E. T., RIDDELL, D. S., and STRUTHERS, J. F. (1967) 'Towards a Sociological Theory of Occupational Choice: A Critique', *The Sociological Review*, **15**, *iii*.

COXON, A. P. M. (1967) 'Patterns of Occupational Recruitment: the Anglican Ministry', *Sociology*, **I**, *i*.

CRICHTON, A. and JONES, E. (1968) 'Youth and Leisure in Cardiff', *Social and Economic Administration*, **2**.

CRINNION, J. (1967) 'Ministry of Labour Occupational Guidance Units', *Occupational Psychology*, **41**, *ii* and *iii*, 121–6.

DAVIS, T. N. and SATTERLEY, D. J. (1969) 'Personality Profiles of Student Teachers', *British Journal of Educational Psychology*, **39**, *ii*, 183–7.

DAWS, P. P. (1967) 'What will the School Counsellor do?', *Educational Research*, **9**, *ii*, 83–92.

DAWS, P. P. (1968a) *A Good Start in Life* Careers Research and Advisory Centre.

DAWS, P. P. (1968b) 'The Planned Development of School Guidance Services', *Papers in Psychology*, **2**, *ii*.

DAWS, P. P. (1969) *Planned Development of School Guidance Services* VGRU, Institute of Careers Officers.

DAWS, P. P. (1969–70) 'Careers Guidance in the 1970's', *Youth Employment*, Winter.

DAWS, P. P. (1970) 'Occupational Information and the Self-Defining Process', *Vocational Aspect*, **52**.

DAWS, P. P. (1972) in Hayes, J. and Hopson, B., *Careers Guidance: the role of the school in vocational development* London: Heinemann.

D.E.S. (1965) *Careers Guidance in Schools* London: HMSO.

DOUGLAS, J. B. (1972) *Young School Leavers at Work and College* In press (to be published 1972).

DOUGLAS, J. B., ROSS, J. M. and SIMPSON, H. R. (1968) *All Our Future* London: Peter Davies.

DUROJAIYE, M. O. A. (1969) 'Occupational Choice and Special Education of Educationally Subnormal Children', *British Journal of Educational Psychology*, **39**, *i*, 88–91.

EL-SHAKARWY, M. and LEE, D. M. (1965) 'A Study of some contributions of the Morrisby Differential Test Battery to Vocational Selection', *British Journal of Educational Psychology*, **35**, 223–41.

EPPEL, E. and EPPEL, M. (1953) 'Young Workers at a County College', *British Journal of Educational Psychology*, **23**, 29–44, 87–96.

ERIKSON, E. (1960) *Childhood and Society* London: Norton.

EYRE, J. H. (1966) 'The Prediction of Vocational Suitability from Secondary Modern School Record Cards', *British Journal of Educational Psychology*, **35**, 48–60.

EYSENCK, E. (1967) 'Personality Patterns in Various Groups of Businessmen', *Occupational Psychology*, **41**, *iv*, 249–50.

FARUDIN, D. H. (1971) 'A Thirty Year Vocational Guidance Follow-up Study', PH D thesis, University of London.

FORD, J. and BOX, S. (1967) 'Sociological Theory and Occupational Choice', *The Sociological Review*, **15**, *iii*.

FULLER, J. A. and JUNIPER, D. F. 'Guidance, Counselling and School Social Work', *Educational Research*, **9**, *ii*, 103–4.

GALBRAITH, N. M. C. (1967) 'Guidance Teams in Fife', *The New Era*, **48**, 3–5.

GILL, C. J. (1967) 'The Trained School Counsellor', *The New Era*, **48**, *ix*.

GINZBERG, E., GINZBURG, S. W., AXELRAD, S. and HERMA, J. L. (1951) *Occupational Choice: An Approach to a General Theory* New York: Columbia University Press.

GOSLIN, D. (1967) *Teachers and Testing* New York: Russell Sage Foundation.

HANDYSIDE, J. and STOTT, M. B. (1958) 'The Effectiveness of Vocational Guidance', *Medical World*, October.

HANKINS, P. (1966) 'The Need for Guidance Services in Further Education', *Youth Employment*, Spring.

HARTOP, B. B. (1966) 'Careers Work in Sixth-Form Minority Time', *CRAC Journal*, **2**, *i*.

HATTON, J. (1967) 'Youth Tutors in Kent', *The New Era*, **48**, 217–18.

HAYES, J. (1967) 'The Role of Occupational Information in Careers Guidance', *Educational Research*, **9**, *iii*. 191–6.

HAYES, J. (1969) 'National Manpower Needs and the Vocational Guidance Counsellor', *Vocational Aspect*, **21**, *xlix*.

HAYES, J. (1970) *Occupational Information and Occupational Perceptions*, VGRU, Institute of Careers Officers, 79–82.

HAYES, J. and HOPSON, B. (1972) *Career Guidance: The Role of the School in Vocational Development* London: Heinemann.

HAYSTEAD, J. (1971) 'Social Structure, awareness Contexts and Processes of Choice', *Sociological Review*, February.

HERFORD, M. (1964) 'Young people at work', *British Hospital and Social Services Journal*, August.

HIGGINBOTHAM and MOUNTFORD (1964) 'Aptitude Tests in the Birmingham YES', *CRAC Journal*, **I**.

HILL, G. B. (1965) 'Choice of Career by Grammar School Boys', *Occupational Psychology*, **39**, *iv*, 279-87.

HOPSON, B. (1970) 'An Experiment in using Psychological Tests in Group Guidance', Vocational Guidance Research Unit, Leeds University.

HOPSON, K. (1973) 'Career development in industry: the diary of an experiment', *British Journal of Guidance and Counselling*, **1**, *i*, 51-61.

HOPSON, B. and HAYES, J. (eds) (1968) *The Theory and practice of Vocational Guidance* Oxford: Pergamon Press.

HOPSON, B. and HOUGH, P. M. (1971) 'Careers Teaching Programme', Vocational Guidance Research Unit, Leeds University.

HOPSON, B. and HOUGH, P. M. (1973) *Exercises in Personal and Career Development* Cambridge: CRAC.

HUGHES, P. (1969) 'Student Counselling Services in British Universities', *The New Era*, **50**, *viii*.

JACKSON, R. and JUNIPER, D. (1971) *A Manual of Educational Guidance* New York: Holt, Rinehart and Winston.

JAHODA, G. (1962) 'Job Attitudes and Job Choice Among Secondary Modern School Leavers. Parts I and II', *Occupational Psychology*, **26**, 25-140 and 206-24.

JAHODA, G. and CHALMERS, A. D. (1963a) 'School Leavers' Recall of the Interview with the Youth Employment Officer', *Occupational Psychology*, **37**, *ii*, 112-22.

JAHODA, G. and CHALMERS, A. D. (1963b) 'The YES: A consumer Perspective', *Occupational Psychology*, **37**, *i*, 20-43.

JEPHCOTT, R. (1967) *Time of one's own* Edinburgh: Oliver and Boyd.

JONES, A. (1969) 'Counselling in Practice', *Education*, 2 May, 599-600.

KEIL, E. T., RIDDELL, D. S. and TIPTON, C. (1963) 'The Size of Firms Entered by Young Workers', *British Journal of Industrial Relations*, **1**, 408-11.

KEIL, E. T., RIDDELL, D. S. and GREEN, S. R. (1966) 'Youth and Work: Problems and Perspectives', *The Sociological Review*, **31**, *i*.

LEE, D. J. (1968) 'Class Differentials in Educational Opportunity and Promotion from Ranks', *Sociology*, **2**, *iii*.

LANCASHIRE, R. (1971) Unpublished Report, NIIP.

LAWRENCE, D. (1971) 'The Effects of Counselling on Retarded Readers', *Educational Research*, **13**, *ii*, 119-24.

LIEPMAN, K. (1960) *Apprenticeship: An Enquiry into its Adequacy under Modern Conditions* London: Routledge & Kegan Paul.

LOCK, H. F. (1951) 'Current Research Needs in Vocational Guidance', *Occupational Psychology*, **25**, *ii*, 142-5.

LOCKE, M. (1968) 'Advice for the Adolescent—from whom?', *Education*, November.

LYTTON, H. and CRAFT, M. (eds) (1968) *Counselling in Schools* London: Arnold.

LYTTON, H., WEBSTER, I. and KLINE, P. (1970) 'Teachers' Attitudes to Guidance and Counselling', *Educational Research*, **12**, *iii*, 220–4.

MACDONALD, B., GAMMIE, A. and NISBET, J. (1964) 'The Careers of a Gifted
Group', *Educational Research*, **6**, *iii*, 216.

MACRAE, A. (1934) *The Case for Vocational Guidance* London: Pitman.

MAIZELS, J. (1965) 'The Entry of School Leavers into Employment', *British
Journal of Industrial Relations*, **3**, *i*, 77–89.

MAIZELS, J. (1970) *Adolescent Needs and the Transition from School to Work*
London: Athlone Press.

MEYER, G. R. and PENFOLD, D. M. G. (1961) 'Interest and Choice of Subject',
British Journal of Educational Psychology, **31**, *i*.

MILLER, G. (1970) *Success, Wastage and Failure in Higher Education* London:
Harrap.

MILLER, G. (1972) *Student Counselling* London: Tavistock.

MONTGOMERY, G. W. G. (1967) *Vocational Guidance for the Deaf* Edinburgh:
Livingstone.

MOORE, B. M. (1970) *Guidance in Comprehensive Schools* Slough: National
Foundation for Educational Research.

MOORE, G., FULLER, J. and WATTS, A. G. (1968) 'Counsellors in British Schools:
Their First Year', *CRAC Journal*, **3**, *ii*, 36.

MUSGRAVE, P. W. (1967a) 'Towards a Sociological Theory of Occupational
Choice', *The Sociological Review*, **15**, *i*.

MUSGRAVE, P. W. (1967b) 'Family, School, Friends, Work: A Sociological
Perspective', *Educational Research*, **9**, *iii*, 175–86.

MUSGRAVE, P. W. (1968) 'Continuities in the Sociological Theory of Occupational Choice', *The Sociological Review*, **16**, *i*.

NELSON, D. (1964) 'National Survey on School Children', *Occupational
Psychology*, **38**, *iii* and **38**, *iv*.

NELSON, D., CARRUTHERS, T., and KILCROSS, M. (1968) 'The Measurement
of Occupational Interests—A Symposium', *Occupational Psychology*, **42**,
ii/iii, 101–33.

NISBET, J. D. and GRANT, W. (1965) 'Vocational Intentions and Decisions of
Aberdeen Arts Graduates', *Occupational Psychology*, **39**, *iii*, 215–19.

O'CONNOR, J. (1971) 'Lying Down on the Job', *Education and Training*, **13**, *ii*,
42–3.

PALMER, F. C. (1964) 'Young Workers in their First Jobs. An Investigation of
Attitudes to Work and their Correlates', *Occupational Psychology*, **38**, *ii*,
99–115.

PALMER, V. C. (1965) *Student Guidance* London: Longman.

PAUL, L. (1962) *The Transition from School to Work* Industrial Welfare
Society.

PIMBLETT, S. (1967) 'Pupil Counselling in an ESN Special School', *The New
Era*, **48**.

RAYNOR, J. M. and ATCHERLEY, R. A. (1967) 'Counselling in Schools—Some Considerations', *Educational Research*, **9**, ii, 93–102.

RICE, R. (1964) 'The Social and Educational Background and Anticipated Career Prospects of a group of Students in a College of Advanced Technology', *British Journal of Educational Psychology*, **34**, iv, 256–67.

ROBERTS, K. (1968a) 'The Entry into Employment: An Approach towards a General Theory', *Sociological Review*, **16**, ii.

ROBERTS, K. (1968b) 'The Organisation of Education and the Ambitions of School Leavers: A Comparative Review', *Comparative Education*, **4**, ii.

ROBERTS, K. (1970) 'The YES, the School and the Preparation of School Leavers for Employment', *Vocational Aspect*, **52**.

RODGER, A. (1951) 'Current Research Needs in Vocational Guidance', *Occupational Psychology*, **25**, i, 44–9.

RODGER, A. (1971) 'C. S. Myers in Retrospect', *Bulletin of the British Psycholog. Society*, **24**, 9–11.

RODGER, A. and CAVANAGH, P. (1964) 'Tests in Vocational Guidance', *CRAC Journal*, **2**, 21–6.

ROWE, A. (1968) 'Counselling in a Comprehensive School', *New Education*, **4**, ii, 9–11.

ROWLANDS, R. G. (1961) 'Some Differences Between Prospective Scientists, Non-Scientists, and Early Leavers in Grammar School Boys', *British Journal of Educational Psychology*, **31**, 21–32.

RYLE, A. (1969) *Student Casualties* London: Allen Lane The Penguin Press.

SCHOOLS COUNCIL (1967) 'Counselling in Schools', *Working Paper No. 15*, London: HMSO.

SHERLOCK, B. and COHEN, A. (1966) 'The Strategy of Occupational Choice: Recruitment to Dentistry', *Social Forces*, **44**, iii, 303–13.

SHIMMIN, S. (1966) 'Concepts of Work', *Occupational Psychology*, **40**, iv, 195–201.

SHOUKSMITH, G. and TAYLOR, J. W. (1964) 'The Effects of Counselling on the Achievement of High-Ability Pupils', *British Journal of Educational Psychology*, **34**, i, 51–7.

SINGH, A. (1968) 'Interests, Values and Personality Traits of Students Specialising in Different Fields of Study in University', *Educational Review*, **21**, i, 41–55.

SMITH, P. (1951) 'Twenty-five years of Research in Vocational Guidance', *Occupational Psychology*, **39**, 93–7.

SMITHERS, A. (1968) 'Some Characteristics of Business Students in a Technological University', *Occupational Psychology*, **14**, iii.

SMITHERS, A. (1971) 'Students' Experience of Thick Sandwich Courses', *Educational Research*, **13**, iii, 171–8.

STARKEY, H. F. (1970) 'Vocational Information Possessed by Secondary Modern School Leavers', *Careers Quarterly*, **22**, ii.

STERN, H. (1961) 'A Follow-up of Adolescents' Views of their Personal and Vocational Future, *British Journal of Educational Psychology*, **31**, ii.

STOCKS, J. C. (1971) 'A Test of Occupational Information for School Leavers', *The Careers Teacher*, Autumn.

STOTT, M. B. (1950) 'What is Occupational Success?', *Occupational Psychology*, **24**, *ii*, 105–12.

STOTT, M. B. (1952) 'Difficulties in the Validation of Vocational Guidance Procedures', *Occupational Psychology*, **26**, *iii*, 158–68.

SWINHOE, K. (1967) 'Factors affecting Career Choice among Full-Time Students in a College of Commerce', *Vocational Aspect*, **19**, *xliii*, 139–54.

TATSUOKA, M. and CATTELL, R. (1970) 'Linear Equations for Estimating a Person's Occupational Adjustment based on information on Occupational Profiles', *British Journal of Educational Psychology*, **40**, 324–34.

TAYLOR, H. J. F. (1968) 'Issues in School Counselling', *The New Era*, **49**, *vi*.

TONKINSON, E. (1962) *Commercial Apprenticeships* London: University of London Press.

TRAVERS, K. J. (1971) *Discovering Careers: A Programmed Textbook* Nottingham Careers Office.

VAUGHAN, T. (1970) *Educational and Vocational Guidance Today* London: Routledge & Kegan Paul.

VENABLES, E. (1967) *The Young Worker at College* London: Faber & Faber.

VENESS, T. (1962) *School Leavers: Their Aspirations and Expectations* London: Methuen.

VERNON, P. E. (1965) 'The Criterion Problem in Selection and Guidance', *Occupational Psychology*, **39**, *ii*, 93–7.

WALTER, A. (1958) *Pupil School Records* Slough: NFER Publication, No. 8.

WALLIS, D. P. (1969) 'An approach to Careers Work with Academic Fifth and Sixth-formers', *Youth Employment*, Spring.

WATTS, T. (1968) 'Using Information on Graduate Employment in Schools', *CRAC Journal*, **3**, *i*.

WIEGERSMA, S. and BARR, F. (1960) 'Educational Guidance: Interest Testing in Educational and Vocational Guidance', *Educational Research*, **2**, 39–64.

WILLIAMS, G. F. (1970) 'Group Counselling', *The New Era*, **51**.

WILSON, J. (1964) 'Vocational Preparation for Dull and Backward Pupils', *Youth Employment*, **16**.

WYMER, I. and BOWELL, R. (1971) 'Constructive Guidance', *Education and Training*, **13**, 78–9.

Further education

ASKHAM, J. (1968) *A survey on the application and recruitment of students to degree level courses at technical colleges* Cambridge: Advisory Centre for Education.

BARNARD, G. A. and MCCREATH, M. D. (1970) 'Subject commitments and the demand for higher education (with discussion)', *Journal of the Royal Statistical Society*, Series A, (General) **133**, part *iii*, 358–408.

BARRY, MARY (1969) 'Cross-validation of selection criteria against success in aircraft apprenticeships', *Personnel Research Report No. 26* London: Manpower Branch Research Unit, BOAC.

BARRY, SUSIE (1971) '2,100 Sixth Formers', *Brunel Further Education Monograph 2*, London: Hutchinson Educational.

BATES, W. T. G. (1969) 'An investigation of interests, aspirations and personality of aircraft apprentices', *Personnel Research Report No. 5* London: Manpower Branch Research Unit, BOAC.

CANNON, J. A. (1969) 'A study of attitudes and aspirations of a sample of BOAC aircraft apprentices', *Personnel Research Report No. 14* London: Manpower Branch Research Unit, BOAC.

CHAPPEL, S. (1967) 'Pre-selection of apprentice motor mechanics: a preliminary validation study', *Personnel Practice Bulletin*, **23**, *iii*, 204–13 Melbourne.

CHARLTON, D., GENT, W. and SCAMMELS, B. (1972) *The Administration of Technical Colleges* Manchester University Press.

COLE, H. and VAN DER EYKEN, W. (1971) 'Survey of Current Research in Further Education', *Brunel Further Education Monograph 1* London: Hutchinson Educational.

COTGROVE, S. (1958) *Technical Education and Social Change* London: Allen & Unwin.

COWELL, M. D. and ENTWISTLE, N. J. (1972) 'The relationships between personality, study attitudes and academic performance in a technical college', *Br. J. educ. Psychol.*, **41**, 84–90.

DOUGLAS, J. W. B., ROSS, J. M. and SIMPSON, H. R. (1968) *All our Future* London: Peter Davies.

ENGINEERING INDUSTRY TRAINING BOARD (1971) *Studies in first year craft training.*

ENGINEERING INDUSTRY TRAINING BOARD (1971) *The relevance of school learning experience to performance in industry.*

ENGINEERING INDUSTRY TRAINING BOARD (1971) 'The analysis and training of certain engineering craft occupations', *Research Report No. 2.*

ENGINEERING INDUSTRY TRAINING BOARD (1971) *Surveys of first year craft training.*

GIBSON, S. (1971) 'A study of the validity of selection criteria for predicting first year aircraft apprentice success', *Personnel Research Report No. 35* London: Manpower Branch Research Unit, BOAC.

GRIMES, A. (1969) *A follow-up study of selection tests for aircraft engineering apprentices*, unpublished project report London: Birkbeck College.

HEYWOOD, J. (1968) 'Technical Education', in Butcher, H. J. (ed.) *Educational Research in Britain 1* London: University of London Press, 297–313.

HEYWOOD, J. (1971) 'Bibliography of British Technological Education and

398   BIBLIOGRAPHY

Training', *Brunel Further Education Monograph 3* London: Hutchinson Educational.

LAYARD, P. R. G., SARGAN, J. D., AGER, M. E. and JONES, D. J. (1971) *Qualified Manpower and Economic Performance* London: Allen Lane The Penguin Press.

LAWTON, D. (1970) 'Preparations for changes in the curriculum', in Tibble, J. C. (ed.) *The Extra Year* London: Routledge & Kegan Paul, 97–116.

LEE, D. J. (1966) 'Industrial Training and Social Class', *Sociological Review*, **14**, iii (new series), 269–86.

LEE, D. J. (1968) 'Class differentials in educational opportunity and promotion from the ranks', *Sociology*, **2**, iii, 293–312.

LEE, D. J. (1972) 'Very small firms and the training of engineering craftsmen—some recent findings', *Br. J. Industrial Relations*, **10**, ii.

LEE, D. J. and HORDLEY, IRENE (1970) 'The "alternative route"—social change and opportunity in technical education', *Sociology*, **4**, i, 23–50.

LIPSHITZ, S. (1971) 'Wastage among craft apprentice students', *Brunel Further Education Monograph 4* London: Hutchinson Educational.

LIPSHITZ, S. (1972) 'Why do they leave?', *Nature*, **235**, **5337**, 313–14, 11 February.

MAGLAN, L. and LAYARD, R. (1970) *How profitable is engineering education?* Association of Colleges for Further and High Education (formerly the Association of Technical Institutions).

MAIZELS, JOAN (1970) *Adolescent needs and the transition from school to work* London: Athlone Press.

MCCREATH, M. (1971) *Factors influencing choice of higher education* Society for Research into Higher Education.

MCMAHON, D. (1962) 'Selection and follow-up of engineering apprentices', *Occupational Psychology*, **36**, 53–8.

MICHAELS, R. (1971) *Survey of social science researches in colleges in the further education sector* Hatfield Polytechnic.

MILLER, G. W. (1970) *Success, Failure and Wastage in Higher Education* London: Harrop.

MINISTRY OF EDUCATION (1961) 'Better opportunities in technical education', *Cmnd. 1254* London: HMSO.

MONTGOMERY, G. W. G. (1962) 'Predicting success in engineering', *Occupational Psychology*, **36**, 59–68.

MOORE, B. (1969) *Block or Day Release?* Slough: NFER.

MORRISON, A. T. (n.d.) *The first cycle—G1 to O2. An investigation into the operation of the General Course in Engineering and the ONC Course in Engineering* Northern Counties Technical Examinations Council.

PENDLEBURY, A. C. and HARDMAN, K. (1967) 'Rolls Royce: the selection of craft apprentices', *Technical Education and Industrial Training*, **9**, viii, 356–7.

PHILLIPS, C. M. (1969) 'Changes in subject choice at school and university',

London School of Economics Research Monograph No. 1 London: Weidenfeld.

POLLOCK, G. J. (1970) 'Wastage in National Certificate Courses', Address to Education Section, British Psychological Society.

R E M E, SCHOOL OF ELECTRONIC ENGINEERING (1968) 'The Prediction of Success in the Basic Electronic Course of the School of Engineering.'

REES, RUTH (1972) 'Difficulties in Mathematics experienced by further education students', *Bulletin Institute of Mathematics and its Applications*, **8**, *viii*.

REES, RUTH (1973) 'Mathematics in Further Education', *Brunel Further Education Monograph 5* London: Hutchinson Education.

ROBERTS, I. F. and CANTOR, L. M. (1971) *Teacher Training and Further Education* Department of Education, Loughborough University of Technology.

ROSS, J. (1962) 'Predicting practical skill in engineering apprentices', *Occupational Psychology*, **36**, 49–74.

SHIPTON, ROGER (1968) 'Validation of selection procedures for apprentice gas fitters at the West Midland Gas Board', unpublished MSC dissertation, Department of Applied Psychology, University of Aston in Birmingham.

SMITH, SELBY C. (1970) *The costs of further education* Oxford: Pergamon.

TIPTON, BERYL (1972) 'Some organisational characteristics of a technical college', *Research in Education*, **7**, Manchester.

TIPTON, BERYL (1973) 'Conflict and change in a technical college', *Brunel Further Education Monograph 6* London: Hutchinson Educational.

VAIZEY, J. (1971) 'The costs of wastage', *Universities Quarterly*, Spring 1971, 139–45.

VAN DER EYKEN, W. (1971) *Craftsman or technician? The recurring problem of 'placement' in technical colleges* Association of Colleges for Further and Higher Education.

VENABLES, ETHEL (1960) 'Placement problems among engineering apprentices in part time technical college courses—Part 1', *Br. J. educ. Psychol.*, **30**, *iii*, 237–43.

VENABLES, ETHEL (1961) 'Placement problems among engineering apprentices in part time technical college courses—Part 2', *Br. J. educ. Psychol.*, **31**, *i*, 56–68.

VENABLES, ETHEL (1967) *The young worker at college. A study of a local tech.* London: Faber.

VENABLES, ETHEL (1972) 'The human costs of part time day release', *Higher Education*, **1**, *iii*.

VICKERY, R. (1969) 'Cast on 500', *Industrial Society*, January 1969, 4–6.

WEIR, A. D. (1971) *A day off work? The attitudes of craft apprentices to further education* Scottish Council for Research in Education.

WILLIAMS, I. C. and BOREHAM, N. C. (1971) 'The predictive value of CSE grades for further education', *Schools Council Examinations Bulletin 24*.

WOODHALL, M. and WARD, A. V. (1972) *Economic Aspects of Education* Slough: NFER.

Teacher education

AINSLIE, P. (1969) 'Personality Characteristics of Student Art Teachers in Two Types of College', unpublished MED thesis, University of Manchester.

ALLEN, D. and RYANS, K. (1969) *Microteaching* New York: Addison Wesley.

ALTMAN, E. (1970) 'Teaching as a Vocation: a Reappraisal', *Education for Teaching*, 82, 28–33.

ASHLEY, B., COHEN, H., MCINTYRE, D. and SLATTER, R. (1970) 'A Sociological Analysis of Students' Reasons for Becoming Teachers', *Sociological Rev.*, 18, *i*, 53–69.

ASPIN, D. N. (1973) 'Values in Teacher Education', in Lomax, D. E. (ed.) *The Education of Teachers in Britain* London: John Wiley.

ASTIN, A. W. (1964) 'Personal and Environmental Factors Associated with College Dropouts among High Aptitude Students', *Journal of Educational Psychology*, 55, *iv*, 219–27.

BAMBRIDGE, G. DE P. (1970) 'The Pedagogic Urge', *Education for Teaching*, 38.

BARR, A. S. (1929) *Characteristic Differences in the Teaching Performance of Good and Poor Teachers of the Social Studies* Bloomington, Illinois: Public School Publishing Co.

BARR, A. S. (1948) 'The Measurement and Prediction of Teaching Efficiency— A Summary of Investigations', *J. Exp. Educ.*, 16, 203–83.

BARR, A. S. *et al.* (1952) 'Report of the Committee on the Criteria of Teacher Effectiveness', *Revue of Educational Research*, 22, 238–63.

BARR, A. S. *et al.* (1961) 'Wisconsin Studies of Measurements of Teacher Effectiveness: A Summary of Investigations', *J. Exp. Educ.*, 30, 5–156.

BEWSHER, L. G. (1966) 'A Study of Attitudes and Incentives Among a Group of Students Training to be Teachers', MA thesis, University of London.

BIDDLE, B. J. and ELLENA, W. J. (1964) *Contemporary Research on Teacher Effectiveness* New York: Holt, Rinehart & Winston.

BROWN, G. A. (1971) 'The Performance of Non-Graduate Student Teachers in University Courses', *Br. J. educ. Psychol.*, 41, *iii*, 314–16.

BUTCHER, H. J. (1959) 'The Opinions of Teachers and Student Teachers About Education', unpublished PHD thesis, University of Manchester.

BUTCHER, H. J. (1965) 'The Attitudes of Student Teachers to Education', *Brit. J. soc. clin. Psychol.*, 4, 17–24.

BUTCHER, H. J. (1968) 'University Education', in Butcher H. J. (ed.) *Educational Research in Britain 1* London: University of London Press, 332–54.

BUTCHER, H. J. and PONT H. B. (1968) 'Opinions About Careers Among Scottish Secondary School Children of High Ability', *Br. J. educ. Psychol.*, 38, *i*, 272–9.

BUTLER, J. R. (1968) 'Occupational Choice', *Science Policy Studies, No. 2* London: Department of Education and Science.

BUXTON, C. E. (1966) 'Evaluations of Forced-Choice and Likert-Type Tests

of Motivation to Academic Achievement', *Br. J. educ. Psychol.*, **36**, *ii*,
192–201.

CAMPLIN, K. (1970) 'Role Transition and The Development of a Professional
Self-image in Student Teachers', MED thesis, University of Newcastle.

CANE, B. (1969) *In-Service Training* Slough: NFER.

CASE, D. (1968) 'Married Women and Young Women Students at a Day
College of Education, and in Their First Year as Teachers', *Br. J. educ.
Psychol.*, **38**, *i*, 102–3.

CASPARI, I. and EGGLESTON, J. (1965) 'A New Approach to Supervision of
Teaching Practice', *Education for Teaching*, **68**, 42–52.

CLARK, J. H. (1968) 'The Image of the Teacher', *Br. J. educ. Psychol.*, **38**, *iii*,
280–5.

CLARK, B. R. and TROW, M. (1966) *College Peer Groups* Chicago: Aldine
Publishing Co.

COHEN, L. (1967) 'The Teacher's Role as Liaison Between School and Neighbourhood', in Croft, M., Raynor, J. and Cohen, L. (eds) *Linking Home and
School* London: Longman.

COHEN, L. (1973) 'Student Characteristics and Attitudes in Colleges of Education', in Lomax, D. E. (ed.) *The Education of Teachers in Britain* London:
John Wiley.

COHEN, L. and BOOTHROYD, K. (1972) 'Need for Achievement in "Committed" and "Reluctant" Teachers', *University of Bradford. School of Research in Education Report* (mimeo).

COHEN, L. and REID, I. (1972) 'Need for Achievement in BED and Certificate
Students', *University of Bradford, School of Research in Education Report*
(mimeo).

COLLIER, K. G. (1973a) 'A Principal's View of College Administration', in
Lomax, D. E. (ed.) *The Education of Teachers in Britain* London: John
Wiley.

COLLIER, K. G. (1973b) 'Teaching Methods in Colleges of Education' in Lomax,
D. E. (ed.) *The Education of Teachers in Britain* London: John Wiley.

COPE, E. (1970) 'Teacher Training and School Practice', *Educational Research*,
12, *ii*, 77–89.

COPE, E. (1971a) 'School Experience in Teacher Education', *Research Report*,
School of Education, University of Bristol.

COPE, E. (1971b) 'A Study of School Supervised Practice', *Research Report*,
School of Education, University of Bristol.

COPE, E. (1973) 'School Experience and Student Learning', in Lomax, D. E.
(ed.) *The Education of Teachers in Britain* London: John Wiley.

CORRUBLE, D. (1971) 'The Vocational Motivations of Primary School Teacher-
Trainees, *International Review of Applied Psychology*, **20**, *ii*.

CORTIS, G. A. (1968) 'Predicting Student Performance in Colleges of Education',
Br. J. educ. Psychol., **38**, 115–22.

DAVIES, J. G. W. (1950) 'What is Occupational Success?', *Occ. Psych.*, **24**, 7–17.

Department of Education and Science (Annual) *Statistics of Education* London: HMSO.

DERRICK, T. (1971) 'Teacher Training and School Practice', *Educ. Res.*, **13**, ii, 101–8.

DERRICOTT, R. (1968) 'The Attitudes of Education Students to Aspects of Their Course of Training', MED thesis, University of Nottingham.

DICKSON, G. E. *et al.* (1965) *The Characteristics of Teacher Education Students in the British Isles and the United States* Toledo, Ohio: Research Foundation of the University of Toledo.

DICKSON, G. E. and WIERSMA, W. (1966) 'Student Teachers—American and British', *New Society*, **201**, 187–91.

DRAKE, K. B. (1973) 'Economics of Teacher Education', in Lomax, D. E. (ed.) *The Education of Teachers in Britain* London: John Wiley.

DUTHIE, J. H. (1970) *Primary School Survey: A Study of the Teacher's Day* Edinburgh: HMSO.

ENTWISTLE, N. J. (1968) 'Academic Motivation and School Attainment', *Br. J. educ. Psychol.*, **38**, i, 181–8.

ENTWISTLE, N. J. and ENTWISTLE, D. (1970) 'The Relationship Between Personality, Study Methods and Academic Performance', *Br. J. educ. Psychol.*, **40**, ii, 132–41.

ENTWISTLE, N. J., NISBET, J., ENTWISTLE, D. and COWELL, M. D. (1971) 'The Academic Performance of Students (1). Prediction from Scales of Motivation and Study Methods, *Br. J. educ. Psychol.*, **41**, iii, 258–67.

ETZIONI, A. (1961) *A Comparative Analysis of Complex Organisations* New York: The Free Press.

ETZIONI, A. (ed.) (1969) *The Semi-Professions and Their Organisation* New York: The Free Press.

EVANS, K. M. (1952) 'A Study of Teaching Ability at the Training College Stage in Relation to the Personality and Attitudes of the Student', unpublished PHD thesis, University of London.

EVANS, K. M. (1957) 'Is the Concept of Interest of Significance to Success in a Teacher Training Course?', *Educ. Rev.*, **9**, 205–11.

EVANS, K. M. (1966) 'The Minnesota Teacher Attitude Inventory', *Educ. Res.*, **8**, iii, 134–41.

EYSENCK, H. J. (1947) 'Student Selection by means of Psychological Tests—a critical survey', *Br. J. educ. Psychol.*, **17**, i, 20–39.

FELDMAN, K. A. (1970) 'Some methods for assessing College impacts', *Sociology of Education*, **44**, 133–50.

FLANAGAN, J. C. (1954) 'The Critical Incident Technique', *Psychol. Bull.*, **51**, 327–68.

FLOUD, J. and SCOTT, W. (1961) 'Recruitment to Teaching in England and

Wales', in Halsey, A. M., Flour, J. and Anderson, C. A. (eds) *Education, Economy and Society* New York: Free Press, 527–44.

GAGE, N. L. (1963) *Handbook of Research on Teaching* Chicago: Rand McNally.

GALLOP, R. (1960) 'A Study of the B ED Student', *Br. J. educ. Psychol.*, **40**, 2.

GARNER, J. (1973) 'The Nature of Teaching and the Effectiveness of Teachers', in Lomax, D. E. (ed.) *The Education of Teachers in Britain* London: John Wiley.

GOULD, R. (1973) 'The Teaching Profession', in Lomax, D. E. (ed.) *The Education of Teachers in Britain* London: John Wiley.

GRACE, G. R. (1967) 'The Changing Role of the Teacher: implications for Recruitment', *Education for Teaching*, **72**, 51–8.

GRIFFITHS, A. and MOORE, A. H. (1967) 'Schools and Teaching Practice', *Education for Teaching*, **74**, 33–9.

GURNEY, P. W. (1970) 'Student Teachers' Self Acceptance, Personality Traits and Attitudes in relation to their Classroom Behaviour', MED thesis, University of Leicester.

HANNAM, C., SMYTH, P. and STEPHENSON, N. (1971) *Young Teachers and Reluctant Learners* Harmondsworth, Middlesex: Penguin Papers in Education.

HERBERT, N. and TURNBULL, G. H. (1963) 'Personality Factors and Effective Progress in Teaching, *Educ. Rev.*, **16**, *i*, 24–31.

HORE, T. (1971) 'Assessment of Teaching Practice: An "attractive" hypothesis', *Br. J. educ. Psychol.*, **41**, *iii*, 327.

JENKINS, R. (1971) 'The Role of the Teacher: A Three Year Study of the Role Conceptions of Students in a Women's Specialist College and Four Mixed Colleges of Education', unpublished MA thesis, University of Wales.

KELSALL, R. K. and KELSALL, H. M. (1969) *The School Teacher in England and the United States* London: Pergamon Press.

KITCHEN, R. D. (1965) 'An Investigation into the attitudes of First Year Students, in a Training College using the Semantic Differential Technique, MED thesis, University of Birmingham.

LAND, F. W. (1960) *Recruits to Teaching: A Study of the Attainments, Qualifications and Attitudes of Students Entering Training Colleges* Liverpool University Press.

LEGGATT, T. (1970) in *Professions and Professionalization* Jackson, E. (ed.) Cambridge University Press, 155–77.

LITTLE, A. and WESTERGAARD, J. (1964) 'Trend of Class Differentials in Educational Opportunity in England and Wales', *Br. J. Soc.*, **15**, 301–16.

LOMAX, D. E. (1969) 'The Characteristics of Successful Student Teachers', PHD thesis, University of Manchester.

LOMAX, D. E. (1971) 'Focus on the Student Teachers', in Burgess T. (ed.) *Dear Lord James* Harmondsworth, Middlesex: Penguin Books.

MANION, L. (1970) 'Attitude Change in College of Education Students during their First Year', unpublished MED thesis, University of Bradford.

MARRIS, P. (1964) *The Experience of Higher Education* London: Routledge & Kegan Paul.

MARSLAND, D. (1969) 'An Exploration of Professional Socialization: the College of Education and the Teacher's Role, London: SRHE, 5th Annual Conference, 47–78.

MAYFIELD, A. (1972) 'An Analysis of Sub-cultures in a College of Education', unpublished PH D thesis, University of Loughborough.

MEHRABIAN, A. (1968) 'Male and Female Scales of the Tendency to Achieve', *Educational and Psychological Measurements*, **28**, 493–502.

MEHRABIAN, A. (1969) 'Measures of Achieving Tendency', *Educational and Psychological Measurement*, **29**, 445–51.

MITZEL, H. E. (1960) 'Teacher Effectiveness', in Harris, C. W. (ed.) *Encyclopaedia of Educational Research* (3rd edition) New York: Macmillan, 1481–6.

MORGAN, C. (1969) 'Predicting Academic and Practical Teaching Success in a College of Education', MED thesis, University of Manchester.

MORRISON, A. and MCINTYRE, D. (1967) 'Changes in the Opinion about Education During the First Year of Teaching, *Br. J. Soc. Clin. Psychol.*, **6**, *iii*, 161–3.

MCINTYRE, D. and MORRISON, A. (1967) 'The Educational Opinion of Teachers in Training, *Br. J. soc. clin. Psychol.*, **6**, *ii*, 32–7.

MCLEISH, J. (1969) *Students' Attitudes and College Environments* Cambridge: Institute of Education.

MCLEISH, J. (1973) 'College Environment and Student Characteristics', in Lomax, D. E. (ed.) *The Education of Teachers in Britain* London: John Wiley.

MORRIS, R. N. (1969) *The Sixth Form and College Entrance* London: Routledge & Kegan Paul.

MUSGROVE, F. and TAYLOR, P. H. (1965) 'Teachers' and Parents' Conceptions of the Teacher's Role', *Br. J. educ. Psychol.*, **35**, *iii*, 171–8.

OLIVER, R. A. C. (1953) 'Attitudes to Education', *Br. J. Educ. Stud.*, **2**, 31–41.

OLIVER, R. A. C. and BUTCHER, H. J. (1962) 'Teachers' Attitudes to Education: The Structure of Educational Attitudes', *Br. J. soc. clin. Psychol.*, **1**, *i*, 56–69.

O'NEIL, W. N. (1965) 'The Criterion Problem in Selection and Guidance', *Occup. Psychol.*, **39**, 99–103.

OTLEY, C. B. (1966) 'Student Attitudes in a College of Education', in *Student Residence: Research Aspects* London: Society for Research into Higher Education.

OXTOBY, R. (1967) 'Reform and Resistance in Higher Education: A Critique', *Educ. Res.*, **10**, *i*, 38–50.

PERVIN, L. A. (1967) 'A Twenty-College Study of Student College Interaction using Tape (Transactional Analysis of Personality and Environment); Rationale, Reliability and Validity', *J. educ. Psychol.*, **58**, *v*, 290–302.

POPPLETON, P. K. (1968) 'The Assessment of Teaching Practice: What Criteria Do We Use?', *Education for Teaching*, **75**, 59–64.

PLOWDEN REPORT (1967) Central Advisory Council for Education, *Children and Their Primary Schools* London: HMSO.

RABY, L. (1970) 'The Motivations of Students in a College of Education for the Choice of Teaching as a Career', MA thesis, University of Keele.

REEVES, J. W. (1950) 'What is Occupational Success?', *Occup. Psychol.*, **24**, 153–9.

RICHARDSON, J. E. (1967) *Group Study for Teachers* London: Routledge & Kegan Paul.

RICHARDS, J. M., HOLLAND, J. L. and LUTZ, S. W. (1967) 'Prediction of Student Accomplishment in College', *J. educ. Psychol.*, **58**, *vi*, 343–55.

ROBBINS, C. D. (1963) *Teacher Education and Professional Standards in England and Wales* Columbus, Ohio: Ohio State University.

ROBBINS REPORT (1963) Committee on Higher Education. *Higher Education* London: HMSO.

RODGER, A. (1965) 'The Criterion Problem in Selection and Guidance', *Occup. Psychol.*, **39**, 77–82.

ROLLS, I. F. and GOBLE, P. M. (1971) 'Future Teacher or Uncommitted Student?', *Soc. Rev.*, **19**, *ii*, 229–32.

ROSS, A. (1973) 'The Development of Teacher Education in Colleges of Education', in Lomax, D. E. (ed.) *The Education of Teachers in Britain* London: John Wiley.

RUDD, W. G. A. (1973) 'Curriculum Development as In-service Education', in Lomax, D. E. (ed.) *The Education of Teachers in Britain* London: John Wiley.

RUDD, W. G. A. and WISEMAN, S. (1962) 'Sources of Dissatisfaction Among a Group of Teachers', *Br. J. educ. Psychol.*, **32**, *ii*, 275–91.

RYANS, D. G. (1960) *Characteristics of Teachers: Their Descriptions, Comparison and Appraisal*, Washington D.C., American Council on Education.

SANDFORD, C. W., COUPER, H. E. and GRIFFIN (1965) 'Class Influences in Higher Education', *Br. J. educ. Psychol.*, **35**, *i*, 183–94.

SANDVEN, J. (1969) 'Do we select the Right People for Reacher Training?', *Paedacocica Europaea*, **10**, 113–36.

SCOTLAND, J. (1973) 'Teacher Education in Scotland', in Lomax, D. E. (ed.) *The Education of Teachers in Britain* London: John Wiley.

SHIPMAN, M. D. (1965) 'Personal and Social Influences on the Work of a Teacher's Training College', unpublished PHD thesis, University of London.

SHIPMAN, M. D. (1967) 'Theory and Practice in the Education of Teachers', *Educ. Res.*, **9**, 208–12.

SIMONS, M. (1965) 'Intercollegiate Differences Between Students Entering Three Year Courses of Training for Teaching', MED thesis, University of Durham.

SIMONS, M. (1968) 'Qualifications of Students on Entry to Colleges of Education', *Education for Teaching*, 75, 44–9.

SMELSER, W. I. and STEWART, L. H. (1968) 'Where are the Siblings? A Re-evaluation of the Relationships Between Birth-order and College Attendance, *Sociometry*, 31, iii, 294–303.

SMITH, B. O. (1969) *Teachers for the Real World* Washington: American Association of Colleges for Teacher Education.

SMITH, B. O. (1971) *Research in Teacher Education* Englewood Cliffs, New Jersey: Prentice-Hall.

SOLOMONS, E. (1967) 'Personality Factors and Attitudes of Mature Training College Students', *Br. J. educ. Psychol.*, 37, i, 140–2.

SORENSON, G. (1967) 'What is Learned in Practice Teaching?', *Journal of Teacher Education*, 18, 173–8.

START, K. B. (1966) 'The Relation of Teaching Ability to Measures of Personality', *Br. J. educ. Psychol.*, 36, i, 158–65.

START, K. B. (1967) 'A Follow-up of the 1961 Group of Teachers: Selection, Training and Professional Progress of Teachers', *Report No. 1*, Manchester University, School of Education.

START, K. B. (1968) 'Rater-Ratee Personality in the Assessment of Teaching Ability', *Br. J. educ. Psychol.*, 38, iii, 14–20.

STOTT, M. B. (1939) 'Occupational Success', *Occupational Psychology*, 13, 126–40.

STOTT, M. B. (1950) 'What is Occupational Success?', *Occupational Psychology*, 24, 105–12.

TAYLOR, J. and DALE, J. R. (1973) 'The First Year of Teaching', in Lomax, D. E. *The Education of Teachers in Britain* London: John Wiley.

TAYLOR, W. (1969a) *Society and the Education of Teachers* London: Faber & Faber, 31–59.

TAYLOR, W. (1969b) 'Recent Research on the Education of Teachers: An Overview', in Taylor, W. (ed.) *Towards A Policy for the Education of Teachers* London: Butterworths, 223–55.

THOMPSON, A. (1965) 'The Criterion Problem in Selection and Guidance', *Occupational Psychology*, 39, 83–9.

THOMPSON, J. W. (1957) 'A Factorial Study of the Values and Attitudes of Graduate Teachers in Training', MED thesis, unpublished, University of Manchester.

TIBBLE, J. W. (1966) 'Practical Work Training in the Education of Teachers', *Education for Teaching*, 70, 50.

TUCK, J. P. (1973a) 'From Day Training College to University Department of Education', in Lomax, D. E. (ed.) *The Education of Teachers in Britain* London: John Wiley.

TUCK, J. P. (1973b) 'The University Departments of Education: Their Work and Their Future', in Lomax, D. E. (ed.) *The Education of Teachers in Britain* London: John Wiley.

TURNER, J. (1973) 'The Area Training Organisation' in Lomax, D. E. (ed.) *The Education of Teachers in Britain* London: John Wiley.

VAIZEY, J. (1969) 'Demography and Economics of Teacher Education', in Taylor, W. (ed.) *Towards a Policy for the Education of Teachers* London: Butterworths.

VERNON, P. E. (1953) 'The Psychological Traits of Teachers', in *The Year Book of Education* London: Evans, 51–75.

VERNON, P. E. (1965) 'The Criterion Problem in Selection and Guidance', *Occup. Psychol.*, **39**, 93–9.

WESTWOOD, L. J. (1967a) 'The Role of the Teacher, I', *Educ. Res.*, **9**, ii, 122–34.

WESTWOOD, L. J. (1967b) 'The Role of the Teacher II', *Educ. Res.*, **10**, i, 21–37.

WILSON, R. (1969) 'Unity and Diversity in the Education of Teachers', in Taylor, W. (ed.) *Towards A Policy for the Education of Teachers* London: Butterworths, 3–14.

WISEMAN, S. and STARK, K. B. (1965) 'A follow-up of Teachers Five Years after Completing Their Training', *Br. J. educ. Psychol.*, **35**, iii, 342–61.

WOOD, SIR HENRY (1970) 'The In-service Training of Teachers in Scotland', in Barr, F. *Advancement of Science*, 129, 265.

WRAGG, E. C. (1971) 'Interaction Analysis in Great Britain', *Classroom Interaction Newsletter*, **6**, ii.

The work of the Society for Research into Higher Education

ABERCROMBIE, M. L. J. (1970) *Aims and Techniques of Group Teaching* London: Society for Research into Higher Education.

ABERCROMBIE, M. L. J., HUNT, S. and STRINGER, P. (1969) *Selection and Academic Performance of Students in a University School of Architecture* London: Society for Research into Higher Education.

AGER, M. (1967) 'University examinations and the employment market', *Universities Quarterly*, **21**, 286–91.

AGER, M. and WELTMAN, J. (1967) 'The present structure of university examinations', *Universities Quarterly*, **21**, 272–85.

BEARD, R. M. (1967) (third edition 1971 with D. A. Bligh) *Research into Teaching Methods in Higher Education* London: Society for Research into Higher Education.

BEARD, R. M., HEALEY, F. G. and HOLLOWAY, P. J. (1968) *Objectives in Higher Education* London: Society for Research into High Education.

BROTHERS, J. (1970) 'Residence in higher education: some findings from the student residence project', in *Research into Higher Education 1969* London: Society for Research into Higher Education.

CARTER, C. F. (1968) 'Structure of university costs', in *Research into Higher Education 1967* London: Society for Research into Higher Education.

CLOSSICK, M. (1967) *Student Residence: A new approach at the University of Essex* London: Society for Research into Higher Education.

COX, R. (1967a) 'Examinations and higher education', *Universities Quarterly*, **21**, 292–340.

COX, R. (1967b) 'Resistance to change in examining', *Universities Quarterly*, **21**, 352–8.

DREVER, J. (1968) 'Information for university admission', in *Research into Higher Education 1967* London: Society for Research into Higher Education.

ENTWISTLE, N. J. and PERCY, K. A. (1971) 'Educational objectives and student performance within the binary system', in *Research into Higher Education 1970* London: Society for Research into Higher Education.

FLOOD PAGE, C. M. (1971) *Technical Aids to Teaching in Higher Education* London: Society for Research into Higher Education.

FURNEAUX, W. D. (1968) 'General introduction to the series', in Beard, R. M., Healey, F. G. and Holloway, P. J., *Objectives in Higher Education* London: Society for Research into Higher Education.

GREENAWAY, H. K. (1971a) *Training of University Teachers* London: Society for Research into High Education.

GREENAWAY, H. K. (1971b) 'Student wastage', in 'Correspondence', *Universities Quarterly*, **25**, 376–9.

HALSEY, A. H. (1969) 'The role of the British university teacher', in *Research into Higher Education 1968* London: Society for Research into Higher Education.

HATCH, S. (1968) *Student Residence: A discussion of the literature* London: Society for Research into Higher Education.

HIMMELWEIT, H. T. (1967) 'Towards a rationalization of examination procedures', *Universities Quarterly*, **21**, 359–72.

JAHODA, M. (1967) 'Examining university examinations', *Universities Quarterly*, **21**, 269–71.

MALLESON, N. B. (1966) 'Preface' to *Student Residence—Research aspects, Report of a conference* London: Society for Research into Higher Education.

MARSLAND, D. (1970) 'An exploration of professional socialization: the college of education and the teacher's role', in *Research into Higher Education 1969* London: Society for Research into Higher Education.

OPPENHEIM, A. N., JAHODA, M. and JAMES, R. L. (1967) 'Assumptions underlying the use of university examinations', *Universities Quarterly*, **21**, 341–51.

Research into Library Services in higher education (1968) London: Society for Research into Higher Education.

ROBBINS, Lord (1963) *Report of the Committee on Higher Education* London: HMSO.

RUDD, E. (1968) 'Graduate studies in the humanities', in *Research into Higher Education 1967* London: Society for Research into Higher Education.

SAINSBURY, A. B. (1970) 'Supplementary predictive information for university admission', in *Research into Higher Education 1969* London: Society for Research into Higher Education.

SILVER, H. and TEAGUE, S. J. (1970) *The History of British Universities 1800–1969—A Bibliography* London: Society for Research into Higher Education.

WANKOWSKI, J. A. (1969) 'Some aspects of motivation in success and failure at university', in *Research into Higher Education 1968* London: Society for Research into Higher Education.

Working Party on Conditions and Careers of Research Workers (1971) *Careers, Conditions and Research Organization in Higher Education* London: Society for Research into Higher Education.

Index

Abercrombie, M. L. J., 185, 203, 333, 336, 338
Abernethy, D., 88
ability
  grouping, 38
  of teachers, 311
academic motivation, 103, 138
achievement
  and parental aspiration, 66–9
  and personality, 89–111
  and social class, 60
action research, 39
Adar, L., 317
Adcock, C. J., 90
Adler, D., 128
adolescence, 272
Ager, M. E., 286, 335
A. H. 4, 310
A. H. 5, 117
Ainslie, P., 313
Aja, K. A., 262
Alderson, C., 88
Allen, A., 113
Allen, D., 322
Allen, K. R., 272, 280
Allport, G. W., 89
Alpert, R., 103
Altman, E., 307
Anastasi, A., 12
Anderson, E. M., 212, 220
Anderson, J. G., 35, 54
apprenticeships, 277
Armstrong, D., 341
Arnot, A., 200
Ascher, M., 195
Ashby, E., 330
Ashley, B., 308
Ashton, B. G., 137
Askham, J., 286
Aspin, D. N., 309
Association for Science Education, 137
Association of University Teachers, 338, 341
Astin, A. N., 302
Atcherly, R. A., 266
attention theory, 239, 244, 247
attitudes to science, 135–8
  social, 92
  of teachers, 177

autism, 181, 205–8
Avent, C., 267, 281

Bachelor of Education degree, 310, 318
Baer, D. M., 251
Bagley, C., 193
Balbernie, R., 227
Ballham, A., 95, 107, 108
Bambridge, G. de P., 307
Bandura, A., 225
Banks, J., 93
Bannister, D., 218
Bantock, G. H., 16, 170
Barker, P., 221
Barker-Lunn, J., 38, 118, 124, 125, 174
Barnard, G. A., 270, 286
Barnes, D., 177, 178, 179
Baron, G., 34
Barr, A. S., 301
Barr, F., 268, 275, 277
Barrington, H., 148
Barry, M., 289
Barry, S., 286, 299
Bates, W. T. G., 290
Batcock, A., 99
Baumeister, A., 244
Beard, R., 333
Bearsley, N. 121
Beech H. R., 225
behaviour modification, 251–4
Bellack, A. A., 178
Belson, W. A., 222
Bender Gestalt Test, 189, 190
Bennett, S. N., 106, 108
Berg, L., 75
Bernal, J., 57
Bernstein, B., 20, 59–60, 66, 67, 168, 172, 176
Berry, P., 239, 240, 243
Betty, C., 173, 176
Bevan, B., 262
Bewsher, L. G., 307
Biddle, B. J., 177, 302, 325
Bidgood, D. K., 262
Bidwell, C. E., 33, 54
Bijou, S. W., 251
Binet-Simon Scale, 9
Birch, H. G., 197
Birnie, J. R., 87

Birney, R. C., 103
Black, H., 330
Blank, M., 176
Blau, P. N., 46
blindness, 180
Bloom, B., 132, 141, 145
Bolger, A. W., 267
Bolton, N., 113, 115, 122, 126
Bookbinder, G. E., 74
Booth, P., 147
Boothroyd. K., 318
Boreham, J. L., 268
Boreham, N. C., 291
Bormuth, J. R., 86
Bortner, M., 201
Bossio, V., 223
Bould, D. J., 147
Boulind, H., 139
Bowell, R., 282
Bower, E. M., 218
Bowley, A. H., 185, 203
Bowyer, L. R., 224
Box, S., 269, 270
Boxall, J., 231
brain damage, 193
Braine, M. D. S., 243
branching programming, 146
Brandis, W., 168
Brandon, S., 223
Brehaut, W., 19
Brennan, T., 105
Brenner, M. W., 203
Bristol Social Adjustment Guides, 189, 216, 222
British Association, 4
British Child Study Association, 3
British Intelligence Scale, 20, 116
British Psychological Society, 5, 197, 237
Bronfenbrenner, U., 62
Brothers, J., 333, 340
Brown, G., 93
Brown, G. A., 310
Brown, W. G., 282
Bryant, J. J., 136
Bryant, P. E., 198, 199
Burdick, H., 103
Burns, R., 189
Burt, C., 4, 10, 13, 15, 19, 90, 115
Burton, L., 228
Butcher, H. J., 1, 71, 93, 96, 108, 115, 116, 117, 122, 123, 135, 307, 309, 315
Butler, J. R., 271, 308
Butler, N. R., 220
Butler, R. A., 10
Buttle, D., 123, 129
Buxton, C. E., 317
Byrne, P. S., 127

Cabot, I. B., 125
Callard, M. P., 93, 229

Cameron, L., 117, 120
Campbell, D. T., 129
Campbell, R. F., 37
Camplin, K., 317
Cane, B., 28, 320
Cannon, J. A., 293
Cantor, L. M., 296
Careers Advisory Service, 262, 264
Careers Research and Advisory Centre, 300
Carlson, R. O., 33, 35
Carruthers, T., 277
Carter, C. F., 330, 340
Carter, M. P., 262, 271, 272
Carver, G., 75
Case, D., 317
Cashdan, A., 80, 243
Caspari, I., 267, 322
Cattell, R. B., 90, 95, 96, 108, 123, 275, 277
Cattell Culture Fair Test, 312
Cavanagh, P., 146, 275, 278
Cavenagh, F., 12
Cazden, C., 176
Central Advisory Council, 25
Central Lancashire Family and Community Project, 50, 55
cerebral palsy, 191–4
Certificate of Secondary Education, 122, 141–3, 145
Chalmers, A. D., 263, 281
Chandler, C., 329
Chanan, G., 28
Chappell, S., 289
Charlton, D., 298
Charters, W. W., 54
Chazan, M., 194, 195, 209, 215, 218, 221, 233
Chesser, E. S., 225
Chester, R., 269
Child Behaviour Scales, 214
Child, D., 113, 114, 115, 117, 120, 121, 270
child rearing 57–70
and maladjustment, 223
Children's Personality Questionnaire (CPQ), 92, 94
Chin, R., 39
Chown, S., 280
Christie, T., 48, 117, 123
Cicourel, A., 52
Clark, B., 51
Clark, M. M., 74, 77–8, 79
Clarke, A. D. B., 197, 198, 200, 236, 256
Clarke, A. M,, 197, 198, 200, 236, 256
Clarke, F., 6, 8, 13
Clarke, J. H., 271, 307
classroom centred research, 15
Clay, M. M., 85, 86
Cleary, A., 255
Clegg, A., 174
Clossick, M., 333
cluster analysis, 105

Clyne, N. B., 221
cognitive bias, 120, 121
cognitive confusion, 82
Cohen, A., 270
Cohen, L., 50, 271, 302, 305, 308, 318
Cole, H., 285, 299
Collier, K. G., 320, 323, 337, 338
Collingwood, R. G., 8
Collins, J. E., 80
colour codes, 83
Comber, L. C., 135
community school, 173
compensatory education, 76, 171–2
comprehensive schools, 34, 43, 48
computer-aided instruction, 146–8
convergent thinking, 112–29
Connolly, K., 186, 187
Cookson, D., 92
Cooley, W. C., 136
Cooper, B., 141
Cooper, G. M., 200
Cooper, J. E., 69
Cooper, M. G., 220, 229
Cope, E., 321, 324, 327
Corbett, A., 173, 176
Corruble, D., 308
Corwin, R. G., 33
Cortis, G. A., 326
Cotgrove, S., 267, 270, 287
Cotton, A. C., 117, 118, 125
counselling, 51, 261–84
Couper, H. E., 305
Cowell, M. D., 100, 103, 291
Cox, A. M., 250
Cox, R., 335
Cox, T., 231
Coxon, A. P. M., 271
Creak, M., 223
Crichton, A., 272
Crinnion, J., 265
Croft, M., 268
Cronbach, L. J., 123
cross-cultural research, 126, 316
Crowther Report, 11, 287, 293
Cuisenaire Method, 67
cultural transmission, 44, 45
Cunningham, C. E., 240, 254, 255, 258
Cunningham, K. S., 7
Cunningham, S., 92, 93
curriculum development, 20, 25–6, 34
    basic premises of, 150–4
    evaluation in, 163–7
    objectives in, 159–61
    research in, 149–67

Dacey, J., 113
Dainton Committee, 135
Dale, J. R., 320
Davidson, S., 220, 228
Davie, R., 220

Davies, B., 67
Davies, J. G. W., 323
Davies, W. B., 34
Davis, D. R., 68
Davis, T. N., 270
Daws, P. P., 263, 266, 267, 268, 273
deafness, 180, 224
Deblinger, J., 128
De Hirsch, 76
delinquescent sub-culture, 42, 174
Denny, M. R., 244
Dent, H. C., 3
Dent, N. A., 210
Dent, W., 298
Department of Education and Science,
    24, 88, 211, 226, 266, 285, 330, 342
Department of Health and Social Security,
    238
deprivation, 71
Derrick, T., 322
Derricot, R., 307
destreaming, 34
Dewey, J., 8
diagnostic tests, 73, 76
dialect, 74–5
dichronic study, 36
Dickson, G. E., 311, 316
Didcott, P. J., 222
Dienes Method, 67
Differential Test Battery, 277
Dinnage, R., 210, 223
disadvantage, 169, 172, 175
discipline, 57, 61–4
divergent thinking, 112–29
Dixon, E., 218
Doniger, C. R., 223
Donnison Commission, 47
Douglas, J. W. B., 19, 59, 69, 220, 223,
    229, 231, 272, 279, 286
Downing, J., 81, 82, 83
Drake, K. B., 303
Drever, J., 340
Duckworth, D., 94, 107, 108
Dunbartonshire Survey of Reading, 77
Durojaiye, M. O. A., 270
Duthie, J. H., 327

Education Reform Council, 5
educational opportunity, 19
educational priority areas, 55, 175
educational research
    British, 1–18
    classroom centred, 15
    decision making in, 24
    definition of, 1–2
    impartiality in, 16–17
    pupil centred, 15
    supervision of, 23
    support for, 19–31, 328–43
    training for, 23

Educational Resources Information Centre, 22
educational technology, 146-8
Educational Testing Service, 139
Eggington, D., 173
Eggleston, J. F., 134, 144, 145, 322
Eggleston, S. J., 41
Eide, K., 30
Elkind, D., 128
Ellena, W. J., 177, 302, 325
Elliott, C., 239, 250
Ellis, N. R., 244, 251
Elton, L. R. B., 147
Elvin, H. I., 11, 16
English Picture Vocabulary Test, 76, 241
Entwistle, D. M., 100, 317
Entwistle, N., 1, 15, 92, 93, 94, 99, 100, 103, 105, 107, 108, 317, 340
enuresis, 228
epilepsy, 180, 191-4
Eppel, E., 272
Eppel, M., 272
Erikson, E., 272
Etzioni, A. A., 35, 303, 320
Evans, E. G. S., 2
Evans, I. A., 225
Evans, K. M., 1, 15, 218, 307, 316
Evans, P., 239, 244
examinations, 138-46, 19
exchange theory, 269
extraversion, 89-111, 230-1, 313
Eyre, J. H., 278
Eysenck, H. J., 90, 92, 102, 103, 108, 270, 312
Eysenck, S., 90, 92, 225, 229
Eysenck Personality Inventory (EPI), 99, 100, 313

factor analysis, 13, 39, 54, 90-2, 316
Family Relations Indicator, 217
Fantini, M. D., 169
Fantz, R. L., 253
Farnworth, M., 78
Farrell, M., 203
Farrudin, D. H., 278
Fee, F., 113, 114
Feldman, K. A., 40, 320
Fensham, P. J., 130, 134
Fiddes, D. O., 182
Fisher, B., 76, 224
Fiske, D. W., 129
Flanagan, J. C., 326
Flanders, N. A., 177, 178
Flood Page, C. M., 333, 337
Floud, J., 304
Ford, J., 43
Forrester, R. M., 188
Foulds, G. A., 12
Fox, D. H., 145
Foxen, T., 240, 253
Foy, J. M., 141

Francis-Williams, J., 202
Frank, G. H., 223
Fraser, B., 108
Fraser, E., 67
Freeman, J., 123, 127, 129, 174
Friedlander, B. Z., 253
Frith, U., 208
Frostig Visual Perception Test, 78, 190
Fuller, J. A., 264, 266
Furneaux, W. D., 98, 229, 336
further education 285-300
selection for, 287-92
wastage in, 293-6
Fyfe, T. W., 83

Gage, N. L., 302
Gagné, R. M., 245
Gahagan, D. M., 176
Gahagan, C. A., 176
Galbraith, N. M. C., 262
Gale, A., 99
Gallop, R., 310
Galton, F., 4
Garfield, A., 185
Garfinkel, H., 53
Garner, J., 327
Garside, S. D., 86
Gear, B. L., 262
Gedye, J. L., 194
General Certificate of Education, 122, 134, 137, 139-41, 309, 310, 317
general systems theory, 35
Getzels, J. W., 37, 112, 114, 115, 117, 122, 129
Gibson, H. B., 217, 229
Gibson, S., 292
Gill, C. J., 266
Gillman, S., 203
Ginzberg, E., 269
Glass, D., 19
Glaser, B., 35
Glynn, E., 148
Goble, P. M., 308
Goffman, E., 46
Goodacre, E. A., 74, 75, 80, 85
Goodier, J. M., 148
Goodfellow, C. L., 93, 229
Goodman, K., 74
Gopal Rao, C. S., 126
Gordon, I. E., 93, 99
Gorton, A., 77, 200
Gorton, K., 200
Goslin, D., 276
Gould, R., 303
Grace, C. R., 317
Graham, D., 195
Graham, P. J., 220
Grant, G., 240
Grant, W., 270
Gray, J. A., 245

Green, J., 239, 249
Greenaway, H., 330, 341, 342
Greenfield, D., 206
Gregory, R. E., 230
Gresty, A., 338
Griffin, A., 48, 305
Griffiths, A., 322
Griffiths, D. E., 33, 35
Griffiths Scale, 188
Grimes, A., 289
Gross, N., 35
Guba, E. G., 37
Guerney, B. G., 225
guidance, 261–84
    tests in, 276–8
Guilford, J. P., 112, 116
Gulbenkian Foundation, 21
Gunzberg, H. C., 256
Gurney, P. W., 313

Haas, W., 84
Haber, R. N., 103
Haddon, F. A., 117, 119, 120, 124, 128
Halliwell, C., 100
Hallworth, H. J., 93, 217
Halping, A. W., 33, 38
Halsey, A. H., 55, 340
Hamilton, M., 219
Hamlyn, D. W., 16
Hammond, D., 74
handicapped children 180–97
    categorisation of, 180–1
    mental, 194–201, 236–59
    physical, 182–94
Handyside, J., 281
Hansen, D. R., 37
Hardman, K., 289
Hargreaves, D. H., 41, 48, 174
Hargreaves, H. L., 112
Harlen, W., 132
Harnquist, K., 23
Hartley, J., 121
Hartog, P., 12, 19
Hartrop, B. B., 267
Hason, P., 116, 117, 122
Haskell, S. H., 186, 187, 220
Hatch, S., 333, 338
Hatton, J., 264
Hayes, J., 266, 267, 269, 273, 274, 275
Haystead, J., 270
Healey, F. G., 333
Hearnshaw, L. S., 3, 13
Heider, E. R., 177
Heim, A., 129
Henderson, D., 60, 64
Henderson, P., 188
Herbert, N., 316
Herford, M., 272
Hermelin, B., 181, 198, 199, 206, 207, 234, 244

Herriot, P., 239, 247, 249, 250, 258
Herriott, R. E., 35
Hersov, L. A., 220, 228
Hester Adrian Research Centre 236–60
    projects, 238–40
    staff, 238–40
Hewett, S., 185, 211
Heywood, J., 341
Heyworth Committee, 20
Higginson, J. H., 11
High School Personality Questionnaire, (HSPQ), 92, 221
Hill, G. B., 270
Hill, G. C., 139
Hills, P. J., 146
Himmelweit, H., 335
Hirst, P., 171
Hoare, D. E., 132, 138
Hobsbaum, A., 241
Hockey, S. W. 132
Hodges, V., 221
Hogg, J., 239, 240, 244, 246, 253, 259
Holloway, P. J., 333
Hopson, B., 266, 269, 273, 275, 276
Hordley, I., 287
Hore, T., 326
Hough, P. M., 275, 276
House, B., 244, 247
Howells, J. C., 217
Hoyle, E., 33, 39, 41
Hudson, B., 132
Hudson, L., 17, 102, 114, 116, 119, 120, 121, 128, 137
Hughes, M., 34
Hughes, P., 268
Hughes, V. A., 186
Humanities Curriculum Project, 149–67, 171, 176
Hutchings, D. G., 138
Hutt, S. J., 206
hydrocephalus, 188–91, 209
hyperkinetic behaviour, 239, 252

ideational fluency, 116
I.E.A., 135–6
Illinois Test of Psycholinguistic Abilities, 78, 203, 241, 242, 251
imitation, 243–4
immigrants, 74, 220
individual differences 244–6, 270
information processing, 85, 250
ingram. T. T. S., 79, 204
inhibition–excitation, 245, 246, 259
Ini, S., 223
Inner London Education Authority, 74, 149
input–output studies, 39–40
in-service training, 131
Institute of Physics, 140
Isaacs, S., 5, 19

Isle of Wight Survey, 181, 184, 193
i.t.a., 71, 81–3, 67
Ives, D. C., 226

Jackson, B., 68
Jackson, L., 217
Jackson, P., 232, 233
Jackson, P. W., 112, 114, 115, 117, 121
Jackson, R., 267
Jacobson, L., 51
Jahoda, G., 263, 280, 281
Jahoda, M., 335
Jeffree, D., 239, 240, 242, 243, 258
Jeffs, P. M., 136
Jenkins, R., 317
Jenning, K. R., 139
Jensen, G., 37
Jephcott, R., 272
John, K., 94, 103
Johnstone, A. H., 133
Jones, A., 268, 272
Jones, C., 146
Jones, D. J., 286
Jones, H. G., 92
Jones, K. T., 83
Jordanhill College of Education, 195
Joseph, A., 58
Joyce, C. R. B., 120, 127
Junior Eysenck Personality Inventory
    (JEPI), 93, 229
Junior Maudsley Personality Inventory
    (JMPI), 218, 221, 229
Juniper, D., 266, 267

Kahn, J. H., 221
Kaltan, G., 46
Kandel, I. L., 16
Karsorla, I., 225
Katz, F. E., 35, 54
Keil, E. T., 269
Keir, G., 87
Kelly, G. A., 218
Kelsall, H. M., 306
Kelsall, R. K., 306
Kelvin, R. P., 98
Kent, W., 68
Kerr, J. F., 131, 134, 144
Killcross, M., 277
kinesthetic feedback, 187
King, R., 44, 48
King, T., 62
Kirk, S. A., 201
Kitchen, R. D., 315
Kitsuse, J. J., 52
Klein, J., 57, 61
Kline, P., 99
Klopfer, L. E., 136
Knight, R., 3
Kogan, N., 113, 114, 128

Kohs Blocks, 127
Kushlik, A., 197

Labour, W., 178, 179
Lacey, C., 41, 48
Lancashire, R., 279
Lambert, R., 47
Land, F. W., 309
language 168–79
    and mental handicap, 240–4
    and reading, 84–7
    and short term memory, 195
    and social class, 58–61
    structure of, 74
Lathan, D., 81, 86
Laughton, W. H., 137
Laurence, K. M., 188, 189
Lavender, J., 85
Lavin, D. A., 98, 99
Lawrence, D., 80, 275
Lawson, K. S., 1
Lawton, D., 59, 168, 289
Layard, R., 286
leadership, 35
learning
    and mental handicap, 236–60
    individual differences in, 244–6
Lee, D. J., 270, 275, 277, 287, 288
left handedness, 79
Leggatt, T., 306
Leisten, J. A., 139
Leith, G., 148
Lennhoff, F. G., 226
Leverhulme Trust, 21, 238
Levien, R. E., 26, 27
Lickorish, J. T., 217
Liddiard, M., 62
Liepman, K., 272
linear programming, 146
linguistics, 84–7
Lipham, J. M., 37
Lipshitz, S., 295
Little, A., 305
Litwak, E., 55
Lloyd, H. A., 148
Lockard, D. J., 136
Locke, M. F., 268, 282, 283
Lockyer, L., 206
Lomax, D., 304, 306, 307, 309, 312, 313,
    327
London Doll Play Technique, 217
London Literary Survey, 74
London School of Economics, Higher
    Education Research Unit, 29
Lorber, J., 188
Lortie, D. C., 54
Lotter, B., 205
Lovell, K., 1, 114, 119, 194, 204, 77
Lucas, C., 98

Lunzer, E. A., 93
Luria, A. R., 245, 199
Lynn, R., 93, 99
Lytton, H., 69, 117, 118, 119, 120, 124,
    125, 128, 231, 268

McAllister, J., 222
McArthur, P., 14
McComisky, J. G., 123, 127, 129
McConkey, R., 239, 249
McCreath, M. D., 286
McDonald, B., 149, 163–7, 271
McFee, J., 74
McGeeney, P., 67
McHale, A., 228
McHenry, R. E., 123
McIntyre, D., 307, 315
MacIntyre, S., 330
Mackay, C. K., 199, 120
Mackay, D., 85
McKerracher, D. W., 225
Maclay, I., 228
McLeish, J., 313, 318
McMahon, D., 289
MacMillan, J., 199
McNeil, J., 69
McNeill, D., 243
McNemar, Q., 122
McQuoid, J. C., 231
Macrae, A., 266
McWhinnie, A. M., 227
Madaus, G. F., 113, 129
Maglan, L., 286
Maguire, U., 231
Maier, I., 239, 251, 252
Mair, J. M. M., 218
Maizels, J., 265, 271, 289
maladjustment 214–35
    assessment of, 215–9
    incidence of, 219–21
    treatment of, 224–6
Malleson, N., 328, 330, 332
Manion, L., 316
Marinosson, G., 241, 251
Marris, P., 306
Marsden, D., 68
Marsh, R. W., 116
Marshall, A., 247, 256
Marsland, D., 313, 318
Martin, E. D., 112
Martin, H. L., 228
Mason, A., 222
Matthews, A., 232
Mathews, J. C., 139
Maudsley Personality Inventory (MPI),
    98, 313
Maxwell, J., 15
Mayfield, A., 308
Meadows, C. E., 220
'Meanings of Words' Test, 114–5, 121, 123

Megson, B., 174
Mehryar, A. H., 218
Mehrabian, A., 318
Mein, R., 243
Melville, N., 9
memory orgnisation, 249–50
mental handicap, 236–60, 194–201
    and language, 240–4
    and learning, 244–9
    and memory, 249–51
    and behaviour modification, 251–4
Meredith, H. M., 137
Merritt, J., 76, 88
Meyer, G. R., 270
Meyer, H. J., 55
Meyer, V., 225
Michaels, R. 285
microteaching, 178
Midwinter, E., 55, 173, 175, 176
Miles, T. R., 79
Miller Analogies, 117
Miller, E., 190, 191
Miller, G. W., 272, 295
Miller, J. R., 40
Millerson, G. C., 222
Mills, J., 120–1
Milne, A., 83
minimal brain damage, 201
Ministry of Education, 20, 293
Minnesota Multiphasic Personality
    Inventory, 313
Minnosetoa Teacher Attitude Inventory,
    316
Mitchell, F. W., 6
Mitchell, S., 220, 221
Mittler, P., 78, 197, 200, 208, 234, 239, 240,
    241, 242, 245
Mitzel, H. E., 324
Moeller, G. H., 54
Mohan, B. A., 168
mongolism, 222
Monks, G., 48
Monroe, W., 12, 15
Montgomery, G. W. G., 267, 289
Moodie, G. C., 330
Moore, A. H., 322
Moore, B. M., 51, 277, 278, 296
Moore G., 264
Moore, T., 217
Moreno, J. L., 218
Morgan, C., 313
Morris, B. S., 2
Morris, R. N., 307
Morrison, A., 92, 217, 307, 315
Morrison, T. I., 133
motor handicap, 182–3
Mouzelis, N., 33
multiple choice examinations, 139
multiple handicap, 208–12
Munday, J. H., 74

Musgrave, P. W., 269, 271
Musgrove, F., 270, 305

Naidoo, S., 79
Naremore, R., 177
National Association for Mental Health, 237
national characteristics, 8–10
National Children's Bureau, 88
National Foundation for Educational Research, 3, 15, 19, 22, 73, 88, 136, 174
N.F.E.R. English Progress Test, 81
National Institute of Industrial Psychology, 261
Neale, P. D., 132
Nelson, D., 271, 277
Nelson, R. O., 225
neuroticism, 89–111, 230–1, 313
Newson, E., 59, 62, 64, 69
Newson, J., 59, 64, 69
Newsom Report, 152, 172
Niblett, W. R., 342
Nicholls, J. G., 128
Nisbet, J. D., 1, 15, 93, 101, 270
Northern Universities Joint Matriculation Board, 141
Nuffield Foundation, 20, 130, 149, 176
Nunn, P., 5
Nurss, J., 75
Nursten, J. P., 221
Nuttall, D. L., 113, 115, 117, 118, 122, 127

objectives in science, 131–5, 139
occupational choice, 269–76
occupational information, 272–6
occupational self-concepts, 276
O'Connell, S., 147
O'Connor, K., 181, 198, 199, 206, 207
O'Connor, N., 234, 244
Office of Scientific and Technical Information, 22
Ogden, J. A., 231
Ojha, A., 98
O'Kelly, E., 76
Oliver, R. A. C., 1, 15, 47, 315
O'Neil, W. N., 324
Ormerod, M. B., 137
Oppenheim, A. M., 223, 335
Organisational Climate Description Questionnaire 38
organisations
  schools as, 32–56
  typology of, 35
Osgood, C. E., 218
Otley, C. B., 320
Ounstead, C., 192
Oxtoby, R., 302, 330

Pace, C. R., 318
Packham, D., 255
Pallant, D., 147
Palmer, F. C., 267, 272
parental aspiration, 66–9
Parsons, T., 35
Paul, L., 272
Pendlebury, A. C., 289
Penfold, A. P., 126
Penfold, D. M., 126
Percy, K. A., 101, 340
personality
  and attainment, 89–111
  and maladjustment, 228–9
  of teachers, 312–6
  traits, 90–2
Pervin, L. A., 313
Peters, M. L., 85
Peters, R. S., 2, 16
Petrie, I. R. J., 226
Philip, A. F., 227
Phillippa Fawcett College of Education, 149
Phillips, C. J., 187
Phillips, C. M., 286
phonic skills, 76
Pidgeon, D., 10, 19, 134, 177
Pimblett, S., 267
Pitfield, M., 223
play, 64–6
Plowden Report, 67, 175, 305
Pole, K., 342
Pollock, G. J., 294
Pond, D. A., 219
Pont, H. B., 120, 135, 148, 307
Poppleton, P. K., 326
Power, M. J., 40
practical science, 131, 144
preschool education, 182
Preddy, D., 239, 244
Pringle, M. L. K., 58, 182, 210, 220, 232, 231
programmed learning, 93, 146–8, 195
Pulham, K., 176
Pumfrey, P., 80
Punch, K. F., 54
pupil-centred research, 15

Q-sort, 218

Raby, L., 307
Rachman, S., 225, 232
Rackstraw, S. J., 60
Ravenette, A. T., 59
Rayner, J. M., 266
reading 71–8
  and linguistics, 84–7
  assessment of, 75
  readiness for, 76
Rees, R., 296, 298

Reeve, J. R., 10
Reeves, J. W., 324
Reid, D. J., 147
Reid, I., 318
Reid, J. F., 71, 79, 82, 86
Regan, G., 221
Remedial Education Service, 80
Remington, R., 240
repertory grid, 218
Revan, R. W., 50
Revans, H. M., 132
Reynell Scale, 189
Rhodes, E. C., 19
Rice, R., 270
Richards, H. H., 216, 218
Richards, J. M., 311
Richards, M. P. M., 57
Richards, P. N., 113, 115, 122
Richardson, J. E., 322
Richmond, P. E., 134
Ridding, L. W., 92, 95, 108
Rigley, L., 79, 80
Rim, Y., 231
Robbins, M. P., 40
Robbins Report, 11, 287, 304, 309, 328, 329
Roberts, I. F., 139, 296
Roberts, K., 262, 270
Robertson, J., 69
Robinson, W. P., 60
Rodger, A., 13, 261, 276, 283, 324
Rogers, C. R., 218
role
    of headmaster, 34
    of teacher, 316–17
Rolls, I. F., 308
Rose, G., 50
Rose, J. J., 218
Rosen, H., 177
Rosenthal, R., 51
Ross, A., 302
Ross, E., 210
Ross, J., 289
Ross, J. M., 223, 229, 231
Rowe, A., 173, 264
Rowlands, R. G., 270
Rudd, E., 106, 107
Rudd, W. G. A., 321, 326, 340
Rushton, J., 92, 94–5, 107, 108
Rusk, R. R., 1, 4, 5, 7, 11, 14
Rutter, M., 74, 77, 181, 184, 193, 194, 201, 205, 206, 214, 215, 220, 231, 234
Ryans, D. G., 312
Ryans, K., 322
Ryle, A., 219, 268, 272

Sadler, M., 4, 5, 11
Sainsbury, A. B., 340
Sampson, O. C., 80, 230
Sandford, C. W., 305

Sandiford, P., 9
Sandvin, J., 325
Sargon, J. D., 286
Savage, R. D., 92, 98, 99, 229
Scammels, B., 298
Schools Council, 3, 20, 24, 82, 88, 141, 143, 149, 176, 268
school
    administration of, 33
    as organisation, 32–56
    community relations with, 54–5
    phobia, 220–1
    subcultures in, 41–3, 47
Schroder, C., 28
Schutz, A., 53
science-arts differences, 101
science-attitude questionnaire, 136
science teaching, 130–48
Scotland, J., 302
Scott, D. W., 139
Scott, W., 304
Scottish Council for Research in Education, 3, 15, 19, 297, 299
Scottish Education Department, 130, 214
Sealey, A. P., 95
self-concept, 218
Selznick, P., 32, 35
Selmes, C., 136
semantic differential, 218
Sembal Trust, 238
Serpel, R., 239, 247, 248
Sethi, L., 190
Shakarwy, M., 275, 277
Shakespeare, R., 185
Shapiro, R. J., 119
Sharp, D. W. A., 133
Sharples, D., 108
Shaw, O. L., 230
Shearer, E., 79
Sherlock, B., 270
Shepherd, M., 220, 221
Shields, J. B., 114, 119
Shimmin, S., 268
Shipman, M. D., 315, 320, 326
Shipton, R., 288
Shouksmith, G. A., 112, 123, 124, 267, 275
Shumsky, A., 177
Silver, H., 333
Simons, M., 311
Simpson, P., 200
Sims, N., 76
Singh, A., 270
16 P. F., 92, 313
sixth form, 47
Skilbeck, M., 134
Skurnik, L. S., 136
Slatterly, D. J., 270
Smelser, W. T., 306
Smith, B. O., 301, 302, 313

Smith, P., 281
Smith, S. C., 286
Smithers, A. G., 99, 113, 114, 117, 120, 270
Smyth, P., 322
Snider, J. G., 218
social attitudes, 92
socialisation, 158, 269
social class
  and attainment, 60
  and potential aspiration, 66–9
  and language, 58–61
  and teaching, 304–6
Social Science Research Council, 3, 20, 238, 285
Society for Research in Higher Education, 328–44
  publications of, 332–5
sociolinguistics, 20
Solomon, E., 313
Sorensen, G., 326
Southgate, V., 82, 83
Spain, B., 188, 189
specific dyslexia, 71, 77–81
specific learning difficulty, 201–5
speech codes, 60, 170
speech defects, 180
spina bifida, 187–91
Stanford-Binet, 196
Starkey, H. F., 274
Start, K. B., 325
Staveley, B., 100
Stenhouse, L., 20, 141, 152, 160, 171
Stephenson, N., 322
Stephenson, W., 218
stereognostic ability, 199
Stern, G. C., 271, 318
Stewart, L. H., 306
Stocks, J. C., 275
Stott, D. H., 83, 216, 217, 222
Stott, M. B., 281, 282, 323
Strauss, A., 35
streaming, 20, 38, 43, 49, 173
Strickland, R. G., 86
subcultures, 41–3, 47, 308
Suci, G. J., 218
Sukhia, S. P., 4
Sully, J., 4
Sultan, E. E., 116
Swann Report, 135
Swansea Test of Phonic Skills, 76
Sweney, A. B., 95
Swift, D. F., 58, 68
Swinhoe, K., 270
synchronic study, 36

Talbot, A. R., 148
Tannenbaum, P. H., 218
Tatsuoka, M., 277
Taylor, J. W. 266, 267, 275

Taylor, L. C., 147
Taylor, P. H., 305
Taylor, W., 13, 17, 21, 26, 27, 30, 34, 302, 303, 320, 323
Teevan, R. C., 103
Tew, B. J., 189
Thakray, D. V., 83
thalidomide, 182
Thomas, B., 239, 247, 258
Thompson, B., 85
Thompson, J. A., 74
Thompson, J. W., 315
Thompson, P., 62
Thomson, G., 13
Thomson, N., 139
Thouless, R. H., 1
threshold hypothesis, 117–18
Tibble, J. W., 321
Tipton, B., 298
Tizard, B., 58
Tizard, J., 29, 181, 191, 197, 209, 211, 214, 218, 220
Tomlinson, E., 240
Tompkinson, E., 272
Torrance, E. P., 112, 119
Travers, K. J., 275
Traxler, A., 13
Troth, D., 148
truancy, 220–1
Tuck, J., 302
Turnbull, G. H., 316
Turner, C. M., 46
Turner, G. J., 168
Turner, J., 302
Turner, R. K., 232
twin studies, 59
Tyerman, M., 220
Tyson, M., 186, 202

Ucko, L. E., 217
Uhl, M., 75
underachievement, 168
Underwood Report, 214, 226
University Grants Committee, 20, 328
Universities
  Aberdeen, 138
  Bradford, 50, 318
  Bristol, 50, 322
  Brunel, 296
  City, 343
  Dundee, 138
  East Anglia, 149
  Essex, 333
  Glasgow, 133
  Hull, 190
  Keele, 121
  Leicester, 50, 134
  London, 98, 343
  Manchester, 7, 41, 237
  Nottingham, 143

Stirling, 322
Surrey, 146
Sussex, 341
Swansea, 171
Ulster, 310, 322
'Use of Objects' test, 114–15, 121, 123, 126

Vaizey, J., 295, 302
Van der Eyken, W., 285, 290, 292, 294, 296, 299
Vaughan, T., 268
Venables, E., 100, 272, 292, 295, 296
Veness, T., 272,
verbal reasoning, 64
Vernon, M. D., 282
Vernon, P. E., 13, 116, 117, 126, 128, 282, 324
Vickery, R., 288
Vineland Scale, 189
visual discrimination, 247–8
visual-spatial tests, 77
visuo-motor ability, 185–6
Vygotsky, L. S., 168, 169

Wakeford, J., 45
Walker, A., 278
Wall, W. D., 15, 17
Wallach, M. A., 113, 114, 128
Wallis, D. P., 267
Walton, D., 225
Wankowski, J. A., 99, 340
Warburton, F. W., 6, 15, 82, 91, 96–7, 99, 116
Ward, A. V., 285
Ward, J., 78, 113, 114, 225
Warnecke, R., 221
Warr, E. E., 210
Warren, W., 227
Warrington, C. K., 204
Watson, J. B., 62
Watts, T., 264, 274
Wechsler Adult Intelligence Scale, 312
Wechsler Intelligence Scale for Children (WISC), 114, 186, 189, 192, 196, 204, 206
Wechsler Pre-school and Primary Scale of Intelligence (WPPSI), 189
Wedell, K., 186, 203, 205, 224
Wedgewood, J., 194
Weinstein, G., 169
Weir, A. D., 297
Weisberg, P., 251
Welsh, J., 108
Weltman, J., 335

Westergaard, J., 305
Westwood, L. T., 316
Whelan, E., 240, 256, 257
Wheldall, K., 239, 240, 241, 242
Wheldall, R., 239
White, B. L., 254
White, J., 171
White, J. P., 2
White, R. R., 187
Whitehead, A. N., 5
Whitmore, K., 181, 214, 220
Wiegersma, S., 277
Wiersma, W., 277, 316
Wilkinson, A., 168
Wilkinson, W. J., 137
Williams, F., 168, 177, 178
Williams, G. F., 275
Williams, I. C., 291
Williams, J. M., 223
Williams, P., 76, 195
Willis, D., 226, 230
Wilson, J. D., 99
Wilson, J., 267
Wilson, R., 301
Winch, P., 16
Winch, W. H., 4, 16
Wing, J. K., 206, 234
Wiseman, S., 15, 59, 134, 325, 326
Wolff, S., 223, 227
Wood, H., 320
Wood, R., 94, 104
Woods, G. T., 139
Woodward, M., 197
Wooster, A. O., 80
Word Blind Centre, 78
work skills, 240, 256–7
Wragg, M., 88
Wymer, I., 282

Yamamoto, K., 118
Yates, A., 19
Yeamans, E. T., 138
Young, D., 66, 69
Young, M., 55, 67
Younghusband, E., 180, 208, 211, 213
Youth Employment Service, 262, 263, 264, 278
Yule, W., 214, 231

Zahran, H. A. S., 218
Zangwell, O. L., 203
Zeaman, D., 244, 247
zonal analysis, 104